The Communist Takeover of Hangzhou

**Studies of the Weatherhead East Asian Institute
Columbia University**

The Weatherhead East Asian Institute is Columbia University's center for research, publication, and teaching on modern and contemporary Asia Pacific regions. The Studies of the Weatherhead East Asian Institute were inaugurated in 1962 to bring to a wider public the results of significant new research on modern and contemporary East Asia.

A Study of the Weatherhead East Asian Institute

THE COMMUNIST TAKEOVER OF HANGZHOU

The Transformation of City and Cadre, 1949–1954

JAMES Z. GAO

University of Hawai'i Press
Honolulu

© 2004 University of Hawai'i Press
All rights reserved
Printed in the United States of America
09 08 07 06 05 04   6 5 4 3 2 1

Library of Congress Cataloging-in-Publication Data

Gao, James Zheng.

   The Communist takeover of Hangzhou : the transformation of city and cadre, 1949–1954 / James Z. Gao.
      p. cm.—(A study of the Weatherhead East Asian Institute)
   Includes bibliographical references and index.
   ISBN 0-8248-2701-5
   1. Zhongguo gong chan dang—History. 2. Hangzhou (China)—History. I. Title. II. Series.
JQ1519.A5 G38   2004
951'.242—dc22   2003019693

University of Hawai'i Press books are printed on acid-free paper and meet the guidelines for permanence and durability of the Council on Library Resources.

Designed by University of Hawai'i Press Production Staff

Printed by The Maple-Vail Book Manufacturing Group

For Laura Liu

Contents

Acknowledgments / ix

Abbreviations / xi

Maps / xii

Introduction / 1

1 On the Eve of the Takeover / 11
2 Training the Cadres / 42
3 The First Efforts / 69
4 One Step Back, Two Steps Forward / 98
5 The Korean War and the City / 125
6 The Trial of Strength / 154
7 Women Cadres / 185
8 The "Geneva of the East" / 216
9 Conclusion / 245

Notes / 263

Glossary / 311

Selected Bibliography / 315

Index / 327

Acknowledgments

My idea of writing a book on the Communist takeover of Hangzhou came up in a conversation with a colleague at the University of Maryland, Shuguang Zhang, in the winter of 1997. As we discussed the current academic concern with a reconceptualization of the 1949 Chinese revolution, I came to believe that an empirical study of the experience of rural Communist cadres in Hangzhou in the "takeover period" would throw a new light on the nature and characteristics of the revolution. In the four years of my research and writing, Shuguang read several chapters of the manuscript and offered insightful criticism and suggestions. I deeply appreciate his help.

I have many individuals to thank for their support, encouragement, and advice at various stages of this project. My gratitude first goes to Jon Sumida, Arthur Eckstein, Jeannie Rutenburg, Chen Jian, Philip West, John Lampe, William Rowe, and Liang Kan. Some chapters of my manuscript were presented at the American Historical Association annual meetings and other conferences, from which I received invaluable feedback. I learned much from the comments of the panelists and other scholars: John Fitzgerald, Guido Samarani, Yelong Han, Quasheng Zhao, Stephen Averill, Weili Ye, Jin Qiu, Christina K. Gilmartin, Susan Mann, Xiaoqun Xu, Jin Jiang, Joseph Esherick, Ruth Rogaski, Xueping Zhong, and Rui Yang. My special thanks are due the two readers for the University of Hawai'i Press, Steven Levine and Stephen Uhalley, who gave the whole manuscript a close reading and provided generous comments and suggestions that guided my revisions and improved this work.

In my fieldwork, I am indebted to numerous friends in China. Some introduced me to the interviewees, who opened my eyes to the human drama experienced by individuals and families. The archivists and local historians in Hangzhou, Shanghai, and Shandong offered support in a number of ways, calling important sources to my attention.

Patricia Crosby of the University of Hawai'i Press is an

encouraging and engaged editor. I am grateful for her editorial acumen and guidance in steering the publication process. I am also grateful to Madge Huntington of Columbia University, who worked with readers to review my manuscript and included it in Columbia University's Studies of the Weatherhead East Asian Institute.

I would also like to thank the University of Maryland for its institutional support. The Graduate School granted me a Summer Research Award, and the Department of History offered me one semester of teaching release, both of which allowed me to pursue the ideas that I present here and made it possible for me to complete this book. Finally, I thank my wife, Laura, who shared the labor and pleasure from beginning to end. I dedicate this book to her.

Abbreviations

CCA	Cangshan County Archives
CCP	Chinese Communist Party
ECB	East China Bureau
ECFA	East China Field Army
GMD	Guomindang (Kuomintang)
HMA	Hangzhou Municipal Archives
LMA	Linyi Municipal Archives
PLA	People's Liberation Army
PRC	People's Republic of China
SMA	Shanghai Municipal Archives
SPA	Shandong Provincial Archives
ZMA	Zaozhuang Municipal Archives
ZPA	Zhejiang Provincial Archives
ZPWFA	Zhejiang Provincial Women's Federation Archives
ZUA	Zhejiang University Archives

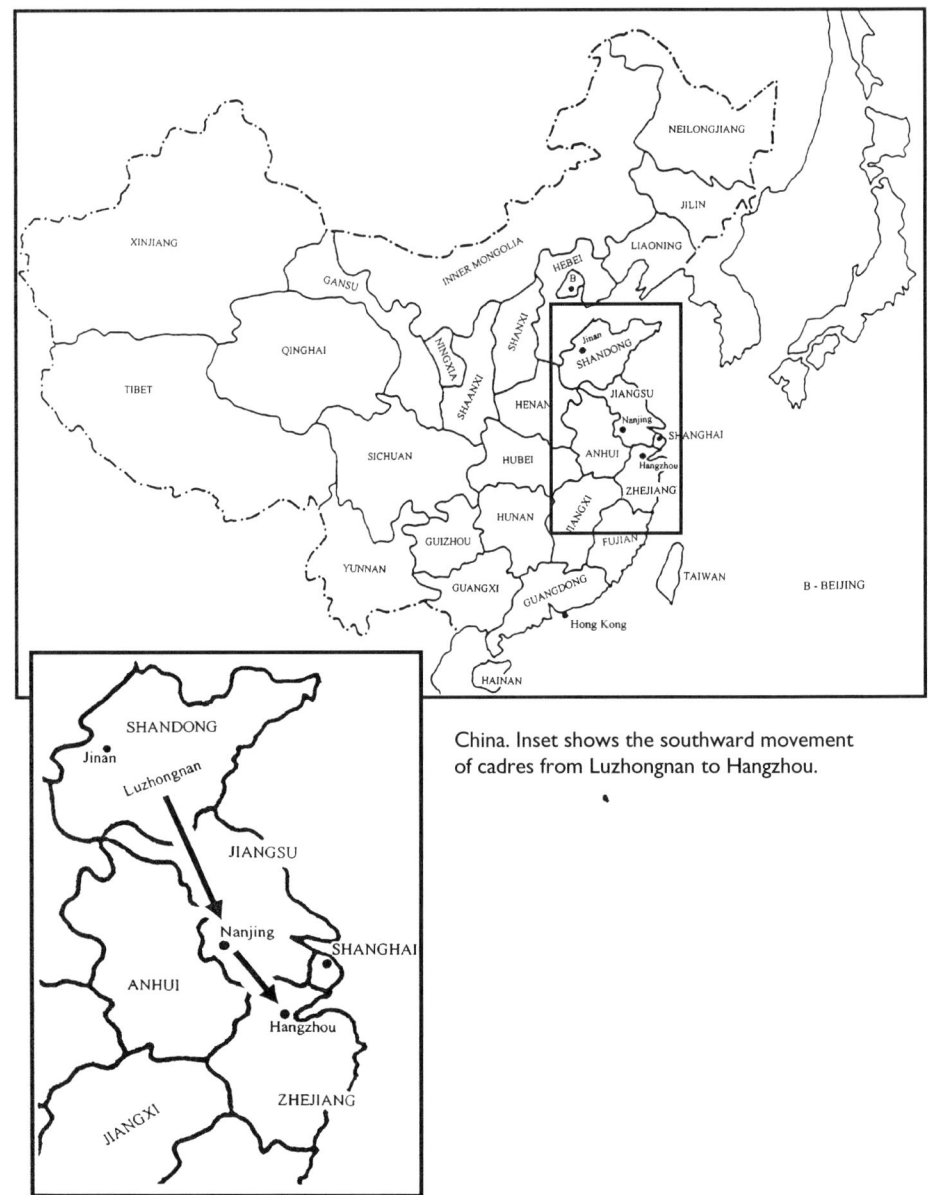

China. Inset shows the southward movement of cadres from Luzhongnan to Hangzhou.

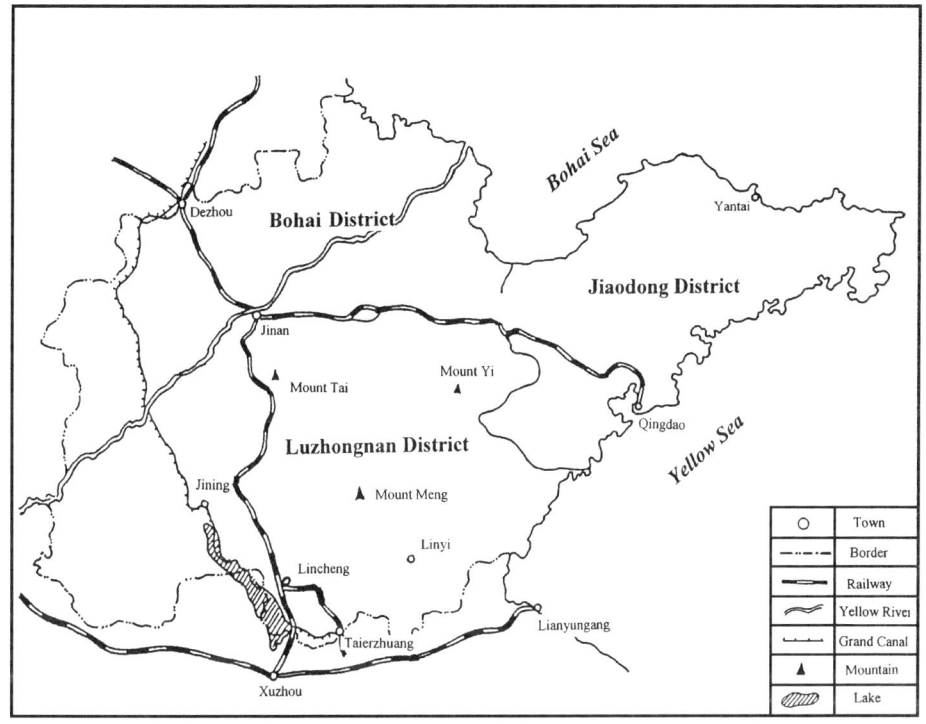

Shandong Province. CCP administrative districts in September 1948.

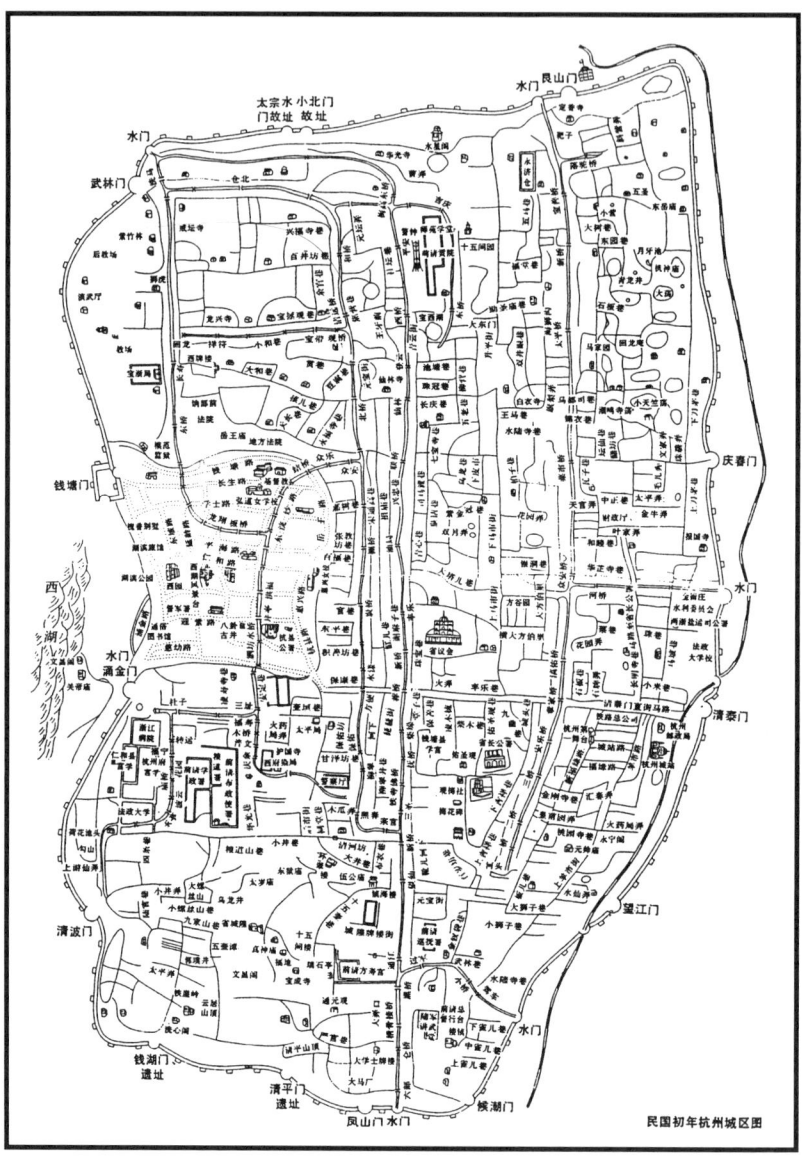

Old Hangzhou. The city in the Republican period (SMA).

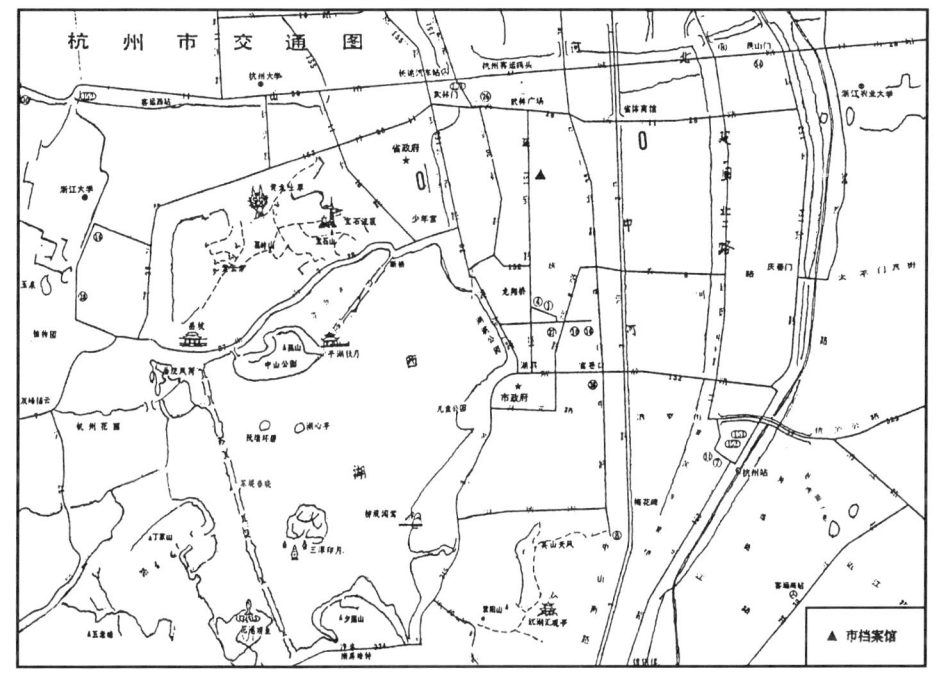

Hangzhou. Major streets and buildings in Hangzhou after 1949 (HMA).

The Communist Takeover of Hangzhou

Introduction

The Communist takeover of China in 1949 brought the promise of fundamental political, social, and cultural transformation. This was to be accomplished through national unification under a government with an idealistic vision of the future mated to discipline and confidence borne of victory after twenty-eight years of bloody struggle. The West, for its part, was skeptical of the capacity of the Chinese Communist Party (CCP) to govern the newly created People's Republic of China (PRC) effectively, let alone implement an ambitious program of national integration and modernization. The new regime had to help the legions of starving and homeless, win over the cynical hearts of urban dwellers, and create a solid institutional base for its revolutionary program. There was good reason to doubt whether revolutionaries from mostly rural backgrounds had the knowledge and skill required to consolidate political control and establish economic stability. Nevertheless, in the early 1950s, the Chinese Communists accomplished these goals.

In the initial period of the new republic, Mao Zedong and his Politburo colleagues agreed that in the first few years in power they would postpone radical revolutionary programs and work with the established urban elites through compromise. It is believed that such an approach suffers from the drawback that the possession of power corrupts the revolution; it is a common pattern of post-revolutionary society that "revolutions die when revolutionaries become rulers."[1]

To explain this pattern of post-revolutionary society, Maurice Meisner writes that when "the new rulers compromise with the traditions and survivals of the past, they ..., consciously or not, come to preside over historical processes that betray their own ideals and hopes for a radically new society."[2] The modern revolutions in France, Russia, and other countries all offered similar stories. Surprisingly, the Chinese Communists succeeded in keeping their revolutionary ideals alive, although they made more concessions to the former upper classes than had the Russians. Why did China present a radical departure from the common pattern of post-revolutionary society? What explains this unique experience of the Chinese revolutionaries?

Both Western and Chinese scholarship has yet to provide satisfactory answers to these questions. The Chinese literature is in large part an exercise in partisan history that stresses military victory, idealizes the CCP's organizational and economic achievements, and ignores the social tensions and crises of the 1950s. Writings that criticize Mao's radical revolution in his later years present the early 1950s as a perfect "golden age" that brought the Chinese people hope for a modern state.[3] Similarly, Western literature fails to explain why there is a gap between the CCP's cautious realism of the early 1950s and its utopian fanaticism in the later years and why the promising beginning of the People's Republic was followed by economic stagnation, political disillusion, and leadership corruption. What is necessary is a thorough reevaluation of the Communists' early governing methods, seeing them as a long-lasting dynamic rather than a temporary expedient, with ultimately large effects on what was to come. The purpose of this book is to carry out the required comprehensive and systematic investigation of these methods and then assess their consequences. More specifically, this study will try to expand our understanding of the cultural dimension of the 1949 revolution.

Why should the study of the Communist takeover be placed in a cultural context? The simple fact is that many of the CCP's efforts in the post-1949 years were focused on the cultural front—the "struggle against the enemies without guns," as Mao Zedong put it.[4] Without a close examination of the CCP's effort to change the basic worldviews of the population, we cannot understand how it successfully made the majority of Chinese people identify with the new regime and its revolutionary goals. To study the cultural dimension of the Communist takeover, this book will examine how the Communists used state power to transform the urban culture and how they employed cultural weapons to consolidate the new regime.

As early as 1948, Mao Zedong realized that the forthcoming military victory of the People's Liberation Army (PLA) would not by itself establish the national legitimacy of Communist authority. Unlike the millions of peasants who had rebelled against the Guomindang (GMD) government, most urban people had not struggled for the CCP's victory. To make the urban populace identify with the new regime, Mao believed the CCP had to invent instruments of cultural transformation. This view is in harmony with Marxist doctrine that only a spiritual weapon can destroy spiritual forces. In the 1950s, Mao's socialist revolution had little in the way of material presence in the ordinary lives of people. For this reason, symbols and objects that could be related to the actions and promise of the new regime were crucial. The Communists exposed the urban dwellers in Hangzhou to the concept of the revolution through several symbols: their special uniforms, bullet-torn flags, pistols with red silk, and Party-organized street performances (among other material objects). In addition, non-material symbols were employed to deliver revolutionary messages, from singing "Without the CCP There Is No New China" to addressing people as "comrades." All these symbols had to be embodied in various ritual performances, of which the most important was the political meeting.

In Chinese history, the founder of each new dynasty made some institutional reforms and ritual changes to demonstrate that he ruled by Mandate of Heaven. The purpose of government-sponsored rituals was to foster a mentality that favored the political legitimization of authority. The Chinese Communists were masters—and indeed had to be masters—of this instrument of regime consolidation. Yet in the field of Chinese studies, there is no study of the relations between the regime change of 1949 and political rituals, and Chinese students can learn about analytic frameworks only from empirical studies of other countries or regions.

Rituals were practiced to reinforce a caste-defined hierarchy in India, to motivate tribal rebellions in Africa, to discourage economic and political differentiation in Latin America, and to give legitimacy to a new revolutionary government in Iran.[5] Ritual performances are not necessarily associated with religious beliefs or preliterate societies. Lance Bennett's study of U.S. elections reveals the contribution of ritual to contemporary American politics. Bennett points out that elections are the most sweeping and popular ritual in American political life. His most thought-provoking argument is that the ritualization of communications in the elections both enhances and limits American political action.[6] Using this conceptual framework for the analysis of culture and political change, this study will examine how communications between CCP cadres and the ordinary people involved a cultural process operating through political institutions and embodied in various forms of ritual that shaped public reactions to political outcomes of the revolution.

The exploration of the cultural dimension of regime change, particularly with respect to political rituals, is a matter of special historical interest because it explains a great deal about the behavior of the Communists following their military victory in 1949. The study of this subject is complicated by the fact that while the CCP elite were revolutionary intellectuals, the rank and file, who were going to be the executors of political consolidation through (among other things) ritual exercises, were peasants with little experience of urban life. The Communist victory of 1949 sent the CCP leaders from their long-time exile in the countryside back to the Party's birthplace in the cities. However, this move exposed the peasant cadres, who had been recruited in the agrarian revolution and guerrilla wars, to an alien environment that posed difficult as well as unfamiliar problems. In a way, the Communist move to the cities was similar to the Macedonian conquest of Greek city-states and the Manchurian acquisition of the heartland of China. Both the Macedonians and Manchus shifted from culturally less developed areas to highly developed areas. To rule the civilized society of the conquered people, they adopted the values of their sophisticated subjects and in the process purposely assimilated their high culture. Yet the Communist cadres with a rural revolutionary tradition were strongly committed to changing the non-revolutionary culture of the urban people and thus met more cultural challenges than military resistance.

This book treats the Communist takeover as no less a cultural event than a political one. The peasant cadres suffered cultural shock upon their arrival in the newly liberated urban areas while they simultaneously tried to revolutionalize these areas, requiring the people to give up not only the old regime, but also their long-established habits and concepts of the world. The historical treatment of Hangzhou analyzes the decisive role of cultural identity in shaping Communist legitimacy and also explores the varied complex and contested ways in which the urban culture penetrated the life of the peasant cadres. The existing works on the Chinese revolution and political culture present solid analyses of how the peasant culture influenced Mao Zedong's ideas and policies.[7] But none of these works discuss a reverse effect of comparable significance: how the peasant cadres were influenced and changed by the urban environment. These peasant cadres were very different from rural students in history who passed civil service examinations and immediately joined the urban elite or talented youngsters today who immigrate to the city for a new profession and are most willing to be assimilated by the urban culture. This book will examine two interwoven processes: the Communist attempt to transform the urban culture in order to facilitate the legitimization of the new regime and the countervailing change in the Communist mentality caused by the resistance and reaction of a resilient urban culture.

Steven Levine writes that "the victory of the CCP may have involved very diverse paths to power in different regions, provinces, and even localities on the complex gameboard of Chinese politics."[8] Similarly, the 1949 revolution reveals many variations in the pattern of Communist takeover. Two pioneering local studies of the Communist takeover of urban China are Kenneth Lieberthal, *Revolution and Tradition in Tientsin, 1949–1952,* and Ezra Vogel, *Canton under Communism: Programs and Politics in a Provincial Capital, 1949–1968.* Tianjin (Tientsin) is China's second largest industrial city in the north, while Canton, located on the southern frontier, represents a more cosmopolitan culture than most Chinese cities. Both the books examine the methodical approach taken by the Communists when expanding their power and marshaling their resources for further revolutionary programs.

The works by Lieberthal and Vogel have directed scholarly attention to the variety of the Chinese revolution in different places and periods, and they have also left some important issues for further inquiry. The history of the Communist takeover of Hangzhou, a smaller, non-industrial, but culturally highly developed city, is particularly interesting. For example, in the absence of a tradition of labor organization, the people in Hangzhou did not show the same degree of revolutionary fervor and optimism as the Cantonese (as Vogel discusses). Also, although Liberthal's argument about the industrial workers in Tianjin generally fits an orthodox Marxist theory, we see a more complicated picture in Hangzhou. From the perspective of the Communist peasant cadres, the major cleavage in the period of the takeover was not the gulf between modern and traditional sections in the city, nor simply between urban dwellers and peasants (as Lieberthal suggests in his book); it was an antithesis between revolutionary rural areas and the "bourgeois city." The views of the peasant cadres on modernity, tradition, and revolution, as well as their political behavior generated from these views, will be a core theme of this book.

There are reasons to choose Hangzhou for the exploration of the cultural dimension of the takeover other than its differences from Tianjin and Canton. First, the Communist leadership decided before the takeover of Hangzhou that all the city's leaders would be replaced by Communist cadres from the rural revolutionary bases in Shandong Province (to the north of Hangzhou), as opposed to elevating indigenous urban Communists—who were in short supply—to positions of power. (See map 1.) This placed the peasant cadres in a strange political and cultural setting, with little or no advice from experienced urban compatriots. It did not take long for cultural conflict to emerge in full force. Hangzhou was an extreme but by no means a unique case, paralleling political development in other parts of China. The study of its particular characteristics will enhance our understanding of the integrated revolutionary program the CCP brought to the entire country.

Second, there is a great contrast between the city of Hangzhou and the Communist rural bases in Shandong. The differences are apparent in terms not only of people's revolutionary enthusiasm, but also of regional imbalances in economic and cultural development. While flames of war and privations owing to economic crises had afflicted the province of Shandong for decades, the city of Hangzhou had enjoyed peace and prosperity. While famines and plagues had struck the home villages of the Communist cadres almost every year, food and other amenities had been adequate if not plentiful in Hangzhou. While generations of peasants in Shandong had had to struggle for survival, tilling poor soil, Hangzhou, in "the land of rice and fish," was the site of ease and luxury. In the eyes of the peasant cadres, prosperity had spoiled the soft southerners, whose values had been corrupted by commercial success and cultural refinement. Thus, the peasant cadres had a commitment to transform what they regarded as the degenerate culture of the city.

This book (which is the result of three years of work at local archives in Hangzhou, Shanghai, and several other cities and counties in Shandong, as well as the archives of Zhejiang University and the provincial Women's Federation), begins with a consideration of materials from the Republican period of the 1940s. Since the PLA entered Hangzhou without fighting, most Republican archives were not destroyed by either war or the GMD government in its hurried retreat. As soon as the Communists took control of the city, they sequestered all government files. The political archives were carefully preserved and turned over to the Public Security Bureau. It was believed that these materials could serve in suppressing counterrevolutionaries, positioning for the Korean War, and preparing for the liberation of Taiwan. In 1987–1989, these materials were integrated with rapidly expanding provincial and municipal archives. In the Shanghai Municipal Archives there is a special section run by representatives of the Public Security Bureau, who determine researchers' access to certain "secret files" that had been turned over to the municipal archives. The reading of all local archive files still requires special permission, but a large part of the "old regime" archives, which used to be called the archives of "the enemy and the puppet regimes," is open to the public. In addition, local archives in Shandong and Shanghai are extremely rich in materials concerning the CCP's activities in the Republican period, especially in the Civil War.

This study of the Communist takeover has benefited in a number of ways from the easy access to the archives of the 1950s. I discovered information that cannot be found in the archives of the later years of the PRC. First, the earlier archives contain not only political and economic but also social and cultural information about the early People's Republic. With very little knowledge of the urban areas, as soon as they arrived in a city, the Communists intensively investigated each factory, school, union, and professional organization, as well as the reactions of various social groups to the CCP's policies. The investigative reports and work summaries were originally for internal circulation only; being staff studies rather than propaganda, they were relatively objective.

Second, these archives reveal the process of policy making at the local echelons of the Party's leadership. China specialists usually know more about the CCP's policies than its policy-making process since most archives include only the final versions of documents and exclude the initial proposals. The archives of the 1950s, however, contain the minutes of the CCP county committees, which convey different voices in discussions of plans for cadres. There are also records of the district governments in Hangzhou that reveal arguments over the scope and speed of mass campaigns. These materials give a clear picture of the contested process of decision making and policy implementation at various Party levels.

Third, document papers and writing styles themselves tell stories. Some of the Communist work reports were written on the back side of the GMD's letterhead, revealing the early scarcity of materials and the CCP's plain living style in the 1950s. A reader can often catch incorrectly written characters and grammatical errors in these reports, which indicate the lower educational level of the peasant cadres. Most impressive is the straightforward and detailed writing style of the early PRC documents. They reported not only progress, but also mistakes, problems, and people's complaints. For example, a report on the First Hangzhou Textile Factory in 1949 details how effectively the original owner of the factory had managed production, how well he had treated the workers, and how much the workers still missed him after the Communist takeover.[9] Such a description of workers' feelings about a capitalist owner was impossible after 1954, when documents began to portray all capitalists as parasites and bloodsuckers.

For this work, I also interviewed a number of rural cadres and urban dwellers who witnessed the takeover. Now in their late seventies or eighties, they are ready to let a researcher record their history. The interviews with women cadres are particularly informative, for they touch on a wide range of subjects: family, children, health, food, money, and husband-wife relations; most details are both illuminating and reliable. These retired women cadres provide a very different impression of Mao's revolution than does the formal party history.

This book is divided into eight chronologically organized chapters. It begins with Communist military victory and preparation for the takeover in 1948, examining the CCP's urban policies and its decision to transfer peasant cadres to Hangzhou. The book then moves to a description and analysis of the training programs the CCP offered to three different kinds of Party workers. These ideologically oriented training programs determined the pattern of Communist rule after the takeover. The following chapters explore the political behavior of the peasant cadres in state reconstruction and cultural transformation after 1949. They examine how Communists created the images of well-disciplined soldiers, capable managers, and revolutionary leaders by using political symbolism and ritual and by solving the immediate political and economic problems. They explore how the peasant cadres avoided being uprooted from their rural revolutionary origins and how they used state power to stage a cultural crusade against American imperialism and compel the surrender of liberal intellectuals and the bourgeoisie. It shows how the CCP used the ritualized political meeting to legitimate revolutionary programs, motivate behavior, and bring about political change. One chapter in this book is devoted to the experiences of Communist women cadres and analyzes their triumphs and frustrations in liberating themselves and their urban sisters. It discusses the takeover from the female perspective in order to explore power redistribution as a gendered phenomenon in both the private and public spheres. The last chapter explores how urban culture negotiated with political power and how political and cultural factors eventually altered the city's development strategy. It analyzes the interplay between the revolutionary and non-revolutionary culture with respect to the different degrees to which they resisted and adapted to each other. As a result of the interplay, both urban dwellers and the peasant cadres created a new sense of identity. The book concludes in 1954, when the Communist government was finally going to initiate the socialist transformation by nationalizing urban industry and commerce in the city.

This study probes local nuances and details while keeping in sight the broader perspective of national revolution. Through the close examination of Communist leaders at middle and lower levels, it highlights the continuity of Chinese political culture before and after 1949 and bridges the gap between the CCP's moderate policies in the early 1950s and its radical revolutionary programs in the later years. It is my hope that this study will provide a broader platform for coming to terms with the human texture of post-revolutionary Chinese society.

1
On the Eve of the Takeover

March 23, 1948, had special significance for Communist leader Mao Zedong. In the early morning, two hundred boatmen assembled at the mouth of a gorge at Chuankou village (the nearest crossing point to Communist headquarters at Yan'an) and began preparing to ferry Mao and his staff across the Yellow River.[1] A year before, Hu Zongnan, a general in the GMD, had launched a massive attack on Yan'an, and the Communists had had to withdraw their heavily outnumbered forces. The Communist headquarters and Mao's entire revolution were both in desperate straits. After he evacuated Yan'an, Mao Zedong took the assumed name of Li Desheng and resumed his guerrilla strategy, fighting in one village after another. Despite all the risks, however, Mao resolutely refused to cross the Yellow River for refuge, believing that his continuing presence in Shanbei, in the area near Yan'an, would boost the morale of the Communist troops and their supporters.

Before long, the tide of the war was reversed. In August 1947, the Communists staged a first counterattack in the battle of Shajiadian and destroyed Hu Zongnan's two brigades. Seven months later, the Communist troops totally crushed Hu, destroying his leading force, the Twenty-sixth Army of twenty-eight thousand men, at the battle of Yichuan. This victory marked a shift of initiative to the Communist side in the northwestern battlefield.

Crossing the Yellow River at this stage, as Mao Zedong saw it, was a symbolic and essential step in spreading the Communist revolution throughout the country. The war would then no longer be fought in Communist enclaves but in GMD-controlled territory.

Many years later, Mao's bodyguard still remembered when Mao said goodbye to the Shanbei revolutionary base before crossing the Yellow River.[2] It was extremely cold on the river in early spring. The turbid yellow water churned up huge chunks of ice and slapped thunderously at both banks. Impressed by the power of the river, as he gazed at the rapids and the whirlpools, Mao said to his entourage, "You can despise anything but the Yellow River. If you despise the Yellow River, you despise the Chinese nation."[3] Mao's feeling of worship for the Yellow River had been shared by Chinese peasants and intellectuals for thousands of years.

An old Chinese proverb says, "Water carries boats and also destroys boats" *(Zai zhou zhi shui yi fu zhou)*. This saying reflects a traditional belief that like water in the river, people could either consolidate or overthrow a regime. At this moment, Mao Zedong was confident of support from growing revolutionary bases in the war with Chiang Kai-shek.[4] But a challenge for Mao and his colleagues was whether the Communists could gain support from newly liberated areas, especially the cities. Excited by the recent military victories, Mao did not forget to warn his colleagues: "If our policy is wrong, we shall fail."[5]

Making Urban Policy

Communist urban policy was closely associated with its rural policy. A few days before Mao Zedong crossed the Yellow River, he received a telegram from Liu Shaoqi, now on the CCP Central Committee and earlier secretary of the North China Bureau (NCB). The letter reported on a meeting of the Executive Committee of the Central Committee held in Hebei. This meeting aimed at correcting the "left deviations" in North and East China. Liu Shaoqi wrote that in both Shanxi and Shandong, a lot of people had been killed in the land reform. The Executive Committee recognized that considerable damage had been done and had to be controlled.[6] Mao replied, "It is a pleasure to hear that all errors and shortcomings with the leadership have been thoroughly examined and corrected at the meeting. Thus [the Party's work] will be put on the right track."[7]

When Mao visited the liberated Shanxi-Suiyuan area, he found that the local government did not drive landlords out of their homes (sao di chu men) but treated landlords and rich peasants quite fairly. In the land reform in this area, landlords and rich peasants were allowed to have shares of land equal to those of poor peasants. Mao praised this moderate measure and told Nie Rongzhen, the party secretary and chief commander in the district, that Stalin's policy of destroying rich peasants had hurt the Soviet economy and that China must learn from the Russian mistake.[8]

The same concern was reflected in two telegrams that Mao sent to Deng Xiaoping, the first secretary of the Party's Central China Bureau (CCB). In one telegram, Mao emphasized that the newly liberated areas "should not be designated for land reform in 1948." The Communists, Mao wrote, had to "make full use of the experience acquired during the War of Resistance against Japan ... [in order to] unite with or neutralize all social forces for the accomplishment of the basic task of wiping out the Kuomintang forces of reaction."[9] In the other telegram to Deng, Mao rebutted the argument that a radical policy would be welcomed by the broad masses of poor peasants and instructed that the Communists isolate and attack only those who "politically side with the Kuomintang."[10] He explained the advantages of these tactics. Since the landlords and rich peasants were pressed to contribute the most to the war fund, they usually bore the greatest part of the war burden. If the Communists did not stage land reforms and continued the program of "rent and interest rate reduction" in these areas, the peasants would gain tangible benefits and the Communists would win more support.[11]

The "left deviations" came out of some Communist leaders' judgment of the rural situation and their desire to speed up the rural revolution in the wake of peasant participation in the revolution.[12] However, in 1948 Mao Zedong was more interested in stabilizing the newly liberated areas than initiating substantial social programs. From Mao's telegrams on the land policy, one can see that his rural tactics correspond with his urban policy. He was seriously concerned that cruelty toward landlords and rich peasants and the exclusion of middle peasants would scare the urban bourgeoisie, that the rural revolutionaries might bring the "left deviation" into their urban work, and that the Communists could not maintain a foothold in the cities without first stabilizing the newly liberated rural areas.

As early as February 1948, Mao suggested that the Party's general policy in the newly liberated areas, especially in the cities, should be "developing production, promoting economic prosperity, giving consideration to both public and private interests, and benefiting both labor and capital."[13] It was clear that if the Communists needed the collaboration of all the social groups in developing the urban economy, they had to be cautious and slow down the radical programs in the rural areas. In 1948, the Party's leadership soon came to a consensus on these issues.[14]

After crossing the Yellow River, Mao and his staff went to Fanzhi County in the province of Shanxi. In the small village of Boqiang, Mao was told that through fierce fighting, the city of Luoyang had been recaptured by the PLA.[15] This time, Mao and his colleagues believed that the Communists were well capable of holding and ruling this city. On April 8, 1948, Mao drafted a telegram to the headquarters of the Luoyang front, instructing the CCP leaders to pay special attention to the following points of fundamental importance in the urban policy:

1. Be very prudent in the liquidation of the organs of Kuomintang rule.
2. Set a clear line of demarcation in defining bureaucrat-capital and do not confiscate all the industrial and commercial enterprises run by Kuomintang members.
3. Forbid peasant organizations to enter the city to seize landlords and settle scores with them.
4. On entering the city, do not lightly advance slogans of raising wages and reducing working hours.
5. Do not be in a hurry to organize the people of the city to struggle for democratic reforms and improvements in livelihood.
6. In the big cities, food and fuel must be handled in a planned way.
7. Members of Kuomintang and Three People's Principles Youth League must be screened and registered.
8. It is strictly forbidden to destroy any means of production,

whether publicly or privately owned, and to waste consumer goods.[16]

Mao Zedong believed that the key to Communist success in the cities was to choose the right people to implement Party policy. Therefore, in the telegram, he instructed his military commanders to "appoint as secretaries of the Party municipal committee and as mayor and deputy mayor only persons who have a grasp of policy and are capable."[17]

Mao's telegram to the Luoyang headquarters was the first document in which he elaborated on Communist urban policy and discipline. History has proved that Mao's urban strategy was very timely. Fifty years later, Bo Yibo, second Party secretary of the NCB in 1949, recalled the chaos and damage that resulted from the Communist takeover of the cities in northern China in 1947–1948. He said the rural Communists "took a roundabout course" before Mao tried to clarify the Party's policy and tactics. Bo writes that as soon as the PLA first stormed the city of Shijiazhuang in November 1947, PLA soldiers started to loot the public houses and private stores, and the new Communist rulers encouraged the urban poor to do the same thing. In addition to this urban havoc, peasants from the surrounding counties were pouring into the city to join the mobs and share the "fruits of victory." Finally, the city had to enforce martial law, and to restore order, "some people were executed."[18] After the PLA captured Handan, Jiaozuo, Yuncheng, and other cities in northern China, Bo Yibo recalled that the Communist newcomers repeated the same mistakes.[19]

On April 19, 1947, Bo Yibo reported these problems to Mao Zedong. In regard to the argument of some rural revolutionaries that "we cannot meet the demand of the broad masses of people unless we destroy urban industry and commerce," Mao commented in the margins of Bo's report: "Such an idea is a reflection of rural socialism. Rural socialism, by its nature, is a reactionary, backward, and regressive ideology, and we must oppose it."[20] On several occasions, Mao emphasized the importance of maintaining a moderate urban policy. He used two phrases to sum up his guidelines for the Communist takeover of the cities: "[Retain] forms intact" (*yuan feng yuan yang*) and "No change in content" (*yuan feng bu dong*).[21]

Nevertheless, Mao's policy of moderation in both land reform and urban work seemed to be ambiguous since he always emphasized that the final objective of the Communist revolution was to turn the whole society upside down. In the final analysis, the landlords and rich peasants would be eliminated, and the next target of the revolution would be the urban bourgeoisie. As a patient hunter, however, Mao always kept his falcons and hounds waiting for the best time and best way to capture the prey. From this viewpoint, one can understand Mao's confusing and contradictory arguments on different occasions. On the one hand, Mao encouraged local Party organizations to waste no time in launching social reforms to satisfy the demands of the revolutionary masses; on the other hand, he asked the Party and government to be patient in areas where the broad masses were not yet awakened and the Party had yet to establish its reputation.

The difficult task left for the local cadres was to judge whether the time was ripe for further social programs. Cadres at various levels used to boast of their achievements in mass mobilization and Party development. They were eager to initiate and speed up radical social programs to prove their loyalty to the revolution and to show the progress they had made. The fanaticism of the local cadres and the ambiguity of the Central Committee's policies were the major reasons why the Communist leadership repeatedly had to fight against "left deviations" without ever really overcoming them.

On the eve of the final victory, Mao Zedong saw a tendency to separatism among Party members. As more urban and rural areas were taken over, the Communist armies were divided up into field, regional, and local forces, giving rise to indiscipline, anarchy, localism, and guerrillaism. Mao sharply criticized Party cadres "who, without authorization, modify the policies and tactics adopted by the Central Committee or other higher Party committees and apply extremely harmful policies and tactics, which go against the united will."[22] In September 1948, Mao called a meeting of the CCP Politburo at the village of Xibaipo, temporary Communist headquarters. Among much else, at the meeting it was decided to train many new cadres.[23]

The Search for Cadres

Before the September 1948 meeting, the Communists staged an offensive against the GMD's vulnerable flanks in Jinan, the capital of

Shandong Province. It was widely assumed that they would overthrow Chiang Kai-shek's regime in five years. However, the progress of the war in Shandong suggested Chiang's earlier collapse.[24] In the rural bases, Mao repeatedly told CCP Party members that "the final objective of the revolution [was] the capture of the cities."[25] Now the military situation was proving that the Communists were on the way to taking over all of China and that they would soon return to the cities, from which they had been expelled in the spring of 1927.[26] Under this situation, the September meeting urged the recruitment and training of new cadres that would follow the Communist troops and take over the newly liberated cities:

> The task of seizing political power throughout the country demands that our Party should quickly and systematically train large number of cadres to administer military, political, economic, Party, cultural and educational affairs. In the third year of the war, we must prepare thirty to forty thousand cadres of lower, middle and higher ranks, so in the fourth year when the army advance[s] they can march with it and bring orderly administration to newly liberated areas with a population of some fifty to one hundred million.[27]

This Politburo meeting, however, did not explain how the Party could have such a large number of cadres ready in a short time. It was also not clear where the cadres would come from to take over Hangzhou.

Since the Communist troops were to start a sweeping advance on all the battlefields, it was a general complaint that the supply of Communist cadres was very inadequate. In his telegram to the Second and Third Field Armies, Mao Zedong suggested turning the army into a workforce: "The occupation of eight or nine provinces and scores of big cities will require a huge number of working cadres, and to solve this problem the army must rely chiefly on itself." He ordered that the Second and Third Armies stop everything and "use the whole month learning how to work in the cities and the new Liberated Areas.... All army cadres should learn how to take over and administer cities."[28] Later the army did play an important role in taking over Hangzhou. However, it first had to continue to hunt down remnants of the GMD and liberate other provinces, so only a few army cadres stayed in the city.

Mao Zedong also attempted "to enroll cadres from the big cities controlled by the Guomindang."[29] He pointed out that many of the workers and intellectuals in these cities were on a "high cultural level," and the Communists could by no means ignore this source of manpower. The areas south of the Yangtze River were the lair of the GMD, and Communists had limited influence there. Before they occupied Shanghai and Hangzhou, they did not have a chance to recruit new cadres in these areas. Most local Party organizations had been destroyed by the GMD; a few survivors lived under very difficult circumstances and could not play any significant role. The CCP Executive Committee summarized the Party's experience in the city of Shijiazhuang: "Membership in the secret Party organization is very complicated,... and we cannot rely on these secret Party members to administer the cities."[30]

One Communist leader, Chen Yun, in charge of the takeover of Shenyang and other industrial cities in Manchuria, submitted a report to the Central Committee endorsing Mao's ideas and suggesting that the PLA and the old liberated areas prepare cadres for the Communist takeover of the cities: "In addition to correct tactics, we need well-prepared cadres capable of all kinds of urban work. To meet the current demand, both the Central Committee and the field armies should prepare special working groups for the takeover of the big cities.... The key members of the working groups should become professional city managers in the process of taking over cities one by one."[31] Chen's basic point was that the army and the local Party organizations could not ask for cadres from the Central Committee as soon as they occupied a city. They should thus train cadres for themselves and support other newly liberated areas. When the war in Manchuria approached its end, the CCP Central Committee asked Chen Yun to organize two groups of cadres—one to work in the Manchurian cities and the other to follow the PLA as it marched south. In fact the number of cadres from Manchuria was limited and did not get to Southeast China.

In May 1948, on behalf of the Central Committee, Liu Shaoqi wrote a letter to the NCB requesting that it immediately establish "a large Party school," "a large military academy," and a university to train young students and intellectuals for urban work.[32] In November, the Central Committee planned "to select a large number of promising cadres among industrial workers and clerks in Jinan, Weixian, and Xuzhou and offer them short-term political training to prepare for the takeover of Nanjing, Shanghai, Hangzhou, and other cities."[33] On March 14, 1949, the NCB issued a document on "The Current Situation in North China and Our Tasks in 1949." In the fifth section, the document read: "In accordance with the progress of the national revolution and the future needs of the revolutionary task, it is necessary to strengthen the cadre schools (North China University, the North China Cadre School, and the School of Professional Cadres). Once we enter Tianjin, we should go all out to recruit students. We must admit 25,000–30,000 revolutionary intellectuals so that we can train them and assign them to the south."[34]

A year before, labor movements and student protests in GMD-controlled cities had gained new momentum. In the areas south of the Yangtze River, Communist guerrilla groups and urban organizations grew quickly. Nevertheless, conditions were not comparable with the rural revolutionary bases in Shandong, where the Communist military victory was overwhelming and a great number of rural revolutionaries were mobilized for the further task of liberating all of China. In the country in general, the rural revolutionary bases remained a major pool of Communist cadres, while the Communist organizations in the GMD-controlled territories could play only a secondary role. According to James R. Townsend, Party members of peasant origin made up 80 percent of the CCP at the end of the Civil War, while intellectual members made up 5 percent and industrial workers less than 1 percent.[35] Mao Zedong and his colleagues were assured that the rural revolutionaries who had been baptized into communism during the eight-year war against the Japanese, the four-year Civil War, and various political campaigns would be fully competent at the urban task. Mao finally came to the conclusion that in preparing cadres for newly liberated areas, "we should rely on the old liberated areas to supply the greater part."[36]

On October 28, 1948, the CCP Politburo issued a "Notice on the Preparation of 53,000 Cadres" for the takeover of the whole country. According to this order, East China had to prepare 15,000 cadres, which were to be assembled by March 1949.[37] On December 25, 1948, the CCP East China Bureau (ECB) decided that all 15,000 cadres should be recruited from Shandong, which was then divided into three districts: Jiaodong (East Coast), Bohai (Northern Shandong), and Luzhongnan (Central and Southern Shandong) (see map 2). Shandong Province had 21 prefectures and 181 counties, with about 25,000 professional Party workers. More than half of them would be sent to the newly liberated areas.

It was estimated that every newly liberated county needed 75 cadres. Groups of 5 counties would establish prefectures and military subdistricts, and each prefecture needed 60 cadres. Groups of 30 counties would comprise one civilian and military district; each district needed 80 cadres. Finally, groups of 120 counties would constitute a CCP central bureau with 300 cadres. These cadres would deal with Party affairs, the military, the government, mass movements, the economy, finance, banking, trade, intelligence, communications, newspapers, and education. The ECB concluded that Luzhongnan should assign 3,680 cadres to Zhejiang Province and its capital city, Hangzhou, to take over power at all three levels (province, city, and county).[38]

Luzhongnan: The Revolutionary Base

To understand why the ECB assigned the task to Luzhongnan, we should briefly focus on this area and its revolutionary history. Luzhongnan was one of three Communist-controlled regions in Shandong Province during the Civil War. It consisted of two areas—Lunan (Southern Shandong) and Luzhong (Central Shandong), which were merged in late 1948.[39] This is a land of paradox. On the one hand, as the homeland of the three greatest Confucian scholars—Confucius, Mencius, and Xun Zi—this populous area is rich in Chinese cultural tradition. Two thousand years ago, Confucius opened his private school in the county of Qufu, setting up an archetype for the numerous village schools that subsequently spread throughout Luzhongnan. For centuries, love of the classics, respect for scholarship, and proper education constituted the most notable features of Luzhongnan. On the other hand, Luzhongnan is equated with the smoke of battle. A recently unearthed manuscript—*The Art of War*, by Sun Zi—has proved that the greatest Chinese military thought first developed in this area. Military leaders of the ancient Qi state created the framework for strategic conceptualization and stimulated the development of battlefield methods.[40] Since then, this land has witnessed the tremendous disasters of war. In the twentieth century, Luzhongnan has been a gateway to the four provinces in Central and South

China. Two main railway lines have crossed in this area, making Luzhongnan a hotbed of military conflicts among warlords. In addition to conflicts among states and warlords, Luzhongnan has a legacy of peasant revolts. In the west, the mountains have sheltered bandit gangs, while in the south several small lakes and swamps have provided hideouts for peasant rebels.[41] One social drama was written into a famous fictional work, *On the Margin of Water*, by Ming writer Shi Nai'an, based on the true story of a peasant uprising in eleventh-century Luzhongnan. Impoverished peasants, government-hunted fugitives, and scholars who had failed their exams joined the revolt and established an antigovernment base in the marshy region. Their romantic tales were spread by storytellers and, arguably, had a greater influence on the local populace than Confucian teachings.

In the twentieth century, several semi-martial, semi-religious organizations such as the Big Sword Society (Dadaohui), the Five Flags Society (Wuqihui), and the Three Rotations Society (Sanfanzi) had grown among the villagers. Traditionally the people in Luzhongnan tend to be tall and stalwart, with dark skin. They possess distinctly Shandong qualities—namely, the capacity to endure hardship, pursue equality, and ignore the authorities but treasure brotherhood and friendship.

Luzhongnan is a poor agricultural region. While the Yi and Chu Rivers did not provide enough water in most seasons to irrigate the farmland, irregular floods caused extensive damage and loss of livelihood. After thousands of years of cultivation without substantial technical innovation, the soil was eroded and the land exhausted, causing the crops to fail and famine to occur every spring.

In the early twentieth century, China witnessed an expansion of urban culture. The development of modern transportation and mass media, particularly newspapers, speeded up the transmission of fresh information and new ideas. By 1910, newspaper reading had not only become a popular pastime in the cities, but also started to take in a rural audience. In Luzhongnan, primary school teachers began to read and explain the newspapers, attracting considerable attention from students and their parents.[42]

In 1919, a group of urban intellectuals launched a crusade against Confucianism, paving the way for the spread of Western radicalism, including Marxism.[43] As Confucian learning declined in Luzhongnan (as well as in China at large), the local gentry sent their boys to the Western-style schools in the coastal cities. In return, these children brought back messages from the outside world and introduced the ideas of the urban New Culture Movement to their home villages.

In 1923, Li Qingwei, a child of the local gentry in Luzhongnan, was the first to be admitted to the Qingdao Business School (in Eastern Shandong).[44] At the school, Qingwei met some founding members of the CCP and joined the Communist Youth League.[45] During the summer and winter school breaks, he brought the Communist magazines *Xiangdao* (Guide) and *Chenzhong* (Morning bell) back home and read them to his countrymen in the villages, where all news had usually come by word of mouth. In the same year, Li Qingwei's brother, Li Qingqi, joined the CCP at Shanghai University and became an activist of the labor movement in the city. The Li brothers encouraged young people in their village to get out of their rural neighborhoods to expose themselves to the outside world and Marxist revolutionary doctrines. In 1926, Li Qingqi became seriously ill and had to return home to recover. He persuaded his father to donate money to open a public school. He recruited fifty students and exposed them to the Marxist doctrine of class struggle. He also published a newspaper, *Peasant Tabloid*, for the local community. Following his example, public schools and night schools spread in other villages.[46]

It was ironic but not uncommon that the children of the local gentry who went to the big cities to study modern science often became organizers of radical rural reforms at home, opposing their own families. In Ju County, Zhao Liangkun, a son of the local gentry, organized the first peasant association and forced his father to reduce rents and interests on loans. Despite his family's resistance, Zhao Liangkun was so devoted to reform that he believed that "to make revolution, one must start with one's own family."[47] In September 1927, the local government started to hunt Communists, and Zhao Liangkun and four other leaders of the peasant association were arrested in Ju County. It was a surprise for the local police to find that all five came from rich families. Owing to the money and social connections of their families, Zhao and his four comrades were merely put under house arrest and luckily escaped serious punishment.[48]

For the most part, the early Communists did not focus their activities on their home villages. Instead they encouraged rural youth to leave the countryside and join the outside revolutionary movement. Such a move, however, was a luxury for the majority of peasants in Luzhongnan. Thus, unlike some southern provinces, Luzhongnan did not experience a whirlwind of peasant movement in the 1920s. When the Communists finally followed the example of the southern provinces and mobilized a small number of peasants to revolt, the uprising was a disastrous failure.

When Mao Zedong created the Canton Institute for Peasant Movement to train rural activists, Communist organizations in Luzhongnan sent representatives to participate in Mao's workshops, where they were inspired by Mao's prediction: "In a very short time in China's central, southern and northern provinces, several hundred million peasants will rise like a mighty storm, like a hurricane, a force so swift and violent that no power, however great, will be able to hold it back."[49] However, unlike peasant leaders from Mao's home province, Hunan, the first-generation Communist leaders of the peasant associations in Luzhongnan, who were descendants of the local gentry, were inept at playing the local political game. They organized reading clubs, offered lectures, taught revolutionary songs, and organized performance parties. They recruited party members among teachers and students, who then approached the peasants as their educators, news providers, and interpreters of the outside world. However, their revolutionary propaganda did not provoke enough movement to engender any substantial political programs.

This problem gradually attracted the attention of the broader Communist organization. In 1932, the Party Branch Committee of the Linyi Normal School, the regional Communist headquarters, called upon Party members "to make friends among peasants and recruit new Party members among peasants."[50] In the winter of the same year, the Party Committee of Yishui County devised a strategy for the Communists to penetrate the Big Sword Society, believing that remolding this popular peasant organization would be the best way to expand the Party's strength and then to stage rural uprisings.[51]

During October 1932 and July 1933, the Communists in Luzhongnan launched several uprisings to "establish a northern soviet." Tragically, the local organizers did not know that the "adventurist line of uprising" had been abandoned by the CCP Central Committee, so their actions did not get any outside support. They had merely followed the outdated instructions that the Central Committee had issued in 1931: "Stage an uprising as soon as [you] get a gun."[52] The organizers assembled students, young peasants, and a few members of the Big Sword Society and revolted. The command word for the revolt was *"Puluo"* (proletariat), revealing their belief that their rural uprising was a part of the world proletarian revolution. As soon as the rebels occupied a village, they declared the establishment of a rural soviet and then laid siege to nearby towns.

The uprisings in all counties were quickly suppressed. The participants were killed, the supporters were decimated, and the Party organization was almost demolished. The abortive uprising indicated that communism had not yet taken root in the countryside. But the CCP did not lose heart, believing that its efforts had at least "planted a number of revolutionary seeds" in the villages.[53]

Luzhongnan: The Cadre Pool

The Sino-Japanese War (1937–1945) gave the Communists an opportunity to revitalize their operations in Luzhongnan. In September 1937, the NCB called for "every good Communist [to] take off his gown to join the peasant guerrillas."[54] In Ju County three hundred students and young peasants formed the first guerrilla unit. In the area affected by the legacy of the Boxer Uprising, anti-Japanese sentiment was strong enough to help the guerrillas find eager supporters. Before long small bands of guerrilla forces had snowballed in a bandit and secret society environment, and all political forces contended for military leadership. Mao Zedong urged the CCP in Luzhongnan to control these forces immediately and assigned capable cadres to lead them, naming all the troops as branches of the Communist Eighth Route Army.[55]

In August 1939, the leading force of the Eighth Route Army, Division 115, moved into Luzhongnan and established a guerrilla base at Baodugu Mountain, a location favorable for Communist expansion. All peasant militias were quickly incorporated into Division 115. In addition to the military buildup, the Communists launched two major campaigns, one for "rent and interest rate reduction" and another for "salvation through production." Through these campaigns and nationalistic propaganda, guerrillas and villagers, gentry and peasants, youth, women, and children—all organized to form a united front against the Japanese. With time and effort, the Communists accumulated strength incrementally and established anti-Japanese bases village by village.⁵⁶

During the war against the Japanese, peasants gradually came to constitute the main source for Communist military forces and Party organizations. Although a large number of students joined the guerrillas, they no longer came as educators of the peasants or natural leaders of Party organizations. Unlike Li Qingwei or other Communist intellectuals who had worked to organize peasants in the 1920s, these students joined the peasant soldiers and tried to become one of them. Nevertheless, in the anti-Japanese armies and organizations, a considerable number of the intellectuals were asked to continue to engage in educational and cultural activities.

The *Mass Daily* reported the development of primary education in Luzhongnan. According to its statistics, the number of primary schools in Yishui County had increased sevenfold in 1944, totaling 260 schools and an enrollment of 12,566 students.⁵⁷ All of the schools used new textbooks compiled by the Luzhongnan New Culture Research Division.⁵⁸ The new teachers were so admired by both villagers and government leaders that they were granted honorific titles of "Hero Teacher" and "Model Teacher."⁵⁹ Moreover, rural publishing houses were set up, local opera troupes were organized, and marketplace performances designed to propagate Party policy became a regular part of rural life in Luzhongnan.

The small number of urban intellectuals who were given the chance to serve in the army or government were regarded as lucky and honorable, but their experiences soon soured. In 1938, a political campaign against "Trotskyist elements" was launched in Luzhongnan. The major victims of persecution were the intellectuals and young students who had come from GMD-controlled areas or Japanese-occupied cities. The persecution campaign was started in Yan'an when Moscow-trained Communist leaders (among them Wang Ming and twenty-eight Bolsheviks) proved to be a failure and Mao's rural-oriented strategy became the hallmark of Chinese revolution. It was a new consensus among CCP members that rural wartime bases were more progressive than the cities and that peasants were more revolutionary than urban intellectuals. The revolutionary army needed to therefore be purified.

The purges of the "Trotskyist elements" in Luzhongnan were

directed at a number of local Party leaders who had a gentry family background or were Western educated. At least thirty young, devoted Communists, including Zhang Xu, the Party secretary of Bianlian County, were accused of being Trotskyists and were executed one by one. As they were purged by the Party, their families were both humiliated and persecuted.[60] Partly because of the heavy casualties of the war and partly because of this organizational decimation, the number of Party members in Luzhongnan decreased greatly in the period between January 1940 and March 1942. In July 1940, there were 7,300 members, but by 1941, the number had decreased by 28 percent, dropping to 5,719. By March 1942, the number had dropped to 3,308, a decrease of 42 percent.[61]

In January 1941, the CCP Shandong Bureau stopped the purges, released those who had been jailed, and reiterated the Party's policy of welcoming intellectuals to join the revolution.[62] However, nine months later, the bureau issued a decree to reconstruct the Party's grassroots units in Luzhongnan, which reflected a similar anti-intellectual tendency. It required all Party branches to purify their organizations and heighten the "class consciousness" of their members. It stressed that the "overwhelming majority of the Party's leadership [of the rural branches] must be workers, farmhands, and poor peasants."[63] After this shake-up, the Party leadership at the provincial and district levels still remained dominated by well-educated professional revolutionaries, but the middle or low-rank cadres were predominantly peasants.

In May 1942, the CCP Shandong Bureau staged the campaign for "rent and interest rate reduction." The head of the bureau's personnel department, Wei Siwen, led a working team to initiate the program. He explained that the purpose of the campaign was not merely to offer peasant economic benefits, but also to reorganize the peasant associations, train rural cadres, and recruit more Party members among peasant activists.[64] By the end of the war, the number of Party members had increased to twenty thousand in Luzhongnan and was overwhelmingly of peasant origin. Students and intellectuals found it difficult to be admitted into the Party, while a significant number of peasant members had been recruited among the villagers.[65] By the end of November, the PLA had easily recruited about sixteen thousand rural youths, using the slogan "Protect your land and protect your home" to convince them to join.[66]

Despite the success in land reform and war mobilization, "left deviations" were soon perceived to be rampant. In the spring of 1947, the ECB issued instructions requiring a reexamination of the 1946–1947 land reform. It accused Li Yu, the former Party secretary of Shandong, of making a "policy of rich peasants." The main charges included the following: (1) in the land distribution the landlords got more and/or better land than the poor peasants, and the self-cultivated lands of the rich peasants were not touched; (2) the families of cadres, soldiers, martyrs, and workers got more land and property than they should have; (3) the landless peasants and the peasants with a little land were given the worst offerings, if any.[67]

The ECB emphasized that the land reform had to go through "a fierce class struggle," and it required all the Party branches in Shandong to reorganize the peasant associations and redistribute land. Under the new instructions, violence and bloodshed occurred. Some radicals even made two colored sticks, a red one for beating landlords and a black one for beating dissidents. In the small town of Dadian (Ju County), 120 people—landlords, their relatives, and sympathizers—were beaten to death, including 2 seven-year-old boys, who were killed by a radical "children's corps." As a result, three hundred thousand people escaped from Luzhongnan to GMD-controlled areas.[68] In June 1947, as GMD troops attacked the Communist areas and temporarily seized Luzhongnan, the landlords' "home-going legions" exacted revenge on the Communists and their families, and more massacres took place in this war-devastated land.

The land reform struggle is a crucial episode in Luzhongnan history in terms of class relations in the villages. Before the 1947 land reform and the revenge of the landlords, there was no serious tension between the landlords and peasants or between the rich and poor in the villages. Orthodox Communist historians used to argue that Chinese villages were characterized by two hostile classes.[69] However, research on Chinese villages in imperial times does not support this argument but rather indicates that "village hostility was predominantly anti-official and anti-tax."[70] In Luzhongnan there was no record of fierce class struggle before this episode of land reform.

Landlord-peasant relations were generally good during the war against the Japanese for several reasons. First, as mentioned above, the first generation of Communist activists came mostly from landlord families, and the children of most gentry joined in the war.[71] Second, most local gentry supported Communist guerrillas in the war.[72] Third, the Communist rural policy of rent and interest rate reduction was acceptable to both landlords and peasants. The villagers were all mobilized in an anti-Japanese united front. After the Civil War broke out, the conditions that had given rise to the social compromise at the village level changed. The peasants had now stepped up to CCP-GMD politics. Equally important, since a considerable number of Communist intellectuals were from a gentry background, their reputation was damaged in the poisoned climate.

The "left deviations" were said to have occurred when the Executive Committee, headed by Liu Shaoqi, supervised the land reform. The committee's call to "light a fire in every village, make smoke in every household" (*cuncun dianhuo, huhu maoyan*) stirred up the local leaders. The supervisors who came from Yan'an stressed the necessity of life-and-death class struggle and ignored the long-standing gentry-peasant cooperation. They advocated attacking landlords without mercy, which immediately triggered social upheavals in the villages.[73]

The alleged "left deviations" finally drew serious attention from the CCP Central Committee. Mao pointed out that the deviations consisted "chiefly in encroaching on the interests of the middle peasants and the national bourgeoisie."[74] Although the radical policy in land reform was abandoned, it helped the local peasants build up their position in the revolution and reinforced their belief that "poor peasants and farm laborers conquer the country and should rule the country."[75] This view shaped their basic attitude toward the city of Hangzhou and its people.

Hangzhou before Communism

Hangzhou is the capital of Zhejiang Province, located in southeast China. During the Spring and Autumn Period (770–476 B.C.), it was the territory of the Yue state.[76] The fertile land, abundant rainfall, and mild climate are most conducive to agriculture. The area offers two harvests of rice a year and produces tea, cotton, and a wide variety of vegetables. In many villages, one can see mulberry and orange trees, cultivated by women who are engaged in sericulture and embroidery. Women's earnings in these endeavors add to family income, making the area's standard of living much higher than in most other provinces. Since the eleventh century this province, known as "the land of rice and fish," has had a higher population density than other parts of China. The small size of the average landholdings has forced local peasants to intensify cultivation and develop sophisticated agricultural skills. The intelligent people of Zhejiang are also successful in the academic, political, and commercial fields. In the Qing dynasty at the provincial and national levels, the Zhejiangnese made up 8.2–10.5 percent of the government officials—the highest proportion in the country.[77] In the twentieth century the "Zhejiang clique" of merchants dominated Shanghai's Chamber of Commerce, and a significant number of the GMD's Nanjing government members were from Zhejiang.

For centuries, Zhejiang paid the imperial governments more rice, silk, tea, and other tributes than most other provinces. Consequently, every government maintained the social stability and economic prosperity of the province in order to ensure a major source of state revenues. At the same time, this nurtured the cynicism of the local people: they did not worry about who sat in the Forbidden City and believed their safety rested on paying the emperor taxes and tribute.

The people in Hangzhou have immense pride in the city's long history. Recent archeological discoveries indicate that the anthropoid Jiande Man inhabited this region as early as fifty thousand years ago. In the late Neolithic Age (about five thousand years ago), the remote ancestors of contemporary Hangzhou dwellers lived in a village called Liangzhu, which is located in the city's northern suburbs today. The Liangzhu Culture, represented by fine pottery and bamboo artifacts, indicates another cradle of Chinese civilization beyond the Yellow River Valley.[78] In subsequent years, this culture was periodically enriched by new elements from the north, as well as by people from abroad, but it maintained its own characteristics and sense of identity.

The city of Hangzhou is on the Qiantang River, building on the deposits of silt from the river. The river is generous in irrigation and well controlled from flooding, allowing for a wonderful place for settlement, suitable for communications and commercial activities. This middle-sized commercial town is renowned for its cultural sophistication and pacific tradition. As early as 2,200 years ago, the first Chinese emperor, Qin Shi Huang, made Hangzhou one of his fifty counties—the county of Qiantang, named after the river. In the following 800 years, however, this small town did not significantly expand since most of the city was still covered with water and the famous West Lake was still a small bay. The real rise of the city resulted from two major factors. One was the Grand Canal. The magnificent project of building a canal from Hangzhou, as the southern terminus, to China's capital, Luoyang, in the north was completed around A.D. 600. As a major avenue of north-south communications, the Grand Canal enabled barges of tribute grain to flow northward to support the imperial court and facilitated the long-distance trade of salt, silk, and other products. Commercial prosperity brought a bloom in business and culture, attracting a lot of merchants and scholars to the city. It was during this time that the great physical beauty of Hangzhou, especially West Lake, became a popular attraction.

The second factor in the city's lasting prosperity was its pacific tradition. History seemed to prove that Hangzhou could never be a significant battlefield that would affect the dynastic fates. In 205–206 B.C., when the warlords Chu and Han struggled for domination, troops from both armies wandered around the area of Hangzhou but finally staged fierce battles in other places. During the Sui and Tang dynasties (sixth and seventh centuries), Hangzhou changed hands five times, but the power transitions were all peaceful and did not interrupt the rhythm of the city's normal life. While North China was usually the hotbed of power struggles, Zhejiang was always at the periphery of the nation's political map. The people at the periphery saw no reason to get involved in military actions in the north.

In 907, the powerful Tang dynasty fell apart, and China was split into two parts. The north (the heartland of China) witnessed five dynasties in sequence, while the south was divided into ten small kingdoms. In what is today's Zhejiang, a salt smuggler, Qian Liu, came to power and proclaimed it the Kingdom of Wu-Yue (including part of today's Jiangsu and Fujian Provinces), with himself as the king. He developed a military force to defend his territory and provide security for the people *(an jing bao min),* but he stressed that this army would never get involved in any wars with other kingdoms or the central power in the north. Whatever dynasty was established in the north, he would recognize its authority and pay it tribute.[79] Although the civil war lasted for eighty years in the north, the people in Zhejiang never got involved in the conflict. Qian's "no war" policy *(bu shi bing ge)* kept the fire away from the city gates.[80] Moreover, the policy appeared to keep the northerners (who were more aggressive and violent) away from Wu-Yue's affairs. Under this tradition, the locals did not organize any military resistance even when foreign invaders, such as the Mongolians, Manchus, or Japanese, came to take over the city.[81] The only war disaster the urban dwellers remembered was during the Taiping Rebellion. In 1860–1863, peasant revolutionaries fought bloody battles with Manchu troops in Hangzhou. The city was stormed and recaptured several times by both sides, and the majority of urban dwellers were killed or died of famine. The urban population dropped from 810,000 to 70,000.[82] This memory shaped the general attitude of the local people toward any radical or revolutionary movement.

Since the twelfth century, Hangzhou had flourished, known as the "Number One Southeast China City" for two hundred years. The basic reason, as the famous historian Tan Qixiang writes, was that other cities (such as Luoyang, Chang'an, and Nanjing) had all been ruined or seriously damaged by wars, while Hangzhou was immune to these disasters.[83] Under pressure from northern nomadic invaders, the Song court moved to the south. A large number of noble families followed the emperor across the Yangtze River; this was known as the southward movement of a hundred noble families *(bai zu nan qian)*. Even more poor people followed the Song court south. In Hangzhou, twenty refugee camps were built in Buddhist temples to receive these refugees, and the government encouraged the local families to adopt children under fifteen years old. As these refugees settled in, the city center and suburbs expanded, and the urban population quickly increased five fold.[84] In 1138, Hangzhou became the capital city of the Southern Song dynasty, and large numbers of people with knowledge and skills from the heartland of China emigrated to the province. By 1156, the number of immigrants surpassed the local population. Today, most Hangzhounese are descendants of the Southern Song immigrants.

Of the newcomers, more than 150,000 were government officials and their families, comprising one-fourth of the population of Hangzhou. Some poor refugees sold themselves into slavery, concubinage, or servitude, and others became actors, actresses, street performers, or prostitutes to entertain the noble and the rich. The second largest group of immigrants consisted of scholars and other literati who either were loyal to the Song court or, because of their cultural pursuits, did not want to live under the northern "barbarian" rulers. It was said that two-fifths of Chinese artists went to Hangzhou. Also, a considerable number of merchants and rich people escaped to Hangzhou with their treasures and reopened their businesses in the city. Since the majority of the city dwellers came from the more developed north and most of them had a good educational background, the political and cultural landscape of Hangzhou changed significantly. The northern influence even altered the local dialect. The people of Hangzhou used their soft southern tongues to pronounce northern phrases, making today's Hangzhou dialect far different from all other Wu-Yue dialects and extremely close to Mandarin in terms of vocabulary and grammar.

Despite being the national capital of the Southern Song dynasty, Hangzhou could not exert as much political influence as the capital cities of previous dynasties (such as Chang'an, Kaifeng, or Nanjing) had done. The city was the temporary residence of the royal family and its government in exile. The court did not have strong ambitions to recapture its lost territory from the northern invaders, and most officials shared a philosophy of wasting no time to indulge in pleasures in this beautiful place. The people criticized the government for its corruption and licentious tendencies and the city for its low morals and profligacy. Despite such drawbacks, with the increasing number of scholars, writers, artists, and musicians moving in, local culture bloomed.

The high-ranking officials were usually armchair scholars who paid great attention to developing the city as a scenic spot. Among the city mayors, two great poets, Bai Juyi and Su Dongpo, made great efforts to scoop up the sludge from West Lake and build new causeways for tourists. Their poetry also described the beauty of the city. It then became the fashion for scholars to visit and recite poems about West Lake; this, in turn, added a cultural arrogance to the natural beauty. Popular culture also bloomed. Novels and local dramas tell love stories taking place around West Lake. No other city has had so many beautiful legends, so many Buddhist temples, or so many scenic spots associated with romance between a prince and a Cinderella, between a scholar and a prostitute, or even between human beings and spirits. In consequence, the city became such a magnet for visitors that, as a local saying goes, "Heaven has paradise; earth has Suzhou and Hangzhou."[85]

Like most traditional Chinese towns, old Hangzhou developed through water commerce via the Grand Canal and local rivers. Foreign traders came form India, Persia, and Europe, bringing Islamic and Christian messages to the locals. In the twelfth century, the western district of the town was a foreign residential area. Korean boots became a new fashion among the urban dwellers; Malay pepper was necessary for their daily cooking; the rich and noble entertained their guests with Uighur watermelon; and the most popular fortune-teller in the town, named Wang Yuewu, was an Arab Muslim.[86] Hangzhou was known as the kingdom of Buddha, with a hundred Buddhist monasteries since the arrival of the Southern Song, but it was also open to other religious beliefs. As early as the seventeenth century, when many people thought the gap between Christianity and Chinese culture was unbridgable, Jesuit fathers Martino Martini and Prospero Intorcetta found that Christianity could reach a "significant degree of enculturation" in Hangzhou.[87] The city was constantly enriched by foreign culture, adding to its charm. It is for this reason that Marco Polo called it the greatest city on earth in the thirteenth century.

At the turn of the twentieth century, locomotives came to the area and gave the city a new drive to expand. In 1911, the population in Hangzhou was 141,859. After the railway connected the city with Shanghai, the population increased by more than 10 percent every year, reaching 817,267 in 1928.[88] Nevertheless, Hangzhou did not develop into a big cosmopolitan or industrial city. Unlike Shanghai, the city lacked banks and other modern financial institutions, it did not have a deep-water port, and its foreign trade was limited. Hangzhou remained a small commercial town. Its major trading firms usually associated with enterprises in Shanghai. They purchased silk, cotton, and handicrafts from peasants and shipped them to Shanghai. A great number of merchants were small, serving the local population and tourists. They ran grocery stores on street corners or gift shops around West Lake. Most stores were mom-and-pop family businesses, with a few apprentices who often were the owners' relatives.

Despite its long history in the silk and textile industry, all the silk factories and cotton mills in Hangzhou remained small in size and traditional in management. At the turn of the twentieth century, the introduction of some advanced technology from Japan and Europe promoted the city's industrial development. Local industry, however, soon stagnated since it could not compete with nearby Shanghai, which was the largest manufacturing and trading center in China and drew the city's skilled workers as well as capital. The rich gentry of the province preferred to open businesses in Shanghai, while Shanghai's enterprises seldom invested in Hangzhou. Although a considerable number of Shanghai entrepreneurs built their villas around West Lake, they went to Hangzhou not for business but for pleasure, and they did not want local businesses to bother them while on vacation. (See maps 3 and 4 for Hangzhou in the Republican period and after 1949.)

By 1949, Hangzhou had about 28,000 workers in 1,786 factories and handicraft mills. There were only 33 factories with more than 100 workers; most had fewer than 10. About 43,189 urban dwellers were involved in business—silk traders, salesmen, peddlers, small shopkeepers, and store employees.[89] The largest industry in Hangzhou was the silk and textile industry, with 1,431 factories and mills and 8,773 workers and clerks. Of these factories, only 101 were equipped with machines, and the others were handicraft mills. Some other small mills worked for and depended upon the silk industry, including 7 reeling mills, 245 raw silk processing mills, and other small businesses.[90] Without quick industrial expansion, Hangzhou did not have a big pool of immigrant peasant labor. Most workers in the city were second-generation immigrants who were familiar with the urban environment and believed in their own skills and contractual obligations. Working conditions and workers' benefits varied in different factories, depending upon the management and market situation. Many families worked in one factory for generations and had a sense of being members of the household. However, most employers did not trust the workers, and a body-search system was established in all the textile factories in order to prevent theft.

In an attempt to protect their interests, the workers in the big factories loosely organized their own trade unions. The unions did not have a clearly political intent; they were most effective in leading a few strikes for increased wages. Since union members had to pay membership fees, workers tended not to join unless they needed the union's help. The CCP, GMD, and various associations and secret societies (such as the Green Gang, a Chinese Mafia) were rivals for union leadership, but none of them controlled the unions to promote their own programs. The influence of semireligious secret societies was mainly among dock workers, porters, and stevedores.[91] In a port city, where land and water transport services were highly developed, the secret societies had nationwide connections, especially with Shanghai. However, the powerful heads of the Green or Red Gangs in Shanghai did not attempt to compete in Hangzhou so as to keep the city trouble free for their periodic visits.

The capitalists and merchants were better organized than the workers. Municipal trade organizations had begun as early as the late nineteenth century and had undergone two major evolutions since then. First, they emerged as associations of people who were born or grew up in the same place, and they evolved into specialized professional guilds. In 1874, the tea merchants and lacquer traders established the first guild—the Hall of Honesty and Loyalty—(Dunyitang) whose major functions were to coordinate market prices and offer sacrifices to the gods. In 1922, associations for the tea merchants from the provinces of Jiangxi, Fujian, Anhui, and Zhejiang were organized in order to help the countrymen from each province and to settle commercial disputes. In 1930, all the wholesale and retail tea traders and lacquer merchants merged into one organization—the Tea Business Association of Hangzhou Merchants and People. Although there was a sharp rivalry between the merchants from Anhui and Zhejiang, both in the market place and for the association leadership, a consensus was reached that every merchant had to follow the professional rules established by the association.[92]

The second change that took place within the trade organizations was an expansion to include members of small enterprises. For example, the Hangzhou Municipal Association of the Silk and Textile Industry was the successor of the Guanchengtang Chouye Huiguan (Silk Guild Hall), which was established in 1908. Each member of the guild hall had had to pay a membership fee of ¥150 and an entertainment fee of ¥150—a price so high that most small enterprises could not afford to join. The guild encouraged its members to make annual donations to the government in order to get protection, as well as to charitable organizations to expand the guild's influence. In 1928, a group of small silk producers challenged the low price paid for silk and unfair standards of measure; it also organized the silk producers' association that replaced the guild. The end of the anti-Japanese war brought about a boom in the city's silk industry. The association was enlarged to include two branches. The 98 members of the first branch were all factories with modern equipment, while the second branch was composed of 1,500–2,200 family-based mills.[93] The major function of the association involved holding rituals for worshipping Guandi; settling disputes; and collecting donations for education, charity, police service, and local security.[94]

It was not surprising that Hangzhou's geographical location well served the city's cultural development. Foreign ideas were filtered through Shanghai and brought to Hangzhou. Western-style schools mushroomed in the city, and modern newspapers won a wide readership. *Zhejiang New Tide Weekly* published its first issue on November 1, 1919, and soon gained national prominence. An early Communist leader, Shi Cuntong, published an article, "Fei xiao" (Decry filial piety), in the journal attacking the core idea of Confucianism, pushing Hangzhou to the forefront of the Chinese enlightenment movement. The Zhejiang First Normal School was one of three cradles of new culture in China (the other two were Peking University and the Changsha First Normal School).[95] A large number of scholars and writers taught at that school. Of the original seven members of the Shanghai Marxist Study Society, five were former teachers or students at the Zhejiang First Normal School. The May Fourth Movement in Hangzhou, as in other cities, ushered in the Chinese Communist movement.[96]

Despite Hangzhou's openness to new ideas, it could not be the center of the revolutionary whirlpool because there were not enough workers, and in any case the workers were poorly organized. The revolutionary activities of the young radical intellectuals did not strike a chord among the urban populace. As public attention gradually shifted from the new culture movement to the country's political crises, Hangzhou seemed to be silent. The revolutionary intellectuals left Hangzhou to join the labor movement in Shanghai or the agrarian revolution in rural China.

In 1925, when warlords were fighting for Hangzhou, Guo Moruo, who had once been a radical intellectual and leading May Fourth writer, wrote: "This is a game of state and nation. It does not need me to offer comments. I am going to West Lake to see my girlfriend. Why should I care about the state of affairs?"[97] Most people in Hangzhou shared Guo Moruo's feelings. Witnessing sweeping government changes in the twentieth century, the urban dwellers in the city always retained their arrogant cynicism. The collapse of the last monarchy brought the rule first of the "Anhui clique," headed by Duan Qirui; then domination by the opposing "Zhili clique," headed by Sun Chuanfang; and finally the Republican government of Chiang Kai-shek, who came from the eastern part of the province. A great number of Chiang's countrymen served in his government, but few were from Hangzhou. None of the new rulers attempted to alter the city's stature as a place of pleasure and cultural activities, and cynicism and pacifism remained the tradition of the local people. In 1938, as Japanese troops approached, the GMD troops abandoned Hangzhou without fighting, and the local populace did not put up any resistance to the marauding enemy either. A local historian wrote, "It was a blessing for the people of Hangzhou that no violent resistance was organized."[98] With a pacific tradition, the people of Hangzhou were seen as moderate and kind, but they were also criticized as soft, vulnerable, and lacking guts.

In the rural areas of Zhejiang there were small groups of Communist guerrillas, but they were ordered to retreat north of the Yangtze River after the end of the anti-Japanese war in 1945. In the following years, the urban dwellers saw almost no Communist presence in the city. In 1947, Hangzhou students joined a nationwide campaign against hunger, persecution, and the Civil War, and one of the student leaders, Yu Zisan, was arrested and killed by the GMD. This touched off a series of protests and demonstrations. Nevertheless, the secret organization of the CCP kept a low-key approach, organizing limited activities and waiting for the coming of the PLA. In 1949, as the GMD's troops were defeated and dispersed along the defense line of the Yangtze River, the Hangzhou Chamber of Commerce organized local militias to block their way into the city. The purpose was not to help the Communists but just to prevent the war from affecting the town.

For centuries, life in Hangzhou had not changed, nor had people's personalities. In peacetime, one had no difficulty finding a job to support oneself and one's family. The Hangzhounese enjoyed life so much that they wanted revolution all the less. They were proud of everything they had, and they despised everything they did not have. They did not have big industry, but what they produced was of excellent quality. Indeed, the beautiful local silk could not be produced anywhere else but in this city, with its natural beauty and talented workers. The Hangzhounese did not have skyscrapers, but they built villas around West Lake in the finest architectural styles of different countries. Most local merchants did not make a lot of money, but what they sold in the shops all reflected the esthetics of the local craftsmen. Even most local monks and nuns were cultural elites with insights into both Buddhism and the arts; the Hongyi master, for instance, was known as the number one scholar-monk *(ruseng)* in China.

It might be because their ancestors had noble blood that the urban people in Hangzhou were very arrogant. They discriminated against peasants, calling them people who bend over to work in the field *(gou lou)*. They also looked down upon the ordinary citizens in Shanghai. In their eyes, Shanghai was a vulgar upstart without a cultural tradition. In joking, they referred to Shanghainese as wretched-looking tramps who live by begging or stealing *(bie san)*. Ironically, the city dwellers used to easily accept and respect successful scholars, officials, and businessmen who came from other parts of the country but lived in the city and assimilated with the local culture. In fact, their discrimination against "outsiders" was a class-oriented cultural prejudice rather than provincialism. Before the Communists pressed toward the city gates, Hangzhou had already become an open city. The old urban elite would soon meet the new rulers of peasant origin. How well would they treat each other?

The Imperial Examination

A couple of months before the peasant cadres in Luzhongnan were dispatched to their new destinations, the Communist headquarters was to move to Beijing. Exactly one year after crossing the Yellow River, on March 23, 1949, Mao left Xibaipo, the last rural headquarters of the CCP in its twenty-two years of guerrilla warfare, and set out on the journey to Beijing.

At Xibaipo, the CCP had just held a meeting on the Party's urban work—the second session of its Seventh Central Committee. At the meeting, Mao proclaimed, "The center of gravity of the

Party's work has shifted from the village to the city." He went on to urge the Communists to do their utmost "to learn how to administer and build the cities. In the cities we must learn how to wage political, economic and cultural struggles against imperialists, the Kuomintang, and the bourgeoisie."[99] Mao and other Communist leaders were ready to embark on an urban undertaking at a hectic pace.[100]

With the long rural experience, the CCP had greatly changed. In 1921, the participants at its first meeting in Shanghai were exclusively intellectuals equipped with Marxist ideology. Twenty-seven years later, the main body of this revolutionary party was made up of the peasantry. The Chinese Communists always say that the Chinese revolution was a peasant revolution and that Chinese soldiers are peasants in uniform. In 1948, the peasants in uniform would soon become the new rulers of the cities. What would happen to these rural revolutionaries as they came to power? Full of peasant banditry, rebellions, and uprisings, Chinese history provided no encouraging answers to this question for Mao Zedong and his colleagues.

On the eve of the takeover of China, Mao asked the Party cadres to read Guo Moruo's book, *Jia Shen san bai nian ji* (In memory of the three-hundredth anniversary of the Jiashen regime). Published several years earlier, the book described how a peasant regime led by Li Zicheng quickly collapsed in Beijing after it took over the metropolitan area three hundred years ago. Li Zicheng had dreamed of building a great empire in Beijing, but city life soon became his nightmare.[101] Mao Zedong urged the Communists to learn from the failure of the peasant rebels and warned the rural Communists of the possibility of being defeated in the cities.[102]

The story of Li Zicheng was adapted into an opera *(The King Li Zicheng)* and other street performances in Shandong and other liberated areas.[103] The opera and performances praised Li Zicheng's rebellious spirit, his strategy of mass mobilization (he promised no taxes), and his early military success, regretting his corruption and collapse. It was not surprising that in the eyes of most Communist cadres, Li Zicheng was a romantic hero. His success rather than his failure was more meaningful to most peasant revolutionaries. As the opera demonstrated and the audience understood it, the key to Li Zicheng's tragedy was simply the fact that he was swollen with pride after storming Beijing. However, Mao Zedong learned more from this story. Mao had broader concerns. First, how could the rural revolutionaries avoid repeating Li's mistake of becoming corrupted? Second, how would they be able to run the urban economy as the Party shifted from low to high culture? Finally, how would the Communist rulers build internal control of the Chinese people?

Mao Zedong's entourage recorded his dialogue with Zhou Enlai on the morning they set out for Beijing. As the eleven cars and ten trucks were to move off, Mao told Zhou, "Today we are going to the capital to take the imperial exam." Zhou Enlai replied with confidence, "We should be able to pass it. We cannot step back." Mao watched Zhou with a meaningful smile and stressed, "No. We won't be another Li Zicheng."[104]

Mao and Zhou's conversation was full of historical allusions. The imperial exam was the highest level of the traditional Chinese civil service examination system. It was the only way for poor students to reach the moon. If a peasant's son passed this exam, he would get a position in the government and become a member of the ruling class. Mao and Zhou were confident in facing a similar challenge when they went to the capital. They also understood that if they failed, they would not only lose the opportunity to rule the country, but they would also bring ruin upon themselves, as had the disgraced Li Zicheng.

Conclusion

On the eve of the takeover, Mao Zedong and his comrades had prepared in two essential ways. One was to make urban policy; the other was to select the policy implementers. In a political atmosphere of "left deviations" from CCP rural policy in North and East China, the Party determined to set a moderate tone for urban policy. Also, there was a consensus within the Communist leadership that the persuasive power of ethical legitimacy should be reinforced as soon as military control was established. By the end of 1948, Mao's urban policy was not only finalized, but also tested successfully in the industrial cities of Manchuria and North China. However, its applicability in some commercial and cultural towns, such as Hangzhou, was still not clear. Mao stressed that after seizing the cities, the Party "must wholeheartedly rely on the working class."[105] Yet in Hangzhou there was neither a significant number of workers nor a labor movement, and Communist influence was very limited. The CCP would have to face this reality before conceiving and implementing any revolutionary policies.

The CCP decided that the main body of new rulers in Hangzhou and other southeastern cities should come from the peasant cadres of Shandong. It was not new for Chinese peasants to move into positions of power. Imperial China, as an open class society, always allowed students of peasant origin to join the ruling class as long as they passed the civil service examinations. Officials of peasant origin were never ashamed of their family background or nervous about their new responsibilities. They were fully able to identify with the elite and its Confucian values. The Communist shift from rural to urban areas meant that "the Party would transfer from culturally lower areas to the culturally higher areas."[106] Mao Zedong referred to this shift as "taking the imperial exam." However, the Communist "peasant students" would not come to identify with the old culture or the old elite. As soon as the peasant cadres became rulers, they expressed both confidence in their revolutionary mission and a narrow defensiveness of their cultural background. They were determined to make the urban people identify with the new regime and change the urban bourgeois culture. Yet in 1948, when the regime was preoccupied with political and economic issues, Mao's urban policy had not yet elaborated the relevance of cultural programs to the consolidation of the Communist regime.

2
Training the Cadres

It was extraordinarily cold in January 1949. As the Huaihai Battle (around Xuzhou) was coming to an end, thousands of wounded GMD soldiers were dying of hypothermia in the snowy weather, making it hard for the PLA to clean up the battleground. The Communist victory in the battle, however, brought a warm feel of spring to Luzhongnan, where every household had paid a high price for the war. The most remarkable contribution was made by women, who bore the double burden of working in the fields and undertaking logistical tasks along with the men. As the war came to an end, the women expected that their husbands and brothers in the military would soon return home and that village life would be easier. War, especially the Huaihai Battle, had brought the peasants both hardship and glory, yet glory always meant more sacrifice. A new directive from the CCP ECB required that all stretcher teams, transport teams, and other peasant laborers follow the PLA on a march south. In addition, about four thousand local cadres were to be transferred to the newly liberated cities.[1]

The move south also affected newly liberated cities such as Jinan. Although Luzhongnan would send four thousand cadres to the south, the occupation of Hangzhou and Zhejiang Province would require more. The ECB therefore started to recruit young intellectuals in the newly liberated cities. These urban youngsters with a good education would help the rural cadres adapt to the new environment of Hangzhou and other cities. But they would have to undergo special training before being assigned to the south.

As soon as the CCP crossed the Yangtze River, its secret organizations in GMD-controlled Hangzhou embarked on a mass mobilization to protect the city from the GMD's destruction. After so many years of secret and precarious activities, the organizations in Zhejiang came out, and their guerrilla forces suddenly expanded. They began to prepare for taking over the cities and organized some provisional local governments. According to the instructions of the CCP Central Committee, they would play a secondary role in the new governments.

In the spring of 1949, the peasant cadres, newly recruited students, and secret Party workers shared the excitement of taking part in the creation of a new republic. The principal task of the CCP was to indoctrinate the three small but dedicated groups of cadres with the Party's political and cultural beliefs and new urban strategies and make them a united force of well-disciplined and qualified state builders.

The Urgent Task for Luzhongnan

In 1948, the Party in Luzhongnan created a new slogan: "Everyone has a slice of the pie; everyone has an obligation to join the army" *(Fenliang renren youfen; canjun renren youze)*. The rural youth in Luzhongnan vied with one another to join the PLA. In October, the Communists recruited seventeen thousand young peasants to expand their troops. In November, another eight thousand new soldiers joined them, and in December 1948, another eleven thousand new recruits left the villages to participate in the decisive Huaihai Battle.[2] In addition, the ECB required the peasants in the Shandong revolutionary base to provide various military services for the war: (1) All 20–45-year-old men (full laborers) should join stretcher teams; (2) All 18–19 and 46–55-year-old men (half laborers) should join transport teams; (3) Children and men over 55 should do auxiliary jobs at home; (4) Women should prepare food, boil water, husk rice, mill flour, take care of the wounded, engage in short-distance transport, and cultivate the land.[3]

In 1948, one hundred thousand peasant militias participated in the battles, and a million laborers, including the elderly, women, and children, were mobilized to deliver military supplies and take care of wounded PLA soldiers. After the PLA Third Field Army fought the GMD's leading force in the Huaihai Battle, Chief Commander Chen Yi observed thousands of peasants assisting the soldiers in the battlefield. The young and old, men and women, made stretcher and transport teams, running a hundred miles to follow and help the PLA army. Chen Yi was moved enough by their efforts to say, "It is the peasants in Shandong with their wheelbarrows who made our victory possible."[4] Given their successful mass mobilization in Luzhongnan, it appeared that the well-organized rural revolutionaries should be perfectly capable of carrying out the CCP's urgent urban tasks. It was a glorious tradition in Luzhongnan that labor and materials were always available to the PLA even on very short notice. This time, however, things did not move as quickly as the Party expected.

Being in a rush and a muddle was inevitable for the Communists as they came to power. Party leaders in Luzhongnan received various directives and work assignments, every one of which was urgent and important. It was difficult to work out a schedule to implement all of them. In the last year of the Civil War, the military advance of the Communist troops was extremely quick, but their preparation for the overall takeover was rather slow. In September 1948, the CCP Central Committee decided to mobilize fifty-three thousand cadres to go south and ordered the ECB to recruit fifteen hundred of them. The ECB did not decide how to implement this directive until December 25.[5] Then the CCP Luzhongnan Committee waited another twenty days to pass on the ECB's decision to its subordinates. And it was only after the PLA won the Huaihai Battle and rapidly marched southward that the people in Luzhongnan began to take active steps. Was this delay because most Communists did not expect their final victory to come so soon or because the rural revolutionaries did not want to extend their local victory to the whole nation?

As a matter of fact, the local cadres in Luzhongnan had other serious concerns. As soon as New Year's Day 1949 passed, the Party organizations in Luzhongnan began to worry about the periodic spring famine. Yang Yuanshi, the Party secretary of Cangshan County, recalls that famine relief required much attention every year, but matters became extremely serious in 1949 because of the war devastation and shortages of labor. It was estimated that 148,000 *mu* of farmland (986,666 acres) in Binhai Prefecture had been wasted or destroyed and that 680,000 people were already suffering from famine. Authorities had to do their best "not to let any one piece of land lie wasted, and not to let one person die of famine."[6] The Party decided to cut down the food supply to government institutions and mobilized all available manpower for the Production and Relief Campaign.[7] In addition, 80–90 percent of the cadres were to be sent to the villages, and PLA soldiers would also join in the spring sowing.[8] Under such circumstances, it was painful to ask local governments to transfer their most needed cadres to other places.

The ECB was well aware of the difficulties. However, it stressed that the CCP had 1 million members and 200,000 cadres in East China, and many of the veteran cadres had not been promoted for a long time. It would be a good opportunity for promotion if these cadres went south. Also, a considerable number of industrial workers and young intellectuals in the newly liberated areas had recently joined the revolution, and they would be available for assignments in the south.[9] The ECB emphasized that the shift of 15,000 cadres to the south was an honorable task for the Party organizations in Shandong. According to the ECB's plan, Luzhongnan, as one of the three districts of Shandong, would have to transfer 3,680 cadres to the south. Of these, 1,766 would be specialists in Party affairs and mass movement, 1,190 would be specialists in administration and finance, and 724 would be military officers. These cadres would include 15 leaders at the provincial level, 100 at the prefecture level, and about 300 at the county level.[10]

The ECB required the CCP Luzhongnan Committee to take two steps toward recruitment: first, the committee would hold a general mobilization meeting of six hundred local leaders. After the meeting, each county or district would make up its list of cadres to be transferred. Second, the 3,680 recruited cadres would immediately assemble for an intensive training program.[11]

From January 17 to January 28, 1949, the CCP Luzhongnan Committee held meetings to relay the instructions from the ECB to the leaders of all the Party's grassroots branches. The meetings began with a report on the military situation of the Civil War. The participants were told that not only had the PLA won some decisive battles, but that it was also superior to the GMD's military forces in terms of size, morale, and equipment.[12] The meeting organizers stressed that the CCP Central Committee and the ECB greatly admired the special contributions made by the people in Luzhongnan, and these words evoked a great sense of pride among the participants. They unanimously approved the "Resolution on Cadre Mobilization and Transfer," expressing their determination to accomplish the urgent task.

In accordance with the resolution on cadre mobilization, Luzhongnan would provide 4,430 cadres (more than the ECB required) for the takeover of Shanghai, Zhejiang, and Fujian.[13] The transferred cadres would be responsible for forming the government in these areas at all four levels: city, prefecture, county, and subdistrict. All major government appointments would be decided before their departure from Luzhongnan, including Party secretaries and (for the cities) directors of departments of personnel, propaganda, and mass movement; for the rural areas, directors of grain departments would also be appointed in advance.[14]

Luzhongnan District had jurisdiction over seven prefectures; each prefecture administered a three-level government: county (*xian*), subdistrict (*qu*), and group of villages (*xiang*). In addition, the district administered three small cities: Zibo, Jining, and Yanzhou. On February 1, 1949, the CCP Luzhongnan Committee worked out the details of the plan:

1. Luzhongnan District will transfer four thousand cadres to the south in order to organize one subprovincial (*daqu*) Party committee and government, ten prefecture (*diwei*) Party committees and governments, fifty county Party committees and governments, and four hundred subdistrict Party committees and governments.
2. The transferred cadres in Zhejiang Province will be assigned to different posts according to the following arrangements: seventy-five cadres for each county (each will lead eight subdistricts), sixty cadres for each prefecture (each will lead five counties), and eighty cadres for each subprovince (each will lead six prefectures).
3. The leading body of the governments at all levels will comprise a Party secretary; a chief administrator; and directors of the personnel department, the propaganda department, the

department for mass movement, the department of finance, and the department for public security.[15]

On February 7, the CCP Luzhongnan Committee issued the "Education Outline on Transferring Cadres to the South."[16] It required that all counties hold a two-day mobilization meeting and finalize the lists of the southbound cadres by February 16, 1949. Then all the transferred cadres would gather to study the urban policy and discipline.[17]

By March 1949, Luzhongnan had formed nine brigades of transferred cadres, organized as follows:

1. Brigade *(da dui)*: The cadres for each prefecture in Luzhongnan formed one brigade (400–500 persons), and each consisted of six companies.
2. Company *(zhong dui)*: The cadres from each county formed one company (about two hundred persons), and each consisted of twelve squads.
3. Squad *(ban)*: The cadres from each subdistrict formed one squad (about twelve persons).[18]

Among the nine cadre brigades, the Fifth Brigade, headed by Liu Jian, and the Seventh Brigade, headed by Xiao Fangzhou, were assigned to take over Hangzhou. Before heading for this destination, they went to Taierzhuang and Lincheng for orientation.[19]

Overcoming the Major Obstacle

The major obstacle in cadre recruitment was localism. Most peasant cadres hated to leave their homes, for in their understanding of the revolution, they were to protect the rights and property they had gained from the land reform and to consolidate justice in their villages and districts. In the final analysis, they were farmers. Since the war was over and their families had land, they should return to farming. CCP leaders assumed that these strong localistic sentiments resulted from the fact that people had long been living in a politically divided China and the Communist revolution was basically taking place at the local level. The self-sufficient rural revolutionary bases had isolated them from the outside world, limited their vision, and localized their objectives. From the standpoint of the peasants, spreading the revolution to the south meant not the prospect of riches and security, but more sacrifice.

In the early twentieth century, a considerable number of impoverished peasants had gone to Shanghai or other cities in Jiangnan (the region south of the Yangtze River) and had become urban coolies. They told their countrymen about the humid climate, strange dialect, bad food, and crafty locals who discriminated against rural people from Shandong. They also said that there were a lot of frightful snakes in the south (many people in Shandong had never seen a snake in their lives). Moreover, the locals in Jiangnan did not welcome any outside rulers. These negative stories made Jiangnan an unattractive place for many cadres in Luzhongnan, although some of them showed a great interest in the new assignment. They were curious about the "land of rice and fish" and looked forward to urban life. Nonetheless, they were not quite prepared for the difficulties they would face in a new environment.

At the orientation meeting in Lincheng, Fu Qiutao, the first deputy party secretary of Luzhongnan District, emphasized the commitment of the rural revolutionaries of Shandong. He said that there would be no more large-scale fighting after the Huaihai Battle and that all China would soon be liberated. The Party needed to dispatch a large number of cadres to the south to rule the country. Fu reminded his audience of the revolutionary tradition treasured in Luzhongnan and then asked the audience: "If we don't go, then who will?"[20]

For revolutionary parties, honor and duty are the conventional means to mobilize members. The "Education Outline on Transferring Cadres to the South" noted that "every Party member, every PLA soldier, and every revolutionary cadre must have an ideal of liberating all of China."[21] For those who hesitated to accept the Party's assignment, the outline explained that "working people in the south are the same as those in the north, and they will welcome us as family."[22] The outline also instructed the cadres to think about the PLA soldiers, the military laborers, and the thousands of martyrs who had died for the liberation of the country. It asked: "If we say no, how can we justify ourselves? How can we not feel ashamed?"[23]

After the two-day meeting, almost all the cadres signed up. Then the Party committees at various levels finalized the lists. In the selection process, the committees were required to follow the criteria of the Comintern. The general principle was, "Pick the stronger cadres for the south and keep the weaker ones home" *(xuan qiang liu ruo)*.²⁴ *"Qiang"* mainly referred to high political consciousness and strong working ability; nobody wanted to be regarded as *"ruo"* (weak) and stay home. In fact, *"nanxia ganbu"* (southbound cadres) soon became a term of honor, synonymous with *"lao geming"* (veteran revolutionaries).

The CCP Zhaobo County Committee held a meeting at Anzhuan, the poorest village of the county, to discuss how to implement the directive of the CCP Luzhongnan Committee. It concluded: "It is not proper to use the proverb, 'Hangzhou is a paradise on earth,' to recruit cadres. Instead, we should emphasize that going south is an arduous but glorious task. The transfer of cadres is not on a voluntary basis. It will be determined by the Party organization after a careful review and selection."²⁵ The CCP Taizhao Prefecture Committee suggested that the selected cadres "should be literate in order to write reports, have a firm revolutionary stand, be hard working, and maintain close contact with the masses."²⁶ Being assigned to the south, therefore, was a form of political recognition, and all the selected cadres were to be promoted, moving up one or one-half rank before their departure.

Almost all of the southbound cadres were young, unmarried men. Anxious about the possibility of losing their girlfriends or fiancées, some wanted to get married or engaged before leaving. However, the ECB believed that the southbound cadres had to concentrate on the new urban task. It therefore issued orders, stipulating that no cadre was allowed to get married for two years.²⁷ Li Xingsheng was twenty-two years old in 1949. When he was assigned to the south, he had no girlfriend. Fifty years later, Li remembers how this bothered him and how his leader tried to comfort him by saying, "Why do you worry? Why should you get engaged here? The girls in the Jiangnan cities are beautiful, literate, and progressive, and they will worship you as a revolutionary hero. You can easily find a girl there." Li took this advice. As soon as he came to Hangzhou, Li met a girl student, fell in love, and tried to marry her. However, the Party intervened and told him that the marriage could not be approved; the urban girl students could not be trusted because most of their families belonged to the non-laboring classes and some had relatives who were GMD members. Despite making a complaint, Li had to give up this romance. After a couple of years, the prejudice against urban girls was gradually dispelled. Li found another urban girl and finally got married.[28]

The directive did not disturb just the men. Women—the wives, fiancées, and girlfriends of the transferred cadres—felt frustrated too. They were worried that the urban girls would steal their husbands or boyfriends. The ECB noticed the women's worries and understood that without the women's support the southbound cadres could not be on their way. Therefore, the ECB issued another order: no southbound cadres would be allowed to divorce under any circumstance for two years.[29]

In the selection process, one problem could not be solved: the poor educational background of the rural cadres. Most of them were not sure whether they were competent enough for the new job. Because of war and hectic political campaigns, the rural revolutionaries had not been able get a systematic education; most of them had merely learned to read and write in the army or in the Party's night schools. According to a survey conducted in Binhai Prefecture in March 1949, among 123 professional Party cadres in the prefectural committee, 69 (56 percent) had 6–9 years of education, 24 (19.5 percent) had 9–10 years, and the rest were almost illiterate.[30] In December 1949, the prefectural committee complained that the literacy level in the area was even lower after a considerable number of cadres were transferred to the south. Among 6,655 cadres at three levels (county, subdistrict, and group of villages), 3,811 (57 percent) had not graduated from elementary school, and 2,162 (32 percent) were illiterate.[31] Of course, as the rulers of the new China, their positions were not dependent upon their literacy level, but rather on their loyalty to the revolution and their wartime service. From the Communist point of view, the virtues of the rural revolutionaries—for example, honesty and simplicity—were both admirable and necessary for the new, vigorous government. These qualities would also be powerful weapons in transforming the decadent urban culture in Hangzhou.

The CCP Luzhongnan Committee criticized cadres who exaggerated the enemy presence in Zhejiang, yet it asked all cadres to be vigilant since the GMD had ruled Hangzhou and other Jiangnan cities for many years and still had influence there. Every cadre was instructed to bring a gun, and guard platoons would escort the cadres south. All platoons would be well equipped, and one-third of them would be Party members.³²

On February 14, 1949, all transfer cadres assembled at Taierzhuang to study the Party's urban policy and to learn about the cities and areas to which they were assigned. The training programs inspired the imagination and were received with enthusiasm. In the past, peasants had migrated from the hardscrabble mountain uplands of Shandong to the fertile river deltas of Jiangnan out of desperation. Now they were being dispatched to Jiangnan to rule the place; they were going on a mission. In their understanding, this mission was to transplant the revolutionary culture from the rural bases to Jiangnan. The whole revolutionary experience had instilled in the peasant cadres a notion of the dichotomy between the revolutionary countryside and the conservative cities.³³ Shandong's contribution to national Communist revolution had given the peasant cadres a sense of leadership. The training program stimulated pride in their revolutionary history, which, in turn, gave them more confidence for fulfilling their commitments. The peasant cadres would enter the cities with their culture and their "little tradition values," which would be incorporated into the dominant values of the PRC.³⁴ Their arrogance as revolutionaries generated a rather negative attitude toward the Jiangnan cities, which were the cultural centers of everything associated with the GMD—foreigners, gentry, and the bourgeoisie: the most luxurious and the most corrupt.

The CCP Luzhongnan Committee finally recruited 4,000 cadres for the move south. After the mobilization and orientation, there were still a few cadres who refused the assignment. The Binghai Prefecture reported that it planned to send 627 cadres, but 14 of them, including two Party district secretaries, refused to go.³⁵ The CCP Luzhongnan Committee announced that these cadres would be purged from the Party.

The Enthusiastic Students

In the turbulent winter of 1948–1949, as the CCP mobilized the peasant cadres and recruited students in the newly liberated cities, in the streets on New Year's Day, one could hear this song accompanied by holiday firecrackers:

Go! Go! Follow Mao Zedong, we go.
We want democracy and freedom.
Go! Go! Follow Mao Zedong, we go.
We won't be imperialist dogs.
Go! Go! Follow Mao Zedong, we go.[36]

The song, "Go with Mao Zedong," was not composed by professional musicians but was popular among the urban youths. The Communist recruiters went street to street, singing the song and waving red flags. They explained the war situation to the urban people and encouraged youngsters to apply to Huadong University. As soon as the applicants were admitted, they joined the recruiters to spread the Party word, explain the duties of young intellectuals in the new society, and stress their opportunity to serve the revolution.

Huadong University in Jinan was the CCP's largest cadre school, and it soon opened new branches in Nanjing and Suzhou. It planned to train students to work with the southbound cadres.[37] It was not very difficult to do so in Shandong, since this area had witnessed anti-GMD and anti-American student movements.[38] Students were greatly concerned about the GMD's corruption and oppressive policies; they were also curious about the Communist alternative. Some student activists were admitted to secret Party organizations; others went to liberated areas to join the PLA. Mao Zedong pointed out that "The fierce struggle between the great and righteous student movement and the reactionary Chiang Kai-shek government was the second battlefront in the Civil War."[39]

Huadong University, however, did not attract just student activists, but also unemployed workers, shop clerks, and former government employees. In a couple of weeks in early 1949, two thousand students had signed up at this tuition-free school. The eager response of many urban youth originated in their economic despair. In past months, they had abandoned their studies because they could not afford to go to school. The majority of graduates could not find jobs, and even professors lacked food and clothing. Haudong and other cadre schools provided the necessities and promised them a career. Despite the fact that these urban youth did not have a clear understanding of the Communist revolution, Huadong University welcomed them with enthusiasm; Liu Shaoqi instructed the school leaders, "Don't blame the students for a lack of revolutionary consciousness. There is nothing wrong with their coming to the CCP for their future."[40]

Liu Bo was twenty-two when he heard the song "Go with Mao Zedong." He immediately decided to apply for Huadong University. As an honors graduate from a famous high school, he had already been admitted to Shandong University. However, he chose Huadong because after one or two years of training, he would be able to serve the new government or join the PLA. Liu Bo was inspired by the ideal of creating a new China, feeling it gave new meaning to his life. He also believed that as a son of poor peasants, he would have a promising career.[41] However, like many students who joined the revolution in 1949, Liu Bo soon had a tough time.

Liu forgot one thing. A couple of years earlier, he and all his classmates had been forced to join the GMD's Three People's Principles Youth League. Although Liu had not taken part in any league activities, his membership in it almost totally ruined his political career years later. From Huadong University, Liu Bo joined the southbound cadres for the takeover of Hangzhou and became a secretary for the city's Military Control Committee. But his application for admission to the CCP was rejected. Then he was transferred from the government to a high school. From that time, in every political campaign, he was a target because he had once joined the GMD's Youth League.

When Liu was admitted to Huadong University, the CCP leaders assured him that his Youth League membership would not affect his future. They did not mean to lie to Liu. In fact, the university admitted a large number of students with "problems," including those who came from bourgeois families or had some minor "spots" on their records. Since these youngsters were determined to devote themselves to the revolution and the CCP much needed them in the struggle against the GMD, nobody wanted to nitpick. Indeed Communist criteria for cadre recruitment and promotion in wartime and peacetime were quite different.

In 1949, the CCP believed that the main problem of Liu Bo and all other students was that they "often tend[ed] to be subjective and individualistic, impractical in their thinking and irresolute in action ... until they have devoted themselves wholeheartedly into the mass revolutionary struggles, made up their minds to serve the interests of the masses and become one with them. The intellectuals can overcome their shortcomings only in mass struggle over a long period."[42]

To be sure, most youngsters did not have a firm belief in Communist ideology, but the widespread song "Go with Mao Zedong" reflected their idealistic sentiments. In the student movements, they advocated "democracy" and "science" and opposed imperialism and feudalism. Added to these ideals were the "liberation of all China" and the desire to "build a new China." And these youth were sensitive and concerned about China's future. They believed that since Zhejiang had been the GMD's final stronghold, marching with the PLA to Zhejiang was their last chance to fight against GMD reactionaries and thus contribute to the new China. Nobody could stop them.

In order to help these youth "overcome their shortcomings," the CCP embarked upon special training programs for them. It was believed that the general tendency among intellectuals in 1949 was to worship Western democracy and to discriminate against physical labor. Therefore, their training was organized around two paramount themes. One was patriotic education; the other emphasized a love of labor. The students were taught about the humiliating chapters of Chinese history since 1840. Finally, everyone would understand that only the CCP could lead the Chinese people to independence and dignity in the world.[43]

Although most of the students were poor, they had not done much physical work and had not experienced the hardships of guerrilla warfare. The education they had received in old or Western-style schools was elitist and looked down upon physical labor and laborers. In the Communist training program, they were taught that labor created the world and human beings. They also read Mao Zedong's criticism of Confucius for never reclaiming land or tilling the soil. Mao encouraged intellectual youths to engage in agricultural work and integrate with the masses of workers and peasants.[44]

After their initial training, the intellectual youths were integrated with the rural cadres from Luzhongnan so that they could learn from them and remember Mao's words: "Compared with workers and peasants, the unremoulded intellectuals were not clean.... The peasants were the cleanest people and, though their hands were soiled and their feet smeared with cow-dung, they were really cleaner than the bourgeois and petty-bourgeois intellectuals."[45] Integrating with workers and peasants was especially important for the young intellectuals who came from landlord or rich peasant families. In 1949, even some non-Communist newspapers expressed the CCP's view that taking part in physical labor would help these youngsters remedy their ideological ignorance and their vacillation in the class struggle.[46] While they had joined the revolution, they had to revolutionize themselves first. These youth hoped that after their training they would be recognized as revolutionary cadres responsible for the implementation of Party policies.

The training program stressed that the young intellectuals would not be able to contribute to the revolution unless they became a part of the workers and peasants. This guideline did not match their self-images. They believed that they were equally devoted to the revolution; furthermore, compared with the veteran peasant cadres, they were more enthusiastic, more energetic, and more capable of running the new republic. Soon after they were assigned to work with the southbound cadres, they were accused of being arrogant and abusing power. They were reminded that they should continue to be students of the guerrilla war veterans and to engage in frequent self-criticism and thought reform. Some of these idealistic intellectual youth could not follow these instructions and were unfortunately purged in subsequent political campaigns.

The Third Group of Recruits

The third group of cadres joining the Communist southward movement was those who were born and had worked in Zhejiang but had retreated to the north in the Civil War. Now they would follow the PLA back to their homeland. In February 1949, a Preparatory Committee for the Provincial Party Committee was formed in Bengbu, Anhui Province. Tan Zhenlin was named Party secretary for Zhejiang and Tan Qilong, deputy secretary. The committee members were the leaders of Hangzhou and Zhejiang Province. The committee decided that Tan Zhenlin would be in charge of military affairs, commanding the Seventh and Ninth Corps to cross the Yangtze River and storm Hangzhou, while Tan Qilong would organize the future government of the city and province.[47]

On April 1, Tan Qilong went to the headquarters of the East

China Field Army (ECFA) and got the list of cadres that would work in Zhejiang. Most of the cadres had been transferred from Luzhongnan. They were organized into "teams," each team covering all essential government positions at a given level. For example, one team comprised the provincial leaders, ten teams held prefecture leaders, and more than thirty teams covered the county and subdistrict level leaders. The CCP Central Committee sent some much needed railway and financial specialists to help Tan Qilong enhance the capabilities of his task force. Additionally, in the early spring, the ECB and the ECFA ordered cadres of Zhejiang origin and cadres that had worked in Zhejiang to leave their posts and form a special team to join Tan Qilong. All together, Tan would have eight thousand cadres to take over Hangzhou and the entire province.[48]

Traditionally, government officials were not allowed to serve in their homelands. It was believed that with relatives and friends in the jurisdiction, an official would not be able to enforce the laws fairly. Moreover, serving at home, an official tended to build up his personal power network. However, for two reasons, many Communist cadres of Zhejiang origin were now being sent back to the province. First, since most of the southbound cadres came from Shandong, they needed some people who were familiar with local conditions. Second, there were about three thousand secret Party workers in Zhejiang who had been engaged in the revolutionary struggle behind enemy lines for many years, and they were to join the new governments. Aware of the potential for localism and factionalism, the new leaders needed some senior cadres of local origin to return to Zhejiang and control the local cadres.[49]

The training program for the local cadres was different from that offered to the southbound cadres. In addition to studying Mao Zedong's "Report to the Second Plenary Session of the Seventh Central Committee of the Communist Party of China," the cadres collected and studied updated information on their homeland to help the cadres from Luzhongnan understand the local situation.[50] In addition, they were asked to take part in some battles. The purpose, as Tan Qilong stressed, was not merely military. First, the cadres would fight to liberate some counties or villages before the leading Communist forces came, thus sending a message of appreciation to the local people who had helped them in the difficult years. Second, the battles would test these cadres and help them establish a reputation as the new rulers of the province where they had worked.[51]

The CCP's history in Zhejiang could be traced back to the first days of its founding. Its first congress was initially convened in Shanghai and then moved to Jiaxing, a small town in Zhejiang. Inspired by the organizational efforts of a group of young CCP members, Zhejiang also witnessed the birth of China's first peasant association and trade union.[52] During the war against Japan, the CCP built two major revolutionary bases in the province—one in eastern Zhejiang with fifteen thousand guerrillas, and one in western Zhejiang with the New Fourth Army of fifty thousand troops.[53] During the Civil War, the Communist forces had retreated, but a few guerrillas remained active in the area. In 1949, the guerrilla branch in eastern Zhejiang quickly expanded from seven hundred to six thousand, while in southern Zhejiang the Communist troops and cadres totaled three thousand.[54] In early 1949, the CCP Shanghai Bureau instructed the Communist organizations in Zhejiang to focus on mass mobilization to protect factories, railways, bridges, and other public properties and to wait for the arrival of the PLA.[55] The CCP leaders in Zhejiang called upon all Party workers and Communist military forces to support the revolutionary war, mainly by organizing pickets of workers to protect the cities and by building up peasant militias into units that would support the PLA.[56]

In fact, the local Party organizations did more than that. In February 1949, the local military forces stormed some small towns and prepared to take over the big cities. Their plans included the establishment of cadre schools to train urban workers and the recruitment of intellectual youth. They planned to use former GMD officials to maintain social order.[57] These hastily amassed troops and organizations were regarded with open suspicion by the southbound cadres, who demanded that all local Party members be reviewed and trained before they joined in the takeover of Hangzhou. It was reported that occasional conflicts occurred between the southbound cadres and local Party members.

To solve the problem, the CCP Zhejiang Committee emphasized the importance of solidarity among Party cadres of different origins and held two meetings to celebrate the unity of the northern and southern cadres.[58] Also, the ECB appointed Yang Siyi as minister of the provincial Organizational Department. Yang was born in Zhejiang and had been one of the leaders of the local Party organization since 1937. In September 1945, the CCP Central Committee ordered Yang and his troops to withdraw from Zhejiang. All military forces left their wartime bases within seven days, and only a few secret Party members and a small band of covert military guerrillas stayed to continue limited operations. During the next four years, Yang worked in northern Jiangsu and Shandong and did not have any direct connection with the Party's secret organizations in Zhejiang. In 1949, however, Yang Siyi found that most of the local cadres were his former subordinates. Because of his knowledge of local conditions and his reputation in the local Party organizations, these people could not flaunt their seniority or parade their glory in front of him. He could also persuade them to accept any tasks the Party assigned them and educate those who complained that they had not gotten the important appointments they deserved. From the perspective of the ECB, Yang Siyi was the ideal person to take charge of personnel affairs in the new government.

Although Yang Siyi and many cadres from Zhejiang had worked in the north for many years and identified with the northern revolutionary bases, most southbound cadres still saw them as southerners, not as "their people." Tan Zhenlin advised Yang Siyi to keep his distance from his former subordinates and warned him not to let familiar local people work around him.[59] This was a serious criticism against Yang, who tried to convince Tan that he was not trying to develop a personal clique but wanted to find people familiar with local conditions to work with the cadres from outside.[60] In 1949, Yang's suggestion of using as many local cadres as possible was both wise and risky. On the one hand, it was good for the city leaders to have a considerable number of local cadres available for the new government. On the other hand, it was worrisome for the new leaders because they feared that an increased influence of local cadres might constitute a challenge to their leadership. Since the main Communist troops had withdrawn from Zhejiang in 1945, the remaining Party organizations and cadres were rather weak. The Communist experience in Shijiazhuang had proved that the PLA could not depend upon local Party workers as it took over a city.[61] Therefore, Yang Siyi's idea did not please the leaders. Instead, he was soon accused of localism and anti-Party factionalism.

The Key Preparations

It was extremely exciting for the thousands of cadres, most in their late twenties, to assemble in Lincheng and Taierzhuang. Attending meetings during the day and watching opera performances in the evening were unbelievable wartime luxuries for them. If there were hardships, the young cadres made light of them. Cui Bo recalls that she and her husband were both selected to be transferred to Hangzhou. Cui was living in a village outside Lincheng, and she had to walk thirty-six *li* (about twelve miles) every day to attend workshops. Moreover, it was regarded as comradeship in the Communist army and government for women soldiers to help their male comrades mend clothes or do laundry. Despite being pregnant, Cui washed clothes for male comrades in a cold river in the winter. Cui was young and did not know how to protect herself, so she eventually had a miscarriage. Nevertheless, she did not tell anybody about it, worrying that the Party would cancel her assignment. For her, the southward moment was both an honor and a chance for family unity.[62]

In the workshops, Cui Bo and her comrades studied the Communist experiences in Manchuria and North China. From the experience in Shijiazhuang, they learned the importance of not letting peasants enter the cities to loot. The experience in Jinan taught them to keep control of all guns and prohibit shootings. Nanjing epitomized the problem of dealing with foreign diplomats and correspondents. And evidence from the CCP's urban programs in Manchuria indicated that the priority should be to restore the country's economy. The intellectual youth read all the documents with great curiosity and tried to remember everything, while the peasant cadres were less interested in reciting the texts since they believed that with their experience and their superiors' directives they would overcome any problems they might encounter.

On April 1, 1949, the ECB published a policy statement proclaiming that as soon as a city in Jiangnan was taken over, an interim military control committee would be established as the highest ruling authority. A municipal government would then be formed to restore the city's economy. The statement stipulated ten categories of city discipline for the PLA troops, as well as city policies for the cadres.[63]

More often than not, the Communists drew great inspiration

from the political wisdom of their Chinese ancestors. Two thousand years ago, Xiang Yu and Liu Bang had contended for state power. Whenever Xiang Yu stormed a city, his soldiers sacked and burned it. Whenever Liu Bang seized a city, however, he made three pledges *(yue fa san zhang)* to protect the life and property of the city residents. Liu's troops observed these pledges, and it won him wide support from the masses. Many historians argue that Liu Bang, founder of the Han dynasty, finally defeated Xiang Yu not merely with military force, but also with his soldiers' sense of discipline.

Chen Yi, the chief commander of the Third Field Army, was known as a "scholar-general." Chen referred to his "Order of the Third Field Army" as his three pledges. The three pledges were the following:

1. To observe all laws and regulations issued by the military control committees and the people's governments.
2. To observe city policy and protect city property.
3. To uphold the revolutionary tradition of hard work and a simple lifestyle.

Chen's order also included ten points for attention, detailed guidelines for the behavior of PLA officers and soldiers. These even required that the rural revolutionaries correct some of their uncivil habits:

1. Nobody may shoot without permission.
2. Nobody may live in a store or house owned by a citizen, and nobody may visit theaters or places of amusement.
3. Nobody may go to town without permission.
4. Nobody may drive carts or ride horses recklessly in the streets.
5. Nobody may eat in the streets or walk arm-in-arm with anyone in the streets or jostle about in crowds.
6. Do business fairly.
7. Keep the guard stations clean and urinate/defecate in latrines only.
8. Nobody may visit a fortune-teller or gamble or visit prostitutes.
9. Nobody may get involved in feudal or superstitious activities or practice favoritism.
10. Nobody may write on the walls.[64]

Chen's three pledges and ten points for attention were adapted into a song that was on the lips of many soldiers and southbound cadres. In April, Zhong Qiguang, the vice director of the Political Department of the Third Field Army, published an article, "Issues on the Ideological Trend and Discipline of the Troops Entering the City," in the journal *People's Front*. Elaborating on Chen's three pledges and ten points for attention, he stressed that "the theory and practice of class struggle in rural areas should not be applied to the cities."[65]

Discipline would not only help the Communists create a good image in the cities, but it would also prove to have a profound influence on political operations in Mao's China. The worker and peasant cadres *(gongnong ganbu)* chosen to meet the urban challenges—actually the peasant cadres of Shandong—had survived the anti-Japanese war and the Civil War, had experienced the land reform, and had gone through rigorous political campaigns. It was believed that their loyalty to the Party, perseverance, and discipline foreshadowed success for the urban revolution.

Primary among the Party's urban policies that the cadres had to study were two articles by Mao: "Telegram to the Headquarters of the Luoyang Front after the Recapture of the City" and "On a Policy for Industry and Commerce." It was stressed that the rural policy of eliminating landlords could not apply to the cities and that all industrial and commercial establishments should be protected and preserved intact. The new city leaders were educated to see the necessity during the transitional period of gaining all possible assistance from different urban groups, especially the intellectual community.

As indicated above, the alliance between the worker-peasant class and the intellectuals was a serious issue within the CCP. A large number of intellectuals had joined the CCP and were known as the intellectual cadres *(zhishifenzi ganbu)*. For years, Mao Zedong had hoped that the intellectual and worker-peasant cadres would gradually merge so that the latter would finally become intellectuals while the former would become workers and peasants.[66] A short-term school or training program, of course, could not meet this goal. As Pepper writes, "These hastily trained intellectual cadres, most of whom were known to be devoid of 'strong ideological belief' in the Party's principles, were regarded with open suspicion by some Party members and older cadres."[67] Moreover, once the

Communists took over Hangzhou, they would meet more intellectual youths and local cadres. Their different cultural backgrounds would result in different reactions to various problems. Conflicts would occur not only between the Communists and city residents, but also among the revolutionaries of different origins. In the postrevolution era, the cultural gap among the Party's different cadres was one factor evoking serious intraparty power struggles.

On April 21, 1949, after a bitter battle, the PLA broke through the GMD's defense line along the Yangtze River. On the following day, the cadre teams crossed the river and marched to Zhejiang. On the way to Huangzhou, the teams were in charge of collecting grain for the PLA. On April 25, the CCP Central Committee approved the ECB's proposal for the takeover of cities in the Jiangnan region. The southbound cadres were immediately notified and instructed to expedite their march to catch up with the advance detachment. Furthermore, they were reminded to pay special attention to five issues when they entered the cities: production, taxation, rent, the labor-capital relationship, and the shake-up of bureaucratic enterprises.[68]

In the spring, Jiangnan was drizzly, and jasmine was blossoming. An impressive and unprecedented march unfolded in the green fields. On the main roads were the PLA troops, while on the winding trails the southbound cadre teams and newly recruited intellectual youth marched in three columns. They recited the instructions of the Central Committee, and drilled each other on urban policies, the three pledges, and the ten points for attention.[69] All of them were excited by the march, the scenery, and the new mission.

Conclusion

The training programs prepared the cadres well for taking over the cities. The most successful part of the programs, perhaps, was building strict discipline among all the participants. The main goal was to avoid the earlier mistakes in Shijiazhuang and some cities in Manchuria. The programs tried to immunize the cadres from the weakness that had usually plagued all new rulers from the Taiping rebels to modern warlords: corruption and abuse of power.

All the training programs were ideology-oriented. Although

Mao Zedong emphasized that "we must do our utmost to learn how to administer and build the cities," the training programs did nothing to expose the trainees to basic administrative skills, commercial knowledge, or technology.[70] The training programs aimed at producing a political leadership, teaching the cadres how to consolidate Communist control and form alliances with urban professionals and other social classes. Such alliances were vital for the new city rulers, enabling them to use the talents and skills of the urban intellectuals, businessmen, and entrepreneurs to serve society.

The underlying idea of the training programs perfectly reflected the political design of nonprofessionals leading professionals *(waihang lingdao neihang)*. The peasant cadres did not have to spend time studying techniques and skills. In Mao's China, Party leaders performed many functions: they were the controllers of order, plan promoters, mass agitators, and policy propagandists. But they were never technical experts or business managers. The new rulers did not worry about their inability to cope with urban problems. They were sure that with proper policies and tactics, they could recruit a full array of people with expertise and experience to work under their leadership.

The peasant cadres depended upon the cooperation of urbanites, but they viewed them with suspicion. As early as 1948, the CCP set forth a policy of using and reforming the intellectuals and urban bourgeoisie, revealing the Party's ambiguous attitude toward people from the pre-1949 society. Since their knowledge, skills, and experiences were urgently needed for national reconstruction, they were welcomed to take part. However, those who hesitated to identify with communism would sooner or later be replaced by a new generation of professionals educated by the CCP in the new China.

From the very beginning, as the Communists put together the broadest possible coalition of urban support, they also foresaw the necessity of organizational purges in the future. In a series of campaigns, from the Thought Reform Campaign to the Anti-Rightists Campaign to the Cultural Revolution, few intellectuals and members of the old urban elite were spared. However, in the early stages, the training programs led the cadres to focus on the two most imminent objectives for the days after the takeover:

stabilization of the political situation and restoration of the urban economy. In this framework, the alliance of Communist political leadership and urban professional skills cemented the new regime into an efficient government. It resulted in the most successful achievement of the CCP in the immediate post-revolutionary period.

A mobilization meeting by the People's Liberation Army (PLA) before it launched the general attack against Hangzhou.

The PLA troops entered Hangzhou, marching along West Lake.

A military demonstration after the PLA stormed the city.

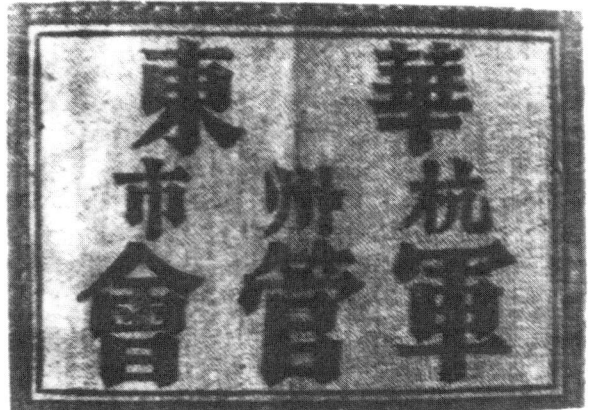

The badge of the Military Control Committee of Hangzhou.

The PLA starting the general attack against the city.

The PLA troops take a rest on the street, with urban dwellers watching.

The PLA arriving at downtown Hangzhou.

3
The First Efforts

The first group of Communist soldiers marched into the city of Hangzhou on May 3, 1949. As soon as they occupied the City Hall, the GMD's blue sky–white sun flag was lowered. Without its own flag to replace it until October, however, the PLA raised a simple red flag to proclaim the regime change.¹ It was obvious that the red color symbolized revolution. The flag without any design seemed to reveal that the new rulers had not yet made a definite plan for the new society.

In front of the City Hall, the president of the City Congress, Zhang Heng, led a group of congressmen and clerks to meet the new rulers.² Their voices were low and their smiles were bleak. Since the government they had served had escaped from the town, part of their own history had vanished, and their future was very much uncertain. The urban dwellers swarmed to the streets to greet the PLA. Since it was not well organized, however, this welcome was not as warm as the one the Communists had received in northern China. Most urban dwellers welcomed peace, but they were ambivalent about this peasant army that had come to take over their city. Yet they were as curious about the newcomers as the newcomers were about the city.³

The Disciplined Soldiers

Although the Communists took the city without bloodshed, they were on guard against any military resistance or political challenges. As the CCP proclaimed itself the people's liberator, many people saw "liberation" as total freedom and personal gain. Before the PLA entered Hangzhou, some aggressive non-Communist mobs had labeled themselves the Democratic Army or the Democratic Self-Defense Army. Some of them flaunted the banner of the PLA to blackmail the local populace; others drove jeeps everywhere to take over public property.[4] As soon as the Communist Twenty-first and Twenty-third Armies took control of the city, they disarmed all non-Communist military forces. In the first day, about one thousand military men surrendered their weapons without resistance to the PLA.

Most likely, the Democratic Army and other openly armed groups were not remnant GMD loyalists but just wanted to take advantage of the chaotic situation to position themselves before the PLA came. It was part of the city's culture that whenever power changed hands, the new rulers would welcome the collaboration of those active in political and military affairs. In the eyes of the Communists, however, all non-Communist organizations, including the Provisional Society for Social Relief and the volunteer police force, might be counterrevolutionary and had to be dismissed. The Communists would not give anyone a chance to share power in their new government.[5]

On the first night, the PLA controlled downtown Hangzhou, and its soldiers slept outdoors under dim street lamps, not disturbing the urban dwellers. Sun Tingfang, a former manager of the Shanghai Zhongyuan Drug Factory, recalled his first impression of the PLA's disciplined soldiers. On an early morning in May 1949, he opened a window and saw all the exhausted PLA soldiers and officers sleeping in the street. He realized that the PLA had quietly entered downtown Shanghai at night and had not wakened the city populace. "The first thought that came to [his] mind was that Chiang Kai-shek would never come back again."[6] His impression of the PLA was typical among the urban dwellers in Shanghai and Hangzhou, where the PLA soldiers strictly observed the rule to not enter a private residence *(bu ru min zhai)*. This impressed the urbanites deeply and made them believe that the corrupt GMD had no chance of defeating these highly disciplined troops in the future. Not entering a private residence was designed to create a telling image that the PLA was different from all troops in the past and that it had come to liberate the people.

On the second evening, local CCP organizations held a grand welcoming rally at Zhejiang University to celebrate the liberation. Approximately seven thousand students and workers attended. When the PLA representative gave a speech, the audience burst into thunderous applause. The students presented the PLA with a silk banner with the inscription, "Devoted to the PLA: Revolutionary Fighter and People's Savior." The enthusiasm of the students and workers finally removed the doubts in the minds of the Communist cadres.[7] They now felt more confident that they could make further efforts to win the trust and support of the majority of the local populace. Before the mass rally was over, Tan Zhenlin moved his headquarters into the city. Tan Qilong and his working team from Anhui would join them the next day, while most southbound cadres from Shandong were still on the way and needed one more week to arrive in Hangzhou. Tan Zhenlin sent the CCP Central Committee a telegraph reporting on the situation: "We arrived on the evening of May 4.... The military organs, the senior government officials, and the GMD's henchmen have escaped, but all other institutions—the railways, telecommunications, banks, factories, schools, public roads, power stations, and water supply companies—all remain in good shape and ready to be handed over.[8]

The local people had hated GMD corruption and wanted order and prosperity, but they wondered whether a CCP takeover would protect their interests. Thus the Communists understood that they first had to create a new image for the city rulers that would facilitate the takeover and win over the masses. A good image could be created by discipline. As the CCP Central Committee pointed out, "Social order in a city depends upon the discipline of the troops, especially upon whether our military and civilian cadres strictly observe our [directives on] urban discipline."[9] This had been proven by the CCP's experiences in Jinan, Nanjing, and many other cities. Moreover, as noted in chapter 1, Mao's general policy for the takeover was to retain forms intact and not change the content. In order to avoid major disturbances and to keep the economy functioning, the new leaders' tactic for the transitional period was, "[Go] rather slow, [do] not hurry, but [make] steady progress."[10]

On May 5, 1949, the ECB issued instructions to intensify the disciplinary education, urging PLA soldiers and officers again to study the Party's urban policies and to check on any violations of discipline. The instructions stressed two points. One emphasized that any concrete measure on city work (e.g., a policy change or a new slogan) had first to be reported to and approved by the ECB or the CCP Central Committee. The other accentuated foreign policy: "Except for the Office of Foreign Affairs, no institution or cadre is allowed to talk to or have any direct contact with foreigners. All foreign diplomatic institutions, churches, schools, hospitals, factories, stores, and private residences should be put under proper protection. Entry into a foreign residence is strictly forbidden. If a foreigner commits a crime, it should be reported to the Military Control Committee."[11]

In contrast to the CCP pattern of building civilian governments in the liberated rural areas, the ECB ordered that military governments be established in the Jiangnan cities in the transitional period: "In a newly liberated city or industrial area with a population of more than 50,000, military control should be exercised for a certain time. In the period of early occupation, you should appoint the chief commanders of the troops storming the city and some local Party leaders to form the city's Military Control Committee."[12]

On May 7, the Military Control Committee of Hangzhou was established, with Tan Zhenlin as the chairman and Tan Qilong and Wang Daohan as vice chairmen. While the CCP had let the old institutions remain intact and continue to function, it felt it was necessary to create a military authority above all other government institutions.[13] This coercive and centralized body was originally designed to consolidate Communist power and control the old institutions, but it evolved into a dilemma of "dual rule" in Communist politics. When the Military Control Committees were dissolved, Party committees took their place. Thus although the CCP had built a government administration, it did not allow it to manage state affairs, putting them under the control of Party organizations.[14]

Another function of the Military Control Committee in Hangzhou was to enforce Communist discipline, which it did in a number of ways. For example, it built a considerable number of toilets in order to change the previous "uncivilized habits" of the peasants. It informed soldiers and cadres that unlike in rural areas, all theaters in the city were moneymaking businesses and no one could enter without buying a ticket.[15] Even the most conservative businessmen could not complain. Although they still had doubts about CCP policy and conduct, they had to admit that so far the Communists had been good.

The majority of new government officials were the peasant cadres from Shandong. Before they came, the local people could associate peasants only with the rebels in a famous work of fiction, *On the Margin of Water*.[16] Probably everyone in the city knew the story about how Wu Song killed his lascivious sister-in-law to avenge his brother—only one of the thrilling scenes in *On the Margin of Water*.[17] From this work, the people in Hangzhou could imagine that the rural revolutionaries might be brave and forthright but also rough, crude, and lawless. But the Communists appeared to be different. The soldiers never forced their way into private residences, and the officers were soft spoken in public and private, conducting themselves modestly. They bought goods at market prices and always returned what they had borrowed on time.

The southbound cadres organized various rallies and meetings in which the veteran soldiers were the popular heroes. For the urban audience, their stories were interesting and their ideas were fresh and sophisticated, offering a promising blueprint for the new China. On July 1, 1949, the first parade celebrating the twenty-eighth anniversary of the founding of the CCP was held in Hangzhou; it included a real demonstration of rural revolutionary culture. Tens of thousands of urban dwellers poured into the streets to watch the contingents of marchers—students, workers, PLA soldiers, and cadres who held portraits of Mao Zedong and other Communist leaders; waved red flags and political placards; and offered street performances of "Peasants Standing Up and Celebrating Victory." The southbound peasant and student cadres were also young, and some were attractive enough to play the parts of beautiful girls in the parade.[18] The performances struck the local people as new and exciting.

Before people could make political sense of the arrival of the peasant revolutionaries, cultural changes began to be evident in the city. On the streets new fashions emerged: for girls, the traditional close-fitting dresses with high necks and slit skirts were no longer popular, and the loose, manly style of cadre uniforms, which came to be known as "Lenin suits," became fashionable. Boys yearned for PLA uniforms. The pistols of the military representatives were a symbol of power, and their red armbands a symbol of the revolution. Many people found good reasons to make such armbands for themselves: a student on campus duty, a temporary guard at mass rallies, a volunteer traffic controller on the streets. Youngsters now went to night schools and to singing parties organized by trade unions or the Communist youth league. Students no longer used local dialect but used Mandarin to communicate with each other.[19]

"A Strange City"

While the Communist soldiers and cadres made a good impression on the urban dwellers, their impression of the city was complicated. They were informed by local CCP agents that as the GMD decided to abandon Hangzhou, the city economy had finally collapsed. Market prices had skyrocketed by a factor of sixteen thousand, and city dwellers tried to spend their last pennies buying anything they could get. Hundreds of small restaurants in the town could not afford to provide a simple breakfast because after they had sold rice cakes in the morning, they did not get enough money to buy flour in the afternoon.[20] The daily meal tickets that colleges issued to students could buy only two and a half small cakes. Rice shops opened for only limited hours to avoid being robbed. As soon as the PLA crossed the Yangtze River, GMD officials knew their days were numbered, closed up offices, and started packing. On the day before the PLA's arrival, Mayor Yu Jimin withdrew 50,000 silver dollars from the bank to pay teacher salaries, but he took 15,000 silver dollars with him and escaped from the city.[21]

The new rulers were not surprised to find that the corrupt GMD had left the government in a shambles, and they prepared to deal with it. From their own experience they believed that revolution always results from poverty and misery, and the current crises in Hangzhou were therefore a catalyst for revolution. However, the newcomers saw more in the city than people's misery. They were puzzled by what in their eyes was the city's "morbid prosperity."[22] Despite the aftermath of war, thousands of visitors and pilgrims continued to pour into the city. About 140 Buddhist and Taoist temples were still open to local and foreign worshipers. Sedan and pedestrian traffic jammed the roads around West Lake. Teahouses were crowded, and wine and sex remained the most profitable businesses in town. From the perspective of most urban dwellers, the city needed more order but not a revolution.

Hangzhou was thus very different from the wartorn cities in northern China. When the soldiers patrolled the streets, they did not see any traces of war or destruction. While Shandong and most parts of North China had been ravaged by successive wars in the twentieth century, Hangzhou had surrendered to every conqueror, including the Japanese invaders, in exchange for peace. In the eyes of the Communists, this was humiliating for any Chinese with a sense of shame. Moreover, even as the Civil War had approached Hangzhou, the city dwellers had retained their tradition of nonviolence. They did not pick a side with the CCP or GMD. As the GMD troops had abandoned the city, the Chamber of Commerce and the city's Security Bureau organized a volunteer police force to maintain order.[23] Most local people were not very concerned about who would win but just wanted assurance that the war was outside their gates.

The CCP was always successful in engaging the peasants in Luzhongnan in the wars against the Japanese and the GMD. Courage and a refusal to bend were the proud characteristics of the peasant revolutionaries. In their eyes, the people in Hangzhou were too soft and had no backbone. Softness might suggest easy control, but it also contains potential power, in the way that dripping water wears through rock. In the past half century, although Hangzhou had witnessed many diverse rulers—the Manchus, Republicans, warlords, and Japanese—none of them had changed the city. Each time, the local commercial and cultural elite had prevailed over the government. While the Communists did not meet any significant resistance upon entering the city, they well remembered Mao Zedong's prediction that in the future they would have to deal with "the enemies without guns."[24]

The southbound cadres disliked Hangzhou—its muggy weather, soft diet, and the people's indifference. The hot and humid summer made them yearn for the dry breezes and scorching sun of home. In Luzhongnan, their staples had been maize and wheat, so they did not like the rice and local vegetables. They missed their wives working in the fields and their children crawling on the edges of clay beds. The urban facilities, modern technology, strange dress, and local dialect caused culture shock. Some cadres were ashamed of their poor education and limited capacity to handle urban problems; a few even deserted their posts.[25] Most suffered keenly from the cultural differences, seeing the city as an inhospitable place. The city leader felt it urgent to accustom these cadres to the new environment and to form a broad coalition of urban support, including the bourgeoisie.

Early Collaboration

Soon after the PLA stormed Hangzhou, the Communists invited representatives of the business community to discuss how to maintain social order and restore production as soon as possible. As a result of this meeting, a consultative committee was established.[26] However, the new leaders did not trust the urban businessmen. In a report to the ECB, the city leaders expressed their concerns: "The city of Hangzhou was one of the bases of the old financial oligarchies. In the beginning, we will adopt a policy to calm [the business interests] in order to reduce the possibility of destructive activities and overcome any possible obstacles.... For this reason, [the consultative committee] should comprise not only Party members and our "red" masses, but also a couple of bad elements who have influence in industrial and commercial circles so that these can be controlled."[27]

Compared with Liu Shaoqi's recommendations in a speech in Tianjin, such a policy was rather conservative. Liu Shaoqi advocated "uniting with the liberal bourgeoisie politically in a struggle against imperialism, feudalism, and bureaucratic capitalism, and also uniting with them economically to develop production." Liu Shaoqi went even further to argue for "rewarding capitalist exploitation": "If we were to go so far as to eliminate the bourgeoisie in the struggle, it would result in the closing of factories, decline of production, and unemployment among workers; that would not be good for the workers, the state, or the people. Today China does not have too much capitalism. China is not overdeveloped; Chinese capitalism is too weak and China is too underdeveloped.... [We] should let the bourgeoisie exist and develop for several decades."[28]

Although some Party leaders, including Mao Zedong, did not

like the terms that Liu used in the speeches, they agreed to the basic strategy Liu designed for Tianjin, and it soon became a guideline for all other major Chinese cities through the early 1950s.[29] Liu Shaoqi called upon centralized control of all aspects of policy making and implementation. He suggested that "the labor-capitalist problems, the disputes between workers and administrators in every city, must be reviewed and handled by the General Trade Union and the city's Labor Bureau."[30] All disputes on wages and working conditions should be regulated by collective contracts reached through negotiation between workers and capitalists, and the Labor Bureau should review and arbitrate all cases.

In working out the general principles for the Labor Bureau, the city leaders of Hangzhou used Liu's suggestions and added two points. First, in labor-capitalist disputes, any radical behavior or violation of laws would be stopped, and workers would be reeducated.[31] Second, "when the Labor Bureau is arbitrating labor-capitalist disputes, it can persuade the workers to make compromises but should never criticize the workers in front of capitalists."[32]

Let us take a conflict at a small silk factory, the Yifen Silk Factory, to see how the Communists dealt with labor-capitalist disputes based on the above principles. The Yifen Silk Factory had six weaving machines, four workers, and four apprentices. On December 14, 1949, the factory owner, Chen Yongzao, said all the material had been used up and he would close the factory. The workers did not agree, and the trade union branch arranged for negotiations. The negotiations started at 4:30 in the afternoon and lasted until midnight, but nothing came of them. Moreover, Chen claimed that the workers abused him during the negotiations by (for example) spraying cold water on his face. Since the negotiations were fruitless, the workers called all their families to move into the factory the next day and forced Chen's family to feed them.[33]

The city leaders took the workers' actions as a serious violation of the law and sent cadres from the Labor Bureau and the Bureau of Public Security to solve the problem, giving them clear instructions: (1) Solve the labor-capitalist disputes in accordance with the government's relevant regulations; (2) Solve the problem of law violation according to the law; (3) The General Trade Union and the Labor Bureau should criticize and reeducate the workers. The cadres from the Labor Bureau spent a day at the factory. They first publicly criticized Chen's attempt to close the factory and ordered him to restore production, but they promised to offer some help. Then they had one-to-one conversations with the workers to teach them the law and proper negotiation methods. The workers' families left the factory and paid for what they ate.³⁴

From the Yifen Silk Factory case, we can see the Party's consideration of both short-term and long-term solutions to labor-capitalist problems. In the first place, the Party was careful not to undermine the reputation of the working class, which was vital for its long-term revolutionary goal of eliminating private industry. At the same time, it emphasized the necessity of making compromises with the capitalists in the transitional period.

Thus for the short term, the southbound cadres tried to build close ties with all possible collaborators. In July 1949 Tan Zhenlin worked up a list of seventy representatives from the business, professional, and intellectual communities and invited them to a tea party in City Hall to celebrate the Party's birthday.³⁵ These seventy people had been carefully chosen as being both influential locally and progressive from the Communist perspective. When the new city leaders, wearing old army uniforms and smiling broadly, came into City Hall, all the guests in Western-style suits and traditional gowns stood up and applauded. Tea parties to entertain non-Party elites on holiday occasions later became a regular practice.

Meeting with government officials in City Hall was nothing new for most of the participants. The GMD government and warlord authorities used to call them in, entertain them sumptuously, and ask them for donations. The Communist tea party, however, had nothing to do with fund-raising. It was a relatively simple reception without food or wine and only green tea. In Chinese tradition, replacing wine with tea *(yi cha dai jiu)* means that the host is simple and honest. With light tea and warm words, the Communists showed the virtue of their simple life and their respect for the non-Party guests. Instead of being asked for money, the guests were invited to contribute their political wisdom—to offer suggestions or comments on the CCP's urban work.³⁶

The tea party served the CCP as a means for political communication and mobilization, while for the non-Party elite it was an opportunity to gain information from the government and to express opinions and concerns. Since the CCP usually invited only those whom it trusted and those who had a high standing in the commercial and industrial circles, local businessmen saw the invitation both as an honor and as political security. In order to remain on the invitations list, most guests would not hazard any negative comments on the statements of Communist leaders, still less on the Party's policy.³⁷ After the city's Party Committee was established and the Military Control Committee faded out, the city leaders took off their military uniforms, and most businessmen started wearing gray jackets (known as *zhongshan zhuang*—Sun Yat-sen-style jackets). What people wore no longer told their social status, and both guests and hosts at the tea parties shared a common concern for the quick restoration of the city's production.

The city leaders held that the "progressive and patriotic" industrialists should be the first to be protected and helped. In their eyes, the general manager of the Minsheng Pharmaceutical Factory, Zhou Shiluo, was one such person. Zhou Shiluo had graduated from the Zhejiang Medical School and was determined to create a local pharmacy to compete with foreigner companies. In 1926, he managed to raise 6,000 silver dollars to set up a factory. Modeling his company on Japanese pharmacies, Zhou innovated in the production line and created some new drugs that imitated American products. In the name of developing China's own pharmaceutical industry, he received all kinds of help in the following years, including technical assistance from his former schoolmates in Beijing and Shanghai and support from the GMD government. He was thus able to remarkably enlarge the factory's production, and he won a great part of the domestic market. His small pharmacy soon developed into the Minsheng Pharmaceutical Corporation and included pharmaceutical and other businesses. On the eve of the Communist takeover of Hangzhou, his friends tried to persuade Zhou to move his factory to Taiwan. Having no confidence in the GMD government and doubting whether the factory would survive in Taiwan, Zhou decided to stay on the mainland. The Communist government took his decision as a patriotic act and believed that he deserved support from the new government. Zhou was one of the first industrialists to come to see the new leaders and ask for help. For these reasons, his factory was granted a 50 percent tax exemption from the city's Bureau of Industry, and soon low-interest loans and government orders were also offered to him.³⁸

The "Lion-Fox" Strategy

The Communist takeover started hectically, but it soon settled into an orderly pattern. The Military Control Committee established sixteen departments to meet the needs of city management and future urban programs. Each department was in charge of the takeover of certain institutions of the GMD government. For example, the Department of Finance and Food would take over the city's Tax Bureau, Grain Bureau, and Bureau of Salt Business, while the Department of Public Security would take over the Bureau of Public Security. The new departments would not replace the old bureaus. The Military Control Committee changed the leadership of the bureaus and made the corresponding departments supervise the work of each bureau. (In most of the discussions below, references are to the old bureaus.) The new departments were as follows:

1. Office of the Chief Secretary
2. Department of Civil Administration
3. Department of Finance and Food
4. Department of Culture and Education
5. Department of Industry and Commerce
6. Department of Transportation
7. Department of Public Security
8. Department of Society (secret policy and intelligence)
9. Department of Military Facilities
10. Housing Department
11. Office of Foreign Residents
12. Supply Department
13. Department for Supporting PLA Operations
14. Municipal Government
15. Garrison Headquarters
16. Office for Cadre Training[39]

Although the whole city was soon under the firm control of the PLA Seventh Corps, accidental attacks on the Communist cadres still occurred. One evening in May, the newly appointed deputy director of the city's Tax Bureau was shot on the shores of West Lake. It reminded the new rulers that it was too early to celebrate victory or enjoy peace. Immediately, 239 new cadres were assigned to take over the city's police bureaus and public security system. These cadres included those from the Security Department of the Seventh Corps, the Security Department of the Twenty-third Army, the southbound cadres, and a few of the intellectual youth who had followed the PLA from Shandong to Hangzhou.[40] A wave of hunting down and arresting GMD spies and bandits was begun by the new Bureau of Public Security.

By the end of the year, 966 GMD spies had been captured and jailed. There were also a number of people who had joined the GMD or its affiliated organizations but had not committed any serious crimes, or who had served in the GMD army, government, and intelligence agencies but did not continue to do so after the PLA came. The Military Control Committee ordered them to register with the government and promised no further measures against them. With their names on the list of the Bureau of Public Security, however, they were targets in the later Campaign for the Suppression of Counterrevolutionaries.[41]

On May 9, the first group of institutions taken over by the CCP included the Tax Bureau, the Bureau of Salt Business, and the GMD's banks and financial agencies. On May 10, the Military Control Committee sent 311 cadres to take over seven departments of the GMD city government, and another 56 cadres were assigned to establish new governments in eight urban districts. The takeover was to be completed in four days.[42] On May 11, the CCP Zhejiang Committee decided to dissolve the CCP city committee that had been established to lead secret activities before 1949. It acknowledged the committee's accomplishments in the GMD occupied city, and it pointed out that "our arduous task requires solidarity and team efforts of the military officers, the new incoming cadres, and the local cadres."[43] The CCP Zhejiang Committee then decided to constitute a new Communist municipal committee for Hangzhou, to be comprised of military men, southbound cadres, and local cadres, reflecting the goal of solidarity and cooperation among the different factions within the CCP. Specifically the committee would have Tan Zhenlin, Yang Siyi, Zhang Jinfu, Lin Feng, Li Fengping, Gu Dehuan, Ke Li, Li Daigen, Zhou Lixing, and Li Yengxi.[44]

The CCP municipal committee was actually in charge of the takeover of the city, while the Military Control Committee was responsible for military and political programs in the whole province. Following Mao Zedong's instructions, the PLA functioned as a working force to take over and administer the cities. At the same time, it remained a fighting force, hunting down the remnants of the GMD's military in Zhejiang. By the end of May 1949, the CCP Zhejiang Committee was established and replaced the Military Control Committee as a policy-making institution, but it continued to issue orders and make public announcements in the name of the Military Control Committee.[45] The CCP Zhejiang Committee consisted of Tan Zhenlin (secretary), Tan Qilong (deputy secretary), and six other members: Wang Jian'an, Ji Pengfei, Yang Siyi, Zhang Deng, Lin Feng, and Long Yue.[46] The appointments reflected a balance of power among the CCP cadres of different origins and experience and well fit the demands of the new urban tasks. Of the eight committee members, five (Tan Zhenlin, Tan Qilong Wang Jian'an, Ji Pangfei, and Yang Siyi) were southbound cadres or military commanders while the other three (Zhang Deng, Lin Feng, and Long Yue) were leaders of CCP secret organizations in Zhejiang and Shanghai. Among the eight, Yang Siyi and Zhang Deng were regarded as intellectual cadres and the others were of rural origin.

Four hundred southbound cadres from the Luzhongnan revolutionary bases were the main body of the new government. The number was very small compared with the eight thousand cadres who were assigned to take over the city of Jinan in Shandong. At best, the three hundred secret CCP members in the city were ready to help, but there was still a serious shortage of administrators. The Communists had to ask a considerable number of previous government employees to stay. Statistics of the city's personnel office indicate that an average of 323 old employees were retained in each municipal bureau in May and 307 in December, while there were only 57 and 81 CCP cadres respectively.[47]

It is important to note, however, that most of the retained employees (*liuyong renyuan*) worked in the Departments of Health and Education or in industrial and commercial enterprises. The major government institutions, such as the Office of the Chief Secretary and the Department of Public Security, quickly reduced their numbers. In June 1949, government offices at all levels had kept 4,144 previous employees, but the number dropped to about 2,200 in two months.[48]

The takeover of GMD government institutions proceeded in three steps. First, the military representatives ordered all these institutions to stop functioning and to hand over documents, inventories, funds, buildings, and other properties. This took between three and five days. Second, the new leaders reviewed the personnel files, checked the records of the previous employees, and decided on new assignments for them. This work was done in a week. The third step was to organize all previous employees to attend "political study meetings" *(zhengzhi xuexi hui)*.[49]

The political study meetings were the key to the takeover. In accordance with Mao Zedong's instructions to retain forms intact and not change content, the first and most urgent task was to re-educate previous employees so that they would serve the new regime. To meet this goal, political study had to be institutionalized and intensified. In the wartime bases of Luzhongnan, the peasant cadres had had a wealth of experience in organizing meetings for pouring out grievances *(suku hui)*, accusation meetings *(kongsu hui)*, and struggle meetings *(douzheng hui)* in the struggle against the landlord class. In the takeover of GMD institutions and private enterprises in Hangzhou, political study meetings were designed to teach Party policy and raise the political consciousness of previous employees. Before long political study meetings became routine in schools and state-run factories. Six months later, even capitalists and merchants were organized to attend them regularly.[50]

Attending meetings was not new for urban people, but the Communists made attendance at the political study meetings mandatory for everyone. The meetings required not only a discussion of Party documents and Mao Zedong's works, but also a critical review of individual behavior. Participants were asked to study the history of the Chinese revolution, know how the CCP had fought for the new China, and engage in self-examinations to find the gap between the Communist revolutionaries and themselves, and then to figure out their "ideological problems."

In the beginning, the cadres were uneasy about calling political meetings. Most urban dwellers were usually cynical about politics. For them, a teahouse was more attractive than a conference room, and gossip was more enjoyable than political discussion. Many non-Party employees even saw the political study meetings as tricks to trap them. They would use every excuse possible to avoid attending them or to keep silent in group discussions. Nevertheless, they gradually understood that that their attitude toward and performances at these meetings would greatly affect their careers.

Based on investigation and observation, the cadres classified the old, non-Party employees into three categories. The first group were bureaucrats. From the first days of the takeover, some bureaucrats tried to show their cooperation and worked to please the cadres. For example, they told the new leaders that they had taken great risks to preserve government documents and property for the Communists; that they had done a lot for the people; and that they now were ready to serve the new regime, not caring about salary, rank, or benefits. The cadres did not trust them but asked them to tell their stories at political meetings. The cadres hoped that this would embarrass the liars and isolate the GMD bureaucrats from the masses. The Communists believed that the bureaucrats would have more or less bad records and would not be suited for the new government. The political study meetings would give them a chance to repent and start anew. If they made sincere confessions, they might still be useful to the people, and the government would offer them jobs.[51]

The second group were professionals. They would stay on in their original posts in cultural, economic, medical, and engineering enterprises. These professionals believed that "they had been oppressed by the GMD government and that they had served the people in the past." Although they denied that they had been influenced by the "pernicious thoughts of the old society," they kept their distance from the new regime or held very ambiguous views toward the Party's policies. They worried that their salaries would be reduced or that they would be enlisted in the PLA. They even feared that the GMD would someday come back. The Communists saw it as definitely necessary to reeducate these people, and the political study meetings would help them to recognize their weaknesses and allow them to better serve the people. If these people did not learn to take the side of the laboring masses, their knowledge and expertise would be useless.[52]

The third group were the service people in the government institutions—for example, plumbers, odd-job men, car drivers, and house cleaners—all from the so-called working class and supposedly the Communists' "own people." In principle, the new government would let them stay in their jobs, but it decided to cut down their number and encouraged the new cadres to do most such work themselves. These people claimed to support the Party's every policy and took an active part in the political meetings.

However, the cadres soon found that the workers were radical, with their demands focusing on better food and improved working conditions. It would therefore be necessary to raise their political consciousness, overcome their narrow-minded concerns for material benefits, and teach them about the Party's political goals. The political study meetings were also a good way to educate these people.[53]

Unlike the meetings that the peasant cadres had held in the wartime bases in Luzhongnan, the political study meetings were designed to educate in order to realize Mao Zedong's goal of "winning over all the people who can be won over and uniting all the people who can be united."[54] Nevertheless, from the very beginning the political study meetings served as tools of control. In the following years the meetings were coordinated with the campaigns for ideological remolding and the suppression of counterrevolutionaries, clearly indicating that behind the educational process stood a cohesive state machine.

In the early days, the old, non-Party employees revered the mysterious Communists from Shandong. As time passed, the halos of the peasant cadres faded. The employees started to look down on them, laughing at their ignorance and weaknesses. They believed that the Communists could not survive without their help. They did not understand that Mao's takeover policy of retaining forms intact and not changing content was but a temporary tactic and that they were doomed to be kicked out of important positions in the new state. The peasant cadres did not know how to draft bureaucratic documents; they could not distinguish green tea from black tea; and they were even nervous about crossing streets in the city's heavy traffic. But they were confident that they could show everyone that the city would be better governed than it had ever been before.

The Communists told the retained employees that their "bureaucratic style from the old society" would no longer work in the new government. They ordered them to spend at least four hours a day in political study meetings.[55] At the meetings, criticism was sharp and showed no forgiveness. Personal shortcomings were interpreted as a "decadent style of life," while any connection with the GMD was spotlighted as a shameful blot on the employees' resumes. Self-examination was intended to make the retained employees confess to their "sins" since they had served the old society for many years. Although there was no violence involved, the meetings were full of psychological pressure. Senior bureaucrats became very worried about being labeled counterrevolutionaries.

After a few weeks of political study, a "resettlement of retained employees" was staged. The military representatives announced that three factors would determine where the retained employees would go: the needs of the revolution, the expertise of the employees, and the progress they had made in the political study meetings.[56] The Communist takeover became an artistic "lion-fox" strategy. Its success was due to the balance between compulsion and persuasion. Everyone now understood that his performance at the political study meetings was vital because the Party kept the repentant activists and purged those who had not been cooperative. That sent a warning to those who did not take Communist meetings seriously.

"Making Smoke Rise"

Making new socialist men was a long-term goal of the Communist revolution, but the immediate task was to revive the city's production. In the last year of the Civil War, Mao Zedong instructed the Communists from rural bases, "From the very first day we take over a city, we should direct the attention to restoring and developing its production."[57] He continued: "If we know nothing about production and do not master it quickly, if we cannot restore and develop production as speedily as possible and achieve solid success so that the livelihood of the workers, first of all, and that of the people in general is improved, we shall be unable to maintain our political power, we shall be unable to stand on our feet, we shall fail."[58]

Theoretically, nobody challenged this instruction; however, it was not immediately followed by many of the cadres who came to Hangzhou and brought their own traditions and values. One of the traditions was to attack local tyrants and redistribute land. As the cadres were eager to help the urban poor, the idea immediately crossed their minds to open the granaries and offer the poor food relief *(kai cang ji pin)*. This was what the Communist troops usually did after they stormed a village or town in wartime, and it had also been the practice of all peasant rebels in the past. The cadres believed that the Communists had to bring tangible benefits to the people in order to win mass support. They could not imagine how their power could hold if livelihoods did not immediately improve.

As the Communists entered Hangzhou, 18,709 famine refugees were waiting for government relief. The city granary provided 105,000 *jin* (52,500 kilograms) of rice in the first two months, such that each unemployed worker got four *dou* (4 decaliters).[59] When the Military Control Committee sent representatives to the main factories, the workers told them that they wanted not only "political liberation," but also "liberation of the stomach," asking for an increase in wages and equal treatment between workers and administrators. In order to spark the enthusiasm of the workers toward production, the military representatives promised to increase salaries by 7 percent (in department stores), 60 percent (in tobacco factories), and 200 percent (in printing establishments).[60]

Such measures to satisfy the excessive demands of the workers and urban poor had been criticized as "a lopsided and nearsighted view of welfarism."[61] Mao Zedong had referred to them as "agrarian socialism," a policy the Communists had followed when they took over the first GMD city—Shijiazhuang—but it had caused nothing but chaos and depression. The experience of running industrial cities in Manchuria also indicated that an early increase in wages simply allowed the workers to sit idle and eat and led the state-run enterprises to go bankrupt.[62]

The city leaders of Hangzhou began to alter the tendency toward agrarian socialism as soon as they tasted sour fruit. The Labor Bureau reported that most cadres tried to immediately change the "unfair capitalist wage system," but it scared most factory owners. In order to cut down on costs, these owners would reduce production, fire a considerable number of workers, or close down their business. As a result, tension and conflict between workers and capitalists on the wage issue escalated, the unemployment rate went up, and production continued to stagnate.[63] With such lessons and those from the northern industrial cities, most cadres began to understand the necessity for a moderate policy to control the scope and speed of transformation.

If one judged by the tourist boats in West Lake and pilgrims in Hangzhou's temples, one could not imagine that economic crisis loomed large in 1949. Only a week after the takeover, however, the Communist mayor began to recognize the serious situation of the fourteen thousand unemployed workers and saw that the city was running out of food, fuel, and power.[64] A market investigation by the Military Control Committee showed that when the PLA had arrived, the price of rice was $4 (silver dollars) per *dan* (about 165 pounds), but a week later it rose to $10 per *dan*. It was estimated that the city desperately needed 150,000 *dan* of rice, but the municipal granary was almost empty. Also, because of a shortage of coal, the power station could provide the city with electricity for only another forty days, and the railway would have to shut down in a week.[65]

As noted, silk production was the city's major industry. About one hundred thousand urban residents—including workers, craftsmen, merchants, and their families—lived from the silk business. But now the market had shrunk, most factories had closed, and everyone was waiting for the government to offer a solution. In May 1949, only 50 percent of the spinning wheels and 7 percent of the looms continued to operate. Moreover, May was the harvest season for tea and silkworm cocoons. If the silk factories did not hurry up and purchase these items, more than two hundred and fifty thousand farmers would hardly survive the second half of the year.[66] In addition, a large number of silk and other companies were subsidiaries or branches of enterprises in Shanghai, and they greatly depended upon Shanghai's markets, capitals, and financial services. Since Shanghai was still in the hands of the GMD, the government had to look for other levers for the city's economy.

Reports from district governments present heartrending pictures of the unemployed living on garbage, begging, or selling children.[67] In the Xiacheng district, a female worker borrowed two *sheng* of rice, took it home, and then went out to borrow fuel. When she got back home, she found that her two hungry children had eaten one and a half *sheng* of the uncooked rice. On the same day, three aged men died of hunger in the city's old folks' home.[68]

What was the proper way to help the urban poor? On May 16, 1949, the city leaders read an editorial by the Xinhua News Agency (the voice of the CCP Central Committee) reiterating that cadres were not allowed to rely on welfarism to obtain unrealistic improvements in workers' living conditions.[69] Following this, the CCP Zhejiang Committee issued "Instructions on Factory Work," which stipulated that increases in wages should be based on negotiation and agreement between the workers and factory owners.

The real monthly salaries of the workers could not exceed the average salaries in the three months before liberation.[70] The CCP advised workers that economic conditions precluded any immediate significant improvements in wages and benefits and they should focus on production to assure a promising future. The chairman of the city's Military Control Committee, Tan Zhenlin, called an urgent meeting and told the Party workers, "We cannot maintain social order or win the public over unless smoke rises from the chimneys of the factories."[71] From this time on, city leaders and cadres focused their attention on "making smoke rise."

Major efforts to restore production started with the creation of new state enterprises. The ECB instructed that "All enterprises of the GMD bureaucrats and all public enterprises, including factories, mines, railways, the postal service, steamships, banks, electricity, telephones, water supply, stores, warehouses, and so on, must be taken over."[72] The Hangzhou Military Control Committee wasted no time in sending representatives to take over these institutions, transform them into the first group of state enterprises, and see to it that production was resumed. The Wufeng Silk Factory was the first state-run enterprise in Hangzhou, and the CCP planned to make it a model for the restoration of production.

The Wufeng Silk Factory had sixty-four looms, making it one of the largest brocade mills in the city. The factory was built by a local gentry-merchant, Wang Wuquan, who had collaborated with the Japanese in the 1930s. After the anti-Japanese war, Wang was arrested, and his property was confiscated by the GMD's Central Trust Bureau.[73] Now the Military Control Committee sent Cai Jingxian as the representative to take over the factory.

Cai was a young officer in the PLA Seventh Corps. On May 23, 1949, he changed into a new PLA uniform that he had just received on crossing the Yangtze River, brought a German pistol, and went to the factory. His assistant, a graduate student of Huadong University, and his bodyguard, a PLA soldier, took rifles and followed him with excitement. As Cai's team arrived at the factory, they saw an extremely desolate scene. The doorman told Cai that the factory owner had fled to Shanghai, the manager had disappeared, and there were no workers there at all.

Cai Jingxian knew nothing about the silk industry, but he believed that "the magic weapon for overcoming difficulties was to depend upon the broad mass of people."[74] Cai began to visit the workers one by one, and he came to the conclusion that the majority of the workers and technicians and even some of the administrators would like to go back to work. What the workers really needed was leadership and a production plan. The Party provided leadership, and the plan would come out of detailed discussions with the workers. Cai called a meeting and asked the workers, "Who fed whom? Did the capitalists feed the workers, or did the workers feed the capitalists?" He encouraged the workers to believe in their own power and act as "the real owners of the enterprise."[75] As Cai and his colleagues worked at the Wufeng Silk Factory, a production campaign unfolded throughout the city. The slogan "To overcome difficulties, restore the economy, and support the liberation war" made the headlines in the local press. All city dwellers, including workers and their families, were asked to respond to the calls to "Let five people share the food of three" and to "Tighten [your] belt and prepare to go through a couple of years of hardship."[76] Under such circumstances, workers had to work longer hours for less pay. Cai first trained and organized a group of young activists, then persuaded the veteran workers to join this group, and finally brought in all the workers, clerks, and technicians.[77] Five days later, smoke rose from the chimney of the factory.

Except for the factory head and the general manager, all administrators were retained in their previous posts with the same salaries. After setting the machine into motion, Cai adopted new measures to promote production. Imitating the Soviet model, he introduced the piece-rate wage system, which encouraged workers to work harder to earn more. By the end of 1949, the factory started to make money. According to its financial report for that year, the monthly profits were ¥40,000 (RMB—renminbi) and the total value of the factory's fixed assets had increased to ¥927 million (RMB).[78] (See below for RMB/silver dollar problems.)

Cai Jingxian ascribed his success to the traditional Communist method of the mass line. The basic idea, as the Party repeatedly emphasized, was to mobilize all social classes—all positive forces—to restore and develop production. For this purpose, three organizations were asked to work together: the trade union for workers, the Association of Industry and Commerce for capitalists and merchants, and the Labor Bureau. As a government institution, the Labor Bureau functioned as a middleman between workers and capitalists and helped solve labor-capital problems.[79] In some big enterprises, the military representatives or the trade union selected worker representatives to form a "Committee for the Restoration of Production" that would be involved in production management.

Nevertheless, it is clear that Cai exaggerated the role of mass mobilization. In fact, state power played the decisive role in restoring the economy. In 1949, a series of state-run trading companies were established to help the local factories open up new markets. The Zhejiang Province Company of Local Products and the Zhejiang branch of the Chinese Silkworm Cocoon Company gave government orders to silk factories, supplied them materials, and used their connections with the old liberated areas to find new customers. The state companies also adjusted production, stabilized the market price, and guided the structural reformation of the enterprises. In order to explore new markets, the government organized a "Delegation of Industry and Commerce" to visit Beijing and other major cities in Manchuria and North China. The Chinese Ministry of Commerce negotiated with the Council of Commerce of the Soviet Union and signed an agreement to export Hangzhou's silk products to the Soviet Union and East European countries. As a result, the silk companies in Hangzhou sold not only all their new products, but also their stocks in storage within a few months.[80]

In 1949, the city leaders of Hangzhou shared with the leaders in Shanghai, Tianjin, and other Chinese cities the aspiration of building highly industrialized metropolitan areas. The provincial Bureau of Industry and Mines was established to first restore production in the former "bourgeois-capitalist enterprises" and then to build as many new factories, mines, and power stations as possible, in an attempt to carry out an industrial revolution in the world's largest agricultural country. Gu Dehuan was chosen to be the head of the Zhejiang provincial Bureau of Industry and Mines. Gu had years of guerrilla war experience in the province and was very familiar with the local people and resources. He was one of the few technical experts within the Party because he had been a college student in electrical engineering before he joined the revolution.

Gu accepted the appointment with enthusiasm. Aware that Hangzhou did not have much industry, he started with a small factory in which the few hundred workers knew only how to repair used cars and change artillery parts.[81] Under Gu's supervision, the factory was converted into making small machines. Gu then reconstructed another factory to make military gunnysacks. As the PLA continued to march south to hunt GMD troops, the demand for gunnysacks was great. The gunnysack factory provided four thousand jobs and made ¥20–30 million in profits each year.[82]

The Silver Dollar War

It is a regular tactic of the CCP to combine economic measures and political means to achieve its goals. The most dramatic example was its efforts to stabilize the financial market in Hangzhou. The local press referred to these efforts as the Silver Dollar War.

Although the political situation was quickly stabilized and industry was gradually revived, the financial picture in the city remained grim. In the light of instructions from Liu Shaoqi, the new bureaus continued to use old employees and the old taxation network to collect taxes. However, military representatives had to accompany the old tax collectors in their duties, and taxpayers got receipts from the Communist government.[83] These measures proved to be essential in solving the financial problems inherited from the GMD.

To establish the new economic order, another measure was taken: the conversion of the GMD currency, the jinyuanjuan (JYJ), into the new Communist notes—the RMB. As in other CCP-occupied cities, the city rulers in Hangzhou believed that this was a decisive step toward stabilizing market prices, ensuring a supply of foodstuffs, and laying down a foundation for improving people's lives in later years. On May 10, 1949, the Military Control Committee sent several working teams out to take over all the public and private banks. Within two weeks, all 193 national and provincial banks and 18 cooperative treasuries throughout the province had been handed over to the new rulers. In addition, the government confiscated all holdings of the GMD's financial institutions—1,365 ounces of gold, 18,560 ounces of silver, 16,834 silver dollars, $1,797 in foreign currency, and 16.1 billion JYJ. Also, 671 cars, 1,039 large vehicles, 311,667 gallons of gasoline, and 5 million pounds of rice became assets of the Communist city government in 1949. The confiscation of bureaucratic capital, which included big factories, mines, railways, telegraph companies, and banks, provided the state with a solid financial basis for the new currency, and the JYJ was strictly banned in the city.[84]

Although the JYJ soon disappeared from the market, the RMB was not immediately accepted, and silver dollars became the popular currency. In rural areas, peasants refused to take RMB, and the government grain-purchasing teams had to carry hard currency to the villages. The exchange rate between RMB and silver dollars on the black market increased every day. On May 11, a silver dollar exchanged for ¥470 RMB, but ten days later, it exchanged for ¥1,020 RMB. Associated with this, the price of rice increased 188 percent, and the prices of other daily necessities also fluctuated.[85]

Money hawkers flashed silver dollars to solicit customers in front of the Tax Bureau building. That made Tax Bureau employees very nervous since they lived on state salaries, which were paid in RMB. They were not comfortable holding RMB. Every time they got paid, they would rush out to the street to exchange their RMB for silver dollars.[86] Under such circumstances, how could the government expect that factory workers and other urban dwellers would not be involved in black market transactions?

In the first weeks, the city leaders tried to take care of the matter in an economic way. Following the instructions of the ECB, the government got involved in the black market. It invested a large amount of silver dollars in an effort to become the biggest buyer of RMB and thus stabilize the exchange rate. However, no matter how many silver dollars the government put in, the black market immediately swallowed them, suggesting that an economic measure alone would not work. On May 16, the Military Control Committee of Hangzhou issued a third announcement banning the circulation of silver dollars. It announced that the People's Bank would open four offices in the city and all exchanges would have to be in these offices. Any street deal was illegal and would be seriously punished.[87] Every day the city's Garrison Headquarters sent an armed patrol to check the market, disperse the masses, and force the money hawkers to sell silver dollars to the government at the official rate.

In late May 1949, two mysterious guests checked into the Golden City Hotel in downtown Hangzhou. Judging from their clothing and accent, they appeared to be rich businessmen from the north. They spread the word that they needed a large amount of silver dollars and were willing to buy at the highest rate.[88] No matter how many silver dollars the hawkers brought them, the two men bought them without bargaining. They asked for the names and addresses of the hawkers for future business. In the evening, all the hawkers were arrested. It was not surprising that the two guests were secret police officers who had been very good at laying a trap for their enemies in the Silver Dollar War.[89] As a result of the subsequent massive arrests, the Department of Public Security destroyed twelve speculators' lairs, and the number of money hawkers decreased from two thousand to one thousand in two weeks. But the general financial situation was yet to be improved.[90]

On May 21, a turning point came in the Silver Dollar War. No longer willing to tolerate the inflation, some tricycle drivers and urban residents attacked the dollar hawkers and forced a grain store to sell rice at a lower price. The government soon took control and arrested the perpetrators, but the incident sent the government a message that tougher measures were desperately needed. On May 22, owing to government intervention, the exchange rate of RMB to dollars temporarily dropped to 850:1, but tension still existed. On May 28, the government ordered all silver dollar hawkers to register with the exchange office of the state bank within three days. Only those who had a good financial record and reliable guarantors could get licenses to operate their businesses. As a result, among 1,000 hawkers, only 273 obtained legal licenses, and only one private exchange office was allowed to reopen.[91] The legal exchange was under control, but the black market revived and became even more rampant.

All the newly liberated cities, including Tianjin and Shanghai, faced the same financial problems and adopted similar measures. On June 6, the *Dangdai Daily* in Hangzhou reprinted an editorial from the Shanghai *Jiefang Daily* that pointed out the following: "Speculators manipulate the silver dollar market and do no less harm to the Chinese people than the GMD's JYJ. It is the general and urgent demand of the overwhelming number of people that these speculators be suppressed so that the problem of the silver dollar can finally be resolved."[92] This editorial was a sign that the Silver Dollar War was a national problem, especially in big cities. It urged the speculators to immediately give up their "dirty deals"; otherwise, "the people would never forgive them." *Dagong bao* reported that on the morning of June 10, 1949, the PLA suddenly laid siege to the Shanghai stock market building and arrested 2,113 silver speculators. Although most of them were released after being lectured, they were too scared to continue in business.[93]

In June 1949, a mass crusade against speculation in silver dollars was initiated in Hangzhou. The peasant cadres from Luzhongnan now began to show their organizational skills and talent. They mobilized 3,100 students from 43 colleges and high schools to form hundreds of propaganda teams. In downtown Hangzhou, 83 cadres from the city government, 12 from the district government, and 100 workers went to major marketplaces to push the Party's policy and to help military patrols search for silver dollar hawkers. They also organized street performances with disgusting characters to represent silver speculators, who soon became hated targets in the city.

The Silver Dollar War gained momentum everywhere in the city. The cadres called various discussion meetings to include different groups of people: administrative heads of household clusters, factory owners, businessmen, shop assistants, teachers, students, housewives, and opera goers. All the meetings were organized to suit the participants: they exposed the conspiracy of the GMD to ordinary people, called on merchants to observe the law, and demanded that shop clerks side with the government. The propaganda teams went to all corners of the city to recruit more workers, coolies, rickshaw bearers, teachers, and clerks. After three days of intensive public propaganda, which included mass rallies, street performances, and cartoon exhibitions, each propaganda team was split into smaller groups. These made door-to-door visits to make the government policy known to every urban dweller.

Everyone in the city was encouraged to watch out for the silver dollar speculators. Based on the reports of informers, the general manager and president of China Bank, Jing Ruiquan and Zhang Renpu, were put on the list of saboteurs and had to live at home under surveillance. While the arrest of illegal hawkers continued, the city government carefully controlled the scope and progress of the efforts. When some unsuitable slogans began to appear—for example, "Send the speculators to Manchuria as coolies," "The state needs silver dollars to buy foreign machines," and "We'll definitely liberate Taiwan next year"—the city leaders immediately put a stop to them and made every team member use the same

Party line.[94] Believing that the Silver Dollar War would make or break the new regime, the CCP made the economic problem into a comprehensive political and social battle.

At the early stages of the Silver Dollar War, some grain speculators rushed to buy rice and stored it, waiting for the price to rise. However, the public grain stores sold it at a stable rate. The provincial government offered Hangzhou 5 million kilograms of rice; the Financial Committee of the ECB shipped another 25 million kilograms from Jiangxi Province to guarantee Hangzhou's grain supply. Moreover, in July 1949 and February and March 1950, the peasants of the old liberated areas in Manchuria and North China offered timely help. A great quantity of grain was shipped to the south, and the government's markdown sale once again destroyed the speculators.[95] The Municipal Trading Company sold 148,486 *dan* of rice at a price 4–5 percent below the market price, and it still had 8 million *dan* in storage. Several hundred grain merchants could not sell what they had stocked and almost went bankrupt.[96] The support from Shandong greatly helped the city government to stabilize the rice price, and this in turn strengthened the RMB. No single grain speculator could beat the government, and all the merchants had to follow the lead of the state grain stores and lower the price of rice.[97]

The Communists attributed victory in the Silver Dollar War to a combination of political and financial measures—cohesion, education, administrative order, and mass mobilization. Actually, these strategies had been repeatedly used by the peasant cadres in their wartime bases. However, the Communists did not see the victory as complete. Government reports pointed out that silver dollars were still in circulation in many rural areas. For transactions in the commodities associated with rural products, such as rice, tea, silk, and silk fabric, the peasants continued to use silver dollars.[98] This clearly indicated that the Communist influence had not yet reached the peasants in Zhejiang. The city leaders were very frustrated since they had come from the countryside and now found themselves separated from the rural populace.

Conclusion

For the first time on May 6, 1949, the city folk of Hangzhou saw Communist soldiers. The performance of the CCP soldiers and cadres in the first months created an image different from the rumors about them that had widely circulated for the past two decades. The PLA troops showed that they were honest and did not disturb normal urban life, and they made a great effort to protect the interests of various social groups. The newcomers further turned out to be not only disciplined soldiers, but also qualified rulers if one were to judge by the impressive work they completed in a short time. They maintained social order and capably ran the city's economy and finances.

From the early experiences of the Communist rulers in Hangzhou, one can see that the political heritage of the peasant cadres played an important role. In the efforts to stabilize social order, restore production, and fight the Silver Dollar War, the peasant cadres continued to—and perhaps had to—use the strategy and tactics they had formulated in their rural wartime bases. As in the rural bases, their primary concern was the "well-being of the masses, from the problems of land and labor to those of fuel, rice, cooking oil, and salt."[99] This "mass line" ensured a successful beginning. In the end, they proved to be kings of the "lion-fox" strategy, using both the fist of mail and the velvet glove to rule the city.

Although the CCP's early tactics stressed rather slow but steady progress, their achievements were remarkable.[100] The unemployment rate started to decline, and inflation was controlled. The victory in the Silver Dollar War and the reopening of the Shanghai-Hangzhou Railway implied economic prosperity. For most of the urban populace, there was no cause for pessimism or doubt about the future of the new regime. Moreover, the peasant cadres from Luzhongnan were a charismatic group: their discourse was fresh, and their accent was attractive.

A good image for the CCP was the key to fortifying its foothold in the city and winning the people over. Image is cultural. It is full of political implications but more visible and direct than any political statement. From the first red flag to the political study meetings, the CCP gradually ritualized the political life of the urban people. The peasant cadres subtly changed people's minds without yet even launching a real attack on the "decadent" urban culture. At the same time, in the eyes of the peasant cadres, the city remained a strange land where they were not yet comfortable.

4

One Step Back, Two Steps Forward

After coming to Hangzhou, the new city leaders moved into lavish villas on Shentang Street, facing West Lake.¹ Through their windows they could see pleasure boats on the water and hear music from nearby gardens. The Western mansions on the shores of West Lake used to belong to the foreign and local rich; boating on the lake was also a privilege of the rich. From their windows, looking around the lake, the Communist leaders were glad to see happy crowds whose dress suggested a working-class background. In a discussion meeting with trade union cadres and worker activists, Tan Zhenlin was glad to point out that thanks to the Communists, the ordinary people could enjoy the beautiful scenery of West Lake, Lingyin Temple, and other city attractions.²

However, a report on his desk soon ruined Tan's cheerful frame of mind. A report by the city's Labor Bureau informed him that a group of unemployed workers, upon getting relief funds after the Communists took over the city's treasury, rented boats and spent all the money entertaining their families on West Lake instead of buying food or paying off debts. That was how they saw the meaning of "liberation." Afterward, they again turned to the government for help.³ The Communists had proclaimed they were the saviors of the people, and the people now took it for granted that they could depend upon government support. The Labor

Bureau report showed Tan Zhenlin how easily working people picked up a "bourgeois" style of life since they were more concerned about tangible, material benefit than Communist politics.

The message of the Labor Bureau report was not difficult to understand. Although the CCP would depend upon the workers in staging all its revolutionary programs, the workers had to be educated and reorganized. For this task, the Party desperately needed a great number of experienced cadres. However, most southbound cadres had gone to rural areas of the province because only one and a half months after the CCP took over the city, the CCP Zhejiang Committee decided that the focus of the CCP's work would again be shifted back to the countryside.[4] The literature has not paid attention to this consequential decision, which raises a number of questions. For example, why did the CCP retreat to the rural areas as soon as it had successfully stabilized the urban situation? If the Communists had not given up their goal of urban revolution, how was this retreat relevant to their future urban programs? If this retreat was part of their well-designed tactic of "one step back, two steps forward," how did the Communists play this game in other spheres of their urban work?

A Temporary Retreat

The first Communist leader to suggest retreat to the rural areas was Lin Biao, chief commander of the PLA Fourth Field Army and Party secretary of the CCB. On June 6, 1949, soon after his troops had stormed and taken over most cities in Central and South China, Lin Biao sent most of his cadres back to the countryside. He warned the Communists of the pitfalls in the cities and argued that "the center of gravity of the Party's work is still in the villages."[5] He pointed out that the rural-urban connection was vital for the Communists to consolidate the new regime, as well as for keeping the revolution alive. Lin's argument clearly conflicted with a resolution of the Party's Second Plenary Session of the Seventh Central Committee, which had called on the Party to shift this center of gravity from the village to the city.[6]

The city leaders in Hangzhou saw good reason to support Lin Biao. The Communists had established solid rural bases in Manchuria and North China through the land reform and other political campaigns, creating the preconditions for the Party's shift to the cities in these regions. South of the Yangtze River, however, the rural areas were still controlled by landlords, rich peasants, and remnants of the GMD. Holding the city of Hangzhou without a nearby rural base, the Communists could hardly sit on the shores of West Lake and enjoy the fishing. In order to consolidate the urban centers, it was necessary to fully command the countryside.

Ten days after Lin Biao's speech, at a CCP Zhejiang Committee meeting on urban work, Tan Zhenlin pointed out that there were about thirty-five thousand bandits and GMD remnants in the rural areas of Zhejiang Province. One of the bandits' military bases was only seventy miles from Hangzhou. Although the bandits had not been active in May or June, they were a potential threat, especially as the PLA's leading force was leaving the city to go south. Tan suggested that the city keep a small number of cadres to deal with routine affairs and shift all other cadres to the countryside to mobilize the peasant masses and launch rural campaigns.[7]

On June 25, the CCP Central Committee approved Lin Biao's suggestions for retreat. On the same day, the CCP Zhejiang Committee started to organize rural work teams. It told the cadres in Hangzhou: "We mustn't begrudge giving up the urban life and going to the countryside. We have to spend two years in rural areas to complete the assignment of the Provincial Committee."[8] The rural assignment was comprehensive: organizing peasant associations, establishing Party branches, arming the peasant militias, wiping out the bandits and GMD remnants, developing agricultural production, and collecting public grain.[9]

According to available documents (including the speeches of Lin Biao and the city leaders of Hangzhou), the security issue was the primary factor in the retreat to the countryside. Nevertheless, this factor should not be exaggerated. As soon as Hangzhou was stormed, the leading force of the PLA Seventh Corps, the Twenty-first Army, and the Thirty-fifth Army continued south to hunt and wipe out the GMD remnants. The Party did not have to dispatch civilian cadres to join the military operation. As for bandits, they had been in the rural areas for centuries; they might bother the local peasants, but they had never constituted a real threat to urban governments in the Qing dynasty or during the Republican years. "Security" did not seem to be a valid reason for most cadres to abandon their urgent urban work and go to the rural areas. At the mobilization meeting, Tan Zhenlin explained that the city's economic needs were a second reason for the CCP cadres to leave for the countryside: "The major purpose in focusing work on the countryside at this stage is to develop the city. Our city remains a backward and consumption-oriented city. In order to develop urban industry, we must wipe out the obstacles in the way of rural development—the feudal land system and the feudal political authority."[10]

In 1949, the city's economy had to be reconstructed. Despite its small scale of production, the major industry in Hangzhou, silk and textiles, had partly depended upon the importation of materials from Japan and other countries, and its products had been for urban or foreign customers. Now the supply and market sources had completely changed. The GMD still occupied most islands off the mainland, thus blocking the local industry from both reaching the global market and importing needed raw materials. Supplies from the countryside and rural markets became vital for the city's survival and development.

To seek rural support, the city rulers first resorted to their wartime bases in North China. In 1949–1950, Shandong Province, though it was much poorer than Zhejiang, organized the urgent delivery of grain to Hangzhou and opened its market to the city's silk products. The city, however, could not depend upon outside help forever. The key step was to establish a commercial network with local rural areas. For this reason, building control over the countryside and improving rural-urban communications was a priority.

Fish Cannot Leave the Water

There was a third reason for the CCP's retreat to the countryside. A well-known Communist metaphor refers to the relations between the army and the people as "fish and water." For the CCP, the "water" was the thousands of Chinese peasants whose support was the source of its energy. When they left their wartime revolutionary bases, the southbound cadres immediately felt as though they were leaving the water, for they arrived in isolated cities surrounded by hostile rural areas and they had to win over the cynical urban masses. Sending work teams to the countryside was an effort to recreate the fish-water relationship between the CCP cadres and the rural masses who had not witnessed Mao's revolution.

The urban programs desperately needed not only more cadres, but also cadres of fine quality. Tan Zhenlin said, "Because the enemy ran away so fast, we had to come in such a hurry that our cadres were really not ready for the urban task."[11] Therefore, the southbound cadres needed more preparation, and other new recruits needed further training as well. Having foreseen a great demand for financial and commercial specialists, the ECB hurriedly recruited a considerable number of them and dispatched them to Hangzhou. These new cadres had neither received systematic political training nor experienced the cruel revolutionary war. The city leaders hoped that the southbound cadres and these new recruits would make up the majority of all the government institutions, with the retained GMD employees comprising less than 30 percent. Actually, the CCP cadres made up a majority only in the Bureaus of Public Security (80 percent) and finance (60.2 percent), while in the offices of health, education, labor, public projects, industry and commerce, and internal affairs, they were in the minority (19–36 percent).[12]

It was even more difficult to find people among the southbound cadres who were qualified for leadership positions in cultural institutions. The CCP Zhejiang Committee asked the ECB for assistance: "If the CCP ECB cannot help us, we have to choose a local person to be the director of the Department of Education. This man may have a good reputation among intellectuals, but he might be a new Party member at best. As far as a director for the health bureau is concerned, it is impossible to find anyone in the city who has received our training and can be trusted."[13] It was clear that in the eyes of the southbound cadres, "local persons" might be qualified technically but not trustworthy politically.

In the early days of the takeover, as noted, students were also recruited to serve in the new government. After a short training, the Party put them into positions responsible for implementing its urban policies. Most of them worked in three institutions of the city government: the Labor Bureau, the Education Bureau, and the Bureau of Industry and Commerce. In the beginning, the city leaders had high hopes for these enthusiastic, energetic, and devoted youngsters, but their performance proved to be far from satisfactory. Most of them could not yet work independently. Sometimes, they had different views on Party policy and their judgments conflicted with those of the southbound cadres. For example, the Department of Industry and Commerce sent three student cadres to help the work team from the Department of Urban Work at the Hangjiang Textile Factory. The work team believed that the most urgent task in the factory was to hold workshops for the political education of the workers, while the student cadres argued that it was to teach the workers how to read and write. The southbound cadres suggested recalling the student cadres for more training.[14]

In the view of the southbound cadres, the major problem with the new recruits and young intellectuals was their lack of a sense of politics. They did not have any experience with class struggle and therefore often misunderstood the leaders' instructions. This indicated that training for these cadres should not be limited to the study and discussion of Marxist books, but should also involve them in the political campaigns. They should, therefore, be included in the rural work teams. It was assumed that the rural experience would remedy twin defects: ideological ignorance and vacillation rather than action. Thus among the multiple purposes of the Communist retreat from Hangzhou was an effort to train the badly needed new cadres. Moreover, it was also intended for the southbound cadres themselves so that they could strengthen their revolutionary virtues. The city leaders had noticed some changes in these cadres that they did not want to see.

In the rural wartime bases in Luzhongnan, no obvious gap had existed between superiors and subordinates in terms of material benefits, and there was no estrangement between the groups in daily life. Jokes, jests, and the sharing of cigarettes or other "luxuries" were common between officers and soldiers and between seniors and juniors, reflecting that the comrades-in-arms were on very intimate terms. Although this was referred to as the "guerrilla style" *(youji zuofeng),* the CCP cadres with extended rural experience still treasured it.[15] However, this relationship could not remain unchanged after these revolutionaries came to power and a new hierarchical society took shape.

The power and wealth of the GMD and the bureaucratic capitalists had to be redistributed after the takeover, but the distribution was not egalitarian. City leaders moved to villas at the lakeshore; district leaders got big houses downtown; and cars, special meals, servants, and other privileges were exclusively available to the top leaders. But the living conditions of most southbound cadres were worse than those of the old employees who had been retained. In addition, many formal occasions required that superiors and subordinates keep a polite distance. Despite the liberation, the old urban elite continued their normal lives, which were unjustifiably luxurious in the eyes of the peasant cadres. Every retained employee received an inflation subsidy of ¥2,000 per month plus a regular salary, while the southbound cadres received only food rations and small stipends—no salary at all.[16] If a cadre embezzled as little as ¥300, he was immediately purged from the Party and dismissed from office. It was not surprising that many of his comrades objected that such a punishment was too harsh.[17] In wartime no one in the CCP had had money, but now some had more and some had less. A considerable number of the peasant cadres did not like the gap between them and their leaders, and they complained about the preferential treatment extended to the retained employees. Some asked for higher positions, easier jobs, and the same benefits as the old bureaucrats.

A report by the city's Propaganda Department highlighted some of the problems in the city's Bureau of Public Security. Since this bureau was one of the most important institutions of the government, its eighteen cadres were supposed to be the best Party workers, appointed after careful selection. The report of the eighteen officers accused thirteen of not setting their minds to work, three of corruption, one of attempted desertion, and one of immoral relations with women. It might be an exaggeration to say that not one of the cadres was a good worker, but the report pointed out that "the Bureau of Public Security was located in the downtown area and the [cadres'] incomes were low; therefore the commercialized urban life could not fail to exert an evil influence on them."[18]

To make matters worse, some corruption among the southbound cadres was exposed. Because the government was still using the "supply system" (*gongji zhi*) to provide necessities to all the southbound cadres, corruption first became evident among cadres who had some financial power.[19] According to reports, these cadres were "petit intellectuals" who had received some economic and financial training, and when they got power, they wanted to live in urban luxury. For example, Yang Qiuxian was a Communist clerk in the Tax Bureau who used tax money to invest in the silver dollar market for personal profit. Xue Changsheng was the manager of a government sanatorium on the shores of West Lake whose job was to arrange entertainment for powerful guests, but he practiced graft in the public dining hall and used what he got for whoring.[20] Both these cases proved Mao Zedong's warning that "there may be some weak-willed Communists who will be defeated by sugar-coated bullets."[21]

The prevention of corruption was a more urgent and arduous task than corrections to agrarian socialism. As noted, it was feared that some revolutionary virtues had faded in the urban environment of Hangzhou. Thus the principal theme of Communist education for the rural revolutionaries became "Never forget our roots" *(yong bu wang ben)*. The slogan was of particular importance in Hangzhou since the overwhelming majority of the cadres were of peasant origin. When these cadres came to lead the urban social classes, they were faced with the same dilemma that had confronted the Manchus in the seventeenth century. Both the peasant cadres and the Manchu warriors came from less-developed areas and were determined to rebuild the society in the places they conquered. On the one hand, the conquering elite had to maintain its virtuous qualities and remain uncorrupted; on the other hand, it had to govern with the help of the institutions and talents of the conquered.[22] However, the culture of the conquered was alien to the conquerors and conflicted with their own traditions. Having come to power, both the Manchu elite and the Communist rural cadres were exposed to a refined and elegant culture that would erode their virtue as sugar erodes teeth.[23]

In December 1949, the Propaganda Department submitted a report to the Military Control Committee. Among other things, it reviewed the performance of the southbound cadres after the takeover. The report revealed what the slogan "Never forget our roots" meant to the cadres. For example, the report offered the case of Wang Xuegong, a military representative to the slaughterhouse under the Bureau of the Treasury. Wang's duty was to verify tax payments on slaughtered animals. In order to catch the early market he got up at four in the morning, and he worked until ten at night. To catch tax evaders, he had to travel throughout the city and visit each butcher. Because of so much walking, his shoes were worn down to holes, so he started going barefoot. It was considered good discipline for all PLA soldiers and officers to be neatly dressed and not walk in the streets barefoot. Wang therefore took off his uniform and changed into civilian clothes to go about his work. In addition, Wang was happy to do whatever work was given to him, even just feeding domestic animals.[24]

The report criticized a cadre named Li Qingyu, who was a branch manager in the Bureau of Public Projects. Li had joined the CCP in 1938. As a combat hero in the anti-Japanese war and a model worker in the land reform, he had had several important positions in the Party, such as standing member of the Party Prefecture Committee in Luzhongnan. In addition, all his relatives had been killed by the Japanese or the GMD in the wars, so Li loved to say, "I've sacrificed my whole family to make the revolution." After entering Hangzhou, he was assigned to be a supervisor of road construction. He believed that this work was less important than his former position and that he deserved a better job. Li stayed in his office all day and refused to go out to construction sites, saying he hated sunshine. Although he was almost illiterate, Li required all Party documents to be sent to him for review. When he went to the hospital, he accepted only medicine in brown bottles and refused that in transparent containers, which he believed to be of poor quality.[25]

One can clearly see from these two examples that what the Propaganda Department praised and what it criticized had nothing to do with policy issues and everything to do with "Never forget[ting] our roots." Working barefoot in the fields was a common practice for peasants. Now it became a symbol of Wang Xuegong's virtue that he had not forgotten his peasant roots. Peasants or other working people could never hate sunshine, so it was evidence that Li Qingyu had forgotten his peasant roots and betrayed his class. The criticism of forgetting one's roots (*wang ben*) was used indiscriminately against any adaptations by the peasant cadres to urban life—wearing a watch, going to a local women's opera, or dining in a restaurant. In many cases, the criticism was based on a misunderstanding of urban life by the peasant cadres. For example, they saw taking a rickshaw as exploitation, wearing Western suits as bourgeois, and women riding bicycles as indecent.[26]

It is not surprising that the peasant cadres misunderstood the urban culture since the Communists' general view of cities was very negative. Maurice Meisner writes, "The dichotomy between the revolutionary countryside and the conservative cities, which the whole revolutionary experience produced, had become a notion deeply ingrained in the Maoist mentality."[27] In Hangzhou, the southbound cadres were disgusted by the mean, soft, and narrow-minded southerners, and they especially hated the bureaucratic style of the retained employees, who did nothing during office hours but hold a cigarette, a cup of tea, and a section of newspaper to read the whole day. At the same time, there was deep-rooted discrimination against the peasantry in the city. The cadres' simple uniforms, strange accent, and different habits of eating and walking could be read as revolutionary characteristics but could also be regarded as less civilized behavior. The urban dwellers accepted the cadres' political authority but laughed at their ignorance of modern city facilities. Gossip circulated that the peasant cadres misused electric light bulbs to light cigarettes, did not know how to take baths, always damaged flush toilets, and took soft carpets to be beds. The cultural hostility of the urban dwellers made the southbound cadres feel like fish out of water. Their strong reaction was, "If you look down on us, we will also look down on you." They firmly believed that those who saw the rural cadres as bumpkins *(tu bao zi)* were the bourgeoisie or those poisoned by the bourgeois culture.

An editorial in the *Tianjin Daily* in 1948 entitled "Transform the Consumer Cities to Productive Ones" enhanced the cadres' beliefs. This widely read article was drafted by the deputy mayor of Beijing, Zhang Youyu. Fifty years later the author recalled that his major theme was to "transform the cities from counterrevolutionary fortresses to revolutionary bases."[28] Actually, what impressed the southbound cadres was Zhang's indiscriminate, emotional criticism against all Chinese cities: "In the semi-feudal and semi-colonial China, the big urban areas occupied by the exploiting classes were all consumer cities. Their existence and prosperity depended upon the exploitation of workers and rural areas. By political, economic, and all other means the cities not only extracted agricultural products to meet their needs, but also sucked the blood of the peasants to exchange for industrial products from imperial countries."[29]

Zhang's argument confirmed the dichotomy of the revolutionary countryside and the counterrevolutionary cities. It caused the CCP to believe that it was necessary for every revolutionary to experience the hardships of war and to engage in agricultural labor.

The retreat of 1949 was a strategic decision of "one step back, two steps forward." It would reinvigorate the southbound cadres' link with the peasant masses, and it would teach the new cadres, young students, and worker activists how to make the revolution a success. For this reason, the CCP Zhejiang Committee ordered Party organizations not only to complete the task of land reform and the elimination of bandits, but also to recruit and train one hundred thousand cadres through rural programs. Tan Zhenlin stressed that no Party organization could take this task lightly because "cadres always determine everything."[30]

The Rural Revolution and Class Consciousness

The first rural work team left Hangzhou on July 8, 1949, and the number of work teams in the countryside quickly increased to thirteen hundred. Three-fourths of the CCP government officials and Party workers were dispatched to the city suburbs and other counties of the province. A few cadres stayed in the city to take care of routine government business, and they took turns going to the countryside from time to time. With the major efforts now shifted to the countryside, substantial urban programs were postponed. In the whole province, ten thousand cadres and students were working in the rural areas by August 1949. Each county had one working regiment of two hundred cadres, divided into several brigades at the *xiang* level and into small working groups in each village.

Since the urgent task of the work teams was to eliminate the bandits, the PLA Seventh Corps sent soldiers and officers to join the cadres. Thus each work team had five or six military officers or experienced soldiers and a well-equipped fighting squad.[31] The work teams helped the peasants to organize local militias to safeguard their villages and support the PLA's offense. The Campaign to Eliminate Bandits could not depend just upon the PLA's military force. The crucial task was to educate the villagers to make a clear break with the bandits and support the work teams. One complication toward achieving this goal was the presence of popular secret societies in the villages that had numerous connections with the bandits. In the beginning, the work teams did not immediately ban the secret societies but told the peasants that GMD spies had penetrated these organizations. The cadres tried to persuade the villagers to stop participating in their dangerous activities and to withdraw their memberships. As soon as the bandits were wiped out, the secret societies were also eliminated.[32]

Another complication was that the bandits were local people who had relatives or friends in the villages. It took enormous effort for the work teams to make the peasants accept the idea that the war against the bandits was a war against the evil exploiting class in which everyone had to side with the government. It was equally important to convince the peasants that the bandits were doomed to destruction and that they had better therefore persuade them to surrender to the government. Zhong Ru recalled the importance of combining the military operation and the political offensive in the Campaign to Eliminate Bandits so as to persuade most villagers, including former GMD officials and local gentry, to collaborate with the Communist work teams. The capture of the bandit leader, Yu Jipeng in a suburb of Hangzhou was an illuminating example of how this worked. The work team first had the former GMD deputy county magistrate send an invitation to Yu and then got help from his cousin to lure Yu into a trap.[33]

The political landscape in the villages in Zhejiang was different from that in Luzhongnan. Unlike the self-sufficient society in the revolutionary bases in Luzhongnan, rural production in Zhejiang Province was highly commercialized. In most villages, agriculture and a household craft industry were organized mainly for the urban markets. (Local products such as tea, cotton, silkworm cocoons, vegetable oil, jute, bamboo, and timber had been major Chinese exports.) The villages depended upon the supply of all kinds of daily necessities from the urban areas. Many village landlords had businesses in Hangzhou and other cities, and, conversely, urban entrepreneurs invested in land in their home villages. Also, most of the landowners were absent and did not directly collect the rents but had them collected by agents. Since there was no "typical landlord" in Zhejiang, as there was in Shandong, some people believed the argument that there was no feudalism in Jiangnan.[34] If the CCP's urban policy was to protect private businesses in the towns, how could it attack entrepreneurs in their home villages?

Although most land was concentrated in the hands of landlords (70 percent or more), landlords in Zhejiang were not as big as those in North China.[35] In addition, not all persons who rented out land were landlords or rich peasants. Some intellectuals (such as doctors, engineers, teachers, and technicians), as well as some self-employed people, also rented out their land to help cover their expenses. Also, some poor peasants, who had only a little land that could not support their families, went to the cities to work while hiring others to till their land. In the villages there also was some land belonging to the community—land reserved for public schools, temples, and official ceremonies.

Debt relations in the countryside were also complicated. Not only landlords, rich peasants, or local merchants issued loans to poor peasants, but a considerable number of urban workers and poor peasants also lent money to others.[36] According to orthodox Marxism, renting land or profiting from loans are forms of economic exploitation and should be the targets of the proletarian revolution. This was a dilemma because if the Communists did target these endeavors, they would hurt a majority of the people. Yet if they did not, what else would they do in the villages?

In July 1949, a dozen cadres from the Bureau of Finance and the Bureau of Internal Affairs (among others) formed a rural work team headed by Zhang Yunxian and went to the sixth district of Hangzhou (later renamed the Genshan district). Seven local cadres from the district joined them in doing a land survey, a necessary preparation for the land reform.[37] The sixth district had a population of 45,000 and 42,000 *mu* of land, so that each person had only 0.8 *mu*. The district was a major producer of vegetables for the city, as well as products such as flax, cotton, rice, and medicinal herbs. Most local farmers were also involved in the cottage weaving industry or had small grocery or transportation businesses. The head of the district, Qi Yaohua (also a southbound cadre), told Party workers that it was still difficult to call a mass rally in the district, and he had to make announcements and publicize the government's policies at local teahouses. When Zhang Yunxian and his group arrived, the campaign against bandits had begun. The work teams had weapons and took part in some battles, but their major task was to guard the villages and passes and watch out for bandit activities. Another task was to hunt salt smugglers, who not only evaded taxes, but also provided the bandits with financial aid and information.[38]

To engage the peasants in land reform, the work teams attacked the argument of "no feudalism in Jiangnan" and corrected the misperception that there was class harmony in the "land of fish and rice." In the eyes of the southbound cadres, the differences in the size of landlords' holdings in North and South China were not important. A Communist proverb says, "All crows are black, and all landlords eat people." The key issue was to make a clear distinction between the oppressor landlord class and the oppressed majority of peasants. The easiest way to make the peasants understand the Communist rural campaign was to tell them that the CCP would unite the majority of the poor to attack the minority of the rich. Thus, ignoring the complicated Chinese classification of farmers into landlords, business-industry landlords, rich peasants, upper-middle peasants, middle peasants, lower-middle peasants, poor peasants, and farmhands, the cadres divided the villagers into the poor majority and the rich minority. It was only the oversimplified version of the doctrine of class struggle that could inspire the peasants to action and allow the CCP to transform peasant consciousness into the necessary support for the Communist regime.

The southbound cadres were good at organizing grievance, accusation, and struggle meetings (as noted in chapter 3), in which they inspired the peasants to denounce the daily abuses of the landlords. Through these meetings, some non-events became serious manifestations of economic exploitation and political oppression by the landlord class. Thus the class consciousness of the peasant participants was enhanced. Nevertheless, the rural work teams acknowledged that it was difficult to find a landlord who had earned the bitter hatred of the peasants in Zhejiang. In order to use the same approach to mobilize the villagers in Zhejiang as they had done in Shandong, they had to organize the meetings in a different way.

First, they changed the focus of the struggle meetings from landlords to bandits and local tyrants. The work teams explained that local tyrants represented a feudal force and should be major targets of the revolution. This strategy was successful in mobilizing the villagers because the peasants had a natural inclination to strike back at whoever abused them. Second, the cadres changed the practice of separate accusation meetings in each village to a "touring accusation" so that well-prepared peasant speakers could accuse the tyrants at a number of villages. The work teams could do a great deal to help the peasants recall all their suffering—

known as *"wa ku gen"* (tracing suffering in every detail and to its roots)—and to enable them to elaborate upon an accusation every time, making it more effective.³⁹

The CCP Zhejiang Committee sent work teams that totaled 30,000 cadres, worker activists, and students to the countryside, and these teams mobilized 1,500,000 peasants in the rural campaigns and organized 220,000 peasants into village militias.⁴⁰ Moreover, 36,000 cadres—many of whom were new—were trained in the countryside and made ready for future urban programs.⁴¹

Winning over the Youngsters

Winning over the youngsters was vital to the Communists' urban programs. As the rural revolution gained momentum, Youth League members and student activists were encouraged to leave the campuses and join the rural work teams. In 1949–1950, there were more than four thousand Youth League members in Hangzhou, responding to the Party's call to take part in the land reform. In following years, more students and faculty were sent to the countryside. As a result, a considerable number of youngsters became active Party workers after training and working in the Land Reform Campaign.

In the meantime, the CCP sent military representatives to the universities and public schools to begin early reeducation. Lin Hujia, the former Party secretary of the first prefecture in Luzhongnan, was appointed the military representative to Zhejiang National University. Zhejiang National University had grown out of Qiushi School, established in April 1897. It became a national university in China's Self-Strengthening Movement, when the country imitated the West to reconstruct its education system. The university made remarkable progress in the Republican period, when a considerable number of Chinese students who had been trained in Europe or America returned to teach there. They won the university a reputation as the "Eastern Cambridge." Lin Hujia was instructed to be very careful in dealing with this institution, especially in light of the general policy of the CCP Central Committee: "Retain the status quo, make a few necessary and possible reforms—for example, abolishing the system of political indoctrination and canceling reactionary courses."⁴² It was too early for the CCP to embark on a new undertaking on the old campus.

Liu Yifu, the deputy military representative to Zhejiang National University, recalled his first day at the school. At the welcoming rally, he announced that all activities of the GMD and its affiliated organizations would be banned and all courses about the GMD would be dropped. Then police came to the conference hall and arrested Hu Buqing, a staff member and head of the GMD agency at the school. Despite the shock of this public arrest, most professors did not worry much about themselves because Liu Yifu promised no mass purges or persecutions. Liu's words also dispelled the fears of faculty and staff who had some connections with the GMD. Secret CCP members on campus came out into the open, and various student activities sprang up—Marxist study groups, singing and dancing groups, and sport clubs. There were two more months left in the spring semester, and the regular teaching schedule was soon resumed.[43]

In a few days, all three public universities and twelve public high schools in Hangzhou changed hands. A few private schools were forced to close for political or financial reasons, including Zhongzheng Middle School. Founded in November 1926 to celebrate Chiang Kai-shek's birthday, this was well known as a pro-GMD school, with a GMD officer as its principal and president of the board of trustees. But most private schools remained untouched. Zhijiang University was a private college originally founded by Americans, and it retained its autonomy.[44] Zhou Zheng, the acting chairman of the University Affairs Committee, found that "the Christian atmosphere on the campus was even stronger than before the liberation." Every day more than two hundred students took part in morning and evening prayers, Bible study groups remained active, and religious lectures continued to be offered on the campus and in the off-campus neighborhood.[45]

As soon as the Communists took over the Education Bureau, they began an intensive investigation of the school system. In July 1949, a report by the bureau to the CCP Hangzhou Committee presented a dim picture of elementary education in the city: (1) schools were dominated by feudal bureaucrats; (2) corruption and degeneracy were rampant; (3) a considerable number of principals were retired GMD officers or spies. The conclusion of the report was pessimistic: "This domination of feudal bureaucrats is powerful and age-old. It will be impossible for us to initiate any programs if we do not smash this clique." The report insisted that "Some changes are necessary; otherwise we will not be able to do our job, and the masses will criticize us for not distinguishing between right and wrong." The city leaders seemed not to agree with the judgments of the report. One of them commented, "I wonder whether the situation [described in the report] is exaggerated." Another said, "[We must believe that] the poor and good people are definitely the majority in the elementary schools." The city leaders reiterated, "As a general principle, we will not push anybody and give them an opportunity to reform themselves."[46]

"Letting them teach themselves and letting them change themselves," the route suggested by the city leaders, was by no means a laissez-faire policy. A series of measures was taken to nudge the teachers and students in the direction of changing and remolding themselves to meet the requirements of the revolution. The first was the incorporation of Communist political education into the curricula. At Zhijiang University, twelve credits in Communist studies became a requirement for every student. Three new core courses (three credits each) included an introduction to Marx's political economy, the Soviet version of the history of social evolution, and Mao Zedong's theory on new democracy. New teachers were hired for political indoctrination, and the curriculum was redesigned by a special committee comprised of administrators, professors, and students.[47]

For college professors and high school teachers, the political study meeting was institutionalized and became a daily routine. Ma Zihua, a teacher at the Anding Middle School, wrote in his reminiscences: "[In 1949] the teachers spent 9–10 hours a week studying basic Marxist theories. One hour of reading after breakfast was inviolable. Every morning, every one of us spent 2 cents buying a cup of bean juice, took it to the office, and slowly drank it reading Marx and taking notes. Every Saturday afternoon was discussion time or, more often than not, we took small stools to the basketball court to join the students' public lectures."[48] This narrative might romanticize Ma's experience, but it was true that the political atmosphere in 1949 was rather easy. The professors and teachers liked to get together to exchange information on the suppression of bandits or the new tax policy and also to gossip about market or neighborhood news.

The Anding Middle School was a private school founded by a Hangzhou merchant, Hu Zixiang, in 1901 in an attempt to save

China through science and education. The maxims of the school were "Honesty, diligence, and love" and "Respect for learning and devotion to teaching."[49] In light of the government's instructions, the teachers offered a new interpretation of "love": "love for the motherland and love for the laboring masses." They believed that the study of Marxism and Mao's New Democracy fit perfectly into their tradition of "respect for learning."[50] Chinese intellectuals had a Confucian tradition of self-cultivation and self-improvement. They were eager to study something new and to contribute to the new China. In the early days of Communist rule, they could hardly foresee that the political study meeting would soon be abused and gradually evolve into political persecution.

Another change on campuses was the popular work-study program for students. It was initiated by a group of students who had tried to solve their financial problems through part-time work. The program was soon supported and encouraged by the CCP organizations at colleges and high schools, in the belief that this was a good start toward changing the Confucian tradition that scholars should not do any manual labor. In the fall semester of 1949, 270 students at Zhijiang University joined the work-study program. They sowed 20 *jin* (about 22 pounds) of potatoes and melons, planned to open 10 *mu* (about 1.6 acres) of land to plant maize, and raised 5 pigs and 20 sheep. With CCP support, the students got a contract from the university to repair the school's sports facilities and to run co-ops and coffee shops on campus.[51] Later the idea of work-study programs was written into the "educator's Bible" (the Party's education policy): "Education must combine with productive labor." In the second semester of 1949, the Anding Middle School organized 100 senior students to join the work-study program; they built city roads and grew rice at a suburban farm. These teenagers participated in the program with enormous enthusiasm, seeing it as very progressive.[52]

Two factors explain the students' enthusiasm for the work-study program. The first was economic. In 1949–1950, most college students and many students in Hangzhou's best high schools were the children of landed gentry or rich peasants. After the land reforms, their families could no longer afford to pay their tuition and living expenses. The work-study program would meet the students' financial needs. Second, the program imitated the model of the Communist cadre school, East China University (ECU) in

Shandong, which believed that participation in physical labor was absolutely essential to revolutionary education. The Education Bureau in Hangzhou encouraged the students to work hard. And it was especially important to the gentry's children, who saw it as a good opportunity to break with their families and make themselves members of the laboring class. Not every student should or could join the work-study program, however. In organizing the work-study teams, the schools had to consider the students' economic needs, academic performance, and health. Since taking part in the program was regarded as a symbol of joining the revolution, students whose applications were approved always felt honored.[53]

The work-study program soon became a formal part of Chinese schooling. In accordance with the Common Program of the Chinese Political Consultative Conference, the Education Ministry in Beijing instructed that the guiding principle for educational reform would be "To combine education with politics and to combine education with production."[54] Based on this principle, all schools had to incorporate physical labor into the teaching schedule. The Hangzhou Normal School (HNS) was an illuminating example of how schedules were restructured. With a mission to train elementary school teachers, the HNS scheduled the following activities for all students: (1) 6–10 hours of agricultural production per week, including growing vegetables, raising poultry, and gardening; (2) industrial work in mechanical, clothing, or shoe factories; (3) voluntary work on weekends and holidays.

The HNS was the first school to work out plans for further reform, which stressed the importance of physical labor in education: "Due to the two-thousand year domination of Confucianism and feudal orthodox ideas, due to a hundred years of slave education by the bourgeois culture, and due to the last twenty years of fascist influence in the name of the 'Three People's Principles,' we have been confused and misled.... In order to abolish the old aristocratic education that advocated consumption but ignored production and talked civilization but ignored labor, we have to first change the views of discrimination against physical labor."[55] In this plan, the HNS made it clear that the major purpose of participation in physical labor was to help students and faculty acquire a revolutionary world outlook. This was the only way the school could produce qualified elementary school teachers.[56]

In the minds of the southbound cadres, the models for revolutionary education were the CCP's cadre schools in the rural revolutionary bases. Like all the Party's institutions in the rural bases, including its government and army, the schools were small, self-sufficient societies. It was the Communist ideal that everybody studied and everybody worked. It was also their firm belief that the spirit of self-reliance and hard work had helped the CCP defeat its domestic and external enemies and had made thousands of revolutionary cadres. This spirit should therefore serve to transform the city schools into revolutionary institutions whose students would be well-educated workers with a socialist political consciousness for the new China.

Nevertheless, most teachers and students did not see the relevance of the work-study program to the Party's strategic goals. They assumed that the program was just a temporary measure to help students continue their education in a period of economic difficulties. They had not yet accepted the notion that doing physical labor was an essential part of socialist education. Most schools continued to emphasize the transmission of knowledge in the classroom, and substantial changes did not take place until the outbreak of the Korean War and the subsequent Thought Reform Campaign directed at the intellectuals in the city.

Organizing the Working Class

As most cadres were sent to the countryside, the CCP tried to find a good way to organize the working class in the city. In 1949, Hangzhou had more than 9,200 stores representing 83 different trades, and the store employees were the main body of the working class downtown.[57] The new government did not take over any stores or shops but helped them continue business as usual. Yet the district government was strongly committed to organizing the store employees. At that time, there were 230 grocery and department stores in Hangzhou. One-half of them were husband-and-wife shops, and about 500 employees and apprentices were the owners' relatives or countrymen.[58] This was also the case in the silk stores and teahouses. The owners imposed parental control over the apprentices and employees. The faith of the workers in the family relationships blocked the way to Marxist unionism. The CCP trade union tried to hold night schools. If apprentices attended the night schools, their bosses did not let them return to their shops.[59] Then the union tried to organize daytime lectures, but in a shop with only two or three employees, obviously the employees did not have time to attend daytime classes.

The situation in the industrial sector was not much better. The Tianzhang Silk Factory was an example. When the military representative arrived to take it over, he found it difficult to call a mass rally because the majority of the employees were old, skilled workers who had no interest in any organizational activities. The young workers showed some enthusiasm for unionism, but their backgrounds were dubious. Most of them were members of secret societies, such as the Green Gang (Qing Bang) or the Brotherhood Society (Xiongdihui), and some had even served in the GMD or Japanese armies. Another group of workers were unskilled, low-paid, seasonal laborers. Before 1949, the skilled workers used the seasonal laborers in their fights against the capitalists. The seasonal laborers were asked to join the skilled workers to argue and bargain with the factory owners for the sake of the skilled workers. If they won, the skilled workers would pay them something from what they had gained.[60]

Although the seasonal and young workers were easily mobilized into a labor movement, from the Communist perspective, their political consciousness was low and they were not reliable. They were fond of eating, drinking, and gambling, and they were averse to work. They welcomed the Communist takeover but refused to work before getting a wage increase. They merely roamed about the streets or sat in teahouses, chatting. When the trade union was established in the Tianzhang Silk Factory, it comprised twelve members. Only one of them was a Party member; five belonged to the Brotherhood Society and three to the Green Gang; one had previously been a GMD member; the remaining two had never been interested in politics. The elected chairman of the union, Xu Daijun, had served in a Japanese intelligence agency for two years.[61] At that stage, the CCP could not find a suitable person to replace him.

In the Tianzhang Silk Factory, as in all the silk factories and textile mills, the overwhelming majority of workers were women, and women workers were another problem. Before 1949, there were some trade unions in several factories, and women workers had been elected to join the union leadership. Because these unions were supported by the GMD or controlled by the Green Gang, the

CCP disbanded them as "yellow unions" and established new ones. The new union leaders were all male, and they had little influence among the female majority. Traditionally, women workers were not as active as their male counterparts, and the dismissal of the former female unionists added to their fear of politics.

Despite having quickly stabilized social order and restored production, the Communists could not as quickly win over the three majorities of the working class: city workers (store employees), the majority of skilled workers, and industrial labor (women workers). More important, two weeks after the Communists entered the city, there was a subtle change in the attitude of the urban workers toward the new regime. From being excited in the first days, they became disappointed. Not seeing an immediate and obvious improvement in their standard of living, some workers complained that "the body was liberated but the stomach was not."[62] Some unemployed workers spent the relief money they got from the government at wine shops and restaurants, and most factory workers asked for big wage increases. When the Labor Bureau tried to persuade the workers to lower their demands and put more effort into production, the workers accused it of "representing the interests of the bourgeoisie."[63] The serious task for the cadres was to educate the workers.

Following the instructions of the CCP Zhejiang Committee, the cadres immediately organized various discussion meetings in the factories. The instructions suggested inviting "middle-aged, mature workers to the meetings and not young workers because the young workers are ignorant and cannot easily be persuaded." The discussion meeting would not simply be a free discussion. It should be well prepared, and all speakers "would be workers appointed by the meeting organizer," so that the major voice would be in support of the Party's policy to protect the interests of both labor and capital. Meetings of different sizes should be organized at each factory. In preparing the discussion meetings, the CCP would find, educate, and organize more worker activists, through whom a majority of the workers would finally understand the government's stance.[64]

The southbound cadres insisted on solving wage disputes through negotiation between workers and capitalists. They did not get involved directly in the negotiations, but worked behind the scenes to offer advice to the workers. At the end of October 1950, the Hangzhou Military Control Committee issued regulations on labor contracts and labor-capital disputes; these required that all wage disputes be settled through legal procedures and following the law.[65] The CCP Zhejiang Committee directly controlled the scope and speed of wage raises and emphasized that neither the municipal Labor Bureau nor the military representatives at the factories had the right to make a final decision on wages. All results of labor-capital negotiations on wage issues had to be reported to and be approved by the provincial committee.[66]

Centralized control over the issue of wage increases appeared to be necessary in order to avoid agrarian socialism, which encouraged workers to make excessive economic demands. Nonetheless, the "yellow trade unions" were urging workers to demand high wages and better working conditions; under pressure from workers, some capitalists would accept whatever they demanded. The southbound cadres saw this as a conspiracy of the urban bourgeoisie, who was attempting to buy the workers' support and upset the city's economy. In their eyes, this was a political struggle. At the First Conference of Worker Representatives of the Province of Zhejiang, Tan Zhenlin criticized workers who had accepted the capitalist offers and become the "running dogs" of the urban bourgeoisie. He continued: "It is necessary to clearly understand that the bourgeoisie has been struggling against us from the very beginning, and it is very experienced and well prepared. If the working class does not have sharp eyes and strong vigilance, we will walk into the bourgeois traps. This requires our comrades who are doing urban work to investigate and research the situation intensively so as to find good methods, tactics, and strategy for the struggle against the bourgeoisie."[67]

What tactics and strategy should the Communists use in this struggle? The CCP had had a wealth of experience with the labor movement since its founding in 1921, but now that it ruled China, it had to make changes. In the past, the CCP had mobilized the workers by exposing the evils of capitalist exploitation, but now its formal policy was to allow and reward the exploitation of workers by the bourgeoisie. The CCP used to argue that once the working class became conscious of its strength, it could learn to use it to defend its interests through strikes against the bourgeoisie, but now strikes would endanger Communist authority, so they had to be forbidden.[68] Under this different political situation, the southbound cadres resorted to a new strategy for mobilizing the urban workers in Hangzhou—not by accusing the bourgeoisie of economic oppression, but by attacking its decadent culture.

From the reports and articles published in the *Zhejiang Daily* in 1950, one can see that the Communists defined the bourgeois way of life as shaped by four evil qualities. The first was reaping the fruits of other people's toil. This had deeply influenced a lot of urban people, causing them to detest and discriminate against physical labor. The second was cheating in business, which led to dishonesty and irresponsibility both in work and in dealing with people. The third, extravagance in production and daily life, went entirely against the rural revolutionary tradition of hard work and plain living. And the last was seeking material enjoyment, including money, wine, women, and amusement; this could corrupt especially young workers and apprentices.

In 1950, responding to Mao Zedong's call, more than a million Party members and other Chinese joined in the campaign to study the evolution of human society. Everyone was required to understand the doctrine that God had not created man; rather, the ape had made itself into a man by doing manual labor.[69] The doctrine was important for the CCP because it was the party of working people. It initiated the Chinese labor movement with the slogan "Labor is sacred," and it constantly recruited working people for the revolution. Moreover, it was particularly significant that Mao emphasized the role of physical work in the first days of the new republic. He believed that only labor would save his Party from the destruction of bourgeois "sugar-coated bullets." The CCP could counterattack the bourgeois culture with the revolutionary tradition of the peasant cadres because in China, nobody worked harder or endured more hardship than the peasants. Thus all urban people, including the workers, needed to learn from these fine peasants.

Based on this belief in the sanctity of labor, the southbound cadres began efforts to educate and mobilize urban workers. In October 1949 several stories in the *Zhejiang Daily* reported changes among urban workers. One was about a railway worker named Tao Aliu, who was a well-known lazybones. After 1949, seeing himself as a "master of the country," he began to work with great enthusiasm and became a model worker.[70] Like many businesses, the Car Repair Factory of the Municipal Military Control

Committee suffered shortages of parts and other materials, but the new working spirit helped overcome the difficulties. The workers there did not wait for state supplies. Instead they went to an abandoned warehouse and searched everywhere to find discarded parts, converting waste into useful materials.[71] The factory was a model in how to confront the pernicious influence of the urban bourgeois culture. A great many similar reports appeared in the *Zhejiang Daily*.[72] All of them reflected the great efforts of the southbound cadres to transform the newly liberated city in the pattern of their old liberated areas.

The military representatives and other cadres also recruited worker activists to join the Democratic Management Committees "to run their own factories." Although the press propagandized that the government would allow and encourage capitalist development, there were "Four Limitations" on private capitalism: (1) tax policy would limit capitalist development; (2) the state would control the market price to limit speculation; (3) the government would limit the operation, scope, and scale of private business; and (4) the Party's labor policy would limit the economic exploitation of workers by the bourgeoisie. One can see from the "Four Limitations" that the final goal of the Communist revolution was to eliminate the bourgeoisie as a class. The CCP was sure that "it would be able to realize this goal in fifteen years," as Tan Zhenlin said.[73] As the first group of rural work teams came back to the city, another group set off for the countryside. The alternative training of the Party's workers in rural areas made more cadres available for the labor movement.

The city's General Trade Union was established, as well as the unions in districts and factories.[74] Some capable cadres, such as Party secretary of Xiacheng district Sun Wencheng, were appointed to leadership posts in the provincial General Trade Union. The trade unions continued to play a role in solving labor-capital disputes, protecting worker benefits, and promoting worker literacy and technical training. However, they could no longer perform certain functions that they had done before the CCP came to power. They could neither organize strikes nor challenge government decisions. Instead, they assisted the Party in communicating with the masses of workers by establishing Party branches in state enterprises and recruiting new members in private factories. The Party organized everyone into political study meetings and offered worker activists special indoctrination, such as a weekly lecture on the Party *(dang ke)*. Before the city government decided to nationalize all private industry and commerce, the southbound cadres had already admitted 1,595 workers into the CCP and established 120 Party branches in the factories, thus preparing for the high tide of the socialist transformation.[75]

The most remarkable progress was worker appreciation of and support for the Communist leadership. In Communist theory, workers are the leading class, and the peasantry is their major ally, while in fact the workers in Hangzhou had to observe the leadership of the southbound peasant cadres in the name of the Party. Clearly the revolutionary experience of the peasant cadres and their previous contributions to the revolution outweighed the class rank of the proletariat. While the workers should never get rid of the Party's leadership, they could distinguish themselves in the Party's urban political campaigns, just as the poor peasants had distinguished themselves in the land reform. From the various political campaigns, the workers had developed a greater appreciation of the concept of class, and this would make them a reliable political force in the Party's socialist transformation of the urban society.

Conclusion

Interpreting the Chinese revolution, Tang Tsou has argued that the Chinese Communists borrowed the ideology, organization, program, and policies from the Soviet Union and the Comintern but that they also introduced innovations that had no Soviet precedents. One of the innovations was the peasant-based revolution, which began in the countryside and then captured the city. Although this was natural for any peasant movement in Chinese history, not all peasant rebels considered securing their rural bases a bigger priority than capturing the big cities. The nineteenth-century Taiping Rebellion is an illuminating example. A vigorous and promising uprising, the rebellion affected sixteen of the eighteen provinces of China and lasted for fourteen years. The Taipings captured Nanjing and proclaimed a new regime. "Then they lost the countryside to the local militia, organized by the gentry and supported by government troops, so that toward the end, the government forces surrounded the cities occupied by the peasant rebels and defeated them rather than the other way around."[76]

This chapter supports Tang Tsou's argument, revealing how the Chinese Communists successfully avoided the mistake committed by the Taipings. They continued to give priority to their rural campaigns even after they took over Hangzhou. A widely accepted explanation for their decision is that they were concerned about rural security.[77] But the new rulers were well aware of the relative precariousness of their hold in the city without a solid rural base. The suppression of bandits and the land reform enabled the Communists to use rural resources to solve urban problems. The rural campaigns provided badly needed personnel and operating models for the urban programs. In the history of the PRC, each time a substantial reform took place in China, it always started in the countryside.

The CCP's retreat to the countryside also resulted from the culture shock of the southbound cadres and their views of urban culture. While committed to remolding the urban culture and society, the Communists believed it was necessary to periodically send the cadres back to the countryside in order to reconnect with their rural roots and revolutionary tradition. Moreover, workers, students, and other urban people should also go to the countryside, where participation in rural campaigns was the principal method of recruiting and training new cadres. The Communists believed that through rural experiences, urban workers, the lower classes, and students were most likely to identify with the Communist ideology and would then become dependable allies of the rural revolutionaries in Hangzhou.

The southbound cadres advocated physical work and a plain life style, as well as loyalty and honesty—traits that were meant to stand in contrast to and attack the culture of the exploiting classes, including the landlords and the urban bourgeoisie. In 1951, Mao Zedong staged a campaign against the film *The Story of Wu Xun*, which told of a nineteenth-century peasant who raised funds to establish Confucian schools for poor children by begging in the streets. Mao characterized Wu Xun as an ugly symbol conflicting with the revolutionary tradition of the Chinese peasants, who had rebelled against the landlord class and Confucian culture. The criticism against this film reflected a similar concern by the Party, which constantly sent urban students to rural areas for reeducation. After this criticism, the position of intellectuals and the urban bourgeoisie became fragile.

5

The Korean War and the City

As it proceeds from the midtown of Hangzhou northward to the Tianshui Bridge or southward to the Song Family Bridge, the Zhongshan Road changes character.¹ It gradually loses its bustle and noise and becomes quieter and cleaner. There were two Christian mission compounds at opposite ends of the road. Both the compound grounds included chapels, schools, and clinics. As a child of one missionary family, Eugenia Barnett Schultheis recalls that the front yard of her compound was full of trees and flowers: "A weigela bush near by bore a shower of pink blossom; there was a scent of mock orange on the air."² The Communist takeover in 1949 did not immediately touch the mission compounds, but it soon changed the peaceful life of their residents, especially when a crusade was staged against the last American ambassador, John Leighton Stuart, who was born and raised in one of the compounds.

The missionary undertakings in the city were closely associated with American diplomacy in China. Soon after Mao Zedong published an article, "Farewell, Leighton Stuart," the religious, educational, and charitable activities of these missions were interrupted. Mao's article touched off an all-out attack on American imperialism that reached its peak during the Korean War. This attack did not conclude with the takeover of the missions or the forced departure of the missionaries, but brought about a series of campaigns—reorganization of urban neighborhoods, suppression of counterrevolutionaries, and ideological reform of the intellectuals.

What provided the southbound cadres with the strongest leverage for mass mobilization in these campaigns was the Korean War. On the one hand, the war induced counterrevolutionary activities and posed a threat to the new republic. On the other hand, it stimulated broad nationalist sentiments, which solidified popular support for the Communist government. For better or worse, this war marked a turning point in the personal lives and professional careers of people who had received a Western education and were fond of American culture.

From the White Paper to the Korean War

On August 5, 1949, the U.S. State Department published a White Paper, *United States Relations with China*. The White Paper goes into particular detail about the American China policy in the five years from the last part of the war against Japan to 1949, when the Communists won the Civil War. In August and September 1949, Mao Zedong wrote "Farewell, Leighton Stuart" and five other articles to criticize this document.[3] The CCP Central Committee called for a nationwide discussion of the White Paper. Beginning in October 1949, the city leaders of Hangzhou first organized the discussion within the CCP, the Youth League, and the trade union, then made it a major topic for political study meetings for everyone in the city. Why should thousands of Chinese discuss an American diplomatic document?

Mao's articles on the White Paper did not argue with the American government on its China policy, nor did they merely express Mao's blueprints for the PRC's diplomacy. Instead, these articles were mainly addressed to the Chinese intellectuals who believed in democratic individualism and had good feelings about the United States. Mao intended to reeducate such intellectuals and "democratic parties" who wanted to take a third road between the CCP and the GMD. This "third road" idea, the CCP believed, had basically been generated by American influence. To win its proponents over to the new regime, it was necessary to change their views of America and American culture.

As we saw in the previous chapters, the Communists' strength rested in the rural areas; even in the newly liberated province of Zhejiang they had quickly won political support from the peasants. The CCP had only a flimsy base in Hangzhou. In the later years of China's Civil War, Western observers noticed that "disillusioned and repressed by the Kuomintang, intellectuals drifted steadily to the Left."[4] But these intellectuals had not yet become Communists; they were still wavering and hesitating. In mid-1949, Mao Zedong wrote, "[Some Chinese intellectuals] think: the Kuomintang is no good and the Communist Party is not necessarily good either.... Some support the Communist Party in words, but in their hearts they are waiting to see."[5] Actually, what the Chinese intellectuals wanted to see was not a Communist state but a democratic society. Mao asserted that the intellectuals were wavering mainly because they believed in Western civil liberties and shared an "idealist conception of history" with American imperialists.[6] For the revolution to continue, the CCP needed to convert the intellectuals and urban residents, and the key issue was to change their attitude toward the United States.

The criticism of the White Paper and Ambassador Stuart had special implications for the people of Hangzhou since this city was Stuart's birthplace and his missionary family had considerable influence among the locals.[7] Stuart started a mission in a northern suburb of Hangzhou where his father had worked for many years. He enjoyed speaking the local dialect, believing that "[the Hangzhou dialect] has a musical lilt and expressiveness lacking in all other [dialects]."[8] As a missionary, Stuart saw no incompatibility between Christianity and the local culture, and he even believed that Christianity would most benefit China when combined with a respect for the ethical and humanistic values of Confucianism. His enthusiasm for studying the dialect actually resulted from his intention to communicate with the illiterate masses.[9] Stuart left Hangzhou to become the U.S. ambassador to China. The city congress presented him a gold key to the city and bestowed upon him the title of "honorable citizen of Hangzhou."[10]

As the GMD government collapsed, John Leighton Stuart had to leave China with all other U.S. diplomats. Yet the American cultural presence still remained. By 1949, for example, about twenty thousand girls had graduated from the American-sponsored Huilan High School (Hangzhou Girls' School). Nobody could ignore the influence of Christian schools on women's education or underestimate the role played by these graduates in their communities.[11] But while American teachers, doctors, and missionaries had once been portrayed in a favorable light, they were now denounced as agents of American imperialism.

The criticism of the White Paper was only the beginning of the anti-U.S. crusade; an intensive campaign did not unfold until late 1950. On June 25, 1950, North Korea's troops crossed the Thirty-eighth Parallel to attack Syngman Rhee's forces in the South. Two days later, the United States and its major allies swiftly intervened in order to halt what they perceived to be the expansion of international communism. At the same time, the U.S. Seventh Fleet was sent to the Taiwan Strait to block the PLA's attempt to liberate Taiwan. On June 28, the Chinese premier, Zhou Enlai, issued a statement condemning America. In July 1950, the CCP Hangzhou Committee asked all four major universities in the city to hold a one-month summer institute on each campus to study the CCP's instructions on the international situation.[12]

People in Hangzhou had not yet felt the effects of the war in July 1950, so the discussions on the Korean situation were rather flexible. In the beginning, some professors even expressed doubts about the government's statement that South Korea had invaded the North. In August, the political climate became more tense and immediately put a halt to such open discussions. On August 1, Beijing held the first anti-American rally as part of the celebration of the founding of the Communist military force. The PLA commander in chief, Zhu De, called upon all Chinese to take immediate action to oppose the American aggression against Korea and Taiwan. By early August, more than two hundred and fifty thousand PLA troops had assembled in Manchuria, and two weeks later the PLA Ninth Corps, stationed in the Shanghai-Hangzhou area, was ordered to take up a position along the Beijing-Nanjing railway line and be prepared to support any military operation in the north. Most people were not aware of the military movements, but from the local press a careful reader could sense the tension. The participants at the summer institutes were required to keep their eyes on the military situation in Korea, and at the end of the institutes, everyone had to make a strong statement supporting the government's stance.[13]

While most professors were holding the summer institutes, the college administrators met to discuss their school's work for the next academic year. Most of them were not fully aware of the seriousness of the situation. On August 19, 1950, the board of trustees of Zhijiang University held its regular board meeting. Not seeing any relevance of the Korean War to the college, the board members planned to discuss how to strengthen ties between the college and the American Presbyterian Church. It was their belief that a connection was extremely important, especially after most American professors had left the college the previous semester. The secretary of the board, L. H. Lancaster, took the minutes, and, as always, he put the university's English name—Hangchow Christian College—on the first line. As usual, the meeting began with a prayer led by Pastor Gu Huiren and concluded with another prayer. The board passed a resolution asking the American Presbyterian Church to allocate new funds for the construction of university buildings. The board members hoped that with new funds they would be able to expand the campus to meet the urgent demands of increasing student enrollment.[14]

It was soon obvious, however, that a Chinese university would no longer be allowed to ask for American aid since Beijing was escalating its involvement in the Korean War. In October 1950, Beijing sent troops to the Korean Peninsula to support the North. In the meantime, China launched a massive "Resist America, Aid Korea" campaign at home. The CCP Central Committee instructed all local governments to make full use of their propaganda apparatuses to mobilize people to join the campaign. As the PLA, under the name of the Chinese People's Volunteers (CPV), crossed the Yalu River, the war became a part of Chinese domestic politics as well as an international conflict.

The following two months were vital for mobilizing the masses to support the government operation. The people in Hangzhou first responded to the Resist America, Aid Korea Campaign with little enthusiasm. Reports from Zhejiang University indicated that most students did not express deep concern over the events in Korea, and still less did they express strong support for China's military involvement in the war. A considerable number of both professors and students kept asking, "Why did the Soviet Union not send troops to Korea?" and "How long will the war last?"[15] The report of the CCP Hangzhou Committee on Middle School Affairs revealed a similar state of affairs. Many schoolteachers argued that the Americans had done some good things for the Chinese, such as opening schools and hospitals in the city. From the Voice of America, they got the news that U.N. troops were advancing in Korea; a large U.S./U.N. force had landed at Inchon. Such news made them pessimistic about the Chinese involvement. Some people worried that American troops would land on China's southeast coast, so that Shanghai and Hangzhou would become the targets of nuclear attacks. At school, teachers had to encourage students to join the CPV, while at home they prevented their children from joining the army.[16]

City leaders faced a particularly difficult task in mobilizing housewives and unemployed urban residents. In December 1950, the government tried to recruit car drivers to form a transport team for the war, but very few people wanted to sign up for it. After lengthy education and persuasion, six drivers were selected for the assignment. But on the day of departure, a driver's wife lay down in front of the cars, crying and shouting, "Kill me first before you go!"[17]

The government-controlled mass media led the people to see the war through a nationalist lens. It was widely taught that China's security to a great degree depended upon the safety of the Chinese-Korean border, and China's involvement in the war was to "defend our nation and defend our home" *(bao jia wei guo)*.[18] The war mobilization was also linked with a peace offensive— opposition to an American conspiracy to launch a new world war. Coinciding with the Moscow-initiated international campaign for world peace, Picasso's dove flew to China, appearing on the covers of magazines, on street posters, and on postage stamps. A new popular song, "Grandma Wang Wants Pease," was broadcast every day and everywhere. Numerous paintings, street performances, news reports, and photographs told the people that the CPV was fighting to defend China and the peaceful life of the Chinese people. At the same time, the American army was portrayed as a cruel enemy and a "paper tiger." This image was intended to remind the Chinese of the nation's suffering and glory in the nationalist war against the Japanese.[19]

Although the distant thunder of the war did not immediately affect normal life in Hangzhou, the nationwide war propaganda aroused strong patriotic enthusiasm among students. The city leaders went to Zhijiang University five times, giving talks on the war situation. The Youth League and student union on campus designed big posters asking, "What have you done for the motherland, schoolmates?" A nationalist sentiment affected everyone, including Christian students and students who were cynical about politics. It was estimated that about 92 percent of the students at Zhijiang University participated in the "Great Patriotic March" on December 9, 1950. After the march, 450 students stayed in the streets and continued the propaganda drive against American aggression, and 170 students immediately enlisted in the army. Zhejiang National University went even further. It suspended all classes for five days, holding all kinds of war mobilization activities, and 968 students submitted their applications to join the CPV.[20]

By the end of December 1950, the city government had made remarkable progress in mobilizing people to join the Resist America, Aid Korea Campaign. The local press in Zhejiang commented that no political movement in the province could compare with this one in terms of mass participation and social impact.[21] In Hangzhou, according to government statistics, forty thousand workers and merchants, four thousand teachers, fifteen thousand students, twenty thousand women, and even monks and nuns had staged demonstrations in response to the government's call.[22] In the meantime, a campaign for increasing production and practicing economy in the factories and fund-raising to support the CPV in Korea gained momentum.

From Beijing Conferences to the Crusade in Hangzhou

As soon as the people in Hangzhou began to take an active part in the Resist America, Aid Korea Campaign, a further call for wiping out the Western cultural presence came from Beijing. On December 29, 1950, the sixty-fifth session of the State Council passed a resolution for a crusade against American cultural imperialism.[23] Deputy Prime Minister Guo Moruo gave the keynote speech at the session. Guo noted that the United States had invested heavily in China's cultural and educational undertakings, including colleges, middle and elementary schools, special education programs, and publishing houses. The Americans ran some major hospitals and orphanages in China and supported various charitable and relief organizations. After World War I, the number of American missionaries had increased very quickly, and thirteen regional bishops in China were Americans. In addition, Chinese theaters were flooded with Hollywood movies, which were 70 percent of China's cinema market. Guo argued that these phenomena constituted American cultural aggression against China that "deceived, poisoned, and imbued the Chinese people with servile ideas in order to enslave them."[24] Guo accused American missionaries, doctors, teachers, and their institutions of reactionary propaganda, espionage, and weapon smuggling after the outbreak of the Korean War. He announced that all American-run institutions had to be taken over by the government or Chinese organizations and that these institutions should cut off all financial and ideological connections with their American counterparts in order to uproot the cultural influence of American imperialism.[25]

As a famous poet, historian, and non-Communist social activist, Guo Moruo was a pioneer in studying Western science and democracy, and he had distinguished himself with liberal writings during the May Fourth Movement of 1919. Because of his reputation in the early Chinese cultural movement, Guo was purposely chosen by the CCP to be the first to attack the American influence. The CCP employed the same tactic when non-Communist female lawyer Shi Liang first demanded the suppression of counter-revolutionaries and American-trained economist Ma Yinchu proposed the Thought Reform Campaign.

Soon after Guo's speech, the government required all foreign-run and foreign-sponsored cultural, educational, and charitable institutions to register with local governments and to report on their work and finances to the government every six months. In the meantime, the local governments were instructed to work out effective measures for the eventual takeover of all these institutions.[26] To prepare for these institutional changes, three conferences were held in Beijing in January 1951.

The first was the Special Conference of Christian Groups with American Sponsorship. Organizers distributed reading materials on American war atrocities in Korea and espionage in China, and the participants were told that they did not have to pick sides between God and the CCP but that they should be "patriotic Christians." On January 21, the conference worked out a declaration: "In order to clean God's sacred territory and maintain the purity of Christianity, we must cut off the connection with imperialism and wipe out all its influence in our churches."[27] The representatives of the Christian organizations believed that the government would ensure their freedom of belief: "God will bless the Chinese Christians who, under the wise leadership of Chairman Mao and with the strong support and encouragement of the people's government, will realize their dream of self-governing, self-supporting, and doing missionary work on their own in China."[28]

At a time when most people believed the Communist propaganda that the Chinese could do everything by themselves, nobody could object to the Three Self-Principles (self-governing, self-supporting, and self-motivated). Compared with the Boxer Uprising of 1900, during which the Boxers burned foreign churches, expelled foreign missionaries, and killed Chinese Christians, the Three Self-Principles was a moderate slogan, but the nationalist sentiment it conveyed was the same as that conveyed by the Boxers. All the documents of the conference expressed a concern for solidarity among the Chinese Christians, calling upon them "to purge the reactionary scum from among the Chinese Christians."[29] As in all political campaigns, the terrible label "reactionary scum" was vaguely defined, but it could be assigned to anyone who made any pro-American speeches.

The second conference was attended by university presidents and representatives of faculty, staff, and students from eighteen American-sponsored colleges. The representatives included Pastor Gu and President Li Zhaohuan from Zhijiang University. They came to Beijing to discuss how to implement the directive of the State Council on disconnecting from the American institutions. In order to persuade all the participants to cut off all economic and ideological connections with American imperialism, the government promised "full financial and moral support so that the universities will not only be able to survive, but will also be able to develop further."[30] Ironically, as many Christian colleges (including Zhijiang University) condemned the Americans for freezing their financial support after 1949, they received telegrams from the American United Board for Higher Education informing them that new remittances from the American sponsors had been sent out, and they were invited to go to Hong Kong to pick them up. This news appeared both satirical and a challenge. It was not surprising that in the tense anti-U.S. atmosphere of the conference, none of the presidents would say anything but "no" to the invitation. The fifty-one delegates to the conference stated in unison that "this is an American conspiracy to buy us.... [It] is a humiliation to the Chinese people." They also expressed their determination "to carry on patriotic and anti-imperialist education to the very end."[31]

The third and largest conference was organized for 118 representatives of American-sponsored charitable and relief institutions from various cities. At the beginning of the conference, the participants criticized the United States in a moderate tone, noting that "some donations [had come] from kindhearted and devoted American Catholics and Christians who saved every penny to help the Chinese people. These American working people could not imagine that their money benefited only imperial agents in China."[32] According to the Marxist theory of class struggle and according to Mao himself, American working people were friends of the Chinese people. However, now was not the time to distinguish who was a kindhearted donor and who was an imperialist agent. The conference intended to wipe out American presence as whole.

The conference organizers invited Party leaders to give talks on the Korean War and on China's domestic situation, exposing the American conspiracy to overthrow the people's government in China. They also asked people who had experience with American nurseries or orphanages to stand up and accuse the institutions of being imperial criminals. According to the materials distributed at the conference, mortality in these American-run nurseries and orphanages was very high because of malnutrition, disease, and poor management. For example, a person from the Canton Holy Baby Nursery told the conference that the mortality rate of its adopted Chinese babies was as high as 98 percent. A government investigation on other American-run nurseries indicated that the situation was not much better and that the death rate was never lower than 60 percent. Moreover, the reports continued: "[In these nurseries] most babies died miserably, while a few children survived but grew up to become anti-Soviet, anti-Communist people. They were taught to be persons who loved and worshipped America and hated their own parents."[33]

Although the mortality figures (68–98 percent) were obviously exaggerated, nobody dared to challenge the credibility of the government investigation. Based on this information, the conference gradually moved to an emotional accusation of imperialism and finally approved a declaration "to refuse American sponsorship, cut all ties with American imperialism, and develop people's relief undertakings relying upon the Chinese people themselves." The participants also expressed their desire to raise funds in support of the Resist America, Aid Korea Campaign and for the relief of Korean refugees.[34]

The three conferences in Beijing not only discussed their relations with American sponsors, but they also issued several documents calling upon intellectuals, religious people, and all urban residents to join the Resist America, Aid Korea Campaign, the land reform, Campaign for the Suppression of Counterrevolutionaries, and other Communist political campaigns. The conferences were the first step in closing off Chinese cultural and educational institutions from the outside world. China decided to bring to a halt its relations with the "U.S.-controlled" United Nations. The Chinese Ministry of Education issued a circular letter ordering all Chinese universities to stop all programs with UNESCO and its affiliated organizations.[35] A new regulation from the State Council stipulated that no university could invite foreign visiting professors or hire foreign experts unless invitations or contracts were reviewed by a special national committee of the central government and approved by the State Council.[36]

On September 11, 1951, the State Council forwarded a notice to all provincial governments informing them that a British journal, *Trade and Engineering in the Far East*, often published articles attacking China and had therefore been put on the list of banned literature. The notice required the local governments to thoroughly check all books and journals from abroad.[37] Moreover, like the policy on foreign culture, China's attitude toward foreign residents became tough. The CCP Hangzhou Committee established a "three-word policy" toward the Americans in the city: Drive [out], arrest, and control *(Gan, guan, guan)*.[38] These policies toward foreigners and foreign-sponsored institutions had important implications for Chinese intellectuals. As the editor of the *Zhejiang Daily* wrote, every intellectual should ask himself "whether he had any ideological connection with American imperialism." Failure to answer this question correctly could ruin one's political and academic career.

Even before the delegates to the Beijing conferences had returned home, the city government of Hangzhou had started to take action. On January 10, 1951, the city Bureau of Civil Administration ordered all foreign-run or foreign-sponsored institutions to register with it immediately, reporting their membership and finances. The registration was completed within twenty days. According to the bureau's summary report, in Hangzhou there were 26 churches, 9 Christian associations, 13 relief houses, 8 hospitals, 4 co-ops, 2 divinity schools, 1 university, 6 high schools, 2 nursing schools, and 11 elementary schools with more or less foreign connections. The churches had 87 foreign missionaries and 851 staff members working for 6,387 local Christians, 2,192 of whom were Catholic. The schools had 1,456 students; the nurseries and orphanages had 249 orphans and abandoned children and kept 142 children under their guardianship; and the hospitals (among other things) took care of 208 lepers. In the previous year, the American sponsors had contributed ¥1,612,000,000, and other foreign sponsors had provided ¥714,000,000. These two sources made up more than three-fourths of the total funding.[39]

As the Zhejiang delegations returned to Hangzhou, the government was ready to move to the next step. On March 6, Yu Zhongwu, the director of the city's Education Bureau, gave a talk to college professors and schoolteachers. He argued that "imperialists had four magic weapons: gunboats, opium, missionaries, and spies."[40] He denounced some Chinese Christians in the city who donated to the Resist America, Aid Korea Campaign but asked that the money be used just for medical purposes. He also criticized students at Huilan High School who continued to wear American jeans.[41]

On April 25, 1951, Guo Chunlin and Feng Yindong (CCP Hangzhou Committee members), Yao Li (director of the Bureau of Public Security), Chen Lijie (director of the Public Health Bureau), and two non-Communist representatives, Ma Wendong and Jiang Zhenzhong, formed a special Takeover Committee. The committee proclaimed that the takeover of foreign-sponsored schools and other institutions was not an anti-religion or anti-foreign act but a patriotic one. The schedule of the takeover was dictated by the government's security concerns.[42] A government bulletin indicated that "all American-sponsored elementary schools had to be immediately taken over, and all church schools near the coast should also be taken regardless of their sponsors because the coastal areas are difficult to control."[43] Although a few American-founded schools such as Zhijiang University tried very hard to "eliminate the influences of American cultural aggression," they could not survive for long.[44] Within two years, all foreign-related institutions had been taken over by the government or just closed down.

Reorganizing the Urban Dwellers

In the first six months of the takeover, the city retained not only foreign-sponsored schools, but also the traditional *bao jia* administrative system. This system organized urban residents on the basis of households; each *jia* had ten households, and each *bao* had ten *jia*. The heads of these units were responsible for tax collection and organizing their units' public service, universal conscription, and crime watches. The CCP declared that the system had been used by the reactionary GMD to enforce its fascist rule. However, since the Communists "did not have experience in running a city and did not have a dependable mass organization in the city," they could not immediately abolish the system.[45]

The outbreak of the Korean War speeded up the reorganization of Hangzhou's urban neighborhoods. At the end of 1950, 507 Residents' Committees and 3,283 residents' groups were established "with purified and effective leadership and working with great enthusiasm."[46] Each committee would cover 150–200 families and would have a chair, associate chair, and five members in charge of security, social welfare, public health, culture and education, and women. The committee's neighborhood would be further divided into ten residents' groups, each consisting of 15–30 households. The Residents' Committees were not government institutions, but they were under the government's supervision and would serve as the principal means to spread the Party's policies among the masses of housewives and unemployed residents. The committees were involved in a great number of areas, including population registration, fire protection, watching out for espionage and bandits, and conveying and implementing the government's directives.[47] There was no election for the Residents' Committees. The Bureau of Public Security would send one policeman to join each committee, and the rest of the members were appointed by the local governments. Selections were made from retired workers or activists in previous political campaigns.[48]

One of the tasks of the Residents' Committees was to organize the urban dwellers, especially illiterate housewives, to listen to the news programs of the central broadcasting system. At the same time, shortwave radio sets had to be registered with the committees and their owners had to pledge not to listen to Voice of America (VOA). From that time, listening to VOA or other "enemy radio" became a serious crime. As a result, there was only one version of war (or other) news—the government's—and all posters, cartoons, exhibitions, and public talks repeated the same story. Any nongovernment rumor about the war would be subjected to intensive investigation and would definitely create lots of trouble for the people who spread it.

Starting in 1951, many housewives arrived in Hangzhou from Shandong: the wives of the southbound cadres came to join their husbands, and their mothers or sisters came to help take care of their children. The government encouraged them to work in the neighborhoods as volunteers. Despite being poorly educated, these rural women were loyal to the Communist regime and worked with great enthusiasm. With a rich experience of the class struggle in wartime, they played an important role in reconstructing the urban neighborhoods and maintaining social security. "Bound-foot scouts" was a nickname for these illiterate rural women who worked for the Residents' Committees.[49] They were devoted and powerful in the Resist America, Aid Korea Campaign and other political campaigns in the following years.

One of the earliest contributions of the Residents' Committees to the Communist regime was their participation in population registration. In February 1950, the government initiated a comprehensive tally of the urban population. It sent 395 policemen to lead this work, while the Residents' Committees mobilized 3,306 activists to assist. Every household was required to fill out a registration form, and then the investigating group of policemen and activists would double-check all the items, especially the history of each family and its social connections. After three months of painstaking work, the groups completed the examination of 120,799 households and put the total urban population at 520,730. More important, as the government declared, "[We] have drawn a distinction between good guys and bad guys."[50] The groups found 99,425 mistakes in previous records and 20,052 "suspicious" people. Among the latter, 7,238 persons were drug abusers, prostitutes, thieves, or other "bad guys" with criminal records; 12,814 were politically tainted: they had been either GMD members, Yi Guan Dao (YGD) activists, or counterrevolutionaries.[51] Most of them could not be put into jail, but they had to be carefully watched by public security groups and the Residents' Committees. A new security system was created—Special Control *(te kong)*, which played an extremely important role in social control in all the years of Mao's China.

The Special Control system was designed to classify the "suspicious" populace into two categories and three classes, according to risk levels. Those on the Special Control lists would usually not be arrested but were closely watched by their neighborhoods. Before the Suppression of Counterrevolutionaries Campaign, there were 13,048 people on the lists in Hangzhou. (About 8,000 of them had been GMD members or soldiers.) After the massive arrests and executions in the campaign, the number dropped to 3,016; 2,166 of these were political suspects and 850 were suspected criminals. In July 1951, the Hangzhou Military Control Committee decided to release 227 counterrevolutionaries and handed them over to 56 neighborhoods for public control *(guan zhi)*. The public control period lasted one to five years, during which all or part of the individual's political and economic rights were denied and he had to do physical work under the supervision of the Residents' Committees and masses.[52]

The people on the Special Control lists were required to report their activities and thoughts periodically. In order to have eyes and ears everywhere, the Bureau of Public Security and the Residents' Committees would let everybody in the neighborhood know who these people were so that they could watch over them. In addition, the Residents' Committees encouraged the suspects to watch and expose each other. Aside from the Special Control category, there was also a small number of marked men under Internal Control *(nei kong)*. They were suspected of being counterrevolutionaries but had no evidence against them, or they had dubious social connections and were thus regarded as potential reactionaries. Some people did not know that they had been placed on the Internal Control list, but they were puzzled that they were often being watched, their movements were always restricted, and their careers were never successful.

Most members of the Residents' Committees did not have a decent education. In mobilizing their residents to join Communist campaigns, they were not very persuasive, but they were extremely patient and persistent. They made door-to-door visits to recruit residents, and these visits could take place every day and last until the resident promised to take an active part in the campaigns.

Accusation meetings were the main form of mass participation in the Suppression of Counterrevolutionaries and Resist America, Aid Korea Campaigns. To expose the crimes of the GMD and American imperialism, every speaker at the meeting had to make accusations "full of blood and tears." In addition, those who had followed the GMD in the past were required to tell insider stories.[53] One obvious difficulty in organizing accusation meetings was that nobody had direct contact with any American soldiers (who were presumably the evildoers in the Korean War), still less was a witness to American atrocities. To solve this problem, the neighborhood of Qianggan Lane and the Hangzhou Waterworks developed a strategy by which people began their speeches by attacking GMD crimes or Japanese atrocities—for example, how the Japanese invaders had burned Chinese villages, murdered Chinese people, and raped Chinese women. Then the speakers should present an analysis, pointing out that the GMD was supported by the United States and that the Americans were as evil as the Japanese. Finally, the meeting would end with the slogan, "Down with American imperialism."[54] The CCP Hangzhou Committee praised this method, noting that it "had grasped the essence of the fact that American imperialism and Japanese imperialism are the same by nature."[55]

Suppression of Counterrevolutionaries

After the consolidation of its rural bases, the CCP in Hangzhou turned to dealing with its urban problems by launching the Campaign for the Suppression of Counterrevolutionaries. This campaign formally began in October 1950 and concluded at the end of 1952. According to the Chinese government, more than 2 million counterrevolutionaries were arrested in the campaign. Among them, 710,000 were executed, 1,270,000 were jailed, and 230,000 were put on watch and control by the masses *(qunzhong guanzhi)* throughout the country.[56]

The CCP did not merely use state power to suppress anyone who opposed the Party's policy. Instead, it attempted to make this campaign a mass movement to attack the enemy and educate the people so as to consolidate the new regime both politically and ideologically. In consequence, the government was faced with two problems. First, it had to make the urban people understand why the government should punish GMD followers to whom the Military Control Committees had promised leniency when the PLA first captured the cities. Second, it had to make some rules to control the massive violence since there was no law or legal procedure available after the takeover. Since the CCP Central Committee gave only a vague definition of "counterrevolutionaries" and only a general principle for punishment, the municipal government in Hangzhou had to deal with both problems on its own.

On June 8, 1950, the Hangzhou Military Control Committee issued a second notice ordering all former GMD officeholders and special agents to register with the government. By July 1, 733 people had done so.[57] Although no immediate action was taken against them, these people could easily sense imminent danger. Soon after, China's involvement in the Korean War made the suppression of counterrevolutionaries even more urgent. On October 10, Mao Zedong ordered all local governments to take active measures to wipe out all counterrevolutionaries.[58] These instructions gave rise to the height of the campaign in all cities throughout China.

Based on the experiences in Beijing, the counterrevolutionaries included five groups of people: (1) leading GMD members (company commanders or above in the army and heads of government for the *xiang* or higher); (2) GMD members who continued with anti-Communist activities (spies and saboteurs); (3) organizers of counterrevolutionary associations (such as YGD); (4) local despots; and (5) bandits.[59] Given the wide range of counterrevolutionary activities, the government was particularly vigilant concerning activities associated with Chiang Kai-shek or American military actions. In 1950, the GMD Air Force bombed Ningbo, a coastal city in the Zhejiang Province. Hangzhou organized serious air defense exercises and intensified preparations of measures against possible espionage and sabotage by GMD and American agents. The local press began to spread the idea that Zhejiang was Chiang Kai-shek's power base, where there were lots of hidden enemies to be exposed and where counterrevolutionary activities had been rampant after the outbreak of the Korean War. The advance of the U.S. Army in Korea revived the expectation of anti-Communists that the Communist regime would be overthrown. The journal of the municipal Party committee, *Hangzhou Work,* reported: "Having heard the news of the American landing at Inchon, a former GMD spy (who was not arrested but under our security control) went to see a local policeman and told him, 'Don't be so active [in the Communist campaigns].... If you now treat me well, I will take care of you in the near future.'"[60]

As the campaign began to unfold, the government made the YGD its first target because the CCP believed that non-revolutionary organizations were the largest threat to the Party. This popular organization had been banned in North China as early as April 1950.[61] However, after the Korean War broke out, it renewed its activities. The city leaders believed that it had something to do with American military operations since the leader of the YGD had asserted in a workshop that "a third world war would break out and China would be destroyed."[62] The workshop called upon people to join the YGD for self-salvation. It also told the participants that "there were some who said they served the people, but they actually hurt other people for their own benefit. God would not forgive them, and the American nuclear bomb was but a tool created by God to kill these evil people."[63] It was clear that the "evil people" meant the Communists.

Hangzhou's Bureau of Public Security concluded that the YGD was controlled by and served American imperialism and Chiang Kai-shek. Moreover, it found that the organization had grown quickly in rural areas and among illiterate urban dwellers.[64] According to the Marxist theory of class struggle, poor people were supposed to be the Communists' major supporters. YGD control over this segment would certainly undermine Communist influence, and such a threat enhanced Communist incentives to destroy the organization.[65] On December 15, 1950, the city's Military Control Committee issued a decree announcing that the theology of the YGD challenged the Communist policy of land reform and threatened wartime security and the government, and it therefore ordered that the YGD be disbanded.

To uproot the YGD, the government combined the persuasion of common members from below with the suppression of leaders from above. On December 13, the Hangzhou Bureau of Public Security arrested 143 leading members of the YGD. After a brief trial, the bureau wasted no time in publishing their crimes: it printed twenty-two thousand copies of the court judgment for distribution. The city propaganda department, the Bureau of Public Security, and the Residents' Committees worked together to organize "persuasion teams," which made door-to-door visits to YGD families. They taught YGD members that the YGD was not only a superstitious society that deceived people, but that it was also deeply involved in the conspiracies of American imperialism and the Chiang Kai-shek clique; therefore any innocent member should withdraw from it. According to a report from the Xiacheng branch of the city Bureau of Public Security, 98 members immediately withdrew, and 243 members confessed their guilt within two weeks.[66] By the end of 1950, 22,277 YGD members had withdrawn.[67] After destroying this organized opposing force, the CCP shifted the focus of its campaign to mopping up all individual counterrevolutionaries.

On April 18, 1951, the second session of the First Zhejiang Provincial Congress of People's Representatives passed a resolution entitled "Strict Suppression of the Counterrevolutionaries." It read: "In recent days, since the outbreak of the Korean War, counterrevolutionaries continue to be swollen with arrogance; their destructive activities are rampant and murders often happen.... The people's governments at all levels must make the suppression of counterrevolutionaries the priority.... Arrest, imprison, and execute those who deserve it."[68] On April 27, the government launched a massive wave of arrests, imprisoning 1,143 counterrevolutionaries in one night. This action went quickly and smoothly mainly because the Bureau of Public Security already had a comprehensive list of targets. Also, those formerly associated with the GMD still believed in the leniency that the government had promised them a year before, so none of them escaped or tried to resist arrest. On April 29, the government planned to hold a public trial. The trial was actually a combination struggle meeting and accusation meeting in which the government not only pronounced the death penalty for 106 counterrevolutionaries, but also exposed and condemned their crimes to educate the masses.

The government planned to have thirty thousand people attend this public trial, and meticulously prepared for it. The southbound cadres were good at organizing such events. They decided first to focus accusations on four counterrevolutionaries: Shao Cunron, a local despot in the Jian Qiao district who had savagely oppressed his countrymen and collaborated with the Japanese; Chen Fenming and Kuang Guoying, two GMD spies who had been involved in the suppression of the student movement in 1947; and a Mafia head who controlled the city's porters and longshoremen. Next, they chose five key speakers to accuse these men of their crimes, and then they had several rehearsals before the trial. Two illiterate rural women, Wan Xiaoxiang and Zhou Aixiang, would tell how Shao had abused them and killed their beloved husbands. A former student from Zhejiang University and one from Zhejiang First Normal School would condemn the GMD's conspiracy that killed Yu Zisan, a leader of the student movement. Finally, a disabled worker would climb up to the stage to accuse the Mafia head of breaking his left foot.

All the speeches were carefully scheduled, slogans were prepared, flags and placards were raised, and the rally location was guarded by military policemen and PLA soldiers. The government ordered the city broadcasting station to telecast the trial live, and it opened special telephone lines to get on-the-spot feedback. The speakers were effective: the women's tears, students' condemnations, and worker's laments successfully mobilized the urban people. In two hours, the organizers of the trial-rally received 199 calls asking the government to execute the four counterrevolutionaries, and 134 letters came immediately after the rally demanding the same.[69]

As the campaign gained momentum, the CCP Central Committee took control of the situation, limiting the number of counterrevolutionaries to 0.1 percent of the total rural population and 0.05 percent in urban areas. Moreover, regardless of the crimes the counterrevolutionaries had committed, 80–90 percent of capital punishment verdicts could be postponed to give them a chance "to repent and start anew."[70] Two weeks after the Hangzhou trial, the campaign reached its peak. Hangzhou organized 1,545 large and small mass rallies that were attended by 468,151 urban residents. The rallies accused GMD remnants of crimes and exposed 1,260 hidden counterrevolutionaries. The city government reprinted three central government documents—*Regulations on the Punishment of Counterrevolutionaries*, *The Suppression of Counterrevolution*, and *General Knowledge for the Anti-Espionage Struggle* (the latter two in cartoon form)—and required that every ten residents have copies. It also required that everybody sing the song: "When a rat runs across the street, everybody cries, 'Beat it!' When a counterrevolutionary walks down the street, everyone shouts, 'Catch him!'" According to a government report, most people supported the Campaign for the Suppression of Counterrevolutionaries. They said, "The sky has finally opened up.... This is the time for revenge."[71]

Under great social and organizational pressure, two thousand former GMD followers surrendered to the city police bureaus and fifty-two people committed suicide (five others were rescued), although almost none of them had been involved in any antigovernment activities since 1949. Zhang Heng was an example. As a famous lawyer, he was the president of the City Congress when the GMD was in Hangzhou. In 1948, as the PLA approached the city, he suggested making Hangzhou an "open city" and rejected the government's plan to construct defense blockhouses. The GMD's garrison headquarters held that "Zhang Heng flirted with the Communists and should be killed." Ironically, Zhang survived in 1948 but became a CCP prisoner in the 1950s. The only evidence for his "counterrevolutionary crimes" was his former service in the GMD City Congress.[72] It was the CCP's belief that a person could not be innocent as long as he/she had once belonged to organizations related to the GMD.

The revolutionary terror was necessary for the CCP in the 1950s not because it faced genuine danger, but because it was determined to eliminate all potential opposition and display the might of "the proletarian dictatorship." Between April and May 1951, more than five thousand counterrevolutionaries were arrested in the small city, causing already overcrowded city jails to overflow.[73] On May 14, the CCP Hangzhou Committee decided to move out those who had less than five years to serve. One thousand prisoners were sent to the Deqing quartz mines for forced labor, five hundred to the Longjing Tea Plantation, and one hundred stayed in Hangzhou to dig mud in West Lake.[74]

The urban people sympathized with the families of the counterrevolutionaries. Some teachers and staff at the Hangzhou No. 2 High School tried to comfort the women whose husbands had been executed: "Don't be so sad. It is not too bad to die. Forced labor would be a more horrible torture."[75] The Party ordered the school to criticize these staff members and teachers and prohibited anyone, individual or mass organization, from showing sympathy for or offering help to these families. The government argued that

American imperialists and Chiang Kai-shek had trained a large number of spies and sent them to penetrate the mainland, and these spies might use the families of the counterrevolutionaries to make trouble. If husbands were arrested, their wives were required to carefully obey the law, as well as to work to support their families.[76]

Perhaps the most important consequence of the Suppression of Counterrevolutionaries Campaign was not the number of counterrevolutionaries the government arrested or executed, but the fact that the campaign changed the traditional concepts of family and neighborhood. The CCP encouraged a son to inform against his father, praised a daughter for exposing her mother, and rewarded a niece for surrendering her aunt to the police. The Communist doctrine of class struggle penetrated into the people's minds, starting a cruel struggle between parents and children, among relatives, and among colleagues in the name of revolution.[77] A high school student, Lu Chengling, sent an open letter to the *China Youth Daily* condemning her father, who had been a GMD spy and had murdered some CCP workers. When people asked her what she would do if the government let her decide her father's fate, the girl answered, "Of course, I would kill him!"[78] In her eyes, her father was now a class enemy, and she believed in the sins of the class enemy and the principle of "an eye for an eye." The young generation of Chinese grew up in this environment of "no mercy to counterrevolutionaries." The cruelty of the class struggle was later expressed in a diary written by a model Communist soldier, Lei Feng: "Be cruel to the enemy like a severe winter."[79] Here one can already foresee the "revolutionary violence" of the Cultural Revolution.

The Thought Reform Campaign

The CPV's military operations against U.S. troops in Korea provoked a cultural war against American imperialism at home. The CCP found that generally urban people loved the United States *(qin Mei)*, worshipped it *(chong Mei)*, or feared it *(kong Mei)*, and it determined to launch a campaign to change people's positive feelings. It began by having the *People's Daily* ask, "Do you have any ideological connection with American imperialism?"[80] Since Chinese soldiers were fighting the U.S. troops in Korea, no Chinese wanted to admit to any connections with American imperialism.

In June 1951, Ma Yinchu, the president of Zhejiang University, was transferred to Peking University, which had expanded to include the American-sponsored Yenching University. To transform this old institution into a new socialist college, President Ma believed the key was to raise the political consciousness of the faculty and staff. Ma believed that regular political study meetings were not enough; an intensive program—a thought reform campaign—would be necessary to help intellectuals reform themselves to meet the demands of the new era.[81]

Ma Yinchu was representative of a group of leftist intellectuals who had fought with the CCP in the struggle against Chiang Kai-shek and wanted to continue to cooperate and even to share power with the Communists after 1949. Despite his Western education, Ma was determined to cut off ideological ties with the United States. He felt that the quickly changing situation made it urgent for intellectuals to keep pace with the majority of working people, and the only way to do so was to reform themselves. Not all his colleagues liked the idea. According to a report by the Political Division of Zhejiang University, in the beginning 54 percent of the faculty stated that political study was important but they did not have enough time for it, 42 percent saw it as unnecessary, and 4 percent used any excuse to avoid it.[82] (According to a 1951 survey, many professors at Zhejiang University had been educated in the United States or in missionary schools; see table 1.)

The government saw Ma's suggestion as vital and timely. Based on the assessment that the majority of Chinese intellectuals still clung to bourgeois concepts and ideas, the CCP felt that a thought reform campaign would help convert them to the side of the

Table 1. Profile of Administrators and Faculty at Zhejiang University, 1951

Position	Total Number	Educated in the United States	Educated in Japan	Educated Elsewhere
President	1	1	0	0
Dean	5	3	1	1
Department chair	37	12	3	22
Professor	190	64	18	98

Source: Zhejiang University, "Report on the Organizational Evolution of Our University before and after the Liberation"; ZUA, Y11/1/1/1, 57–58.

working class. On September 4, 1951, Zhou Enlai met with Ma Yinchu and discussed how to stage such a political study campaign, starting at Peking University.[83] A week later, Mao Zedong endorsed Ma's plan and suggested that the CCP Central Committee send some leading cadres to the university to give talks.[84] On September 29, Zhou Enlai made a speech to three thousand college teachers on "the thought reform of the intellectuals." Zhou stated that the purpose of the thought reform was for intellectuals to "pick up the right standpoint." Every intellectual should "gradually shift from a nationalist standpoint to the stance of the people and then move further to the standpoint of the working class." Zhou added that as soon as the problem of standpoint was resolved, intellectuals could well serve the country, the nation, and the Chinese people.[85]

The Thought Reform Campaign first unfolded at twenty universities in Beijing and Tianjin, then spread throughout the country. It was expected to take four months, but it lasted for one year. On January 24, 1952, the Education Department of the ECB issued a formal notice to city leaders in Hangzhou: "The Thought Reform Campaign is the current priority. In order to promote this campaign, your schools must allocate special time for the political indoctrination of teachers and staffs; thus do not schedule any classes on Friday afternoons."[86]

To implement the ECB's instructions, Zhejiang National University organized two months of intensive political study; 362 professors and 149 staff members were divided into 29 discussion groups to study Party documents.[87] The program had two steps: first was patriotic education and second, revolutionary education. Patriotic education was to help intellectuals understand that the United States was the enemy of the Chinese nation and that the Soviet Union was its friend. In the Thought Reform Campaign, students, especially returning students, were the driving force that criticized teachers and pushed them to confess their mistakes.[88]

The CCP Committee of the university arranged accusation meetings in every department in order to attack American imperialism, and the Thought Reform Campaign first focused on instilling patriotism and wiping out pro-American sentiments.[89] Professors were asked to recall whether they had been discriminated against when they were students in the United States (see table 1). Those who could not remember any such experience were regarded as politically conservative and in need of more help. The help involved more intensive political study and conversation with Party leaders. Finally, some professors could state, as Professor Liang Shoepac did, "My experience in the United States was terrible. The longer I stayed there, the more I hated American imperialism."[90]

Most professors and staff members did not like the Soviet Union.[91] The Thought Reform Campaign therefore required that they study Lenin's book *On Imperialism,* Mao Zedong's "Analysis of Chinese Social Classes," and Chen Boda's book, *How Stalin Supported the Chinese Revolution.* After reading and discussion, they would have a better understanding of the aggressive nature of American imperialism and more appreciation for the strategic importance of the Sino-Soviet alliance. In the meantime, the university encouraged all professors to study Russian, use Russian textbooks, adopt the Russian grading system, and follow Russian theories in their own scholarly endeavors.[92]

To raise their class consciousness, intellectuals needed not only to read and discuss the required books, but also to engage in introspection and confess their mistakes. Everyone had to go through three stages of confession: self-confession, help from the masses, and approval by leaders. The faculty and staff were required to use the southbound cadres as models, comparing the cadres' dress, hairstyles, hobbies, and language (among other things) to their own. The differences between them would be politically significant and would be interpreted as the influence of bourgeois culture on the intellectuals. The professors' scholarship, teaching methods, and attitudes toward students from poor peasant families were also examined from the political perspective. After an intellectual's self-confession, his/her colleagues would expose his/her hidden thoughts and personal scandals. The confessor would be frustrated and humiliated. With the intense organizational and social pressure, he/she would finally have to plead guilty.[93]

For the second step of the campaign, revolutionary education, professors were organized to study the Marxist doctrine of class struggle. According to a government investigation in 1949, 64.9 percent of the faculty and staff at Zhejiang University were from families of landlords, bureaucrats, or the bourgeoisie, while those from families of workers or poor peasants made up only 10.5 percent. In addition, 42 percent had once belonged to the GMD or other reactionary organizations. Influenced by their teachers, 20 percent of the graduates and 9.4 percent of the junior and sophomore classes had joined various pro-GMD organizations.[94] The major part of this step, therefore, would be for the participants to make a clean breast of their personal and family histories, including their former associations with reactionary organizations and connections with foreigners or foreign institutions.

The Party used the so-called "criticism and self-criticism" method to run the confession meetings. Su Xingbei, professor of physics, had once made some casual remarks: "Wherever the red flag is, I see desolation all round. The Communist regime can hardly survive for twenty years." Before the campaign, many people had admired Professor Su for having the guts to speak the truth. In the confession meetings, however, Su became the focus of attacks. He had to make many tearful confessions and ask for forgiveness. Tan Jiazhen, a professor at the School of Science, confessed that many years ago he had suggested "giving China to the Americans to run," and after 1949 he had hoped the CCP would follow Tito's example and keep its distance from Moscow. Both Su and Tan were accused of hating the Communist revolution. After their confessions were approved by the CCP school committee, they were required to improve their teaching methods and reconstruct their scholarship by learning from Russia.[95]

Although everyone had to make confessions, the intellectuals were treated differently, and the treatment did not depend just upon their confessions. In the first stage of the campaign, the Party had classified all faculty and staff into five categories, according to family and educational background and political performance. The Party's policy was to protect the first category of people and take care of the second category because those in both groups had been activists in political campaigns and would be "forgiven" after making a couple of confessions in small meetings. The third category comprised people who did not work hard or had minor political problems. In general, they would be criticized in small groups, and a few would have to confess at large meetings. The fourth category had to make various confessions at both small and large meetings, as well as confess to Party leaders personally. This group used to be unfriendly toward the southbound cadres and thus deserved a hard time in the campaign. The Party would focus on the fifth group (3 percent of the faculty and staff); these people had dark spots in their histories, resisted the campaign, and refused to confess even when the evidence against them was obvious. The Party suspended them from work and sent them to a special "workshop."[96]

At all confession meetings, the professors' attitudes toward mass criticism and toward the Party leaders were more vital than what they actually confessed. Among other things, the Thought Reform Campaign was intended to make the intellectuals recognize the Party's authority and respect the Party cadres who did not have a good education. It was designed to lecture the intellectuals, whether or not they had done something wrong. Their family and educational background determined their "original sin," and they would have to learn to always be modest and prudent and "tuck their tails between their legs." The major function of the confession meetings was to destroy the political confidence of the intellectuals and make them feel inferior to the peasant cadres. The CCP believed that only if the Party controlled the intellectuals both politically and psychologically would its takeover of the universities be complete.

The Thought Reform Campaign created a new campus culture. In the summary reports at the conclusion of the campaign, many professors at Zhejiang University denounced the crimes of their landlord or bourgeois parents. Not all of them were optimistic or confident about their future, but they recognized the crucial importance of the "class standpoint," and they dearly wanted to have the standpoint of the working class.[97] The students who were to graduate in the fall submitted written pledges to accept government assignments in frontier and rural areas and to work where the state needed them the most.[98] The CCP Committee of Zhejiang University reported that through the campaign it had trained 141 "first-echelon" activists who were ready to be admitted to the CCP and 452 "second-echelon" activists who would soon be ready after further training and testing. With the rapid expansion of the Party's organization and its increasing influence among the students, the Communist leadership in the educational sphere was finally consolidated.[99]

Conclusion

For the Chinese Communists, the Korean War created a good opportunity to launch urban revolutionary programs. Nothing would be more powerful than the slogan to "defend our nation and defend our home." Similarly, nothing would be more effective in mobilizing people than associating the revolutionary programs in China with the life-and-death struggle in Korea. In addition, since the city leaders had to depend upon the southbound cadres, it was convenient to let them use their tried-and-true weapon—nationalism—to unfold these programs. In the war against Japan, the Communists had exploited nationalist reactions to Japan's invasion by providing Party leadership for rural resistance. Through the nationalist war, the Communists had infused "a new moral and political outlook into the peasantry."[100] In the 1950s, the CCP peasant cadres led another war in Hangzhou—the cultural crusade against American imperialism—and they exploited nationalism (or call it patriotism) to infuse a new moral and political outlook into the urban dwellers and intellectuals.

The Korean War was "a mixed blessing" for the CCP.[101] The city leaders of Hangzhou skillfully combined the Resist America, Aid Korea Campaign with other urgent tasks. The war gave them a good reason to call on workers to increase production. More than twenty thousand workers took part in the so-called Patriotic Production Competition, and the ten major factories in Hangzhou overfulfilled their production plans.[102] Yet the most important political consequences of the war were the suppression of counterrevolutionaries and a crusade against American cultural imperialism. Increasing anti-American sentiments gave rise to the Thought Reform Campaign, which divided the Chinese people into anti-American and pro-American groups. The pro-American intellectuals were faced with only two options: confess or perish.

The Thought Reform Campaign was the most important event in the PRC's early history, representing the first shift from a moderate Party policy to a radical revolutionary program. While in the first days of the takeover the Party had tolerated the independent thinking of intellectuals as long as they were not overtly anti-Communist, the Thought Reform Campaign attacked all hidden non-revolutionary thoughts and left no room for any non-revolutionary ideology. The campaign imposed a sense of "original sin" on Chinese intellectuals and destroyed their political confidence and moral integrity.

Intellectuals were the soul of the city of Hangzhou, representing its fine culture, esthetic elegance, and independent personality.

Now they were forced to leave the central space of this city. However, it was as yet too early for them to come to the painful assessment of their changing position in the new regime. After the Thought Reform Campaign most of the intellectuals were required to read Mao's books with more respect and follow the Party's instructions more actively. As they started to struggle for survival in the political net of the Party, one could see that the cultural city of Hangzhou was changing. Now only one social class remained a challenger to the CCP's goal of totalitarian control over the city: the urban bourgeoisie. The bourgeoisie's power in industry and commerce and its influence in social values still predominated, and no ruler in the city's history had changed its role and function. However, with the cooperation of the urban intellectuals, the Communists were sure that this problem would soon be resolved in a new campaign.

6

The Trial of Strength

"To serve the people, the best cigarettes on sale."[1] This was an advertisement in a grocery store window in Hangzhou. To link everything with revolutionary slogans, such as "to serve the people," was the fashion since the Communist takeover. To no one's surprise, Communist discourse had a great impact on the urban dwellers. At the same time, some commercial concepts penetrated the Communists. The southbound cadres who had joined the CCP to devote themselves to the revolution were now talking about "repayments," "benefits," and "bargains."[2]

The economic situation in 1951 was remarkable. According to a report by the provincial government, industrial output had increased by 40.7 percent and the volume of commerce by 42.31 percent that year.[3] However, every time China's economy made progress, Mao Zedong sensed a political crisis. Mao feared that the growth of industry and commerce would increase the influence of the urban bourgeoisie and make the bourgeois way of life more tempting.[4] This would also increase the risk that CCP members would be corrupted by the bourgeoisie and give up their tradition of plain living and hard struggle. Mao saw a love of pleasure and a distaste for hard work among the CCP cadres. It seemed to him that this meant war between the CCP and the urban bourgeoisie. Who would be the winner? How could the CCP maintain complete control over business and industry? Was it possible to make the urban bourgeoisie wholeheartedly accept the new regime and dare not resist the CCP's social transformation? This would be a real trial of strength.

The Changing Cadres

The years since 1949 had seen considerable changes in Hangzhou, as well as among the southbound cadres. The two changes were different. The former had been rapid, visible, and mostly institutionalized by the CCP in light of its revolutionary ideals. The latter were slow, subtle, unconscious, and complicated—changes that hit the southbound cadres in the process of the city's transformation.

Let's take tea as an example. Drinking tea was a major part of the daily life of urban dwellers. Male adults usually hurried to teahouses as early as dawn; it was known as "catching the early market." After having tea, people began doing business. Then every afternoon they had a long break to have "noon tea" to chat, gossip, and exchange market information.[5] In the early days of the takeover, the southbound cadres went to the teahouses to spread the Party's policy, but they could hardly draw the attention of the tea drinkers. The cadres believed that the "unhealthy" tea culture of drinking and doing nothing and the lax bureaucratic working style must be changed. "If I am thirsty, I drink water," a southbound cadre said. "Why tea?"[6]

However, Mao Zedong liked tea. He not only drank tea, but he also ate soaked tea leaves.[7] He went to visit the famous tea-producing village of Meijiawu in the suburbs of Hangzhou, showing great interest in tea production and the life of the tea farmers. Zhou Enlai also visited Meijiawu and wrote about what he saw to his wife, Deng Yingchao (who loved drinking tea and was good at making it): "Unless you have a concept of the whole process of tea production, including planting tea trees, picking tea leaves, and roasting them, you cannot be a 'queen of tea' but just a 'tea pot.'"[8]

The old urban elite of Hangzhou talked about the best water, the best temperature, and the best season for making tea, while Mao and Zhou added a concern for tea production and tea farmers. That implied they saw tea not as a luxury for the upper classes but a business for working people. The southbound cadres gradually understood that they had to support the tea industry, which brought the city great profits from both the domestic and global markets. As noted above, the Communist government invited urban businessmen and non-Party friends to come to tea parties, and before long, this practice was picked up by cadres to entertain their private guests since tea was cheap, tea making was easy, and tea drinking was regarded as a positive and healthy lifestyle by Mao and Zhou.

The local tea in Hangzhou was not very strong but delicate. Once one tasted it, one would certainly enjoy it. Tea gradually became a regular drink for the southbound cadres. As they held cups of tea in conference rooms; or entertained their guests with Dragon Well (a famous local tea); or presented their friends, relatives, and comrades-in-arms with a box of fresh Cloud Fox tea, they no longer associated tea drinking with a bourgeois way of life. They even agreed with the notion that one could not be a leader in Hangzhou unless one knew something about tea. Gradually, they also became skillful at adjusting the water, temperature, and proportion of water to tea to make the best beverage. In this manner, the southbound cadres were assimilated by the local tea drinkers.

This change was not the result of orders from Mao or Zhou, although some southbound cadres might use Mao's interest in tea to legitimate their new interest in it. In fact, the urban way of life—including delicate tea, better food, fine clothes, public amusements, and modern facilities—was seductive and easily became part of the life of the newcomers. Drinking tea appeared to be such a small and natural part of the lives of the local people that they probably did not notice when the southbound cadres accepted this practice. However, it was precisely their adaptation to urban culture that brought the southbound cadres closer to the local populace. Unfortunately, not all changes that the southbound cadres experienced were pleasant or popular.

After the new regime was consolidated, people became disappointed with the various levels of Communist bureaucracy. The first complaints had to do with women's issues. In November 1951, the Party's newspaper, the *People's Daily*, reported the maltreatment of a woman worker, Hao Jianxiu, by the Tianjin First Textile Factory. The factory leaders squelched her efforts at innovation and persecuted her supporters. The *People's Daily* sharply criticized the factory leaders, referring to them as typical bureaucrats. This was the first time that the slogan "Struggle against bureaucratism" hit the headlines. Starting with this report, a special column against bureaucratism began to appear in the newspaper.[9]

From then on, several reports were published in the "struggle against bureaucratism" column, and all of them were about family violence and abuse against women. Some reports also revealed shocking cases of individual or group suicides, all committed by women in different provinces, including Zhejiang. Throughout the country strong demands were voiced to confirm women's economic and social equality and wipe out all kinds of ignorance, discrimination, and violence against them. It seemed that the women's complaints had aroused social attention and that a crusade against bureaucratism would soon unfold. At that time, nobody foresaw that the criticism against government bureaucratism would finally develop into the Three Antis and Five Antis Campaigns, in which not the abuse of women but the urban bourgeoisie would finally become the major target.

The turning point was a report by Gao Gang, the Communist leader of Manchuria, and Mao Zedong's comments on it. In 1951, Gao Gang initiated a campaign against corruption, embezzlement, and bureaucratism in Manchuria. Gao's definition of "bureaucratism" included more than just women's issues. He argued that bureaucratism was the most dangerous change to befall the Party cadres, and it was manifested in their ignorance of the revolutionary mission, pursuits of personal pleasures, arrogance, pomposity, and the like. His report divulged that a lot of Communist cadres abused power, practiced graft, and stole huge sums of money from the state.[10] The corruption originated when the CCP changed from being a revolutionary force to a ruling party. As the peasant revolutionaries seized the cities, they were exposed to various pleasures and luxuries. Like rulers in all previous dynasties, some peasant cadres begun to indulge in the worldly pleasures of wine, women, and song. Gao Gang argued that this suggested the possibility that the Communists would repeat the tragedy of Li Zicheng, who had fought for eighteen years but held power for only eighteen days (see chapter 1). Some reports from Beijing confirmed Gao Gang's assertions. For example, the city government had ferreted out 650 corrupt officials who had more than ¥1.5 billion in illicit money.[11] Numerous individual cases of corruption reflected a general danger, and they were a warning for the Party to take strong action.

Mao held Gao Gang's report for twenty days without commenting. He tried to figure out how the women's issue and cadre corruption were related and what was behind these problems. Based on his famous theory of the bourgeoisie's "sugar-coated bullets," he assumed that the bourgeois influence was at the root of the bureacratism and corruption. He urged the masses to mobilize to expose the corruption and force corrupt officials to confess. Mao suggested that it was necessary to send the corrupt cadres a serious warning, transfer them to other posts, purge them from the Party, and arrest and even execute the chief criminals.[12]

In the early years of the takeover, Mao Zedong personally approved the death sentence of two high-ranking officials,[13] asserting that only with the meting out of such severe punishment could twenty, two hundred, or even twenty thousand Communist cadres be saved from making similar mistakes.[14] At this stage, Mao Zedong believed that it was not just a matter of punishing a few corrupt individuals. Rather, he had to launch a nationwide campaign because corruption was an epidemic affecting a great many Party members, and the virus came from the bourgeoisie. It seemed that former guerrilla fighters were not immune to the corrosive influence of bourgeois ideas. Mao Zedong concluded that without repelling the attack of the bourgeoisie, the revolution could not develop.[15] Finally, Mao commented on Gao Gang's report: "This report is correct.... [We should] launch an attack against corruption, waste, and bureaucratism."[16] Mao decided to issue Gao Gang's report and his comments to Party organizations and government institutions at various levels. In his comments, Mao formally defined three targets for the new campaign, the Three Antis Campaign.

On January 1, 1952, the central government held a big party in Beijing, inviting 479 Party and non-Party leaders to come to celebrate the New Year. Mao Zedong gave a speech to greet the guests and said, "I wish for victory on the newly opened front, which is a large-scale attack against corruption, waste, and bureaucratism so as to cleanse away the filth and poison left over in our country from the old society."[17] Judging by both Mao's primary goal and the consequences of the mobilization, we can see that the Three Antis and the following Five Antis Campaigns were the second revolution. In the pre-1949 revolution, the national bourgeoisie had been the CCP's ally; now it had become the enemy of the socialist revolution. The Three Antis and Five Antis Campaigns ultimately changed commonly held views about the way people were related to each other personally as well as politically and economically.[18]

In 1952, a Western observer described the Three Antis Campaign as "a sign of self-confidence on the Communists' part that they could openly and successfully attack deviations, corruption, and other weaknesses in their own ranks."[19] Indeed, Mao Zedong was fully confident of success. A year ago, he had heard his little daughter singing a song entitled "Without the CCP, There Is No China." Mao told his daughter that was not correct since China had existed for thousands of years before the CCP was founded. Mao suggested changing the song to "Without the CCP, There Is No New China." "New" was the key word. The new China would be an ideal society in which there would be no abuse against women or corruption in government. It was Mao's belief that his cadres would never be changed by the bourgeoisie but that they would change the world.

The Three Antis Campaign in Hangzhou

The Three Antis Campaign was directed against the three "evils" of corruption, waste, and bureaucratism. In Hangzhou it began on December 12, 1951. Since the corrupt cadres were called "tigers," the campaign was also known as a "tiger-hunting" campaign. The city organized "tiger-hunting teams" at all government institutions. Comprised of a group of professionals, the teams were to audit accounts and mobilize workers and other activists. In the winter of 1951, the tiger-hunting teams and the "suspects" were called to attend workshops at the Workers' Sanatorium on Mount Pingfen. A big slogan was hung on the trees at the pass of Mount Pingfen: "Without a confession, no tiger can leave the hill!"[20] All those who attended were asked to sing "Two Roads for You to Choose":

> Open your eyes, you corrupted,
> Two roads for you to choose.
> One is bright, another is a dead end.
> Think about which one you choose.
> Leniency to those who confess,
> Severity to those who resist.[21]

Before the tiger-hunting teams began to square accounts, the Party organized political study meetings to launch a psychological offensive against the suspects. At the meetings everyone was asked to study Party policy, examine his/her work, and to engage in self-criticism. The tiger-hunting teams would analyze what the suspects said and get clues for further investigation or find criminal evidence to force the suspects to confess.

A month after the campaign began, the tiger-hunting teams caught the biggest tiger in Hangzhou, Feng Mengdong, director of the city's Department of Civil Administration. Feng had come from the Communist rural base in Luzhongnan. The son of a poor peasant family, Feng had joined the revolution in his teens. He had fought bravely in the anti-Japanese war and the Civil War and was wounded several times. With some elementary education, Feng was regarded as more knowledgeable and capable than other peasant cadres and was therefore promoted rather quickly. When the CCP took over Hangzhou, he was appointed director of the Division of Civil Administration under the Military Control Committee and then director of the Department of Civil Administration.

Entering the city, Feng was intoxicated with self-satisfaction and believed that it was time for him to enjoy life. He soon became a fan of *yueju*, the local women's opera.[22] He was very enthusiastic about organizing a new opera troupe, raised money for it, watched its performances, and helped the actresses with financial difficulties. Most southbound cadres did not like this type of opera. They saw it as nothing but a mixture of decadent music and silly conversation. Its themes were love stories or trifling personal problems—totally irrelevant to the revolution. Since Feng was fond of something that most southbound cadres did not like, he was soon isolated from his comrades-in-arms and thus became a "stranger." A "stranger" was always the easiest target in Mao's political campaigns.

When the Three Antis Campaign started, Feng Mengdong was accused of ignoring his duty and using illegal means to collect ¥96 million (old RMB) in funding for the *yueju* opera troupe. As Feng refused to participate in self-criticism, the auditing team found additional "crimes": Feng had used his power to hide and embezzle an American car (a Buick). This car was supposed to belong to the Shanghai Public Bureau, but Feng had taken it for his personal use.

He had also sold another government-owned car without permission. Although there was no evidence showing that Feng had pocketed the money in question or that he had had affairs with any of the *yueju* actresses, everyone believed Feng was guilty. To make matters worse, Feng remained arrogant and denied all the accusations, saying, "I will have none of your nonsense." Therefore, as the first offender caught in the campaign, Feng was purged from the Party and arrested.[23]

Though the Three Antis Campaign was directed against three specific "evils," Mao required all the Party organizations to focus on perpetrators of crime against the economy—the "hidden tigers." He sent a telegram to local governments and Party organizations to warn them: "In all our institutions, be they Party, government, or military, as long as there is a lot of money and property involved, there will be a large number of big 'tigers.' Nevertheless, it is not correct to assume that in the departments with little money, such as the Department of Propaganda or cultural and educational institutions, there will be no big 'tigers.'"[24]

Mao's telegram indicated that corruption could be found everywhere, but what kinds of cadres would most likely be the "tigers"? Mao forwarded Gao Gang's report to the city leaders of Hangzhou, who suggested that the following cadres could be major suspects: (1) those who used to be merchants or owners of small factories before they joined the revolution; (2) those from bourgeois or petty bourgeois families; (3) those who had close ties with businessmen or industrialists; (4) those who had financial power and lived luxuriously; (5) those who always made government purchases at one or two private companies.[25] Two groups of cadres met all these criteria. One group had previously been GMD employees in North China. They had received short-term revolutionary training and followed the peasant cadres from Luzhongnan to Hangzhou. With expertise in business and commerce, they served in various government offices, dealing with financial and monetary affairs. The second group was the student recruits and cadres of local origin. With a better education than the peasant cadres, many of them had been assigned to work with urban intellectuals and businessmen and had thus established close relationships with them. In addition, some of them came from "non-working-class" families, making them very untrustworthy.

In 1952, Mao wrote more than two hundred telegrams and articles urging the Party organizations to hunt down more big tigers. In a telegram to the leaders of the NCB, Mao praised their achievement: "The large number of tigers you have caught indicates that you have a better understanding, higher confidence, and great enthusiasm."[26] In other telegrams, Mao criticized Shandong Province and the South Central Military Region for having caught too few tigers. The CCP Zhejiang Committee sent a report to the CCP Central Committee estimating that it might be able to find a thousand tigers in the province. Mao Zedong argued that this estimate was too conservative. He suspected that there were probably two or three thousand tigers or even more in the province.[27] Following Mao, every leader quantified specific tiger-hunting goals for his subordinates and evaluated their performance by the number of tigers they caught. Under strong pressure to meet the quota, the cadres had to use all means possible, including physical torture, to fulfill their task. One can only image how many innocent people were victimized under such circumstances.

Mao stressed that the Party cadres should "hunt tigers with the same determination and courage that they struggle against American imperialism."[28] The language used in this campaign—for example, people's warfare *(renmin zhanzheng)*, a battle of annihilation *(jianmie zhan)*, and storming the fortifications *(gongjian zhan)*—reflected the cohesive nature of the movement and the military legacy of the Party. Although there was not much violence, the morning-to-night confession meetings became a real torture. Moreover, as soon as people were mobilized for "warfare," the Party's promise that verdicts would rest on the weight of evidence and investigation became mere lip service. The tiger-hunting teams in various enterprises competed with each other for the most tigers caught and the most illegal earnings uncovered. They were content to obtain confessions via compulsion and to give them credence. One accountant in Taizhou Prefecture confessed that he had embezzled ¥5.5 from his institution, but the tiger-hunting team forced him to acknowledge that he had stolen ¥500,000 of the institution's money—even though the entire annual budget of this institution was only about ¥2,000.[29]

The final statistics revealed the absurd nature of the mass movement. It was reported that the Three Antis Campaign had caught

290,000 economic tigers. Only 105,000 of them could be proved guilty, and the remaining (more than 65 percent) had to be released.[30] The CCP argued that the government had corrected the mishandled cases in the concluding stages. Not all the tigers, however, were strong enough to survive the massive attack. Unable to stand the psychological pressure and torture, a number of them collapsed, lost hope of proving themselves innocent, and committed suicide. The secretary of the Youth League at the Zhejiang Medical University, then in his late twenties, committed suicide.[31] Worse yet, people would not forgive him because suicide was regarded as a refusal to be educated by the masses and the Party.

In the Three Antis Campaign, Mao and his Party were faced with a dilemma. On the one hand, they wanted to catch as many big tigers as possible. On the other hand, they did not want to give the people the impression that so many Communist cadres had become corrupt in such a short time after coming to power. Therefore, Mao Zedong emphasized that this campaign was actually an educational movement, teaching all Communist cadres that wartime heroes must stand up to the tests of peacetime. The major approach of the campaign, therefore, was supposed to be persuasion, with verdicts based on evidence.

In order to protect the majority of the southbound cadres, the Party organizations controlled the campaign to make sure that criticism against bureaucratism would remain moderate. In most cases, Party leaders had only to go through some self-criticism and express appreciation for the masses' criticism. In fact, these cadres did not welcome all the criticism from the masses, and they even suspected that some criticism was a blind to shift people's attention and protect a real tiger. Although these Party leaders had to be humble during the campaign, they remained powerful after the campaign, and some of them used every means possible to retaliate against subordinates who had criticized them in the campaign.[32]

On March 13, 1952, the city government in Hangzhou made a final review of all the cases and reported its verdicts to the provincial committee. Two months later, the CCP Zhejiang Committee announced that the Three Antis Campaign had been successfully concluded and that the goals of purifying the Party and educating the people had been reached.

The Five Antis Campaign: An Economic Struggle

While the Three Antis Campaign was still in progress, another one, the Five Antis Campaign, was initiated. The new campaign resulted from hostility toward the bourgeoisie, especially the Party's theory that all corrupt cadres must be connected with the illegal activities of businessmen. The illegal activities specified were bribery, tax evasion, theft of state property, cheating on government contracts, and stealing economic information for the purposes of speculation; these were known as "the five poisons" (*wu du*). The government claimed that an audit of private companies in Shanghai had indicated that 99 percent of the businessmen had committed one or several of the five poisons.[33] It was reported that these crimes were so rampant in Hangzhou that they had caused huge losses in state revenues.[34]

In January 1952 on many occasions, Mao Zedong stressed that it was necessary to launch a timely, large-scale, and resolute campaign in all cities against the bourgeoisie who had violated the laws. The CCP Zhejiang Committee moved quickly to implement Mao's instructions. On January 16, 1952, the committee launched the campaign in seven cities of the province; Hangzhou was the first on the list.[35] On February 2, the city leaders convened a joint meeting of the Political Consultative Conference and the Committee for Increasing Production and Practicing Economy. Plans were discussed in detail so as to meet Mao's criterion that all large cities take action in the first ten days of February.[36]

There were 16,561 registered industrial enterprises and commercial firms in Hangzhou in 1952. In addition, it was estimated that around 3,400 small shopkeepers and peddlers had not yet registered with the city's Bureau of Industry and Commerce. Before the campaign was launched, the city government made a survey of the assets of all private enterprises (see table 2). In addition, the majority of industrial and commercial enterprises in the city were classified into seven categories, according to their capital assets (see table 3).

Although the capital assets of the majority of the firms in the city amounted to less than ¥100 million in 1952, the government found that the total illegal income of the city's enterprises was as high as ¥140 billion.[37] Clearly this illegal income, especially from tax evasion, caused serious deficits for the government. The Five

Table 2. Assets of Private Enterprises in Hangzhou, 1952

Type of Assets	Volume of Assets (Billion ¥)[a]	Percentage of Total
Total	398.8[b]	100
Industrial	148.2	37
Commercial	202.1	51
Handcraft industry	48.5	12

Source: CCP Zhejiang Committee, "First Summary Report on the Current Progress and Further Plans for the Five Antis Campaign" (March 8, 1952); in Zhejiang zibenzhuyi, 115.

[a]Figures in old RMB.

[b]This was the volume registered with the city's Department of Industry and Commerce. The city government estimated that the real volume might be more than ¥597 billion.

Table 3. Categories of Private Enterprises in Hangzhou by Volume of Capital, 1952

Volume of Capital (Million ¥)[a]	Number of Enterprises	Percentage of Total
<100	15,895	96.00
100–500	588	3.55
501–1,000	47	0.28
1,001–2,000	17	0.10
2,001–5,000	9	0.06
5,001–10,000	1	<0.01
10,000+	3	0.01

Source: CCP Zhejiang Committee, "First Summary Report on the Current Progress and Further Plans for the Five Antis Campaign" (March 8, 1952); in Zhejiang zibenzhuyi, 124–125.

[a]Figures in old RMB.

Antis Committee called on 1,400 cadres from the provincial and municipal governments, as well as students from the Party school and school for worker cadres, to form 22 work teams to audit the accounts of the major private enterprises. The work teams recruited new members among factory workers and were then divided into 1,608 working groups that focused on six major industries and businesses—tea, timber, medicines, hardware, silk, and textiles. To prepare for the campaign, the Five Antis Committee held training sessions for 5,000 shop assistants. The committee also received some 50,000 letters denunciating those who had committed the five poisons. These provided important clues for the work teams to hunt down the criminals. In addition, the tiger-hunting teams in the Three Antis Campaign, which comprised 15,900 workers and shop assistants, quickly shifted their attention to the investigation of the five poisons. At the same time, the Union of Industry and Commerce organized the merchants and industrialists to attend intensive political education sessions to help them study Party policy and make confessions about their wrongdoing.[38]

In order to coordinate with the ongoing Three Antis Campaign, a new slogan hit the headlines of the local press: "Smash the fierce onslaught of the bourgeoisie!" At first, the urban people could not understand the slogan, wondering how businessmen and industrialists could possibly stage an onslaught since they did not have any arms or weapons. Moreover, the businessmen argued that it was the corrupt Communist cadres who should be "smashed": they were so greedy that they demanded bribes, practiced graft, and violated the law. It was they who had "slipped and fallen into the water." Why should the government blame the bourgeoisie?[39] Some merchants simply claimed that the Five Antis Campaign was nothing but a way to squeeze money out of them and that "under communism, businessmen are doomed, sooner or later."[40]

The first person who publicly refuted the arguments of the businessmen was a non-Party economist—Ma Yinchu. On February 8, 1952, he met with a journalist from the *Liberation Daily* to express his support of the government. He said that after the Communist victory in China, the bourgeoisie was not able to organize a nationwide struggle for state power, but it had not given up the attempt, and it was purposely making assaults on the people's government. Ma said that the Communist cadres were corrupted not in the countryside but in the cities, which proved the corrosive influence of the urban bourgeoisie on the cadres.[41] Coming from a non-Communist intellectual, Ma's comments were more convincing than the government's propaganda.

The Association of Industry and Commerce in Hangzhou was instructed to study Ma's comments and make a formal statement to support the Five Antis Campaign. Every businessman, at this stage, tried to prove his hands were clean and urged other businessmen to confess their "five poisons" in order to maintain his own status as a "friend" of the CCP.[42] It was good enough for the Party at this stage that nobody decried the campaign, and it now had a free hand to organize a massive attack against the silenced enemy. After the Thought Reform Campaign, most intellectuals took an active part in the Five Antis Campaign in order to prove that they had made progress. In addition, the newly established Residents' Committees were glad to organize residents to criticize the nasty speculators and "dirty rich people." Thus a united front against the five poisons was formed in the city among different social classes and groups.

For historical reasons, as noted, Hangzhou's industries were closely associated with industries in Shanghai. On January 21, 1952, the chairman of the Central Supervisory Committee, Bo Yibo, was sent to Shanghai to oversee the Five Antis Campaign. The political situation in Shanghai would greatly affect the progress of the campaign in Hangzhou. In Shanghai, Bo Yibo called meetings of the leading businessmen and urged them to confess their five poisons by February 1 (later postponed to February 15). A similar deadline was set up by the Hangzhou municipal government. At the municipal Department of Industry and Commerce numbers of businessmen, dressed in blue tunics and trousers, waited in line to make confessions to government officials, and others paced up and down outside the building, wondering what they should confess. Every time they made a confession, officials would urge them to confess more. They kept going back to the Bureau of Industry and Commerce to make additional confessions but never felt relieved.[43]

The main thrust of the Five Antis Campaign was not a face-to-face struggle. Employees were organized to expose their bosses' crimes without directly confronting them. Soon the city government in Hangzhou learned the following tactics from Shanxi Province: (1) urge businessmen to confess and promise to reward them for informing against their partners or other companies; (2) urge corrupt cadres to admit who had bribed them and induced them to commit crimes; (3) use women workers to persuade the wives of the businessmen to push their husbands to confess.[44]

In the early stages, the businessmen had some illusions. They thought that the CCP could not really know what they had done and would not punish them in any case since the law does not punish the majority *(fa bu ze zhong)*. It was very common for businessmen not to reveal all their assets in their reports to the government. It was also not unusual for them to use poor materials to cheat contractors or profit at the expense of the government and customers. Initially the businessmen were not asked to hurry and confess. Instead, they were asked to read the reports on "five poisons" cases in other cities and to denounce these crimes. When the leaders of the Association of Industry and Commerce were asked to make confessions first, other association members just listened and made comments. The easy beginning made many businessmen believe their problems were minor and that they could easily survive the campaign without confessing to anything. They did not feel serious pressure until auditing teams entered their factories or stores and started to take action.

As soon as the tiger-hunting teams came in, the businessmen were plagued with morning-to-night interrogations. They had to account for every penny of their illegal earnings, not knowing when their confessions would be accepted. This enormous psychological pressure soon led many to suffer nervous breakdowns or even commit suicide. They tried to find other ways to resist. A few expressed their enmity by closing their businesses, firing some worker activists, or announcing bankruptcy to avoid paying workers' salaries. Two shopkeepers beat their shop assistants, who were seriously injured and finally died; the bosses were immediately arrested and then sentenced to death.

Soon the Hangzhou city government decided to adopt tougher measures to push the campaign forward. On February 22, 1952, a rally was held to publicly denounce the targeted businessmen and force them to confess. During the rally, the government arrested five businessmen who refused to confess and denounced four businessmen by name, ordering them to make full confessions. Yet it was also announced that three serious offenders had been exempted from punishment because they had made thorough confessions and denounced other criminals. After the rally, the Five Antis Committee mobilized three hundred thousand urban residents to carry out a one-week propaganda drive and demanded that all businessmen submit a second round of written confessions. In early March, the city government was ready to finish up its first round of investigations.[45]

Just as the CCP Zhejiang Committee was preparing to submit its first report on the Five Antis Campaign in Hangzhou to the CCP Central Committee, the city government in Beijing worked out detailed measures for classifying businesses. Its classification into five categories was approved as the model by the CCP Central Committee: (1) law-abiding: establishments that did not break the law or made very little in illegal earnings; (2) basically law-abiding: establishments with illegal earnings of less than ¥2 million, or illegal earnings exceeded this amount but the crimes were not serious and the responsible parties' confessions were satisfactory; (3) semi-law-abiding: establishments with illegal earnings of over ¥2 million but whose crimes were not seriously harmful to the state; (4) seriously law-breaking: establishments with fairly large illegal earnings and serious infringements upon the interests of the state and the people, or whose responsible parties refused to confess; (5) completely law-breaking: establishments guilty of the most serious economic crimes, causing extensive losses to the state and the people. The Central Committee instructed all city governments to use the Beijing model to consider their local conditions and thus work out their classifications for businesses and businessmen.[46]

Initially the Hangzhou city government had divided all the industrialist and merchants into three categories: (1) law-abiding (illegal income was less than ¥2 million in industry and ¥1 million in commerce); (2) semi-law-abiding (illegal income was less than ¥100 million); and (3) law-breaking (illegal income of more than ¥100 million). The first category accounted for 41.66 percent of the total private enterprises, the second 53.57 percent, and the third 4.77 percent. The city government planned to arrest one hundred businessmen, severely punish fifty, and sentence two or three serious offenders to death.

In a report on March 8 to the CCP Central Committee and the ECB, the CCP Zhejiang Committee optimistically estimated the possible conclusion of the campaign by the end of March. About five thousand enterprises had been cleared by the government as "law-abiding establishments," and their cases were closed. Final reviews of the other categories would soon be completed. The committee estimated that the financial gain to the city government from repayments and fines would be about ¥150–¥250 billion.[47]

Three days later, the ECB replied to the CCP Zhejiang Committee, praising Hangzhou for the progress it had made in the campaign and requesting the CCP Hangzhou Committee to adjust its criteria so as to include a category for "basically law-abiding" establishments and to divide the "law-breaking" category into "seriously" and "completely." In Shanghai, an enterprise with illegal earnings of less than ¥10 million was regarded as a "basically law-abiding establishment." The ECB suggested that the dividing line between "basically" and "semi" law-abiding should be between ¥2 million and ¥10 million. However, the most important thing, the ECB stressed, was that the total number of law-abiding and basically law-abiding establishments make up at least 50 percent of the total enterprises. (The figure was 70 percent in Beijing and 52 percent in Shanghai.) In any case, the Communist political strategy was to unite the majority and punish only a few.[48]

On March 13, the CCP Zhejiang Committee forwarded the ECB's directives to Hangzhou, instructing the city government to complete its classification by March 20; bring conclusive verdicts for the law-abiding, basically law-abiding, and semi-law-abiding establishments; and quickly go through these cases group by group. After March 20, the city government needed to focus on the few seriously law-breaking and completely law-breaking establishments so that the campaign could end no later than April 5. According to the ECB, by April it would be time to restore normal economic life in the city.[49]

All the businessmen with illegal earnings had to make repayments and pay fines. In Hangzhou, most small businesses fell into the "basically" and "semi" law-abiding categories and had to turn in all illegal earnings to the state. Some serious offenders could also be treated with leniency if they denounced other offenders. The business establishments in the last category would be subject to a confiscation of assets and punishment by criminal law. This punishment, as Mao Zedong said, could include "arrest, imprisonment, and execution by firing squad."[50]

On March 25, 1952, the Five Antis Committee called a public confession meeting for 520 major law-breaking establishments. About 3,000 workers and cadres participated in the meeting, at which, after a brief policy announcement and a few speeches by the worker representatives, 248 businessmen made public confessions and promised to pay fines totaling about ¥75.4 billion. After the meeting, attack was focused on those who had refused to make public confessions. By April 5, all of these businessmen had confessed as well.

It was obvious that most confessions were made under pressure, and the offenders had to exaggerate their crimes (or misdemeanors) in order to survive. In the early stages, the CCP was very eager to uncover widespread "five poisons," and it forced the businessmen to emphasize them in their confessions. Chen Yun reminded the city leaders of Hangzhou of fake cases: "There are several factories in Zhejiang where the volume of illegal earnings to which the offenders have confessed is even greater than the total income of the factories. These figures are too high to be true."[51] Finally, the city Five Antis Committee had to review its findings and cut down the total volume of "five poisons" earnings from ¥452.7 billion to ¥270 billion. Consequently, of all the industrial and commercial companies only 0.5 percent were labeled as seriously law-breaking and only 0.03 percent as completely law-breaking.

On April 19, 1952, the CCP Zhejiang Committee forwarded a report by the CCP Hangzhou Committee to the ECB and the CCP Central Committee declaring that the city's Five Antis Committee had reached a final verdict for 545 law-breaking establishments and had worked out the following arrangements to end the campaign:

1. Of the 545 law-breaking establishments, 439 (91.5 percent) would make repayments without fines; 30 (5.5 percent) would make repayments and pay fines; 14 (2.6 percent) would not only make repayments and fines, but also be subject to confiscation of all or part of their assets; the city government would confiscate all the assets of 2 establishments (0.4 percent); and the 2 merchants who had murdered their store employees would be sentenced to death.
2. Fifteen establishments (9 industrial and 6 commercial) would make repayments without fines. All these were big enterprises with about 4,000 employees. For political reasons, the city government made a one-grade reduction in their criminal status, moving them from seriously law-breaking to semi-law-abiding establishments.
3. The city government would take over 16 establishments (3 industrial and 13 commercial) that would go bankrupt after

making repayments and paying fines of ¥15.9 billion since their capital totaled only ¥9.8 billion.
4. The city government would not take over 14 establishments (all commercial) that would also go bankrupt after making repayments and paying fines of ¥12.5 billion (their capital totaled only ¥1.3 billion).
5. Four establishments—the Huafeng Paper Mill, the First Textile Factory, the Liuyi Knitting Mill, and the Jianzhen Ironworks Factory—were the biggest and most influential enterprises in the city. The government would reduce their repayments and fines or extend the deadlines for payments in order to help them avoid bankruptcy.
6. The Five Antis Committee found that 14 enterprises were assets of "enemy and puppet governments" and decided to confiscate them.[52]

Hangzhou's plan was approved by the ECB, especially its appropriate treatment of the big enterprises and leading industrialists, and the ECB praised the city's efforts to win over the offenders to the people's side. By the end of May 1952, the Hangzhou municipal government declared that the Five Antis Campaign had been successfully completed, although the campaign continued in other parts of China until November. The ECB recommended Hangzhou's procedures to other cities, such as Nanjing and Jinan, suggesting that they adopt similar moderate measures at the final stages of the campaign.[53]

The Five Antis Campaign: A Political Message

The Five Antis Campaign jeopardized the operation of many private enterprises, so the state had to offer them financial aid to keep them from bankruptcy. At the same time, the campaign helped to improve the general financial situation of the country and ensured government control over the private sector of the economy.[54] In November 1952, the turnover in private commercial firms dropped 29.91 percent, while the total volume of business in Hangzhou increased 8.12 percent.[55] Politically, the Five Antis Campaign was a great success in the battle against the bourgeoisie and in communicating the revolutionary message to various social classes. The campaign proved the applicability of the strategy and methods that had served the revolutionary programs in Shandong. The southbound cadres employed their technique of mass mobilization to organize various meetings, public trials, and a propaganda offensive to involve all urban people, some of whom used to be very cynical about politics.

In the past, businessmen's wives had done nothing more than shop, go to operas, or play mahjong to kill time. They did not care about politics, and no government cared about what they did. In the Five Antis Campaign, however, the Women's Federation, the Association of Industry and Commerce, and neighborhood committees began to visit these bourgeois women and began to keep them busy with all kinds of political meetings. As a result, the women began to show an interest in the political situation and in Party policy and tried to help their husbands survive the "disaster."[56] The southbound cadres also successfully instigated "class struggle" between workers and poor urban dwellers, on the one hand, and merchants and industrialists, on the other. Thousands of urban dwellers, most of them retired workers and housewives, took active part in the rallies against the five poisons. The persistent resentment of the poor against greedy merchants and their hatred for the "evil rich" now took expression in revolutionary discourse.

The most important advances were made in sharpening the class consciousness of the working class. In most factories, the CCP held grievance meetings, at which workers for the first time since 1949 denounced economic exploitation by the bourgeoisie. In investigating and condemning the five poisons, the worker representatives partly took over the management of private enterprises. The city government called this a "combination of the Five Antis and democratic reform." Among shop assistants, the CCP stressed the importance of smashing the feudal yoke of kinship and encouraged the assistants to denounce their law-breaking boss-relatives. Workers now began to feel their own strength. They were proud to have made "the industrialists and merchants unable to sleep and have no appetite to eat" in the campaign. One report by the CCP Hangzhou Committee cited the workers: "In the past we were nervous to see the boss; now the boss is trembling with fear to see us. We have really stood up now. We have never been this happy since we were born."[57]

After the campaign, the CCP Hangzhou Committee wanted to

institutionalize mass mobilization. It wanted to make short-term political workshops a regular part of the training program for three or four thousand more worker activists, recruit young workers into the Youth League, and gradually develop the Party organizations in all factories. In addition, the city government planned to use part of the businessmen's repayments to build one thousand houses for working-class families, five health centers for poor urban residents, one night school, and several dining halls to serve unemployed workers so as to enhance the reputation of the government among the workers.[58]

The bourgeoisie, for its part, fared very badly during and after the campaign, but there was no sign that the CCP would indiscriminately eliminate all businessmen. In the classification and treatment of offenders in the Five Antis Campaign, illegal earnings had been a principal factor, but political attitude was equally crucial. The CCP believed that seeking profits was instinctive to the bourgeoisie and that there was not a single businessman who had not violated the law. In addition, before 1949, the Chinese bourgeoisie could hardly have survived under pressure from both foreign and bureaucratic capital. Tax evasion, bribery, cheating, using official connections, and speculation were perhaps the only way for businessmen to make money. Thus the CCP did not believe that there was such a thing as a completely law-abiding establishment. The category of "law-abiding establishment," therefore, was used to pacify the economically influential and politically "progressive" businessmen. In the final stages of the campaign, the CCP Central Committee issued several directives on the "deliberate protection of big businessmen."[59] On April 24, 1952, Zhou Enlai sent a telegram to Bo Yibo in Shanghai, instructing him that "In all large cities, we should purposely put those upper-level bourgeois who have previously cooperated with the government into the category of law-abiding establishments."[60]

The case of Rong Yiren, a leading Chinese entrepreneur, was a good example. In the beginning, the illegal activities of the Rong family were exposed as major revelations in the newspapers in Shanghai. According to the amount of Rong's illegal earnings, his enterprises had to be ranked as semi-law-abiding. However, his economic power and political attitude made the Communists see his case in a different light. When the Communists took over Shanghai in 1949, most members of the Rong family left for Hong

Kong. Only Rong Yiren stayed. He helped the Communists stabilize the economic situation in the city, and he offered the new regime political support in the following years.[61] In view of his national influence, the Shanghai municipal government decided to classify his establishment as basically law-abiding. When Mao Zedong reviewed Rong's case, he instructed the Shanghai government to make further adjustments: "Why should we be so narrow-minded? Let's be more generous and put him into the category of completely law-abiding establishments."[62] To correct the misunderstandings of some Party members who took the campaign as the final step for wiping out the bourgeoisie, Mao Zedong pointed out, "[The Five Antis Campaign] does not mean any change in our policy toward the bourgeoisie. We are still developing a new democracy rather than socialism. The campaign is not to eliminate the bourgeoisie but just to weaken its influence. We will continue to pound on the bourgeoisie for several months, hurt it severely, and then embrace it. We won't beat it to death."[63]

At the concluding stages of the campaign, the city leaders of Hangzhou adopted moderate measures to make the final verdicts because they believed that they had hurt the bourgeoisie badly enough and now could soften the policies and appease it. The city leaders saw many good reasons for a shift from suppression to "leniency." Among other things, the city still needed the economic cooperation and political support of the bourgeoisie, especially its upper echelons. Ninety-nine industrialists and merchants were regarded as the upper stratum of the bourgeoisie, having positions in the government or in organizations sponsored by the government. According to the CCP Hangzhou Committee, thirty-two of these businessmen used to be close to the Party and should be given preferential treatment in order to show that the CCP would never abandon those who had supported it. As a result, only two of the businessmen were removed from their positions, while two-thirds of them were finally classified as law-abiding or basically law-abiding and continued to hold their positions after the campaign.[64]

The general manager of the Liuyi Knitting Mill, Hu Haiqiu, regarded as one of the industrialists who had always followed the Communist Party, benefited from the city's moderate measures. In 1949, Hu went to Tan Zhenlin to relate his experiences and show his loyalty to the new regime. Thirty-one years ago, Hu and six other students from the province had gone to France to study industrial technology, dreaming that one day they could save China via science and industry. In 1924, Hu Haiqiu opened the Liuyi Knitting Mill in Shanghai. Unable to compete with foreign and bureaucratic capital, he could not maintain a foothold in Shanghai, so he relocated the factory to Hangzhou and gradually took root there. Unfortunately, the anti-Japanese war soon extended to the city and destroyed all his buildings and equipment. After the war, Hu made a great effort to restore production and kept the business operating in the chaotic times, but his enterprise never really flourished. By the end of the Civil War, his factory had a few buildings, 16 machines, and 160 workers, but he had totally exhausted his capital reserves. Tan Zhenlin appreciated that Hu had come to the government in the early days of the new regime. Tan believed that Hu was a Chinese patriotic national bourgeois and could serve the Party's urgent task of economic restoration. He assured Hu that the people's government would support every enterprise that benefited the people and the national economy. The Military Control Committee in Hangzhou instructed the provincial bank, state-run department stores, and government institutions to provide loans for, order goods from, and offer technical assistance to the Liuyi Knitting Mill. Responding to the new regime's call for the restoration of production, Hu sold his other valuables, including his wife's jewelry and his brother's house, to invest in the factory and increase production in the mill.

Hu Haiqiu was appointed vice chairman of the city's Association of Industry and Commerce and often invited to the government's tea parties, at which he expressed his appreciation for the government's help and his support for the Party's policies. In the Five Antis Campaign, however, Hu was accused of "violating laws" and "seriously endangering the state and the people." Wu Xian, the deputy mayor, told Hu that the Communist Party still trusted him and that he should not worry about the accusations. Hu was finally labeled as basically law-abiding.[65]

The Huafeng Paper Mill also benefited from the city's flexible policy. This factory was also classified as a law-abiding establishment, although its general manager, Jin Runxiang, confessed to very serious "five poisons" crimes. The manager's political connections with the government could explain the classification. As we know, grievance meetings were usually used to make accusations against the bourgeoisie. According to Mao Zedong, they could also be used for the national bourgeoisie to pour out grievances against foreign imperialism and the GMD. It would be considered a patriotic and progressive act if an industrialist made an accusation against the GMD or America. And that is what Jin Runxiang did, thus gaining the trust of the Communist government.

Jin Runxiang began his career as a comprador of an American company in Shanghai. In order to make more money, he opened his own business and then reinvested all the earnings in the American company. Unfortunately, the American manager ran away with all the company's money, thus bankrupting Jin's business. For help Jin turned to a friend (who was the director of the division of military supply in a warlord's government), and the friend asked Jin to work with him in running a speculative business in Shanghai. Through smuggling, tax evasion, and embezzlement, Jin made a lot of money and resumed his own business. In the early 1930s, he bought a poorly managed paper mill, renovated the equipment, increased its production, and sold his products in the name of "saving China by industry." Under the protection of Du Yuesheng, chief of the Green Gang, Jin gradually monopolized the paper-making industry in Jiaxing, a small town in Zhejiang, as well as in Suzhou and Hangzhou. As soon as his business began to flourish, the war with Japan broke out, and Jin fled to Hong Kong empty-handed. In 1941, Wang Jingwei's puppet government in Nanjing decided to return some factories to Chinese owners if they were willing to collaborate with the Japanese. Jin went back to Shanghai and worked with a Japanese co-owner to keep his factory running. The justification for this behavior, as Jin said in his defense, was "to keep alive the seed of nationalist industry." After the anti-Japanese war, Du Yuesheng became more powerful. He helped Jin get a position on the Takeover Committee of the Economic Department of the GMD government; the committee was in charge of taking over the properties of the Japanese and of Wang Jinwei's government. Taking advantage of his position, Jin got his paper mills back and used some resources from Wang's puppet government to develop his business, and he thus became rich again. But the good times did not last long. Although the GMD government issued Jin an official permit for the exclusive right to produce and sell cigarette paper, it also permitted the company of a GMD government official to import American cigarette paper (and financed it as well). American imports would beat out all Chinese paper-making enterprises. For a third time, in 1949 Jin Runxiang was faced with imminent bankruptcy.[66]

It is clear that Jin tried his best to please and collaborate with anyone in power—the warlords, the Japanese, the Mafia, and the GMD—so as to develop his own businesses and prosper. He did not have any political or moral principles. From the Communist perspective, he had a dirty history, but his self-criticism after 1949 was considered thorough. Jin confessed to his collaboration with the "people's enemies" and regretted that he had profited at the expense of many small Chinese businesses. He said that every time he seemed about to be successful, his business was ruined by fierce imperialism and bureaucratic capitalism. At political study meetings or in personal conversations with Party leaders, Jin repeatedly said, "In retrospect, I have witnessed three ups and downs in my forty years of experience, and finally I have understood Mao Zedong's comments that the Chinese nationalist bourgeoisie was not the master of its own fate in the old China. Without CCP leadership, my factory could not survive and develop."[67] Jin sounded perfectly honest and correct to the Communists. After 1949, he was appointed as a member to the Provincial People's Congress and vice chairman of the Provincial Union of Industry and Commerce.

In the Five Antis Campaign, the city government received more than one thousand letters of accusation against Jin Runxiang. The local press exposed all his scandalous activities, calling him "a big thief," making Jin think that the CCP no longer trusted him. He came to believe the GMD's prediction that all businessmen would be killed under Communist control. Worrying about possible arrest, he rushed to make confessions, exaggerating his illegal earnings to ¥1,040 billion. To his big surprise, however, the government did not accept what he said but classified him as a completely law-abiding entrepreneur. His seat in the Provincial People's Congress was held for him, and he was invited to give a talk at the congress about his experiences and his gratitude to the CCP for educating other businessmen.[68]

When the Five Antis Campaign was initiated, Mao Zedong said, "The bourgeoisie made a lot of money from the government's purchase orders during the Korean War, and it thus had certain political capital and became arrogant.... Now it is time to seize its "pigtail" and deflate its arrogance. If we do not make the name of the bourgeoisie stink and its members humbled, the people will surely turn to the bourgeoisie."[69] The treatment of Hu Haiqiu and Jin Runxiang by the Hangzhou government reflected Mao Zedong's very purpose in staging this campaign. It was not to eliminate the bourgeoisie physically nor merely to weaken it economically. It mainly was to destroy its prestige so that it could only quietly follow the CCP and no longer exert a separate influence in the Chinese political arena.

The New Three Antis Campaign

The CCP staged several rectification campaigns in its history and set up an ironical, if not cunning, pattern. It began by encouraging people to criticize Party members; then it took a sudden turn to counterattack an "enemy's onslaught"—to retaliate against those who had responded to the Party's call for rectification; after the Party was sure that it had smashed the "enemy's offensive," the movement returned to its starting point to welcome all "well-meaning" criticism. The campaigns of 1952–1953—beginning with the Three Antis, followed by the Five Antis, and then the New Three Antis—demonstrated this CCP pattern.

Theoretically, the Three Antis Campaign was launched to correct the Party's mistakes and to preserve the CCP's image as an uncorrupted leadership for whom the people came first. In fact, the campaign did not really touch most Party leaders in Hangzhou. In the beginning, some young cadres of student background were quite enthusiastic about criticizing bureaucratism. They criticized their bosses for not being concerned about people's hardships and not listening to suggestions from junior Party members or ordinary people. They pointed out that some Communist leaders were ignorant but acted self-important and used a "GMD style" to run the revolutionary institutions.[70] These young cadres had joined the revolution because they had been inspired by the idealism of Communist utopianism. They were sorely disappointed with the power abuse of some southbound cadres after they took on important positions in the Party and government. With little knowledge of the economy or education or the workings of an urban area, these leaders usually made decisions arbitrarily. The young cadres hated these leaders, who sought only fame, wealth, women, and luxury.

The criticism was sharp and emotional but did not last long. The Three Antis Campaign was unfolding under Communist leadership, and most of the leaders were the peasant cadres. Although Mao Zedong had pointed out that harsh leadership and commandism were central problems that would strain the Party's relations with the masses, the city leaders believed that the key targets of the campaign were newly recruited cadres and the employees retained from the previous regime. The young cadres could by no means channel the direction of the campaign. Their criticism against their supervisors was interpreted as a lack of discipline on their part and disloyalty to the Communist Party. Their supervisors would give them negative evaluations for their performance in the campaign, and these evaluations would be put into their personal dossiers to ruin their political future. The applications of such youngsters for Party membership were no longer considered, and the young cadres who were working in major government departments were transferred to less important divisions.[71]

Despite the accomplishments of the Three Antis and Five Antis Campaigns, complaints about the work style of CCP leaders at various levels continued to mount, in Hangzhou as well as in other parts of the country. Recognizing this, Mao Zedong drafted the following for the CCP Central Committee: "Our Party has corrected two major mistakes [in the Three Antis Campaign]—corruption and waste. However, bureaucratism—that is, ignorance of people's sufferings, not knowing what is going on at the lower levels, harsh leadership, commandism, and the violation of laws and discipline by our cadres—has yet to be corrected."[72] On January 5, 1953, the CCP Central Committee issued a directive for Party organizations from the central to county levels to "wage a resolute struggle against bureaucratism, commandism, and the violation of laws and discipline." This became known as the New Three Antis Campaign.

Twenty-two days later, the CCP Zhejiang Committee worked out a plan to implement the directive. The Party secretary, Tan Qilong, called on Party cadres to correct bad work practices. He identified bad leaders as those who (1) maintained no contact with people at lower levels and did not listen to the voice of the masses; (2) assigned tasks without explaining Party policy or appropriate methods; (3) welcomed only good news but did not want to hear the bad; (4) did not regularly visit the Party's grassroots organizations or show interest in the thoughts of their cadres; (5) got bogged down in routine matters; and (6) ignored the hardships of the masses.[73]

Mao instructed that the New Three Antis Campaign should be a mild rather than turbulent rectification movement.[74] Nonetheless, the campaign in Hangzhou became a sharp, inner-Party struggle. On the one hand, ordinary people had strong sentiments against bureaucratism and commandism. They were also strongly critical of the patriarchal behavior of some southbound cadres. On the other hand, Party leaders were determined to mute the people's voice in order to avoid damage to their own reputations and an undermining of the Party's leadership. The rural areas presented even more serious problems: it was reported that the cadres there implemented only the policies they liked, forced the peasants to turn in extra public grain, got involved in superstitious activities, and made arbitrary policies by themselves.[75] The city government had sent some work teams to help local Party organizations solve these problems. However, when criticism was directed against the leaders of the city and the province, the story was quite different. The Moganshan Conference of 1953 was an illuminating example.

From July 21 to August 4, 1953, the CCP Zhejiang Committee held its Fourteenth Extended Committee Meeting at Moganshan (Mount Mogan). The meeting first discussed how to develop agricultural production that had been damaged by natural disasters and how to work toward a better harvest that year. The meeting then turned to reviewing the progress of the New Three Antis Campaign in the province. Some participants, such as the director of the Organizational Department, Yang Siyi, began to criticize the number one provincial leader. In his diary, Yang wrote that this leader's bureaucratism was evident in several ways: (1) he often considered the opinions of the masses insignificant; (2) he always criticized the "liberalism" of other people but ignored the correlation between liberalism and his bureaucratism;[76] (3) he was opposed to the tenet that self-criticism and self-examination should begin with higher-level leaders; (4) he wanted to hear only good news and rejected reports on the bad; (5) he criticized subordinates arbitrarily but never wanted people to criticize him.[77]

Although many people agreed with Yang, they did not support him because most southbound cadres believed in patriarchal rule. In their deep-rooted peasant culture, the number one leader was their patriarch, and his leadership was unchallengeable. In the New Three Antis Campaign the southbound cadres might criticize patriarchal rule in their subordinate units, but they would not directly confront their own patriarchal leadership, still less criticize their bosses. Many did not support Yang, believing that his viewpoint challenged not only a specific leader, but also the entire Party leadership. Moreover, Yang Siyi was a local cadre with an intellectual background. As the director of the Organizational Department, he had recruited a considerable number of local people and talented intellectuals, and he maintained good relations with the old urban elite. These factors made him a "stranger" to the southbound cadres.

At the meeting, some members of the CCP Provincial Standing Committee defended the number one leader and accused Yang of being a captive to bourgeois individualism and liberalism. Yang was forced to engage in self-criticism and confession.[78] The campaign against bureaucratism eventually became a crusade against bourgeois liberalism. It was not until July 1954 that the ECB finally affirmed Yang Siyi's stance against bureaucratism.[79] In August, the Provincial People's Congress elected Yang Siyi deputy governor of Zhejiang Province, marking the peak of his career. Nevertheless, for Yang Siyi, the New Three Antis Campaign was a turning point. Afterward, he could no longer enjoy the trust of Party leaders. Four years later Yang was purged from the Party. That was the price he paid for criticizing patriarchal leadership at the Moganshan Meeting.[80]

Conclusion

The Three Antis, Five Antis, and New Three Antis Campaigns were important steps in Mao Zedong's permanent revolution. For the southbound cadres, Mao's revolution was not just an abstract concept. It directly affected their political interests, for they felt that their personal power embodied the unchallengeable Party's leadership. Thus they committed themselves to the fight against the urban bourgeoisie. Their rural revolutionary tradition was the Party's glorious asset, believed to be immune to erosion from the bourgeois culture. However, new cadres and intellectual cadres had to be trained long and hard to experience the tough revolutionary struggle; otherwise, they would be easily "pulled out" by counterrevolutionaries. At the same time, the urban bourgeoisie could also corrupt a few "weak-willed" veteran cadres. It was based on these beliefs that the CCP took the campaigns in 1952–1953 as a life-and-death struggle for the Party, as well as for the southbound cadres. The campaigns solidified CCP control by tarnishing the reputation of the urban bourgeoisie; they also solidified the leading position of the southbound cadres by purging those who could not resist the bourgeois influence and those whom the Party did not trust.

In a discussion of the political consequences of the Three Antis and New Three Antis Campaigns, Frederick Teiwes writes: "During the 1950 rectification campaign, the official statements valued the administrative abilities of new cadres as well as the political achievements of old cadres. In fact, the emphasis was on the need to promote administratively competent newcomers at the expense of old revolutionaries as befitted the needs of the situation."[81] The experience of Hangzhou, however, proved otherwise. The major concern of the rectification campaign was not to improve the administrative ability of Party workers but to test their loyalty to the Party. The predominant theme was power. Indeed, it was a major challenge for the peasant cadres to govern cities. Since the new rulers desperately needed knowledge, expertise, and management experience, it was a stopgap measure to let the urban bourgeoisie continue to run the economy and for old employees to remain in their government jobs. Not only in Hangzhou but all over the country, the CCP reconciled political loyalty and technical proficiency in two ways. First, it tried to train its own experts to gradually replace the old ones; this inevitably provoked periodical purges in the country. Second, it upheld the principle of nonprofessionals leading professionals *(waihang lingdao neihang)*, insisting that politics command technology in all spheres of state affairs.

To be sure, China's modernization after 1949 would enhance the influence of technical bureaucrats. The Party, therefore, had to employ all measures to avoid two dangerous consequences: its own experts being outdone by the bourgeoisie or its veteran revolutionaries being undermined by the increasing influence of technical experts. That is the reason Mao Zedong always redoubled his calls for class struggle when China had overcome economic difficulties or made progress in state reconstruction. In no case would the CCP like to "promote administratively competent newcomers at the expense of old revolutionaries." The Three Antis Campaigns and others of Mao's political campaigns were all used as control mechanisms to inhibit any political change that would threaten the Party's leadership or upset the political interests of the peasant cadres. To this end, the Party employed all means—its propaganda machines and its ritualized meetings—to glorify the rural revolutionary tradition and demonize the bourgeois culture. Mao's political campaigns communicated these messages to the Chinese people on a continuous basis, making them public knowledge.

7
Women Cadres

After the establishment of the PRC, the state-run film studios began to use a three-person image (male worker, soldier, and female peasant) as their new emblem.¹ As Chinese movies were showing throughout the country, images of women repeatedly emerged on the screen to represent the Chinese peasantry. This emblem reflected a wide perception that associated Chinese women with poor and backward rural life and implied the subordinate position of women, who were under the leadership of male workers.

As spring came to the city of Hangzhou in 1953, however, some eye-catching posters appeared on the streets that portrayed women as PLA soldiers, textile workers, and urban intellectuals. Some posters simply presented young women in Russian-style long skirts *(blagi)*, with broad smiles on their faces and families in the background, implying a happy life for women in the new China.² These posters were part of the propaganda for a nationwide educational campaign to publicize the 1950 Marriage Law. Two years previously, soon after the Marriage Law was first issued, the practices of polygamy and concubinage were abolished, the marriage registration system was established, and a mass campaign was initiated to criticize arranged marriage and family violence and to advocate free-choice marriage and freedom of divorce.³ Now, as these posters indicated, the campaign had a new focus. Combined with preparations for the first general election in the country, the second Marriage Law Campaign would not only propagandize marriage reform, but also emphasize women's new roles in society, encouraging them to cast ballots for the representatives of people's congresses at various levels in the PRC.[4]

As the first major legislative enactment of the PRC, the Marriage Law had a revolutionary impact on both women's social status and their political participation.[5] However, not all women's stories were as pleasant as the street posters intimated. This chapter is devoted to a group of women cadres who joined the revolution during the anti-Japanese and civil wars and contributed to the Communist takeover of Hangzhou. It will trace their experiences back to the rural bases of Shandong and move to the lives of the southbound women cadres in the urban setting of Hangzhou so as to shed new light on the question of whether socialism liberated women and reveal both the triumphs and the frustrations of women cadres in Mao's revolution.[6]

Women Shaped the Revolution

If we can argue that Mao's revolution relied basically on male peasants, this should not be exaggerated into a myth that it was exclusively male.[7] The revolution in Luzhongnan saw a growth in women's associations and opportunities for women's political participation. As most male adults in villages went to the battlefield, local Party organizations had to depend upon the women for many of their campaigns.[8]

In 1923, the CCP began its activities at the Third Women's Normal School in Xuzhou.[9] Six years later, it established the First Lunan Branch (south of Shandong), which admitted five Party members from among elementary school teachers; two of them, Zhang Huiyi and Bo Jingzhen, were women.[10] The next year the Party recruited three more women from the Fifth Provincial High School.[11] The strong ideals of women's liberation that came with Marxist ideology greatly inspired these young ladies. Like their predecessors—women revolutionaries such as Qiu Jin, Xiao Chunu, and Zeng Xing—the first group of CCP women activists in Luzhongnan were intelligent, radical girls who rebelled against their "feudal" families by refusing family-arranged marriages or asking for the freedom to study and work in the cities.[12] The CCP taught the female students to link women's suffering with national crises, so that they came to believe that the goals of the Communist revolution and women's emancipation could be perfectly blended, and they devoted themselves to the revolution with enthusiasm and pride. Unfortunately, most of these early CCP members, including the first group of women revolutionaries, were killed in abortive uprisings in 1932–1933.

In the years of the anti-Japanese war, the issue of women's emancipation no longer commanded public attention, but with bold attempts to draw women to the revolution, the CCP continued to use women's emancipation for mass mobilization. Ren Xiurong recalled that her motivation for joining Mao's revolution was to get out of an arranged marriage. After Ren's father joined the Communist army and left home, her adopted mother wanted to force the seventeen-year-old girl to get married. She arranged for Ren to either become the second wife of a schoolteacher or marry a bandit chief. Ren hated both options and decided to leave home to join the Communists.[13]

Although it was not uncommon in Luzhongnan for girls to make such a brave move and break their family's control, as Ren Xiurong had done, most rural women in Shandong joined the Communist movement in a rather more passive way. Some just followed the examples of their brothers, and others were sent to the Communists by their "liberal gentry" fathers. Wang Huaizhen explained about her motivations for joining the Communist revolution: she interrupted her schooling and joined the medical team of the Eighth Route Army after she saw her three brothers join the Communist army one after another. She wanted to be with her brothers and believed that she could do what the boys were doing.[14]

In January 1939, the Communist Anti-Japanese Military and Political College in Shandong began to recruit students. The school planned to admit six hundred new students in military, political, and mass movement classes, and the school was open to both boys and girls.[15] The story of one of the female students, Liu Qi, explains why some parents sent their daughters to the school. In the war, Liu Qi's brother was killed by the Japanese, and her father was determined to get revenge for his son. He sent Liu Qi to the college and audited her classes. The lectures he heard assured him that this was the right place to make his daughter strong and useful for the anti-Japanese war. Afterward, he encouraged his other two daughters also to join the Eighth Route Army.[16] Zhang Xia tells a similar story. She remembers that as a poor village girl, she was attracted by the school's promise of free tuition, free accommodations, and placement in a job after graduation. However, Zhang was surprised to find that many of her forty classmates came in nice dresses, indicating they were from rich gentry families.[17] Some gentry families had sent their daughters to the college because they admired the Communist strategy for national salvation, while others just believed that the college would be the safest place for their daughters in wartime.

In addition to running military and political colleges, the Communists held reading classes for women of all ages *(funu shiziban)* in villages. Girls and housewives did not have to leave home and could learn how to read and write. In the classes, they were also taught about the war. The Japanese atrocities in Shandong, especially the raping of women and the killing of children, were often cited. It was most dangerous, they were told, for women whose family members were involved in anti-Japanese activities. Thus, the Communist movement became a family movement in the villages: one family member joined, and others would automatically follow. This was also the case in the Civil War, when the rural population was split between supporters and opponents of the GMD. The peasants chose sides not as individuals but as a family.

To appeal to women, the Communists portrayed the Eighth Route Army as the ardent proponent of China who would create a safe haven for women. This was part of the Communist propaganda calling for every Chinese to stand up to save the country. Drawing sustenance from this inspirational nationalism, many women came to the revolution in this period. The reading classes interpreted the theoretical language of Maoism for them and translated it into practical terms. While the reading classes might take a couple of months, the teacher-student contacts and the solidarity among the rural women themselves lasted much longer. This short-term education was a decisive factor in arousing women's political consciousness.

Women's participation in the Communist political and military campaigns had a great impact on village life. The peasant response to the women's revolutionary behavior was not as negative as some of the literature describes. Luzhongnan is an area full of female heroism. The legend of Mu Guiying is well known from local operas, oral tradition, and cartoons. Mu Guiying, a young girl with extraordinary talent and courage, beat out all other candidates in a competitive selection for military commander during a national crisis. Then she commanded her husband, uncles, brothers-in-law, sisters-in-law, and government troops in a decisive battle against foreign invaders.[18] For generations, Mu Guiying had been far away from the daily life of rural women, but her legend could become a reality in the war, when everyone picked up a weapon to join the battle.

As rural girls strove hard to emulate Mu Guiying and help toward national salvation, peasant boys did not want to fall behind. The most powerful slogan for military recruitment was "Send the beloved to the army" *(song lang can jun)*, which reveals that women were key to the success of military recruitment. In order to get the honorable title of "Model Women's Village" in Luzhongnan, women had not only to provide the best logistical services, but also to mobilize and send many new soldiers to the Communist army.[19] In addition, a girl serving in the Communist army as a nurse or propagandist or working in the Party organizations was the "dream girl" of the boys who joined the revolution, and they wished to have a wife like that.

Although the Communist army welcomed women's participation, the overwhelming majority of soldiers and officers were male bachelors. More often than not, girls were frustrated in this man's world. Cui Bo recalled that in the early years, because there were only a few unmarried girls in the army and government and most male comrades were bachelors, the girls were always being chased by the men. It was difficult to stop being pestered, and still harder to refuse offers of marriage from superiors. In addition, the Party organizations were happy to act as go-betweens for the unmarried senior leaders and girls. Ren Xiurong recalls that when she was working on the medical team of the local militia, a regimental commander of a Communist troop wanted to give her team some guns in exchange for her to be his wife, and the leader of the medical team was glad to make such a deal to get the weapons the team most needed. If the commander had not changed his mind in the end, she would definitely have married him.[20]

In most cases, a girl could not refuse a marriage arranged by the Party organization *(zuzhi)* since her attitude toward such an arrangement was regarded as her political statement. The only way for girls to stop from being bothered was to marry someone as soon as possible. However, as soon as they got married, another problem arose. The big headache, as Cui Bo said, was that it was very easy for these young women to get pregnant. Most of them were devoted to the revolution and wanted careers other than as mothers and housewives, so it was very common for them to go to great lengths to terminate a pregnancy. They stomped and thrashed, took herbal medicines, and even pounded their own stomachs in order to cause miscarriages. It was also common practice for young mothers to turn their newborn babies over to strangers—peasant families—so that they could return to full-time revolutionary work. Since married couples were usually separated in wartime, sometimes the husbands did not even know that their wives were pregnant, had miscarried, or had given birth to babies and then turned them over to villagers.[21]

In January 1939, the CCP Lunan Special Committee was established, and a women's department headed by Li Rupei was instituted. Two months later in the four counties controlled by the Communists, three major mass organizations were formed: the Workers' Association (later renamed the Peasant Association), the Youth Association, and the Women's Federation.[22] The division of labor among the three associations became more clear in the following years: the Peasant Association was in charge of labor services for the Communist army, the Youth Association was armed for village self-defense, and the Women's Federation had the task of organizing women to take care of the agricultural work and provide logistical support in the anti-Japanese and the civil wars.[23]

Soon after she joined the Communist Party, Cui Bo served as a correspondent for the Communist newspaper, the *Lunan Times*. In 1947, she wrote a news dispatch reporting of a model women's federation in the village of Luwangzhi, Changcheng County. This association had a hundred members who were organized on a regular basis to study, hold rallies and singing parties, and provide a variety of services for the anti-Japanese troops. As these troops approached the village, the women always lined up to meet them. They not only offered them food and drink, but they also did laundry, mended clothes, and took care of the wounded. Cui Bo also wrote for *Mass Daily*, reporting on the roles women played in the guerrilla war as spies, propagandists, and grassroots organizers.[24]

As the wartime bases were consolidated in Luzhongnan, the Women's Federations shifted their focus to women's issues: unbinding women's feet, promoting literacy, abolishing polygamy, banning imposed marriage, and condemning family violence. Feminist concepts of gender equality penetrated into village life. Women worked diligently in all areas to support the Communist wars. For the CCP an easy way to call mass rallies in the villages in wartime was to gather the women together to "cook food or make shoes" for the Communist troops. From a quiet beginning, women's power grew slowly but steadily in the villages.

The revolution shaped the rural women cadres and was in turn reshaped by them. First of all, rural gatherings, at which housewives came to work and chat, were organized by women cadres. In addition to lots of gossip, the villagers also got news, including news of the military advance of the Eighth Route Army. On these occasions the women cadres naturally became educators, explaining Party policy on the reduction of rents and interest rates and land reform. Second, when the demands of Communist military logistics increased as a result of the prolongation of the war, the women cadres began assigning work to each family.[25] Landlords and rich peasants were usually required to make more contributions than the peasants to both the anti-Japanese and the civil wars. They had to pay more public grain and make more shoes for the Eighth Route Army (and later for the PLA). Sometimes when they could not make enough shoes themselves, they had to buy shoes from other peasant families to meet their quotas. The women cadres set the quotas based on the army's needs and the political behavior of the landlords. Gentry families who were supportive of the CCP would get lower quotas, while those who did not take an active part in Communist campaigns would have to spend more time or money to fulfill their quotas. They were evaluated mostly by the women cadres in their villages.

Women's power was also evident in several of the Party's agrarian campaigns. Landlords and rich peasants tried to maintain good relations with the village cadres, both male and female. These relations, in turn, shaped the moderate tone of the reduction of rents and interest rates and the land reform campaigns, in which women cadres had a strong voice.²⁶ Poor peasants were encouraged to "speak with bitterness" about the degrading poverty they had suffered for generations. Most likely, the landlords would be called to mass rallies and be denounced and humiliated. Different landlords were treated differently, according to what they had done during the wars. In this regard, the evaluations by village women cadres were the key to the general attitude of Communists toward the local gentry, thereby determining the fates of the landlords and rich peasants in the villages. During the anti-Japanese war, some "evil gentry" who had collaborated with the Japanese were severely punished. But in most villages a coalition of all classes against the Japanese had been formed; this coalition lasted even into the Civil War. In January 1947, peasants in Luzhongnan were urgently mobilized to prepare food for the PLA troops. In Fei County, the women were divided into seven groups to work day and night. Some groups husked 2,000 *jin* (2,222 pounds) of grain for the PLA, while one group worked at one of the gentry houses and baked 1,800 *jin* (1,999 pounds) of cakes overnight.²⁷

In the fall of 1947 work teams sent by the Executive Committee of the CCP Central Committee came to Luzhongnan. They criticized the "rightist opportunism" of the local Party organizations and the peaceful land reform in Shandong. This caused conflict between the local Party workers and women cadres, on the one hand, and some cadres from Yan'an, on the other. Local cadres were criticized for having lost the class perspective, and the women cadres were said to lack political consciousness. The work teams started a new land reform to attack all landlords and rich peasants indiscriminately; in the process the reputations of the local and women cadres were ruined. Mao and the CCP Central Committee then issued some instructions to correct the "left deviations" of the work teams and directed that all Party members, women, and the masses in the old liberated area focus their efforts on the forthcoming Huaihai Battle.²⁸

Bound Feet in the Revolution

Well before the Huaihai Battle was over, the CCP started to recruit cadres to follow the advancing PLA troops to take over the southern cities. As we have shown, in the selection process, the Party committees in Shandong were required to follow the principle of assigning the stronger cadres to the south and keeping the weaker ones at home *(xuan qiang liu ruo)*.[29] Within this vague general principle, one criterion was clear: "No foot-bound women cadres should be selected."[30]

The "no foot-bound women" dictum appeared in the minutes of the CCP Cangshan County Committee on February 11, 1949, and the policy was carried out all over Luzhongnan.[31] Why did foot-binding become an issue in cadre selection? The formal explanation was that women with bound feet could not endure a long march to the south. The major concern, however, was that foot-bound women would damage the image of the liberated rural areas since foot-binding had been terminated in modern cities as a corrupt custom. The policy excluding foot-bound women from the southward movement itself suggests an association of these women with the Communist movement in Shandong. If foot-bound women had not played a special role in Mao's revolution, they would not have been an issue in the first place. Indeed the contribution of foot-bound women to the wars merits closer examination.

Foot binding was a centuries-long tradition, but it was more popular in Shandong than in southeast coastal areas.[32] In 1912, Sun Yat-sen issued an order prohibiting it, and the order became a law of the Republic of China in 1932. The CCP was a firm opponent of foot binding. Communist activists such as Deng Yingchao shared the feminist goals of "prohibiting prostitution, the sale of women, and binding women's feet," referring to the termination of these activities as a part of women's emancipation.[33]

Foot-bound women entered into the revolution in the first place owing to the successful mass mobilization by the CCP in the old liberated areas of Shandong during the war against Japan. In the war, the Communists recognized that a coalition of different classes and groups was the only feasible way to "save the country." On December 21, 1939, the first Women's Federation was established in the county of Lingtan. More than three hundred women attended the inaugural meeting, and Yuan Ming (a foot-bound woman known as Grandma Fu—Fu Daniang) was elected president.[34] Surely there were disadvantages to being a foot-bound woman, but there were advantages as well. Although foot-bound women were unable to participate in military operations such as rapid marching or combat, they could do some types of both public and secret work much better than men in the revolutionary bases or in the Japanese-occupied and GMD-controlled areas.

One example is Grandma Ren (Ren Daniang), a rural woman who was born in the village of Sahua, Shandong Province, in 1903. She married into the Ren family very early, and when her husband died, she was still young. Grandma Ren remembered the spring famine after her husband's death and how, owing to CCP relief, she and her children survived it. So when she was asked to work for the Party, her only hesitation was, "What could I do as a foot-bound widow?" The year 1941, however, was to prove her special value for the revolution. From January to October, the Japanese focused on wiping out the Communist guerrillas. The Japanese policy of "Burn all, kill all, loot all" almost depopulated some villages in Shandong. People saw Grandma Ren walking out of her yard, limping along the village trails between the Japanese-controlled and guerrilla areas, but nobody imagined that this foot-bound woman was delivering crucial messages for the resistance movement. It was in that year that Grandma Ren joined the CCP and got a new name—Liu Lan.

After the Communist guerrillas recaptured this area, Liu Lan became an official Party worker. The villagers continued to call her Grandma Ren—but with more respect. Her new reputation gave Grandma Ren a greater voice in recruiting new soldiers for the Communist army in the anti-Japanese and civil wars. Liu Lan spent a huge amount of time making door-to-door visits in villages, talking with rural women, soliciting opinions, explaining policies, discussing their concerns, and defusing conflictual situations. Liu Lan was extremely successful in encouraging parents to send their boys to the front, persuading women not to be drags on their husbands and organizing all people remaining in the villages for logistic services.[35]

During the war, guerrillas frequently went back and forth, and local Party workers were often transferred from one county to another. However, foot-bound women cadres, like Grandma Ren, even after they joined the CCP, never went beyond their nearby villages. That made them more suitable for local organizational work. Not needing any written records, they knew by heart all the relevant names and networks. These foot-bound women cadres were instrumental in maintaining communications between the Party's grassroots organizations and its higher bodies because they met two essential requirements for the Party's secret activities: efficiency and safety. A few foot-bound women also left home to join the Communist army. When Zhang Xia went to the Anti-Japanese Military and Political College in 1938, she found that in the women's brigade, there were some rural foot-bound women as well.[36]

By the time Grandma Ren was admitted to the Party, Cui Bo was already an experienced activist and leading member of the CCP Pi County Committee. As the daughter of a railway employee, Cui Bo had never had her feet bound. She remembered the day when her teacher made an emotional speech in class, telling the students about the Japanese invasion of Manchuria. The whole class cried. When Cui Bo grew up, she saw the Japanese atrocities in her homeland. "China will never be conquered as long as a single Chinese remains alive," words from the most popular song in that period, inspired both boys and girls to join the anti-Japanese war. In 1943, the Communists lost most of their wartime bases in Luzhongnan to the Japanese, some Party institutions had to be dissolved, and all women cadres were asked temporarily to go back home. Cui Bo had nowhere to go and was about to bear her second child, so she arranged to hide in a family of local gentry near a Japanese-occupied town. Her hostess was a little, middle-aged, foot-bound lady who managed the family business.[37]

This mysterious foot-bound woman claimed that Cui Bo was her daughter-in-law. She explained to her neighbors that she had called the girl home since she was pregnant; although this "big-footed" daughter-in-law was an urban girl, she still had to obey the local custom and bear her children at the in-laws' home. Cui Bo discovered that several other women, including two concubines of a bandit chief, were hiding in this lady's manor. In addition, sometimes strangers would come at night; the hostess would feed them and see them off. Although the house was very close to the Japanese blockhouse, nothing happened to the guests who came and left in a hurry. Cui Bo was sure that this mysterious place must be a well-established link in certain underground activities, and she even guessed that the hostess was a secret CCP party worker.[38] She did not ask her since it was not rare that foot-bound women shielded guerrillas and Party workers. It was a common practice for the CCP to assign a woman to a male partner to do underground work under the guise of a married couple. Sometimes, the Party also made its underground units look like a middle-class family—for example, a husband, wife, and old, foot-bound woman servant all could be Party workers.[39]

In the 1940s, among the Communist Party workers, there was also a group of cadres who were "women with renovated feet" (*gai zu pai*). It was said that even Mao Zedong's fourth wife—Jiang Qing, whose hometown was also in Shandong—was among these.[40] Releasing the bound feet was easier for girls whose ankle-bones had not been broken and distorted, but it was much more painful for adult women.[41]

Ren Xiurong was born in 1928. Her grandmother forced her to bind her feet when she was a little girl. The grandmother was a foot-bound woman who joined the CCP with her brothers in the 1930s. During the day she worked for the Women's Liberation Society, yet at night she carefully checked to see whether her granddaughter had wrapped her feet properly. Ren asked why her grandmother supported revolution publicly but continued this savage practice at home. The grandmother said she worried that nobody would marry Ren if she had big feet. It was still commonly believed in Luzhongnan that compressing a girl's feet would not merely make her look dainty, but would also signal that she was destined not for work but only for marriage. For bound feet, a girl had to endure the torture of wrapping the feet in tight swaddling in the morning, removing the bloody bandages in the evening, soaking them, and then rewrapping and tightening them again. Through this ritual, it was thought, women would become even tempered and docile. But Ren entertained the idea of becoming a strong woman and entering a school that trained soldiers and social workers in the anti-Japanese war. So every day as soon as her grandmother had left her bedroom, Ren took the bloody bandages off. Later the grandmother found out about the trick, sighed, and accepted Ren's wishes because even the older generation of rural women had begun to recognize that the war had made everything very different for girls. A girl with natural feet would have an advantage in working, fighting, or merely running away from the Japanese. Thus Ren Xiurong never had her feet bound again and became a "woman with renovated feet."[42]

Releasing the bound feet (*fang zu* or *gai zu*), of course, required a rebellious spirit and tremendous courage for the women at the time. A considerable number of the women with renovated feet had run away from their families and entered the Party schools or the PLA southbound teams. The brief period of foot-binding left unhealed wounds, which meant that they would never be as strong as the women with natural feet. In 1949, a group of these women were allowed to follow the southbound teams to take over the Jiangnan cities. Ren Xiurong recalled that she struggled to endure the pain in her feet in the daily marches with the army. Although her husband, an officer, had a horse, she could accept his help and ride his horse only at night. With this help, she finally arrived in Hangzhou.

The Southbound Cadres and Their Rural Wives

The southbound teams were comprised almost entirely of male cadres, while female cadres were persuaded to "return to production and normal village life."[43] Village life, however, was no longer "normal," but seriously damaged by the war. The "military grain" extracted from each peasant family exhausted the village economy. Shortages of seed, draft animals, and male labor made the prompt restoration of production impossible. Every spring peasant families in Luzhongnan suffered rampant famines, but in 1949 food had run out as soon as winter had come. In December 1949, the CCP Binhai District Committee found that after the male cadres were dispatched to the south, a large number of their families, bereft of their breadwinners, had also left their famine-stricken villages and become beggars in nearby cities. It was a shock for the Communist government to see some women who had been longtime loyal Party workers or wartime heroines begging from door to door. The district government decided to take immediate measures to offer them desperately needed help. It was emphasized that this was not only a local problem, but one that would certainly demoralize the southbound cadres if they knew what had happened to their wives and children.[44] In fact, it was reported that a few southbound cadres deserted along the way because of homesickness and worrying about their families.

The CCP Binhai District Committee urged local governments and Party organizations to bring the departed women and children back to their villages. The Beihai Bank (a government-run local bank) appropriated special funds for low-interest loans or relief funds for families of the southbound cadres. Every county and village government was asked to provide these families with maize or wheat seed for spring sowing. In Yi County, which had transferred forty-two cadres to the south, the local Department of Internal Affairs visited every village to make sure that the cadres' families were well taken care of. In the department's report, Cao Daishan's family was a typical case. Cao had served in the county's Bureau of Public Security before being transferred to the south in April 1949, leaving four females at home: his elderly mother, a sick wife, and two little daughters. His family had only sixteen *mu* of land, but when the village tried to give them more land, they refused to accept it since there was no agricultural labor available in the family. The county ordered that their neighbors till the land for them, and the government offered them thirty *jin* (thirty-four pounds) of wheat to offset the spring famine.[45] Like the Cao family, most families of the transferred cadres had the same problem. The county government asked villagers to sharecrop with these families or sent the militia to help them work the fields in the busy season.[46]

The local governments in Luzhongnan believed that the best way to solve the problem of destitute families such as the Caos was to help the women join their husbands in the south as soon as possible. Some counties opened women's workshops to train the spouses of the southbound cadres for government work.[47] In accordance with CCP admissions policy, all who were legally married or formally engaged to members of the southbound cadres (with approval by the Party) were qualified to apply for such work. While they studied, the women could bring their children to the nurseries attached to the workshops. In May 1949, about three hundred young women were admitted to the workshops, and arrangements were made for reuniting them with their husbands after graduation.[48]

The local governments bought discount train tickets and saw these women off to the south. The CCP Zhejiang Committee set up a reception center in Shanghai to meet them and take care of the next leg of their journey. Xu Jingxin remembers the moment when she and her three children finally arrived at the reception center—after leaving their village and taking many buses and trains. This was the first time they had seen a big city, and everything—even wall-to-wall carpeting—seemed amazing. She asked the receptionist a thousand questions about urban life, while her children were happy to roll about on the carpet all day.[49]

The government did not have enough resources to bring all the rural women to Hangzhou to join their husbands, however. Some of the women themselves did not want to go; they were worried that they might be discriminated against in the city because of their poor education.[50] Consequently, only a small number of women actually came to the city, and eventually 90 percent of the southbound cadres divorced their rural wives. As noted, the ECB had issued instructions prohibiting new marriages or divorce for two years.[51] Moreover, it was a traditional Chinese moral principle that a man should not divorce his wife after rising from poverty to wealth. It was especially unacceptable to villagers for a husband to abandon his wife after she had served her in-laws well. However, the Communist Marriage Law offered the southbound cadres the freedom and legitimacy to divorce.

Although the Marriage Law stipulated that "Divorce is granted when the husband and wife both desire it," the southbound cadres could easily find some grounds for divorce, such as that the marriage had been family-arranged. For ordinary people, mediation was necessary before divorce was granted, but nobody would bother to mediate between a husband in Hangzhou and a wife in Shandong. Moreover Article 19 of the Marriage Law gave the cadres sufficient reason for divorce—namely, divorce could be granted to a member of the revolutionary army if he had not corresponded with his wife for a period of two years since 1950. The CCP Hangzhou Committee extended the period to three years. Most southbound cadres could easily satisfy this requirement since they usually had not written home, and even if they had, they had addressed the letters to their parents and never to their wives or children.

As everyone knew, the real reason for divorce was that the southbound cadres had gotten used to urban life and no longer wanted to live with their rural wives. Most of them remarried urban girls who were young, pretty, and well educated. The Marriage Law provided new political and ideological language for such family changes. It read that "husband and wife are duty-bound to love, respect, and assist each other,"[52] but in the Communist vocabulary, love is never class-blind. The southbound cadres therefore could petition for divorce by saying that their marriages lacked political grounds or that their wives no longer worked for the revolution, and therefore no love or common language existed between them. The southbound cadres did not even have to go to court; their petitions would be reviewed and approved by Party organizations, and all legal papers would be prepared for them by the courts. The Party stance was to "protect the Party's cadres" and to do whatever was good for the "revolutionary cause."[53]

This stance was clearly expressed in a circular order from the Chinese Supreme Court that instructed "all local courts to grant a divorce to the southbound cadres who asked for one as soon as possible." It stressed that "any delay would hurt the feelings of the southbound cadres and affect their revolutionary work." The Supreme Court noted that most wives of the southbound cadres were still living in their home villages in Shandong, and it ordered "the local governments to educate and persuade the wives to accept the court's judgments." According to the court, women who refused to divorce were lacking in political consciousness and had to be "educated."[54]

Divorce was not only exclusively decided by the southbound cadres, but also was very unfair for the women. There was no financial compensation for the wives, and husbands had no legal responsibility to provide support for either the women or their children. In wartime, the local governments had carefully protected the dependants: benefits and all kinds of help were offered to the rural women in order that soldiers and cadres not worry about their spouses. The local governments in Luzhongnan were then asked to continue to take care of the divorced wives in order to help the southbound cadres avoid family problems.

For this purpose, there were two things the local governments in Luzhongnan could do and did do: (1) allow the rural ex-wives to continue to live with their in-laws, and (2) continue to treat them as spouses of PLA soldiers or cadres. In fact, living with in-laws was a local peasant practice; it was said that wives were divorced by their husbands but not by the husbands' families *(lihun bu lijia)*.[55] For several reasons, the local governments wanted to retain this practice. First of all, they wanted to placate the rural women since most of them had taken an active part in the revolution and had good reputations in the villages. Second, the local governments (especially at the subdistrict and village levels) liked to keep track of the number of PLA spouses *(jun shu)* and cadre spouses *(gan shu)* so that they could get appropriate relief funds or subsidies from the state. In this way, the benefits for the families would not change and local financial burdens would be lowered. Moreover, living with their in-laws would prevent the divorced women from becoming homeless or helpless, conditions that would increase the problems of the local governments. Also, there were no easy alternatives for housing assistance.

Women Cadres in the City

Although the Party ordered the majority of rural women activists to return to their villages in Shandong, a small number were allowed to follow the PLA troops in the southward movement.[56] The Party recruiters first decided on the male cadres to be transferred and then considered women's requests. The women candidates for the southward movement had to be the spouses of the transferred cadres, and they had to be on active duty in the army or local governments; in no case could they take their children with them. After a brief orientation, the lucky chosen women caught up with their male comrades in the rapid march, crossed the Yangtze River, and took part in contact battles with the remnants of the GMD troops.

The women cadres were proud of having been selected for "the last battle between light and dark," and they were deeply inspired to participate in creating a new China. They identified themselves as Party cadres rather than women workers. They believed that women could achieve greatness in politics if they were devoted to the revolution. Shen Yi recalls that when she joined the southward movement, she was young and strong. Her team had to walk forty to fifty miles every day, but she never dropped out of the rapid march. In charge of collecting grain for the PLA, she always set out in advance to make arrangements for the troops that would follow.[57]

Because of the shortage of cadres in the takeover, the revolutionary experience and skills of the women cadres were much in demand, and they were appointed to various important positions in the new government. For example, in the southward movement Cui Bo was the head of a small group of the southbound cadres.

After the cadres arrived in Hangzhou, she was appointed associate director of the Education Division of the Personnel Department of the provincial government. Later she was sent to a chemical factory to be the Party secretary. Xu Jingxin had been a director of personnel in a county government office in Luzhongnan. In Hangzhou, she first worked as a personnel officer in the city government and was then promoted to be the director of the Personnel Office in the Bureau of Commerce. Fang Jing was sent to the Bureau of Agriculture and Zhang Min to the General Trade Union.

In the institutions where they worked some of the old employees who had been retained liked to ask who was whose wife. The women cadres hated these questions and condemned the employees for using bourgeois nepotism to explain the Communist work assignments, which were supposed to be based on need and merit. The women cadres were determined not to live in the shadow of their powerful husbands. In any case, dealing with the challenging tasks of the takeover, they had to work independently and in different areas. In the new setting they adjusted quickly and took charge efficiently. They were excited by the challenge of having to establish themselves as independent urban Party workers in their own right.

In the early days, the southbound women cadres did not just work among urban women. The Military Control Committee of Hangzhou was busy reestablishing social order, restoring production, and reconstructing the urban bureaucracy, and the women cadres did not want to be kept away from these urgent tasks. The government provided the families of the southbound cadres with some subsidies and assistance. It provided one housemaid for a one-child family and two for three-child families. Indeed the women cadres were too busy to take care of their children. Cui Bo recalls that as one of four secretaries for the provincial government, she was in charge of communications among the ten prefectures of the province and with the central government. Every day she worked until nine or ten P.M. and slept in her office.

The women cadres had been good mass organizers in Luzhongnan and adept at working in the grassroots units. However, in the city most of them had problems communicating with the local people. The urban dialect was difficult for them to understand and might cause misunderstandings, so the southbound cadres needed local language assistance. Nevertheless, language was not an insurmountable obstacle for the Communists. As noted, from the first day the women cadres appeared on the streets of Hangzhou (in a special gray uniform known as a Lenin suit), they aroused the curiosity and admiration of the urban dwellers,[58] and they quickly won themselves a place in hero worship. Although not all women cadres were good orators or agitators, their revolutionary experience made them idols in the eyes of urban youngsters. Regardless of gender, the local people referred to the southbound cadres as veteran Eighth Route officers *(lao balu)* or veteran revolutionaries *(lao geming)*.[59] To a great degree, women's political and social participation was inspired by the example of the southbound women cadres.

The earliest success in gaining women's participation was their enthusiastic response to the social education program launched by the Communists as soon as they took over the city. To accommodate the massive number of applications, 88 adult schools were opened, of which 34 were exclusively for women. By the end of 1949, 1,792 men and 1,582 women had been enrolled in reading, writing, and political education courses.[60] The students included women workers, shop assistants, and housewives; some of them became women's activists after graduation. Other kinds of study sessions were also organized to help women learn or increase technical skills so that they could find jobs. In 1953, as Women's Federations at various levels were established, many southbound women cadres, including Cui Bo, were shifted to them. Although the women cadres always identified themselves as professional revolutionaries rather than workers on women' issues, the Party believed that the most suitable task for them in the new period was to help educate and organize their urban sisters.

As all the southbound cadres made remarkable progress with the urban programs, major problems arose in their own families. War and peace had different impacts on the family life of the southbound cadres. All the southbound women cadres had met their husbands after they joined the army or Party organizations. Their husbands felt very lucky to have married girls who shared their political beliefs and revolutionary careers. However, peace, which made it possible to settle down, also brought gender hierarchy into the family. The husbands believed that they had more important positions and should devote themselves to their work, while the wives' major duty should be to take care of their husbands and be committed to family affairs, not their own careers. The women cadres, who had begun to work with full confidence and pride, did not accept this notion. They believed that if they were able to overcome the same difficulties in wartime as their male comrades, they could be equally competent at all tasks in peacetime. Politically conscious and with a wealth of revolutionary experience, the women cadres felt they deserved the Party's trust and promising careers. They could not tolerate being treated as ordinary urban housewives.

The deputy governor of Zhejiang Province, Yang Siyi, described his family life in his diary after he and his wife, Wenjun, came to the city. He was critical about his own "selfish attitude toward [his] family and [his] wife." He wrote that he asked his wife to do everything concerning the children, his mother, and himself, but he forgot that she also had her own revolutionary job to do and that she, moreover, was in poor health. Yang wrote that he was sorry for hurting Wenjun and making her cry. He believed he had to change his attitude toward his wife; otherwise, their family and their relationship would be ruined.[61]

There was a typical belief among the southbound cadres that the wife's position was secondary within the family and that she should subordinate her wishes to her husband's demands. Under such circumstances, the women cadres felt the double pressure of work and family, but not many male cadres recognized this as Yang Siyi did. Most southbound cadres were peasant revolutionaries, and it comes as no surprise that they shared the peasants' patriarchal ideals. They wanted wives to serve husbands, and they wanted to have a lot of children. The early 1950s witnessed the first baby boom in China.[62] Frequent pregnancies and childbirth ruined the political careers of the women cadres. The more children they had, the fewer opportunities were available to them for promotion. Sometimes the women themselves asked the Party to assign them easier and less important work so that they could be closer to their families and have more time to spend with their children. The gap between husband and wife thus widened quickly, even though the male and female cadres had begun from the same starting point when they came to the city.

Two events in 1953 speeded up changes in the political lives of the southbound women cadres. One was an order issued by China's defense minister, Peng Dehuai, asking all women soldiers to retire from active duty.[63] The major argument was that peacetime no longer required women to sacrifice their family life, and they could make greater contributions to the country's economic reconstruction in other ways. Some women officers were transferred to nonmilitary positions, while others just became full-time mothers. It was now felt that women's major responsibility was at home and that their main concern should be to assist their husbands in performing their duties. Clearly this was a setback for women who sought emancipation from the traditional patriarchal family order. Like it or not, the women cadres were now dependent on the power of their husbands, becoming a new group of officials' wives *(guan taitai),* a privileged class the women cadres had been determined to eliminate when they joined the revolution.

The second event was the replacement of the supply system *(gongji zhi)* by the salary system *(gongzi zhi).* The Communist cadres no longer got payments in kind and generally equal benefits. Instead, they got different salaries and privileges according to their ranks. This automatically brought about changes in people's ways of thinking. The peasant cadres abandoned their belief in egalitarianism and accepted the hierarchical order that had long existed in urban society. One example of this change was reflected in the concept of work assignments. Party appointments were no longer just work assignments but political rewards for the male participants in the revolution.

The distribution of power in the government came to resemble that in the patriarchal system. A woman could work as her husband's chief of staff or the director of his personnel department, but these appointments were made and accepted as extensions of the power of the husband. Cui Bo became the chair of the provincial Women's Federation because her husband was the deputy governor of Zhejiang. When Chen Xiuliang's husband was promoted to be the governor of Zhejiang, she was appointed acting director of the provincial Propaganda Department.[64] Despite the Communists' theoretical commitment to gender equality, the political reality after the takeover of the city boiled down to a wife's honor coming from her husband's status *(fu gui qi rong).* By the same logic, a wife's career would also be ruined by her husband's bad luck. Again, Chen Xiuliang is a good example: when her husband was labeled an anti-socialist rightist, she too was purged from the Party.

In campaigns to publicize and implement the Marriage Law after 1950, the Party and government advocated gender equality in family life, employment, education, and political participation. They worked hard to abolish polygamy and prostitution, to ban imposed marriages, and to create more educational and job opportunities for women. Ironically, most Communist cadres did little to realize genuine gender equality within their families, and the Party did not abandon its prejudice against women cadres in its work assignments.

The Women's Federation

In 1950, the Zhejiang provincial Women's Federation was established. The director of the Women's Department of the CCP Zhejiang Committee, Wu Zhongliang, was elected chair. Since Wu had other positions in the new government, the associate chair, Li Zhihui, was in charge of the routine operations of the federation.[65] Later, Cui Bo and a considerable number of southbound women cadres joined her to work in the federation.[66]

The Women's Federation proclaimed itself to be a mass organization responsible for the channeling of female participation in economic development and sociopolitical reform rather than a feminist group in either theory or practice.[67] The Women's Federation, Youth League, and General Trade Union were the three major mass organizations under direct CCP control, but they varied in terms of organizational form. Like the CCP, not everyone was able to join the Youth League; applicants could be admitted to this "vanguard" of Chinese youngsters only after the organization reviewed their records and found their pasts satisfactory. In contrast, every worker could be a member of the trade union, although registration was required. In the early days, the organizational principle of the Women's Federation was similar to that of the trade union. Any woman could be a member as long as she expressed a willingness to join and be registered with the local branch.

In the wartime bases in Shandong almost every adult female in a village joined the Women's Federation. However, the southbound cadres were surprised to find that very few women in Hangzhou or in other parts of the province applied for membership to the federation. By September 1950, there were 645,600 members in the province—only 6.1 percent of the total female population. Based on initial surveys, the southbound cadres were aware that most of the women in the province were not active politically and that fewer still were members of any institution. It was obvious that the "membership system" did not suit the Women's Federation, and it was not in harmony with the behavior patterns of women in Zhejiang.

In 1951, the membership system was replaced by a "representative system." Everywhere, especially in the countryside, women's assemblies were formed, and any woman who participated in the election of women representatives would be regarded a member of the Women's Federation with no registration required. By the second half of 1951, the number of Women's Assemblies at the *xiang* level had increased to 1,613, and 86.7 percent of the women in the province's rural areas had become members of the Women's Federation.[68] The first political activity organized by the federation in Hangzhou was a mass parade on New Year's Day, 1951. About twenty thousand urban women, including workers, students, and housewives, swarmed into the streets carrying small, colored flags and shouting, "Oppose Japan's armament by American imperialism!" Other cities and counties responded by organizing their own parades or petitions for peace. Eventually the federation got 1,615,000 women's signatures in petitions for peace.[69]

In August 1951, Tan Zhenlin gave instructions to the federation: "Women who work in the city should focus on the development of production."[70] This message had obvious political implications. In order to support China's war in Korea, Hangzhou launched a campaign to increase production and tout economic measures, and women were called on to do their part for the war and the country's reconstruction. It is fair to say that partly owing to the women workers' contribution, the total output of the textile industry in the city increased 40 percent in 1951. In that year, twelve women workers in the province were awarded the title of "Model Worker" in the province, making up 26.3 percent of the province's total Model Workers.[71] This percentage was still very low, since the province's major industry was textile and silk production, in which the majority of the labor force was female.

Coinciding with the effort to increase production, the Women's Federation was involved in a series of reforms, including those to abolish discriminatory regulations against women laborers and improve their working conditions. Before 1950, women worked

12–16 hours a day and got very little pay (8–12 *dan* of rice a month). In most factories women had to endure very humiliating treatment—for example, a body search before the end of work every day. A veteran worker, Ye Jingxiang, said: "Only veteran workers can understand what the body search means to us. In the summer after twelve hours of work, we are soaked with sweat and want to get home to take a bath. But at the gate there is always a long line of workers waiting for the body search. In winter, the guards put their cold and dirty hands under our clothes to touch any parts of our bodies they want to."[72]

On May 1, 1950, almost one year after the CCP came to the city, the First Hangzhou Textile Mill abolished the body search system, and another eight hundred factories followed suit. Nothing could have pleased the women more. At the gates of the Wanxin Textile Mill, women erected an arch with flowers and the slogan: "Long live the working class!"[73]

In 1951, the Women's Federation launched a campaign "to save children" in both urban and rural areas.[74] In urban areas it was associated with the anti-American crusade, in which some American charitable organizations were accused of murdering Chinese children. In the rural areas the crucial work was to rescue thousands of pregnant women and babies who might die because of traditional childbirth methods.

Before 1949, as discussed in chapter 5, a number of nurseries and orphanages were managed by foreigners or sponsored by foreign charitable organizations. When the CCP came to the city, it did not immediately take over these institutions. It was reported that from May 1949 to February 1951, an American-run nursery, Yuyingyun, adopted 379 children, but 181 of them (48 percent) died afterward.[75] During the Civil War and in the early days of the new regime child mortality rates in these institutions were high for several reasons: shortages of food and medical supplies, a lack of experienced nurses, poor management, and the fact that most abandoned babies were already in imminent danger when they were picked up on the streets. Tan Zhenlin argued that the main cause was an imperial conspiracy: "The imperialists set up nurseries and orphanages in our cities, but they purposely killed 80 percent of the children they adopted."[76] In July 1951, all the nurseries and orphanages were taken over by the government, and the

Women's Federation sent its cadres and professionals to join in the management.

In the rural areas there were no foreign nurseries or orphanages, but the mortality of infants was even higher. The CCP Zhejiang Committee understood that 70 percent of the deaths were caused by the old method of delivering babies. It therefore instructed the Women's Federation to work with health institutions to train all midwives to adopt a new delivery method within three years. When the Women's Federation sent work teams to the rural areas, they were shocked not only by the high mortality rate of infants, but also the miserable situation of women.

According to a 1950 survey, 37.9 percent of newborns in rural areas died of tetanus, and the total mortality rate of infants in most counties was 43–50 percent. The more babies were born, the more infants died. Infanticide was common and easy since most babies were born in nightstools. When some families found that a newly born child was a girl, they just closed the nightstool and suffocated her. Although villagers considered pregnancy good news for a family, childbirth was regarded as a dirty matter. The delivery room was called a "dark room" and was isolated in a thatched shed, cowshed, pigsty, or even toilet. In certain villages, in order to avoid offending the gods and ghosts, women could not lie down on a bed to give birth, but had to be in a kneeling or squatting position. In the villages, there was no medical treatment for pregnant women, and many of them died from postpartum hemorrhage or puerperal fever. As an old saying had it, "Giving birth to a child, a woman has one foot on earth and the other in the grave."[77]

The campaign to publicize the new delivery method began in every county. Exhibitions were held in villages as well as at market festivals. Along with its primary focus, the campaign also appealed to husbands and families to abolish all discriminatory practices against women. The old midwives caused the death of a great number of newly born children. They were poor and illiterate grannies who moved from one village to another to offer their services. One midwife named Michun, working in Xiaoshan County near Hangzhou, had used rusty obstetric forceps for more than forty years but had never sterilized or even washed them. The midwives got a little payment from the babies' families, but most villagers discriminated against them for their "dirty job." Working with the medical clinics, the Women's Federation directed these grannies into medical workshops, and after a program of study, the medical institutions issued them licenses. Between 1951 and 1953 Hangzhou held 12 workshops that trained 690 midwives. In the countryside, 14,376 grannies received medical training, and more than 5,000 nurses had been educated and were working in the province by 1953. Perhaps the most impressive efforts of the Women's Federation were in stopping infanticide, especially the killing of girls in the rural areas.

Remarkable progress toward protecting women's rights was made in the Land Reform Campaign, which supported the Communist belief that women's liberation can be realized only through the liberation of all working people. Because of the principle of gender equality in land distribution, a female family member had an equal right to possess land and other property. When a girl was born, her family would report the birth to the peasant association in the village and thus obtain a piece of land. The land reform also raised the social status of women. Women were encouraged to attend struggle meetings to condemn landlords, and weapons were given to militiawomen to defend the villages. The local governments reported that women usually made up 40 percent of the membership of the peasant associations and some became village cadres.[78]

Such gains, however, were undercut by the difficulties of eliminating the centuries-long prejudices against women—not only among villagers, but also among local cadres. In February 1951, a widow named Bian Xiangqiu, who lived in Dongjiacun, near Hangzhou, did not get the share of land she deserved in the land reform. She complained to the cadres of her district. But they saw her as a troublemaker and hung her up and beat her. Bian did not give up but went to the county court to sue the cadres. The county government did not honor her complaint but arrested her and kept her in jail for eighty-six days. She was released only when the CCP Zhejiang Committee happened to come across the case and intervened. As Bian's case indicated, there was still a long way to go to eliminate the entrenched power of the existing rural order and the deep-rooted prejudice against women.

In June 1953, the Women's Federation held its second congress in Hangzhou, and Cui Bo was elected the first associate chair. Women representatives from all parts of the province came to the consensus that the main new task for the association was to publicize the Marriage Law and to encourage women's political participation.

New Women Cadres

Two preconditions to women's political participation were education and economic independence. In the past, women's education had been basically an urban phenomenon, and only elite and professional families, such as doctors and teachers, would send their daughters to school. According to a general survey by the Women's Federation in 1951, 90 percent of the adult women in Zhejiang Province were illiterate.

Since 1949, the new government had made progress in enrolling more girls in various schools. In 1953, the five colleges in the province admitted 1,900 girls—four times more than in 1948. In addition, 41,000 girls were in high schools and about 570,000 were enrolled in primary schools. Although the absolute numbers of girl students had significantly increased, the proportion of girls in the total student population was still much smaller than that of boys.[79] Thus the city government launched two campaigns for women's education: "Study Culture" (1949–1951) and "Quick Literacy" (1953). The Women's Federation and the city government worked together to open 987 night schools and admitted 27,714 women workers for literacy education. In the Jianggan district, a woman worker named Xia Cailian knew 200 Chinese characters before going to the night school. After seventy-five days of intensive study, she learned 2,400 new characters and could read *Zhejiang Daily* and write simple notes.[80] The CCP stressed the political implications of the education campaigns by putting forward the slogan, "If women want to count, they must first be literate." As the education campaigns projected a new vision of women, the government encouraged them to join the country's economic development. At the second Provincial Women's Congress, Governor Tan Qilong stressed that the Party should mobilize women to engage in all types of production and make them understand that they could not be fully liberated unless they joined in production and gained economic independence.[81]

Most villages in Zhejiang did not have enough arable land, so women did not usually have to work in the fields. Instead, a large number of them were involved in a home-oriented crafts industry. It was estimated that more than 150,000 women were engaged in making straw hats, and others made straw mats, paper umbrellas, embroidered quilts, and fishing nets.[82] However, it made a lot of sense to encourage women's participation in agricultural work in terms of their economic independence. The Women's Federation saw it as a major advance in the women's movement in the province when women went beyond housework and into the fields. For example, in Xindeng County in 1950, 2,579 women did field work, while one year later the number increased to 15,471. It was reported that 80 percent of the rural women joined the agricultural work in the plowing and harvest seasons. The women also took part in government-sponsored irrigation work. In 1953, the provincial government bestowed the title of "Model Worker" on 18 women.

In order to promote women's political participation, the CCP called on women to join the Campaign to Build Democratic Government. This campaign had two objectives: to have as many women as possible take part in the first general election of the republic, and to train women cadres in the process. In the early 1950s, the CCP's first movie studio in Manchuria produced *Zhao Yiman*, a movie that had a tremendous influence on youngsters' understanding and memory of the Chinese revolution. Zhao Yiman was a Communist martyr who started her revolutionary career in the urban labor movement and then moved to a rural area to lead guerrillas during the anti-Japanese war. The movie's depiction of her as a lady wearing a red scarf and riding on a white horse made her legendary, and she was worshipped by young girls in the 1950s. Inspired by stories of Zhao and other revolutionary heroines, urban girls responded to the Party's call to join the army and the government. Most of the new recruits worked in offices of education, public health, the local press, and the Women's Federation. Without enough work experience, none were put into leading positions.

Women were eager to take part in the first general election. In preparation, 70–90 percent of them attended orientations for the election, and 83.93 percent, including women in mountain areas, cast votes in the election. More important, as table 4 indicates, a considerable number of women were elected as people's repre-

Table 4. Zhejiang Women Representatives in Various People's Congresses

People's Congress Level	Number of Women Representatives	Percentage of Total Representatives
Xiang or *zhen*[a]	35,895	17.11
County	3,383	18.29
Province	73	16.19
National	6	17.1

Source: The Women's Federation, "Active Participation in Developing the Country's Democracy" (1953); ZPWFA, 11/1/2.

[a]*Zhen* are small towns whose residents are peasants.

sentatives at various levels and became the Party's grassroots cadres.

In Hangzhou, women representatives made up a small percentage of the Municipal People's Congress (22.26 percent), while more worked as members of the city's neighborhood committees (41.36 percent).[83] Since the People's Congresses not were policy-making bodies, the women cadres could not play a significant role in running the country. The Women's Federation, however, still had much to be proud of because this was the first time many women, especially in the rural areas, had cast votes and the first time they had been elected as people's representatives.

Conclusion

In both the Chinese and Western literature, the Communist takeover of China has usually been described as an all-male affair. By rescuing the forgotten stories of women cadres from the dustbin of history, we can deconstruct the myth and see their vital part in this human drama. It was women's support and participation that made the PLA's military victory possible and fueled the success of the CCP's southward movement. In all Communist campaigns after 1949, women's voices can be heard. Even the Three Antis and Five Antis Campaigns were triggered by women's struggle against bureaucratism.

What, then, was the impact of the Communist takeover of

Hangzhou on rural women cadres and their urban sisters? In wartime, when men were drawn into the army, women's power grew in the revolutionary bases in Shandong, and the women cadres achieved decision-making positions at village and county levels. The CCP's southward movement, however, excluded most women cadres and called them back to "normal production." This revealed that the Communist takeover in 1949 was a power redistribution not only among classes but also between genders. In 1949, therefore, the Communists lost a considerable number of experienced women cadres. The CCP did not immediately feel a shortage because it soon recruited new women from students in the cities. The new recruits, however, were not on the same level as the southbound women cadres in terms of revolutionary experience or organizational skills.

Communists espouse two types of women's rights. First is a group of basic rights, including property rights, the right to an education, and the freedom to marry. The second groups involves equal opportunities in the new society, and these rights are by and large a luxury for Chinese women.

The CCP did a great deal to secure women the first group of rights as soon as it came to power. It abolished polygamy and prostitution, encouraged women's participation in production, opened all schools to girls, and established the Women's Federation for the protection and support of women. The southbound women cadres helped their sisters gain these rights, including the abolition of the humiliating body search system in factories. However, the emancipation of Chinese women was not complete. It was just as Lenin had warned: women and men were equal under the law but not in reality.[84]

On the eve of the takeover, foot-bound women were deemed unqualified for the Party's new task of taking over the cities. There is no doubt that foot-binding was associated with patriarchal concepts of women's "vulnerability." "Vulnerability," however, does not necessarily have to be associated with foot-binding or other physical weaknesses of women or with rural backwardness. The CCP also did not believe that female intellectual cadres should be assigned to leading posts in the Communist government, even if they had a wealth of revolutionary experience.[85]

Although the 1950 Marriage Law offered men and women equal rights in marriage and divorce, the biased verdicts in favor of male southbound cadres in divorce cases indicated the persistence of traditional discriminatory attitudes toward women and the continuing strength of the patriarchal social structure. Moreover, the CCP recognized women cadres not merely based on their own merits, but also depending upon the political success of their husbands. That indicated the persistent peasant belief that "A hen cannot herald the break of day" *(Muji bu sichen)*. And it implied that women could not run a country. Therefore, when the young and intelligent urban girls recruited after 1949 grew up and became mature women cadres, they were faced with the same old problems. Among other things, leading positions remained practically inaccessible to them.

8

The "Geneva of the East"

It was comparatively quiet in the city in late 1953 and 1954. The CCP's original plan was to spend five years restoring the economy and then ten years developing it. Now the task of economic restoration was completed, and China's First Five-Year Plan for the country's industrialization was on track.[1] In the suburbs of Hangzhou and in nearby counties, collectivization unfolded in keeping with the strategy of advancing steadily and progressing slowly rather than rashly, while in the city the government made plans to nationalize all private industry.[2] However, the high tide of socialist transformation was yet to come in both urban and suburban areas.

Four years had passed since the takeover, and life in the city had started to revolve around the Communist economic and political campaigns, but no change was easy. Even the place names in the city resisted "revolutionary changes." To the local people, Jiefang Lu (Liberation Avenue) was still Yingzi Lu, as it had been before the PLA came; the Provincial Guest House was still the Xinxin Hotel, the Children's Palace was still Zhaoqing Temple, and "Ten Views of West Lake" were still those inscribed by Qing emperor Kangxi. Nevertheless, since the main street connecting the downtown and the railway station had been renamed Liberation Avenue, anyone who came to Hangzhou and took this road would immediately be exposed to the key concept—liberation, the departure point of fundamental changes in the city.

In a sense, the railway station, which had greatly expanded to meet the increasing demands of transportation and communication, represented the combination of change and continuity. It had been rebuilt on the site of the old station, but the new building shared the architectural style of the new buildings of the municipal administration. The traditional palace-style roof and the huge, bright waiting rooms reflected the designer's idea of making both Eastern and Western elements serve the city. In 1953, the station had two special groups of passengers. One was the first group of students selected and sent to study in the Soviet Union. The other group involved high-echelon leaders of the Party and government. In this chapter, we will see that their visits had immediate implications for the urban development of Hangzhou.

A Changed Strategy

Beijing announced the First Five-Year Plan in 1953. To travel the same road as the Soviet Union, China decided to put priority on heavy industry for the country's modernization. This plan, however, was not favorable to industrial development in Hangzhou. The 156 magnet projects sponsored by the Soviet Union and major state-funded enterprises were all located in inland provinces, and none of the 697 projected major industrial enterprises would be built in Hangzhou. That meant that no major investment from the central government would be available to develop the local economy.[3]

China had good reasons to develop its major industries in the inland provinces. First were the security considerations. The coastal areas were regarded as vulnerable, exposed to possible GMD counterattacks from Taiwan and to foreign invasion.[4] Second, in order to guarantee a power supply to Shanghai, the largest industrialized city in China, the government did not want Hangzhou to develop much industry because this would lead to a competition for electricity. Third, Zhejiang Province, the famous "land of rice and fish," was the major grain contributor to the country. Since the Chinese government saw food production as the foundation of the national economy, it felt that Hangzhou should not build many factories because they would draw agricultural labor from the countryside. However, to guarantee state revenues, Beijing also wanted to keep the coastal economy prosperous.[5] The central government would not give the province significant financial or technological assistance, but it would continue to ask Zhejiang to contribute capital and manpower for the magnet projects in the interior. What could Zhejiang Province and the city of Hangzhou do to meet the country's inland-oriented development strategy? Were there any alternatives for the city's economy? The reorientation of urban development was a subject of protracted discussion among local leaders.

In 1953, a Soviet urban specialist, A. C. Maxim, was invited to attend a city work-planning meeting. The Russian was certainly impressed by the city's scenery and cultural resources, and at the planning meeting, Maxim presented a sophisticated plan that would develop Hangzhou as a city for recreation, tourism, and cultural activities.[6] The city could also become a center for international conferences and be known as "the Geneva of the East." Maxim approached urban design from the perspective of the Soviet model. He said that function, economy, and beauty were the basic requirements of the Soviet Communist Party and government for urban development. Not every city had to develop its own industry since the Soviet people deserved a variety of living spaces.

In accordance with Maxim's suggestions, the Hangzhou city planners decided to divide the city into four districts. The downtown (Shangcheng and Xiacheng districts) would remain the commercial areas; the scenic areas around West Lake would be reserved as public space for recreation; the belt along the Qiantang River would be developed into a special zone for higher education; finally, the city would have a limited number of factories, all of which would be concentrated in the districts of Gongshu and Jianggan, the areas farthest from downtown and from West Lake. Maxim also insisted that the Genshamen Power Station be moved out of the city since it produced too much smoke. The government and the people should treasure West Lake, and most residences should be kept a certain distance from the lakeshore.[7]

The planning meeting also discussed how to control the size of the urban population. Some people suggested that the population of Hangzhou could increase to 1.2 million. Maxim countered that a city with a population of 1.2 million had to be an industrial city, and this did not match the nature of Hangzhou. He suggested that the total urban population should not exceed 800,000.[8]

Many years later the Chinese started to criticize their early economic policy in the 1950s because it had blindly followed the "Russian model." However, it should not be forgotten that Maxim offered Hangzhou valuable advice for building a "Geneva of the East." Maxim was not the first person to initiate such a plan, but in the early 1950s, advice from a Soviet expert was influential, and it helped the city leaders make their final decision on the development of the city.

There was no doubt that Hangzhou had all the advantages to become a city for recreation, tourism, and cultural activities. Tourism had long been a local industry. Its scenic beauty and cultural facilities had won Hangzhou the reputation of "a paradise on earth." In addition, the local hotels and restaurants, teahouses, gift stores, temples, and handicrafts products served to make the city prosperous. An American missionary described the unique appeal of the city: "Scenes of [West] Lake and hills and valleys and bamboo groves and the Chi'en T'ang [Qiantang] River, pagodas and temples and tombs and grottos were celebrated in poetry and prose, in painting and (in more modern times) photographs, and were familiar to people everywhere in China."[9] Since everyone wanted to see it at least once, tourists from all parts of the country came to the city. In 1932, the artist Lin Fengmian wrote: "Aren't spring and fall the best seasons for the sale of the local products of Hangzhou: silk, tea, umbrellas, bamboo sticks, and paper fans? Aren't they the best seasons for the hotels and restaurants in Hangzhou? Why? It is because West Lake is most beautiful in spring and fall and thus attracts the most tourists, isn't it?"[10]

Indeed a great number of urban dwellers—boatmen, rickshawmen, waiters, handicrafts makers, shopkeepers, prostitutes, actors and actresses, and thousands of monks and nuns—made their living by serving the tourists and pilgrims. As noted in chapter 1, before 1949, high-ranking officials in Nanjing and millions of residents in Shanghai regarded Hangzhou as their backyard garden. Moreover, in the last two years of the Civil War, feeling the approach of doomsday and wanting to enjoy life while they could, even more rich people poured into Hangzhou and spent money like water, boosting the city's thriving economy.[11]

When the Communists came, they did not destroy this structure but made an effort to keep the city clean and tidy. As soon as the CCP took over the city, it initiated several projects to construct new roads, develop new gardens, and clean up the lake water. These projects were a part of the social relief programs to help unemployed workers and the urban poor.[12] When Jiang Hua was appointed the first Communist mayor of Hangzhou, he issued an administrative order protecting the trees, flowers, temples, and historical relics. The order prohibited fishing or washing vegetables in West Lake, and peddlers were not allowed to do business on the lakeshore.[13] The city government, however, did not intend to develop a tourist industry but to make West Lake a big fish pond that would raise eighty thousand green carp, sixty thousand silver carp, and sixty thousand abalone in the first year. In addition, a great number of trees and flowers, most of economic value, were planted around the lake and in the nearby mountains.[14] It was clear that although the city leaders treasured the natural resources of Hangzhou, they were heeding the Party's general call for "transforming consumer-oriented towns into productive cities." The plan to "reform West Lake" was a combination of preserving the lake's scenic beauty and exploiting its productive potential.[15]

Now, in his visit to Hangzhou, Maxim suggested that the city leaders give up the attempt to make Hangzhou an industrial city, thus totally changing the urban development strategy. This was not merely an economic issue. First, it meant that the city could not expect a quick increase of industrial workers. This might be a setback for the Communists, who urged the expansion of the political force of the proletarian class in the cities. Second, Maxim's proposal would require the city to preserve a more traditional culture. That would have an important bearing on the city's management of the temples, historical sites, and artistic activities, and it would affect the government's policy toward cultural celebrities and cause difficulties for the Communists in consolidating the new regime and pursuing social transformation. Third, the proposal frustrated local cadres, such as the head of the Bureau of Industry, Gu Dehuan, who had fought and worked their whole lives to achieve quick industrial growth.

In the final analysis, the urban development strategy was a political issue. The southbound cadres came with a sense of mission to liberate the city. They believed that after the Communist takeover, Hangzhou would no longer belong to the rich and powerful but to working people, and therefore its function and appearance had to be changed. Could the city continue to exist in its traditional form? Was the Russian suggestion a rational choice for this city's long-term development?

In the winter of 1953, Mao Zedong made his first visit to Hangzhou; the visit offered the city leaders an answer to the above questions and legitimized the changing development strategy. Mao introduced a new viewpoint: the city's natural beauties and cultural facilities were its capital in the country's political game. Hangzhou would and should play a special role in the country's economy, as well as in Communist politics.

Mao's Manors at the Lakeshore

On December 24, 1953, the General Office of the CCP Central Committee advised all members of the Politburo that Mao Zedong would leave Beijing for a vacation and Liu Shaoqi would be in charge of the routine work of the Central Committee. Three days later, Mao Zedong arrived in Hangzhou. He was supposed to stay there for one month, but he did not leave the city until March 1954. His chief assistants, Hu Qiaomu, Chen Boda, and Tian Jiaying, accompanied him to the city, and they would work there to draft the first PRC constitution for Mao's review.[16] From 1953 through 1975, Mao made more than forty visits to Hangzhou, during which he usually stayed at two luxurious manors at the lakeshore—Liu Zhuang and Wang Zhuang. Following Mao's example, other top leaders, such as Liu Shaoqi, Chen Yun, Lin Biao, Ye Jianying, and Li Xiannian, also frequently went to the city for pleasure or business, and at most times they arranged to stay at Wang Zhuang.[17]

Liu Zhuang was built by the bureaucrat-merchant Liu Xuexun in 1905. The most beautiful part of the manor was a bamboo garden, which reflected the owner's belief in the Confucian ideal that one would "rather eat no meat than live without bamboo."[18] To meet Mao's needs, a swimming pool, conference room, and other modern facilities were added. Wang Zhuang was built by the rich tea merchant Wang Zixin in the 1920s. Located near a Buddhist temple, Wang Zhuang was constructed in a nice combination of Chinese and Western styles. The garden was famous for its various tea trees, rare chrysanthemums, well-designed rockery, and exquisite pavilions. The owner was a lover of music who devoted special rooms to his collection of more than a hundred ancient *qing*.[19] The manor was usually quiet since it was surrounded by dense trees and had only one trail leading to the street. The owner, however, welcomed all visitors. The beauty of the manor and the host's elegance and hospitality helped him to advertise the family's tea business.[20] After the Communist takeover, these manors became the "forbidden city" of Hangzhou. Ordinary people could no longer get near them since security guards blocked the trails and the nearby water. From the other side of West Lake, people could only see a few villas looming in the distance and wonder what important decisions would come out of this mysterious place.

Why did Mao leave Beijing, and why did he choose to go to Hangzhou? The official reason was that because of illness and exhaustion, Mao Zedong needed a rest. One popular guess was that Mao's leaving had something to do with his distress at the news that his eldest son had died in the Korean War. These reasons might all be true, but the decisive factor for Mao's leaving Beijing in December 1953 was a sharp power struggle within the Communist top leadership.

The power struggle finally ended in the purge of the PRC's vice president and Politburo member Gao Gang and Party Organizational Department chief Rao Shushi.[21] Both Cultural Revolution sources and the Chinese literature after Deng Xiaoping's "policy of reform and openness" reveal that Gao and Rao were first supported by Mao Zedong in the Party struggle against Liu Shaoqi.[22] Mao's dissatisfaction with Liu Shaoqi resulted from a speech Liu gave in Tianjin in which he emphasized the necessary development of capitalism. This speech contradicted Mao's strong commitment to the elimination of capitalism (the theory of "permanent revolution"). At the same time, Mao Zedong greatly admired Gao Gang's advanced socialist measures in Manchuria. Encouraged by Mao, Gao and Rao began attacking Liu Shaoqi. Unfortunately, Gao and Rao went too far and attempted to replace Liu Shaoqi and Zhou Enlai and control the Politburo. They got support from Generals Peng Dehuai and Lin Biao, but they met with the collective opposition of Deng Xiaoping, Chen Yun, and other Politburo members. At that point, Mao Zedong decided to side with the majority in the Politburo in order to maintain the unity of the leadership. Also, Mao found that Gao Gang's personal ambition was dangerous, and his "undercover activities" became a serious threat to Mao's own authority.[23] It was not a pleasant matter for Mao to purge Gao Gang. They had had a very close relationship since the Yan'an years, and Gao initially had Mao's firm support against Liu. Mao felt that he had better leave the matter to other Politburo members so that he could intercede later if necessary.[24] It was against this background that Mao left Beijing.

At the Politburo meeting convened in Beijing to discuss the Gao-Rao situation, Liu and Zhou launched a counterattack. Gao Gang asked to see Mao Zedong, but he was not allowed to go to Hangzhou. Gao Gang then sensed danger and Liu Shaoqi was encouraged. In Hangzhou, Mao met with Yang Shangkun, the chief of the General Office of the CCP Central Committee, and confirmed his approval of what was going on in Beijing. Then Mao met with Gao's major supporter, Lin Biao, who was ill and recuperating in the city, and Mao pulled Lin away from Gao.[25] Soon after New Year's Day 1954, Mao invited the Soviet ambassador, Pavel Yudin, to visit Hangzhou. In a brief conversation with the ambassador, Mao told him that a crucial personnel change would soon take place in the Party and government. Since Gao Gang had developed close ties with the Soviet Union, Mao believed that an early hint to the Russians before the final blow to Gao was necessary.[26]

Mao's most important decision in Hangzhou was a telegraph to Liu Shaoqi on January 7, 1954, that suggested that the Central Committee hold the Fourth Plenum and informing Liu that Mao would neither attend the plenum nor deal with any daily Party routines. It was the first time that Mao put into practice his idea of dividing the Politburo into two tiers.[27] In the following two months, Mao was not involved in any of the Party's activities, nor did he show up on public occasions. He continued to issue instructions to the Party, government, and the PLA and had a few necessary meetings with people in his manor.[28]

During his stay, Mao called Hangzhou his third home (after Hunan and Beijing). He needed a place distant from the formal political stage to watch other political actors, test their loyalty and ability, manipulate them, and make decisions without hurry. Observing the political drama from a distance, Mao was confident that he could still control the situation while remaining flexible. No Party leaders could go to Hangzhou without Mao's permission. Whom Mao called, whom Mao met, and what conversations Mao had—all sent vital messages to Beijing and greatly influenced the formal policymaking of the CCP. Following Mao's example, other CCP leaders began to play similar games of informal politics. They went to the city to look for a chance to approach the supreme leader or contact the local leaders to get information about Mao's intentions or plans. The city also became a meeting place for political allies and a refuge for Party leaders, such as Chen Yun, who often went there to escape from the political whirlpool in Beijing. Thus national politics became a dynamic force shaping the city and its culture.

While the local leaders in Hangzhou had the responsibility for providing security and all the comforts to Mao Zedong and other leaders, they also had the advantage of being able to approach the top leaders, a step that was vital to their political careers. With daily contact, they had a chance to develop their communication networks with the top leadership. They might have brief meetings with Mao and thus get some important piece of information that would help them understand the politics at the top and judge the political climate. Knowing and being known by the top leaders was important; it explains why a considerable number of local leaders in Zhejiang were promoted to higher positions in the central government or in other provinces.[29] It also explains why, in the early days of the Cultural Revolution, Mao Zedong made the decision to attack Liu Shaoqi in Hangzhou, and why, five years later, he traveled to the city again and told the city leaders of his opposition to Lin Biao. Since informal politics was extremely important in China, other CCP leaders, including Madame Mao and Lin Biao, also used their local connections in Hangzhou to keep themselves informed about Mao.

As we have discussed, its natural beauty was the city's treasure. It was the reason that the first convalescent home for the CPV was built there in 1951. Then the air force, navy, the national General Trade Union, the railway department, and other departments in the central government also built sanatoriums in the city.[30] Moreover, Party and government leaders from other cities and provinces wanted to come to Hangzhou for vacation. The new rulers of the city, the southbound cadres, were aware of the city's special advantages, and they knew it was important to develop political and commercial relations with Beijing and other areas because Zhejiang was a small agricultural province and desperately needed support from the central government and other provinces. The leaders were very hospitable hosts, and their guests from other provinces no longer saw the southbound cadres as rural revolutionaries from Shandong but as the "comrades of Hangzhou." The southbound cadres were happy to become "comrades of Hangzhou" and to learn and teach visitors about the city. Actually, they were proud to introduce their guests to the local products and culture. They would say to the visitors, "Watching West Lake in sunshine is good, in the rain it is better, in moonlight it is wonderful, but in the snow it is splendid."[31] At the lakeshore manor, Mao Zedong enjoyed the full moon, the local opera, and taking pictures in the snow. One of his famous photos, "Mao Zedong in Hangzhou" (published in *China Pictorial* and other magazines), was printed on local silk scarves.[32]

The Temples: Not Just Religion

To develop Hangzhou for recreation, tourism, and cultural activities, the southbound cadres had to resolve how to deal with the very many places of worship in the city.[33] Most of the temples in Hangzhou are Buddhist, a few are Taoist, and there are churches and even some Islamic mosques. As early as the eleventh century, more than four hundred temples existed in the city, and the number had increased to a thousand in the early twentieth century. Hangzhou was therefore called "the land of Buddha."[34] The largest temple, the Lingyin Temple, was built by an itinerant Indian monk in 326 A.D. (It was said that after a long journey this monk arrived in Hangzhou and saw a peak among the local hills that looked like one in his homeland; he called it "Flying Peak" and decided to build a temple in front of it.) In its golden age in the Southern Song dynasty, the temple had more than five hundred rooms accommodating more than three thousand monks and thousands of pilgrims.[35] In the following centuries, the temple was destroyed by wars or fires fourteen times, but every time its buildings were reconstructed and the monastery extended. When the Japanese stormed the city, the temple sheltered more than six hundred refugees, thus further enhancing the reputation of merciful Buddha. At the time of the arrival of the Communists, the temple had more than two hundred resident monks who had originally come from all parts of China.

Most Chinese temples are located in quiet and secluded places, keeping away from the uproar of the secular world. They are nestled in forests, hidden in mountains, or surrounded by waters. A famous scholar, Lin Fenmian, wrote about the Hangzhou temples in the Republican years: "The temples stand in great number around West Lake, which is an indication that Hangzhou and West Lake are richer in natural beauty than other places."[36] As noted, these famous temples and the picturesque scenery acted as magnets for thousands of secular visitors as well as for pilgrims.

Chinese temple culture was closely associated with art and literature. Some senior monks and nuns were not only familiar with Buddhist scriptures, but also engaged in poetry, painting, calligraphy, and music. Also, most well-known and respected scholars in traditional China were devoted Buddhists and had cultural links with temples. Conversations between pilgrims who were of the nobility and the temple's Master of Law might touch a broad range of subjects in religion, philosophy, art, and literature. Many poetic and artistic works by the senior monks of the Lingyin Temple were handed down from ancient times; from these we can see their cultural associations with famous contemporary scholars and even emperors.[37] In modern times, Li Shutong (1880–1942) was representative of these well-educated monks. Li was born to a rich salt merchant family and studied art and music in Japan for five years. After he returned to China, he became a famous scholar, educator, and composer. He composed "Goodbye," which was a favorite song among students throughout the country. In 1918, he abandoned family life and took the tonsure to become Master of Law Hongyi at the Hupao Temple in Hangzhou. Every year a great number of visitors went to the temple not to worship Buddha but to ask for artistic or calligraphic works from the master.[38]

Temple culture was a complex phenomenon. The temples did not merely serve the elite, but were also open to ordinary people. Everyone could visit them and meet with monks or nuns in the halls or in their living quarters. All visitors could ask for a cup of tea or some vegetarian food, whether they gave a donation or not. All the temples in Hangzhou used to provide simple accommodations for pilgrims or tourists who had not booked hotels.[39] Such a service enhanced the charm of the tourist-oriented city.

From the perspective of the southbound cadres, however, the monks' hospitality was but a means to woo more pilgrims. The crucial problem with temples was the parasitic lifestyle of their residents. The monks and nuns did not produce anything but lived on the donations of pilgrims and on income from temple lands. The city leaders decided to reduce the number of temples and to organize the monks and nuns into various productive work teams.

On November 21, 1949, the *Zhejiang Daily* published a report entitled "The Monks in Lingyin Temple Are Changing." According to this report, two-thirds of the monks had been sent back to their home villages, and the rest were now engaged in various production activities. They had been organized into three groups in accordance with age and health: full labor, semi-labor, and non-labor. The full laborers were thirty years old or younger and would farm, cut firewood, dye silk, and weave cloth. The semi-laborers would assist the full laborers with all these tasks. The non-laborers were more than sixty years old and were in charge of maintaining the temples and their scriptures. All the monks got up before dawn; after half an hour of reading Buddhist scriptures, they started to work; after three and a half hours of physical labor in the morning, they had lunch. In the afternoon they would spend four hours working and half an hour studying scriptures. One hour of Buddhist study per day was surely not enough for religious pursuits—even if it was not interrupted by frequent "political studies." Moreover, the monks worked even harder than factory workers since they had only two days off a month. A slogan on the pillar of the temple hall facing a statue of Buddha seemed to be half-explanation and half-warning: "From now on, all monks must support themselves by their own labor and overcome their parasitism through real work!"[40]

The changes in temple life were in line with the CCP's general goal of transforming the consumer-oriented city into a productive one. However, they resulted not only from government policy or from the negative attitude of the southbound cadres toward Buddhism. Regime change had caused a decline in religion, and the Communists' efforts to transform the urban culture had speeded up this process. After the Communist takeover, the temples failed to bring harmony in the quickly changing city because the temple culture had been forged by a pattern of urban life that no longer existed.

To celebrate the first anniversary of Hangzhou's liberation, the local press published several articles on social changes in terms of the general mood of society. According to the press reports, these changes embodied new tendencies toward a "love of labor," "enthusiasm of study," and "fraternal unity" among urban people.[41] The *Zhejiang Daily* came to the conclusion that the city was moving toward the ideal society, where "no one has to pick what's left by the wayside."[42] Needless to say, these reports were hardly objective descriptions of the real situation, but rather reflected the views of the southbound cadres about their new society and immediate goals. It is not surprising, therefore, that the press also reported the decline in religious activities as additional progress toward the new society.

In previous years the Lingyin Temple used to receive several dozen *dan* of candles and oil, but in the first five months of 1950, the donations were less than one *dan*.[43] In the past, the temple had performed rites for rich families on various occasions: birthdays, funerals, sickness, or festivals. Payments for such services plus pilgrims' donations amounted to a daily income as high as 7–8 *dan* of rice. The seventh month in the Chinese lunar calendar used to be the busiest time for Buddhist rituals. In the past, the monks and nuns were invited to chant scriptures at people's homes, and the sound of their reading and Buddhist music prevailed even over the noise of the city's major shopping area—Zhongshan Road. After the PLA came, however, there was not a rite ordered in six months. Although the temple had land in Xiaoshan County, the monks worried about losing it since the land reform was imminent. To meet the new economic situation, the monks had to change their way of life.[44]

Under the CCP slogan, "Make yourselves self-supporting working people," a great number of monks and nuns were forced to leave their temples or nunneries. On the eve of the PLA entry into Hangzhou, there were about 3,500 monks and nuns; the number had fallen to a couple of hundred by 1950. In the following years, the situation continued to deteriorate. A government survey in 1953 indicated that Lingyin Temple, which used to have more than a hundred monks, now had thirteen; the Hupao Temple had even fewer—four. To make the situation worse, these large temples did not have abbots and could not find qualified senior monks for the abbot positions.[45]

For several reasons, however, the Communists could not destroy either the temples themselves or Buddhism. First, although the Communists were atheists, the constitution of the PRC proclaimed respect for freedom of religion and claimed to protect legal religious activities. The CCP Zhejiang Committee established an Office on Religious Affairs, which cooperated with the CCP Department of the United Front, the Bureau of Public Security, the Bureau of Urban Construction, and the Bureau of Urban Gardens to handle the issue of temples. No single institution could decide on the size of a temple or its plan of reform. Second, as already discussed, the temples in Hangzhou were not just religious institutions, but also brought considerable income into the city. Third, the temples in Hangzhou were not just of local concern. A plan to destroy the temples would have met with great resistance from believers all over the country, especially Buddhist pilgrims from Tibet and Muslims from China's northwestern provinces. Fourth, the famous temples in Hangzhou, such as Lingyin, Hupao, Jingci, and Qinglian, had international reputations, especially in Southeast Asia. Maintaining the temples, therefore, had major political implications, indicating that the new regime appeared to be moderate.[46]

Finally, the city government had also to consider the great number of women pilgrims from the rural areas south to the Yangtze River. In the spring, their pilgrimage was a great event in Hangzhou. These women were not organized but wore uniform outfits as if by prior agreement: blue, handwoven clothes and colorful scarves; they all carried paper umbrellas and yellow satchels with the words "pilgrim and incense" on them. They walked in groups of dozens or hundreds to visit all the Buddhist temples around West Lake and in the surrounding mountains. As pious adherents of Buddha, they would not miss a single temple, nor forget to pray to every god; they spent most of the money they had saved for a whole year on joss sticks or donations to the monks or nuns. They would bring cold steamed rice or cakes with them for lunch and buy little additions in grocery stores.[47] Since they came in great numbers, the shopkeepers would be eager to serve these customers. Street peddlers and vendors' stands occupied every inch of land along the roadsides to the major temples. Business from the pilgrim season in the spring surpassed sales in the other three seasons combined.[48]

Whether they liked it or not, the southbound cadres could not stop the pilgrimage, which was the greatest event in the lives of the rural women in the villages of Jiangsu and Zhejiang Provinces. It was a holiday exclusively for rural housewives, and no men or unmarried girls could join them. Most of these women had married as teenagers and had started to worship Buddha at home. Buddha was the only one to whom they could communicate about their daily hardships and suffering: a husband's abuse, an in-law's maltreatment, a child's sickness, or natural disasters. The pilgrimage was a happy event, offering them their only chance to get away from their husbands' control and enjoy a journey with their sisters. Although there were some young women in the group, most of the women had uninterruptedly gone on the pilgrimage for many years, so the people in Hangzhou call these visitors "Grandma Pilgrims."[49]

The Great Canal and the network of numerous rivers and lakes in Jiangnan brought the rural women pilgrims to the city. In 1909, the Shanghai-Hangzhou railway started operation, and it offered a special tourist train to bring urban people to join the pilgrims.[50] The Grandma Pilgrims came no earlier than the end of January and no later than the first week of February. They would stay in Hangzhou until the willows turned green, spring flowers bloomed, and the silkworms were about to break from their eggs and had to be fed. And then they returned home to work and to look forward to the next year's pilgrimage. In the city's history, only two events had interrupted this activity. One was in 1860–1861, when the Taiping rebels had stormed the city and destroyed many temples; the other was the Cultural Revolution of 1966–1976, which closed all the temples and sent the monks and nuns to the countryside to work.

In 1953, Mao Zedong visited the Lingyin Temple and often climbed nearby Mount Beigao, from where he could get a bird's-eye view of the temple. Unlike previous emperors, who had come and left inscriptions, Mao did not leave any comments on the temple. In his poem, "Three Climbs on Mount Beigao," there was not a word mentioning Lingyin. Mao might admire the Chinese cultural heritage, but he would not publicly express it. This attitude seems ambiguous, but the truth is that by and large the Party's policy on religion was very ambiguous. It did not prohibit people from maintaining their religion, but it encouraged them to give up their religious beliefs.

In July 1953, the CCP Zhejiang Committee instructed that the number of monks in Lingyin, Jingci, Qinglian, and Hupao should remain at the current figure, no more and no less, and that the troops, public offices, and schools that had occupied the temples' buildings should gradually move out. The government appropriated money for the renovation of the damaged halls of the temples.[51] These measures could not solve all the temple problems, but at least they would help to preserve something valuable for the city. In later years, Zhou Enlai accompanied foreign guests to the Lingyin Temple many times, and he praised the efforts of the "comrades of Hangzhou" in maintaining these Chinese historical relics. As hosts to foreign and domestic visitors, the southbound cadres had to tell the guests about the temples; from local scholars they learned the stories behind the halls and the forests, and gradually the "comrades of Hangzhou" understood the cultural value of the temples. It is not an exaggeration to say that the temples finally became something the southbound cadres treasured. During the Cultural Revolution, when a group of radical Red Guards attempted to burn the Lingyin Temple, thousands of college students and local cadres went to stop them.

Reforms in the Cultural Heritage

The southbound cadres came to realize that to make Hangzhou a socialist "Geneva of the East," the natural scenery, including the temples, would have to be preserved, but places of recreation and cultural activities would have to be reformed. In 1949, the Military Control Committee formed the Office for Cultural Affairs to supervise all cultural activities and embark upon reform. The office believed that the *yueju* was the largest and most influential local opera in Hangzhou and that it should therefore be the first to be reformed.[52] After a brief survey, however, the office found that reforming the *yueju* would be a most difficult task.

Yueju originated in the Shenxian County, which had belonged to the Yue state in ancient times (and from which it got its name). Unlike the Peking Opera, the rise of *yueju* was a modern phenomenon. In 1916, *yueju* came to Hangzhou and soon became the most popular opera in the city. Afterward, *yueju* was introduced to Shanghai and reached its peak of development in Shanghai's foreign concessions during the Sino-Japanese War. As numerous middle-class refugees, most from Zhejiang Province and the Japanese-occupied districts of Shanghai, fled to the French and other international concessions, *yueju* was their major form of recreation and spiritual sustenance. It was said that in the concessions, an "isolated island" surrounded by Japanese-occupied districts, more than a dozen *yueju* performances were presented at different theaters every night.[53]

In acting, scenery, and lighting, *yueju* borrowed techniques from modern drama and Western film. It was designed to use the facilities of modern theaters to produce elaborate stage effects. *Yueju* is also noted in Chinese drama for its beautiful costumes and props; clearly *yueju* could develop in the Hangzhou-Shanghai area, where the best silk and the best tailors were available. The themes of *yueju* were exclusively love stories. At first, males performed in *yueju*, but then it changed to only females, whose voices were more suitable for the sweet tunes and soft stories.

Yueju did not have its own playwrights; its operas were adapted either from stories that had traditionally been sung or from the Peking Opera or other local operas. *Yueju* chose to adapt only well-known stories. *Yueju's* music was beautiful—lyrical and suitable for amateurs to sing. The *yueju* gradually became the second largest opera in the country (next to the Peking Opera). When the Communists attempted to transform it, resistance came not only from the performers, but also from the audience, who did not want changes in the famous stories and the lovely music.[54]

Aware of these difficulties, the Office of Cultural Affairs began by organizing "talk show" performers into the Association of Folk Art Reform. These were actors and actresses who sang ballads, told stories, performed comic dialogues *(xiangsheng),* and gave clapper talks *(kuaiban).* They did not have permanent sites of performance, and they were often bullied by local ruffians. With much lower incomes than *yueju* performers, they were mostly looked down on. After being organized by the government, they had regular theaters in which to perform and gained some security. The first members (a group of fifty-two), therefore, were very eager to create new productions, such as "The PLA Crosses the Yangtze River," "Buy Public Bonds," "Collect Public Grain," and "Salute the PLA." The titles in themselves told the main purpose of the productions—propaganda for the government's policies and support for the CCP's political campaigns.[55]

For two reasons the southbound cadres showed a great concern for these street performers. First, they liked the "talk shows," and they were familiar with the stories. For example, *On the Margin of Water* (mentioned in chapters 1 and 3), about peasant rebel-heroes from Shandong, was in the repertoire of these storytellers.[56] Performances of the story had been repeatedly improved and enriched and had thus become even more entertaining. One of the storytellers, Zheng Jinfang, had become famous in the 1940s, and after the Communists came to power, he was often invited to do special performances for the city leaders and their guests. *The Romance of the Three Kingdoms* was his specialty.[57]

The second reason was that the content of the "talk shows" was easier to revise to serve current political ends. It was customary for "talk show" storytellers to connect their stories to the present, making jokes about contemporaries or commenting on present events. The CCP therefore wanted to use them to quickly adapt their "talks" to new revolutionary works.[58]

In April 1952, the owner of the city's largest amusement center, Big World, committed suicide during the Five Antis Campaign, and the government decided to take over the center and rename it the People's Recreation Center.[59] Some *yueju* troupes in Big World were dismissed and others reorganized. In structuring the People's Recreation Center, the Bureau of Labor suggested that the center should first hire the employees who had worked at Big World so as to avoid an increase in the unemployment rate, but the Bureau of Culture and Education insisted that it was necessary to dismiss "unqualified" performers and employees so as to thoroughly reform all areas of culture and entertainment. Following the instructions of the Propaganda Department, the Bureau of Culture and Education sent some Party and Youth League members and worker activists to Big World to completely wipe out its "degenerate style of management."[60] In the following year, the center was restructured again and became the Hall of Sino-Soviet Friendship, showing Russian movies, holding Soviet exhibitions, presenting lectures on Russian literature, and organizing other cultural activities.

In order to encourage all cinemas and theaters to show revolutionary movies and new dramas that "could heighten people's political consciousness," the government offered them tax deductions or exemptions to run such shows.[61] The cinemas and theaters were also asked to review the movies or programs, collect audience responses, and include them in monthly reports to the Bureau of Culture and Education.[62]

From the first week of the takeover, all actors, actresses, and playwrights were organized into three study groups. Every Monday the playwrights were assembled to report on the progress of their political studies and to discuss new writing plans.[63] In the following years, the government-led Association for Drama-Opera Reform admitted 1,024 actors and actresses to its membership. Among them 471 were allowed to continue to perform in Hangzhou, and all others were organized into several troupes to tour the countryside and other cities. Working with the association, in 1951 the city's Bureau of Culture and Education held two workshops for 384 actors and playwrights at which they were required to criticize old works and old ideas. For example, an old opera, *The Regret of the Ming*, tells the story of the collapse of the Ming dynasty and the suicide of the last Ming emperor. It was decided that the opera would not be performed any more because "the opera speaks for the feudal ruling class, and the emperor's 'regret' should not appear on the stage of the working people."[64] By 1952, the Bureau reported that 60 percent of the *hangju* performances (another form of local opera) and *qu yi* (folk art) in the city had been revised.[65] But little progress was made in creating new *yueju*.

In the early days of the takeover, every government institution believed that it had the right to oversee urban cultural life. It was reported that some policemen in the Jianggan district ordered the opera troupe there to submit its scripts for their review—otherwise it would not be allowed to perform in the district. The city government saw that it was necessary to stop such arbitrary censorship and announced that only the Bureau of Culture and Education would have the power and responsibility to censor programs. Actually the department proved to be quite discerning when it came to opera reform.[66] In 1953, there was a debate about a *yueju* opera, *The Green Jade Hairpin*. The story was about a woman whose loyalty was questioned by her husband and in-laws because she had a green jade hairpin that was suspected to be a gift from another man. The woman was therefore maltreated and abused. Eventually the husband learned that the green jade hairpin was a legacy from his wife's parents. The misunderstanding was cleared up, and the wife finally got her husband's love and respect. *The Green Jade Hairpin* told a simple story, but its humorous dialogue, graceful dancing, and beautiful music made it a favorite of many *yueju* fans. With the Communists' arrival, there was a debate. Some argued that this was a good opera that expressed how a woman suffered in "feudal society"; others criticized it because it advertised a "feudal idea" in that the woman's dream was to become a noble lady.[67] In the early 1950s, the political climate was moderate enough that a compromise was still possible, and the opera could be shown with a minor revision.

Revisions of old operas had to conform to the Communist interpretation of history. Even a play based on legend, such as *The White Snake (Bai she zhuan)*, could not be an exception. *The White Snake*, based on a famous Chinese legend, was also very popular in East Asia, and it had some Korean and Japanese versions. The story is as follows. A young scholar visited West Lake on a rainy day. He saw two ladies and lent them an umbrella. A romance started between the scholar and one of the ladies, and the seed of love grew. Then the scholar and his love (White Snake) got married. The problem was that the two ladies were not human beings but snake spirits. Despite the fact that White Snake and her sister (Green Snake) were good and honest, marriage between a human and a snake was not allowed by society. Finally a monk came to separate the couple. He caught White Snake and put a pagoda on her to hold her down. For centuries people sympathized with the two lovers and offered many alternatives to this sad ending. (One was that Green Snake got help from fish, shrimp, and crabs, who created a flood to destroy the pagoda and release White Snake.)

The Communists interpreted the snakes as oppressed Chinese women and the monk as a symbol of feudal rulers, so they changed the end of the opera to correspond with Mao's revolutionary theory: Green Snake mobilized the Chinese peasants to launch a people's uprising that finally smashed the "feudal pagoda" and brought about a family reunion. As a result, the legend became politics and the love story became a class struggle. Although the playwright and the performers tried very hard, the audience took the revised opera as an absurd joke. The audience did not understand how the snake, crabs, fish, and shrimp could become guerrilla fighters. The lovely images they had known for centuries had been totally distorted.[68]

It was obvious that in treating the *yueju* and other local cultural products the southbound cadres tried to follow Mao's instructions to discard the dross and select the essence. But the standards for distinguishing the dross from the essence were always changing, depending upon the political climate. A dramatic diplomatic incident in Geneva in 1954 eventually influenced the "comrades of Hangzhou" toward *yueju*.

On June 8, 1954, the Chinese delegation at the Geneva Conference invited the British premier, Anthony Eden, to a special reception. Premier Zhou Enlai entertained him and other Western guests by showing a Chinese movie, *Liang Shanbo and Zhu Yingtai*. The movie, adapted from a traditional *yueju*, told the story of two students, a boy named Liang Shanbo and a girl named Zhu Yingtai, who meet in school in Hangzhou. Their friendship develops into love, but family interference prevents the young lovers from being together. Before long the boy dies of lovesickness. With a broken heart, the girl jumps into her lover's grave and commits suicide. In order to help the Western audience make sense of this story, Premier Zhou suggested that the movie title be translated as "the Chinese Romeo and Juliet." Indeed there were similarities between these Eastern young lovers and the Western ones. As a result, the Western audience was deeply moved by the tragic story and the beautiful end: after their deaths, the couple turn into butterflies and fly off, wing to wing, in the sky.

Liang Shanbo and Zhu Yingtai introduced the Westerners to a pretty Chinese town—Hangzhou—and to its beautiful opera, *yueju*. Zhou Enlai introduced the story to the world as a Chinese cultural treasure, and this sent the southbound cadres in Hangzhou a political message. Earlier, one southbound cadre had been condemned for his absorption in this "degenerate" women's opera, and he was purged from the Party. Now the southbound cadres had to change their views on *yueju* and other traditional local operas. Two years before, the *yueju* version of *Liang Shanbo and Zhu Yingtai* had been performed at the First Chinese National Theater Festival and won a medal, but people did not notice it. After being shown in Geneva by Zhou, the movie version won two awards in international film festivals. Then it became a great hit in Hong Kong, where it was shown for 187 days and set a new record in ticket sales (650,000).[69] At home the movie inspired Chinese writers, artists, and composers to create various works on the subject; it also renewed the enthusiasm of the Chinese to visit the city.

The southbound cadres gradually accepted *yueju* opera. Despite its local color, the singing and dialogue of *yueju* are all in Hangzhou Mandarin (Mandarin with a Zhejiang accent), so it can be understood by people from other provinces. In 1953, when the CCP Zhejiang Committee convened a meeting at Moganshan, the Zhejiang *yueju* troupe was called upon to perform. In addition, the young actresses were invited to dance parties with CCP leaders. The deputy governor of Zhejiang, Yang Siyi, noted in his diary that in twenty-four days, there were eleven dance parties organized for the Communist leaders at Moganshan.[70]

It is not surprising that many southbound cadres became deeply involved in dance parties since ballroom dancing was extremely popular among the CCP leaders in the 1950s. Mao Zedong, Zhu De, Zhou Enlai, and their Politburo colleagues were always attending dance parties with great enthusiasm. The city leaders of Hangzhou simply followed their example. Although most southbound cadres had not known how to dance before, they learned quickly. If for no other reason, the city needed a *yueju* troupe to provide dance partners for the CCP leaders.

If *yueju* performances remained almost untouched in the 1950s, other big changes affected the city's political atmosphere, and this had an impact on people's feelings toward both traditional and foreign culture. Before 1949, the International Cinema specialized in showing American movies. At that time, the streets also advertised American cigars or gramophones playing American jazz. Men wore Western suits and ladies had on Western makeup. Signs of American culture were all around. After the outbreak of the Korean War, several theaters continued to show Hollywood movies, but for many people the pleasure was gone. In one case, a high school student wanted to see an American movie. Along the street, he saw the red flags and anti-American slogans, heard the song "Beat the American Wolves" on radio sets in the stores along the way, and noticed people with red armbands staring at him with suspicion; he sneaked into the cinema and felt guilty.[71] Similarly, *Liang Shanbo and Zhu Yingtai* continued to show in the theaters, but people could no longer just enjoy the love story. The government insisted that the audience take the movie as a "textbook of class struggle," not just seeing a tragedy of two lovers, but also understanding "the evils and cruelties of the feudal system."[72]

Toward Socialism

In keeping with the new strategy for urban development, cultural activities were carefully managed and almost all historical relics were preserved. Walking along the lakeshore, one could see the graves and monuments of historical figures. Among them were the graves of two special women—Qiu Jin, a martyr of the Republican revolution, and Su Xiaoxiao, an ancient geisha.[73] In the Cultural Revolution, the two graves—and others—were destroyed, and the city leaders were accused of protecting a GMD ally and a prostitute. This was evidence of their betrayal of the revolution.

In the 1950s the city leaders and the southbound cadre had not given up the goal of the revolution. From the moment the CCP entered the city, the crusade against bourgeois ideas and culture rose or fell in intensity, but it never stopped. For these revolutionaries, the "Geneva of the East" still had to be a socialist society. The city leaders also believed in the Marxist theory that a profound cultural revolution was possible only after a successful reconstruction of the national economy. The urgent task for the southbound cadres in Hangzhou in 1953–1954 was the final economic expropriation of the urban bourgeoisie.

Although the southbound cadres took over the government economic enterprises in the first days of their entry into the city, a large number of private enterprises remained untouched. In 1953, there were 1,459 private factories employing 28,000 workers and 16,401 commercial firms of various sizes. In the city, 43,189 people engaged in commercial activities. Despite remarkable progress in the development of state industry and commerce, the southbound cadres believed that private enterprises had remained disproportionately high in the city's economy. In the first year, private industry accounted for 91.5 percent of the total output value, and private stores accounted for 94.1 percent of the turnover from retail trade and 77.6 percent from wholesale trade.[74] This structure would not change quickly in favor of state enterprises since the new urban plan did not encourage the development of industry in the city.

With time and effort, however, the government gradually gained control of the city's finances. The state-run trading companies manipulated the urban market and established solid connections with peasant suppliers and consumers. In Hangzhou, private commerce was mainly relegated to gift shops, groceries, other small shops, and peddlers. Despite their small scope of operations, these retailers well served the city's tourist industry, and state-run companies could hardly be tailored to the city's needs in a short time. In May 1953, the CCP Zhejiang Committee sent a report to the ECB suggesting that "private commerce should be reduced steadily."[75] On June 23, the ECB replied, instructing Zhejiang "to maintain the status quo for a while; wait and see."[76] The ECB agreed with Zhejiang that it was necessary to control private commerce. The third secretary of the ECB, Tan Zhenlin, who had worked in Hangzhou for a couple of years, noted in a speech at the Party's convention in Zhejiang, "Besides America and Chiang Kai-shek, speculators are the major enemies of industrialization and the realization of state capitalism."[77] However, the ECB believed that "[transformation] is a long process," and "at the current stage only those who pose a threat to the leadership of state enterprises have to be pushed out.... [Zhejiang] should wait for new instructions from the CCP Central Committee, then take proper action at the proper time."[78]

In October 1953, the CCP Central Committee proclaimed that the state would henceforth monopolize the purchase and marketing of grain. In November, the CCP Zhejiang Committee announced measures to implement this new policy.[79] The policy cut off the commercial connections of capitalists and merchants with the peasantry. Thus they could not obtain materials freely and lost their access to the domestic market, making it impossible for them to organize production as they saw fit. They now had to follow the government's planned economy. This was a key economic measure in pushing China to the point of no-return on the way toward socialism. The CCP Zhejiang Committee took a further step in December 1953 by issuing instructions to start the socialist transformation of capitalist industry and the handicrafts industry.[80] As collectivization in the countryside progressed quickly, the urban transformation would soon abolish the private ownership of property. According to the prevailing Marxist criteria at the time, China would be a genuine socialist society after it completed this transformation.

Although the southbound cadres had a strong desire to nationalize private industry and commerce, they were careful to avoid any reckless actions. The city government first took over thirteen private enterprises to test the idea of joint state-private ownership and analyzed the problems that emerged at each stage of the experiment. The Five Antis Campaign had dealt a heavy blow to urban capitalists and merchants, and their businesses had not yet recovered. Policies on nationalization had to be relaxed for a while, as the ECB suggested. In January 1954, as the market situation improved, the ECB issued another directive, urging Zhejiang to adopt strong measures to reverse the declines in private commerce and slow down the process of the socialist transformation.[81]

The CCP Zhejiang Committee had planned to establish 409 joint state-private ventures in 1954, but it soon found that this number had to be reduced to 46.[82] In the initial experiment with joint ventures, all of the enterprises had had to deal with tense state-private relations and a decline in production. The urban bourgeoisie now understood that the final goal of the socialist revolution was to eliminate it. This frightened some capitalists not only because they would lose their property, but also because they would become "enemies of the people." People who had stocks in private factories did not dare to claim their investments. They preferred to lose their shares rather than be labeled as part of the bourgeoisie. At the Hangzhou Textile Mill, 14.6 percent of the shares remained unclaimed, and at the Huling Silk Factory 48 percent of the shareholders were unknown.[83] Under such circumstances, the city leaders stressed that the most important thing was not to nationalize more enterprises but to make each joint state-private enterprise an appealing model: highly productive, profitable, well managed, and benefiting both the state and the bourgeoisie. The new strategy emphasized "consolidating [our] position, focusing on key enterprises, building up models, and intensifying preparations for final nationalization."[84] Once again, the CCP promised that the revolution would not touch the way of life of the urban bourgeoisie, and capitalists were told they were allies of the working class in the country's economic reconstruction. There was no timetable for nationalization at this stage, and the transformation seemed to have been postponed into the distant future.

In the propaganda campaign for socialist transformation, the local press argued that "the necessary conditions for socialist transformation included socialist enthusiasm on the part of the workers, a progressive tendency on the part of the capitalists, and the development of the Party's organizations."[85] In practice, there were more specific criteria. First, the enterprises that were taken over had to be profitable so that they would not be a burden to the government after they were nationalized. Second, the private owners had to either have bad records or be suffering economic difficulties so that they dared not resist. Third, the CCP had to have a strong ideological influence and organizational presence in these enterprises.

The Mingfen and Huafen Paper Mills are examples. First, the two factories belonged to one enterprise with 2,621 workers and modern equipment. They produced high-quality paper for books, typing, currency printing, and color pictures. The two factories controlled 80 percent of the national market in cigarette paper, and their annual output was ¥340 billion in 1953. Second, the factories had had to pay a fine for tax evasion and other economic crimes in the Five Antis Campaign and thus owed the state bank ¥97 billion. Moreover, Mafia members in Shanghai controlled 25 percent of the enterprise. These people could be arrested at any time, and their stocks could be confiscated by the government. Finally, the CCP had penetrated the factories and had established seven party branches before 1949. There had been 109 Party members by September 1953, and they controlled most workshops in the factories.[86] On the basis of the factories' economic value, their susceptibility to state control, and the Party's influence within them, the CCP Zhejiang Committee asked the CCP Central Committee to approve its plan to institute joint state-private ownership in a group of enterprises to include the Mingfen and Huafen Paper Mills and four other factories.[87]

Experiments in a few of the joint enterprises indicated that socialist transformation could not be completed by simple administrative orders. In the previous four years, the CCP had already institutionalized the political study meetings, so they could easily be used for intensive mass mobilization toward socialist transformation as well. Not only in government institutions, but also in factories, trading companies, and neighborhoods, political study meetings had become a ritualized and routine activity. One hour a day or a half a day per week was exclusively devoted to them. The meetings were organized by the CCP, the Youth League, the Chamber of Commerce, the trade unions, the Women's Federation, and neighborhood committees; the idea was to involve workers, capitalists and their spouses, shopkeepers and artisans, illiterate housewives, and the unemployed.

Two major points were emphasized at the meetings. First, all private industry, commerce, and handicrafts would have to be nationalized to meet the goals of the socialist planned economy. Second, only nationalization would finally solve the problems of state-private and labor-capitalist conflicts.[88] For factory owners and merchants, special discussion meetings were organized to study the Party's "buyout" policy toward private industry and commerce. According to this policy, the capitalists would be paid dividends of 20 percent of the monetary value of their assets every year after nationalization, and they would be given suitable managerial appointments that would fully use their talents and skills. Thus the socialist transformation would transform the urban bourgeois into self-supporting working people.[89]

The political mobilization lasted more than two years, starting in 1954. In this protracted process the southbound cadres showed incredible patience and persistence, while the resistance from the urban bourgeoisie was fierce. In this period, the number of joint state-private enterprises steadily increased, and their successful operation was not only always reported by the press, but it was also a central topic at political study meetings. Some workers even asked, "Why didn't our factory become a joint state-private enterprise? When will it be our turn?" In the meantime, capitalists felt the increasing social and political pressure. If Communist propaganda did not persuade the urban bourgeois to accept socialism, it at least made them realize that nationalization was inevitable. Once the new policy of a state monopoly on grain, cotton, and vegetable oil was implemented, it became more difficult to operate private businesses. Under these circumstances, the capitalists wanted to "put an end to the matter as soon as possible."[90]

Now the CCP saw that the time was ripe, and dramatic changes took place in the city. Within three days in January 1956, almost all private factories, mills, trading companies, and major stores were suddenly declared state-private enterprises. Tens of thousands of city dwellers swarmed into the streets for parades to celebrate the victory that "the city had entered into socialism ahead of time."[91]

This socialism, of course, was not complete. Mao Zedong had stressed that the Five Antis Campaign had simply exposed and criticized the corruption of the urban bourgeoisie but had not touched its ideology. Similarly, nationalization was only a change in the ownership of the means of production, but to create a socialist "Geneva of the East," further and greater efforts would be required on the cultural and ideological fronts. In the 1950s, Mao Zedong repeatedly reminded his Party members, "The question of which will win out, socialism or capitalism, is still not really settled."[92] This reminder was a foreshadowing of uninterrupted political campaigns throughout his life.

Conclusion

In the early years of the People's Republic, bureaucratic centralism favored institutional standardization, but an imbalance in regional economic growth necessitated many local variations in development patterns. Therefore, while most Chinese cities followed the Russian model, with a priority on heavy industry, Hangzhou designed its own plan for urban development—to become the "Geneva of the East." Consequently, the traditional tourist and other businesses were preserved and developed at the expense of the city's industrialization. This strategy was dictated not only by economic rationality, but also by the need for a convenient meeting place for the central and local governments. The city provided a pretty location for personal networking and informal politics, which were vital in the Chinese political culture. Because Mao Zedong and other CCP leaders often went to Hangzhou, the scenic beauty and cultural heritage of the city became a resource for the southbound cadres in negotiating their careers.

The phrase "Geneva of the East" never appeared in formal government documents, reflecting the desire of the southbound cadres to distinguish their socialist city from the Western city of Geneva. Nevertheless, people talked about it and tried to make it such a site. This development strategy required that the city leaders honor the local culture, but at the same time they embarked upon programs of social transformation, especially to control religious life and reform the local operas. The year 1954 witnessed both progress and compromise. In the long process toward socialism, the southbound cadres developed a better understanding of the city's cultural resources and became the "comrades of Hangzhou." In building a "Geneva of the East," the southbound cadres could legitimately enjoy their new life. Nevertheless, the "comrades of Hangzhou" never forgot their political goal. They made significant preparations for the socialist transformation of the city's industry and commerce and thus built the capacity for new ideological programs and cultural change.

9
Conclusion

The historical treatment of the Communist takeover of Hangzhou reveals a two-pronged approach toward socialism. First, in the new setting the Communist southbound cadres were saddled with all sorts of political and economic constraints and had to use the debris of the old order to build a new one. Second, in pursuit of their revolutionary goals, they initiated a gradual social transformation with policies that were acceptable if not attractive to a population with an outlook on life that had not yet been reshaped by Communist ideology. This approach was vital to both the survival and the development of a Communist regime in China. Moderate policies in the early 1950s were a pragmatic response to what were believed to be short-term political and social realities; they were intended to provide a platform for much more radical action later on and were not compromises that were manifestations of waning revolutionary fervor. The radical policies that followed were thus a natural outgrowth of the apparent temporizing at the start, not a sharp change of course. This direction not only challenges a seemingly universal pattern in which revolution dies out in the postrevolutionary era, but also explains the controversy over the CCP's political behavior during different periods, a phenomenon that was observed by Meisner and other scholars.[1]

The official Chinese view has ascribed this unique direction to Mao's doctrine of "permanent revolution."[2] On the threshold of the People's Republic, Mao Zedong proclaimed that the nationwide triumph was but the first step in a long march of ten thousand *li*.[3] He pointed out that the CCP had just completed a "bourgeois-democratic revolution" and should waste no time in making all the necessary preparations "to transform it into a socialist revolution."[4] Mao's theory itself, however, could not provide effective models for coping with the immediate and massive problems of practical governance. To set the Chinese revolution on a continuous process, in which the socialist phase was the logical and ineluctable sequel to what had preceded it, the CCP had to demonstrate its ability to rule effectively. At the local level, this task had to be carried out by Communist cadres from the CCP's poverty-stricken rural wartime bases. In 1949, it was by no means clear that these former guerrilla fighters would be capable of performing in the new role.

Although the most popular and lasting expression of the difficult but successful transition was Mao's constant stress on the Party's leadership and its overriding revolutionary goal, this study has shown that Mao's opportunist approach and political ritual shared major credit for the achievements. For the majority of CCP members, the opportunist approach and ritual activities were not Mao's creation but part of peasant culture. They already existed in their rural lives and were then transferred into the new, urban-centered regime. Less than five years after the founding of the People's Republic of China, the CCP had made significant progress in rebuilding state institutions and changing people's ways of thinking. In 1955, Mao and his colleagues decided to speed up agricultural collectivization and the socialist transformation of urban industry, reflecting their judgment that the conditions for socialist revolution were now right. This outcome was a result of the successful implementation of the new urban policy, combined with the upholding of the revolutionary tradition by Communist cadres, most of whom were of peasant origin. It suggests that in the early years of the PRC, rural revolutionary culture contributed to the Communists' new tasks even in a sophisticated urban environment.

Opportunism

At first glance, the PRC appears in its early years to have pursued a gradualist approach to revolution: it executed a series of well-designed political campaigns—each solving a specific problem and one following another—to reach the final goal of a fundamental reconstruction of China's society.[5] This study of the Communist experience in Hangzhou, however, reveals that the ends of policy were not immune to significant modification dictated by local conditions—in other words, those who were to be transformed influenced the goals of the transformers in ways that had a significant effect on the ultimate transformation. Mao Zedong provided the new rulers of Hangzhou with a general vision of his objectives: a New Democracy, the predominance of the working class, the remolding of the bourgeoisie, and a Communist future. There was, however, neither a comprehensive plan nor a specific timetable for China's development. The southbound cadres in Hangzhou appear to have been astute opportunists, carefully seizing every opportunity to push Mao's program forward.

Opportunism was indeed the only approach possible at the local level. The Communist takeover of Manchuria and North China offered little in the way of general guidance for political and social transformation. In these cases, the CCP's stance had been ambiguous, confusing, and sometimes contradictory. The city leaders in Hangzhou first heard Liu Shaoqi, in a speech in Tianjin, proposing to "consolidate the New Democratic system." Then they were informed that Mao Zedong questioned Liu: "Consolidate the New Democratic social order? How?"[6] They first heard that Mao admired Gao Gang's radical socialist measures in Manchuria; then they received Party documents condemning Gao's policy as left deviation.[7] Moreover, in a commercial city such as Hangzhou, the CCP faced problems different from those in the industrialized cities of Manchuria and North China. There was no industrial working class, no tradition of a labor movement, no organized resistance against communism, and no big bureaucratic capitalists. The city leaders had to understand the specific conditions in the city in order to decide how to apply Mao's general principles appropriately. They had, in short, to invent an ideologically sound governing approach suitable to the particular conditions of Hangzhou.

A most telling example of the opportunist tactics was the cadres' success in dealing with the so-called "third group" of people, which included the urban bourgeoisie and intellectuals. Liberal intellectuals and their democratic parties had been the CCP's allies in its war with the GMD. Most of them preferred American democracy rather than Russian communism, but they were eager to contribute to the country's economic and political reconstruction as soon as the Civil War ended. Since the CCP still needed their support and cooperation after 1949, it gave governmental positions or honorable titles to these intellectuals and social notables. Similarly, in order to restore production and develop the economy, the CCP allowed—and from time to time even encouraged—the capitalists and merchants to expand their businesses. Of course the goal of absolute proletarian control made power sharing with any other social groups unacceptable in the long run. The political and cultural influence of liberal intellectuals and democratic parties had to be weakened, and the urban bourgeoisie as a class had to be eliminated. In the early years of CCP rule, these objectives were not abandoned but only postponed.

The outbreak of the Korean War gave the Communists a great opportunity to intensify domestic campaigns to uproot the Western cultural presence and to bring liberal intellectuals to heel. Similarly, the economic malpractices of some businessmen offered the CCP a good reason to launch the Three Antis and Five Antis Campaigns to destroy the political influence of the urban bourgeoisie. To initiate these urban programs of the Communist offensive, the CCP began with defensive slogans—"Resist the American aggression" or "Counterattack the bourgeois onslaught." Although neither the Korean War nor the Antis Campaigns could provide complete solutions to the issue of intellectuals or the urban bourgeoisie, they prepared China for a new and higher stage of revolution. From a study of the campaigns of the early 1950s, one can discern the beginnings of a decisive strike against bourgeois intellectuals in the Anti-Rightists Campaign of 1957.

In Hangzhou we can see several important manifestations of opportunism. First, tactical opportunism meant that Mao's campaigns often changed objectives and themes. This study has indicated that the Five Antis Campaign actually began as a movement against gender abuse and then became an attack on the bourgeoisie; the New Three Antis Campaign began as a criticism against bureaucratism but soon turned into a crusade against "liberalism." These switches were the products of an imaginative and adroit political strategy. But such opportunism had serious drawbacks as well. The campaigns were always fraught with sudden turns, breaks, and restarts. Each campaign destroyed some enemies but created new ones, leaving as many problems as it had solved and necessitating another campaign to deal with them. As a consequence, the combination of revolutionary idealism and opportunist tactics generated a vicious circle of divisive and distracting campaigns that disrupted the economic development of the new republic.

Second, opportunism allowed different and often opposing voices to represent Party thinking. The varied interpretations of Party policy, or arbitrary emphases on different aspects of its meaning, in turn prompted frequent changes in the political climate. For example, in order to quickly stabilize the urban situation, the Communists in 1949 promised leniency to all those who had served in the GMD government, but two years later they stressed that it was necessary to suppress all potential enemies and that all those with "bad historical records" must be arrested, executed, or controlled.[8] Thus the interpretation of policy by Party cadres was substantially dependent upon the cadres' needs, capacity, and resources in different times and places. In most cases, the leaders' policy statements did not get translated directly into general policy but required additional rounds of negotiated interpretation at the local level. While the text and spirit of a policy would be communicated to thousands of cadres who were to put it into practice, more often than not, they distorted and transformed it to meet the circumstances. Our analysis of the CCP's takeover of Hangzhou indicates that the response of the southbound cadres to Mao's policy was not unthinking obedience but creative interpretation.

Third, opportunism allowed flexibility in responses and rationale, and the Party cadres at various levels used the flexibility to incorporate their own concerns in policy implementation. At the same time, Mao could avoid having to take responsibility for potentially unpopular actions and could shift the blame for failures onto policy implementers. Thus, Mao exploited the old Chinese saying, "The scriptures are really good, but the monks distorted them." Even if a person was a victim of the Party's persecution, he could believe that "Chairman Mao knows that I am innocent, but local cadres have abused their power and made up a bogus case against me." So, people complained about the policy implementers but never found it necessary to direct their anger at Mao. For many years, the political opportunism of the top CCP leadership thus enabled the myth of the Party's greatness to survive its crises of trust. The provincial committees and the city leaders in Hangzhou employed the same approach to protect themselves and to cast their subordinates as scapegoats for any policy errors. In the best cases, this type of opportunism empowered Mao and other leaders to make policy adjustments or reorient policies in order to avoid further damage. However, it never helped them face their own mistakes or make fundamental changes.

Opportunism is rooted in the Chinese peasantry. Few opportunities were available to peasants, and rural life was not easily changed. Chinese peasants were usually passive, reactive but not creative. Their potential as a dynamic revolutionary force would not be released unless they saw a real opportunity for change. In China it is said that there are three keys to success in all undertakings: opportunity, geography, and human resources *(tianshi, dili, renhe)*. Opportunity was ranked the most important. It was said that a person should not make any rash moves unless the opportunity was right. This idea was at the basis of famous historical novels such as *The Romance of the Three Kingdoms* and *On the Margin of Water*. Mao Zedong had read such stories many times, and the influence of his early reading in shaping his later strategy is obvious to all scholars.[9]

The Chinese revolution was permeated with opportunism. Mao's guerrilla war strategy was marked by opportunist tactics— "Fight if we can win and run if we cannot." In the early days of the takeover, the southbound cadres implemented Mao's policy of keeping forms intact and not changing content, and they underlined an opportunist choice: taking one step back when conditions offered no immediate gain. They believed that the key to the success of the takeover was not rushing the social transformation, but bringing people order and prosperity, thereby demonstrating the new regime's capacity to run the war-devastated country.

In 1949, Mao and his peasant cadres started to operate in the arena of modern politics, but they did not give up their opportunistic tradition. Thousands of peasant cadres started to run all kinds of modern enterprises without alternative methods. However, opportunist tactics, which had proved successful in the guerrilla war and the takeover, invariably conflicted with the demands of China's modernization in later years. Having accumulated some experience from the early successes of the regime, Mao began to prepare blueprints for ambitious economic programs—such as the Great Leap Forward—that plagued the country with failures and disasters. In a sense, Mao Zedong should not single-handedly shoulder the blame for the failure of China's planned economy since the majority of peasant cadres, like the southbound cadres in Hangzhou, were used to the opportunist approach but not ready for the well-defined development programs of a modern state. In the post-Mao era, the guiding slogan in China's reform has been "groping stones to cross the river." Obviously, this remains an opportunistic strategy, indicating that one part of Mao's legacy has persisted.

Political Ritual

After military victory in 1949 the CCP was still faced with the issue of political legitimation. A fundamental political shift would require that people give up not only the old regime, but change their long-established habits and concepts as well. To make the urban populace identify with the new regime, Mao believed the CCP had to resort to cultural means to change people's way of thinking. For centuries, as China witnessed periodic civil wars, people had upheld the notion that "The winner is the king and the loser is a bandit," implying that "the Mandate of Heaven" came with military conquest. It is important to note, however, that this was not good enough for Mao Zedong, who attempted not only to hold power, but also to continue his revolution.

Mao's permanent revolution after 1949 seemed too vague for most Chinese, so it needed to be symbolized and objectified. All the symbols the CCP employed to make sense of the revolution were embodied in various types of ritual performances. These ritual performances took several forms, with *huiyi* (or *hui*—meetings) the principal ones. The GMD's taxes *(shui)* and the CCP's *huiyi* are pet phrases with which the Chinese describe the political behavior of the two parties: the GMD forced people to pay too many taxes while the CCP demanded that they attend ceaseless meetings. Both served as symbols of state power, though. In paying heavy taxes to the GMD government, the people felt the oppression and exploitation of the state. Tortured by endless Communist *huiyi*, they felt the social pressure and coercive power of the state. Indeed, the CCP's *huiyi* had a ritual function, for they were the symbols of revolutionary power.

This study of Hangzhou provokes a further discussion of the relations between political ritual and regime change. First of all, how much can one consider the Chinese Communist *huiyi* as ritual performances? Ritual is a means of symbolic communication and, at the manifest level, non-instrumental.[10] Moore and Myerhoff explain, "[Rituals] may accomplish tasks, accompany routine and instrumental procedures, but they always go beyond them, endowing some large meaning to activities they are associated with."[11] This study has indicated both the instrumental and ritual aspects of the Communist *huiyi*. These were manifested not only in the ritual forms within *huiyi*, such as singing revolutionary songs, reciting Mao's sayings, or shouting the Party's slogans. More important, *huiyi* were often designed not to solve specific problems but merely as performance. Numerous *huiyi* required self-criticism or confession, but in many cases, people exaggerated their confessions. These "false" confessions, made under pressure, were a performance, but they were taken as expressions of revolutionary enthusiasm and a step in the right direction. It is no surprise, therefore, that leniency or rewards would be offered to those who exaggerated their "guilt."[12] As evident in the Five Antis Campaign, the city leaders of Hangzhou encouraged the capitalists to confess their economic crimes at public meetings. The meeting organizers saw no problem in the gap between what those people confessed and what they had actually done. The meetings had without doubt gone beyond an investigation of crimes and moved to the level of ritual performance.

Lance Bennett writes that ritual is a set of routine procedures used by participants in recurring situations to establish and display the social principles embodied in myth.[13] The Hangzhou experience indicates that the ritual performance of *huiyi* played several crucial roles in Communist politics. From the early political study meetings for government employees to those for the spouses of the capitalists, the *huiyi* system was institutionalized and charged with major functions of Chinese politics.

First, the *huiyi* legitimized the new political order. They were of particular importance because they were part of a perpetual routine. In Hangzhou government institutions, schools, factories, and neighborhoods were required to spend a couple of hours every day or half a day a week holding *huiyi*, which repeatedly delivered the message of Communist leadership and the Communist revolution, instilling these concepts into everyday life.

After Mao's death, the CCP started to criticize the deification of Mao Zedong during the Cultural Revolution. In fact, Mao's deification had started as early as 1949. As the Communists encouraged everyone to sing, "Mao Zedong is the great savior of the people" at public meetings, they forgot the *Internationale,* the song they had learned in the early revolutionary years that taught them, "There never is a savior; neither God nor emperor can save us."[14] The deification of Mao and the mystification of the CCP went on simultaneously. The *huiyi* indoctrinated the participants with the correctness and greatness of the CCP and nudged diverse segments of the urban population to repeatedly express their loyalty to the Communist Party. No *huiyi* were organized to criticize the Party, the government, or their policies. "Symbols," Ted Lewellen writes, "make power sacred."[15] As an activity wrapped in a web of symbolism, *huiyi* helped the CCP make its power sacred and last longer. This helps explain the fact that although the disastrous failure of Mao's Great Leap Forward caused rampant famine, the Chinese people still did not dare revolt against the "sacred" leadership of Mao and the CCP.

Second, *huiyi* helped the CCP establish a monopoly over the "truth" and created a new elite. Party documents were strictly classified, and cadres and Party members could read only the documents permitted for circulation among their own ranks. The masses could not get direct access to most public information but knew only what cadres reported at various *huiyi*. The cadres transmitted selected information about the political situation and Party policies. Their words became the lenses with which people saw the world, and their words became the truth that was unquestionable. As Mao Zedong and the Party were deified, the Party cadres became the middlemen between God and human beings, the brokers of the revolution.

In the 1950s, the peasant cadres in Hangzhou, most at middle or lower levels, had not had a significant voice in the Party's policy making. But the Party's policy could reach the people only through these cadres. In addition, the policies made by the CCP Central Committee were deliberately ambiguous, leaving room for interpretation. Thus in Hangzhou the solutions to political and economic problems were localized. Interpreting the text and spirit of CCP policy, the southbound cadres brought in their values, feelings, and beliefs and then transmitted instructions to the people. *Huiyi* thus created the revolutionary elite who monopolized the truth. At *huiyi,* the manners, style of dress, and accent of the southbound cadres, became the symbols of a new elite, and the local people developed a sense of inferiority. These cadres became symbols of the Party, and any criticism against them was regarded as an attack against the Party.[16]

Third, the most obvious role of *huiyi* in the political process was to inspire the masses to take revolutionary action. Participation in *huiyi* was in itself a symbolic statement about following Mao's revolution. This study has shown how intensively *huiyi* were applied to various political campaigns in Hangzhou. Campaigns would usually begin with mobilization meetings *(dongyuan hui).* They would be followed by study meetings *(xuexi hui)* and move on to struggle meetings *(douzheng hui),* criticism meetings *(pipan hui),* and confession meetings *(jiantao hui).* They would finally conclude with sum-up meetings *(zongjie hui).* Lucian Pye writes that "the dominant emotion of modern Chinese politics has been a preoccupation with hatred coupled with an enthusiasm for singling out enemies."[17] One major purpose of the *huiyi* was to discover who the enemy was. The enemy, according to *huiyi* organizers, might be one's colleagues or oneself, one's wrong behavior or one's wrong thoughts. The symbol of "the enemy" was most important in legitimizing radical actions in the Land Reform, Five Antis, and Thought Reform Campaigns. The CCP liked to use criticism meetings to identify landlords as traitors to the nation, capitalists as greedy profiteers, and intellectuals as the running dogs of American imperialism. A study meeting or a struggle meeting would begin with condemnation of American imperialism and American atrocities in Korea in order to create an atmosphere in which the actions taken against landlords, capitalists, or intellectuals could often be rough, sometimes even violent, and always unreflective. In the 1950s and the following years, *huiyi* were a potent force in the periodical Communist purges and political campaigns to topple the old political order or bring about revolutionary change.

Finally, *huiyi* could bring people together, uniting them in the revolution, and they could also separate them, marking a line between friends and enemies. On the one hand, *huiyi* bound people together and gave them a sense of common purpose. At *huiyi* everyone was required to use the same formal language, including Marxist-Maoist terms. Since people had widely differing interests and pursuits, the symbols used at *huiyi* helped integrate them, and this integration was vital for the new Communist order. On the other hand, different *huiyi* were offered to different people—Party members, non-members, activists, workers, intellectuals, merchants, and the "four categories of evil"—to define their positions in the political hierarchy.[18] *Huiyi* thus also became markers of social classes.

No matter what kinds of *huiyi* people attended, all were required to participate in self-examination and self-criticism so that a sense of "original sin" was instilled in everybody. As this study has indicated, not everyone wanted to attend the *huiyi,* but resistance was regarded as opposition to the new rulers, and those who resisted were quickly marginalized or punished. Thus in the Communist political process *huiyi* were effective not only in distributing Communist values, but also in eliminating unwanted elements. Through both persuasive and coercive means, the CCP ritualized *huiyi* and solidified its political control.

Dual Identities

The Communist takeover of Hangzhou led to a process involving two sorts of search for identity. In one the urban dwellers attempted to find a new sense of belonging and to locate, in Pye's words, "an appropriate paternalistic form of authority."[19] In the other, the southbound cadres strove to establish themselves as the unquestionable political elite in a new geographical and cultural space. This was a process of cultural confrontation and convergence in which both the southbound cadres and the urban dwellers penetrated each other's ranks and both, in the end, emerged with a dual identity.

The southbound cadres came from culturally less developed areas, but their rural culture was now associated with power. They could and did use government resources, including administrative means and propaganda, to spread their culture. No matter how strange their dialect and accent seemed, their language was officially used at the political meetings, and the soft and beautiful Hangzhou dialect became virtually unpresentable on most public occasions. After the Five Antis Campaign, Western suits and traditional gowns disappeared from the streets, and the gray uniform of the Lenin suit became the fashion—a good example of how Mao's revolution penetrated into everyday life. The urban dwellers participated in the Communist rituals and gradually accepted the new beliefs, norms, and symbols that constituted a new culture and formed a new identity—Renmin (people of the New China). This, in turn, helped to legitimize the new state and generated solidarity among its citizens. Although the overwhelming majority of urban people accepted the new identity of Renmin, their class identities did not disappear altogether because the CCP constantly assigned them class labels. These assignments were not always logical. For instance, the Party labeled all doctors, teachers, engineers, and artists as members of the bourgeoisie or petty bourgeoisie. Despite the arbitrary classification, the class labels had an important function: they distinguished the powerful from the powerless in the new republic. In political campaigns as well as in everyday life, the Chinese people would be hopelessly aware of their dual identity: belonging to a broad and ambiguous category of "the people" but at the same time confined to a specific social class.

An identification of the ruled with the rulers is the very foundation of patriarchal authority in Chinese culture. Although a considerable number of top CCP leaders had had "violent and even traumatic confrontations with their fathers,"[20] they believed that the majority of the Chinese would accept the totalitarian family structure in the political arena; the government would have full responsibility and would take on the absolute power of the father figure. In an American presidential campaign, the candidates usually ask whether people's lives are better currently than they were four years ago. Such a question suggests that a president's policy and performance should be the basis for continuity or for a change of administrations. In China, however, as long as people accept the ruler as their official father and mother *(fu mu guan)*, the government has a free hand. Any challenge to it is regarded as the revolt of an unfilial son against his father—a great outrage in Chinese society.

In addition to the wise use of political ritual and opportunist tactics, the southbound cadres in Hangzhou also had the advantage of leadership in the post-revolutionary society. Schram writes that Mao Zedong resonated with "peasant virtue and the vocation of the intellectuals, revolutionary theory and Chinese tradition."[21] Such a characterization can also be used to describe the southbound cadres. First, the southbound cadres were not merely peasants. They had some basic education, had read some books on communism and, more important, had received revolutionary training in wartime, which developed their belief in Mao's theory and inculcated a sincere spirit of devotion. Second, the tough rural environment endowed them with the fine qualities of Chinese peasants (e.g., hard work, endurance, persistence, and the pursuit of a Utopian society of total equality and justice). Mao himself argued that the positive elements of peasant culture combined with Marxist ideology would constitute the ideal revolutionary.[22]

While it had traditionally been traumatic for peasants to leave their homes and long-established way of life and emigrate to cities, the southbound cadres were not poor peasants driven by poverty but war heroes and new rulers. They themselves felt that this understanding and self-identity were imperative. As they used symbolism to push the revolution forward, they also used it to construct their own unique subjectivity and social networks, in which their cultural values were embedded. Their mode of dress, discourse, and accent demonstrated their richly detailed associations: veteran revolutionaries, from a rural background, and CCP members. In addition, they developed a regular ritual to keep the CCP on a pedestal as the people's savior and to make themselves appear glorious and virtuous. It is a Chinese belief that supposedly "rulers are more virtuous than others and thus they deserve more status and power."[23] Although the peasant cadres had only a little education, they did not doubt that their virtue would provide infallible answers to questions in the new regime.

The glorification of the rural past of the peasant cadres determined their persistent prejudice against urban culture. The strong contrast between the poor villages in Shandong and the prosperous commercial city of Hangzhou caused culture shock for the southbound cadres. Although they had to adapt to the new environment, their hostility toward capitalism and market-oriented society resulted in their determination to transform Hangzhou. This sentiment often manifested itself in a distinctly romantic idealization of their self-sufficient society in the wartime bases. In their eyes, the city's consumer culture weakened people's revolutionary will, and even the regional differences between Shandong and Jiangnan, such as the southern dialect, food, and music, were indications of the feeble spirit of the local people.

The CCP's policy in the post-revolutionary society, as noted, was not to physically eliminate the urban bourgeoisie but to expropriate it economically and remodel it culturally. However, cultural transformation was not a one-way process. First, it was hard to define "bourgeois culture," and more often than not, the southbound cadres confused it with urban culture. Actually, the dynamics of urban culture lie in its mixture of different subcultures and in its constant assimilation of new elements to its own benefit. An intense and ever-changing diversity characterizes urban life. As Edwin Chapin wrote, to identify the "diversities of human conditions" was "the first lesson of the street."[24] In Hangzhou diversity created a very resilient culture. Hangzhou, as a consumer city, produced prosperity, facilitated economic and political operations, and provided convenience and enjoyment. No newcomers, including the Communists, could refuse to enjoy them. In this way, Hangzhou quietly changed the southbound cadres as well.

Second, as the old urban elites lost their political and economic influence, they used their cultural capital to renegotiate their living space.[25] Their cultural services were needed by the Communists, who wanted to show that they were not savage conquerors but civilized rulers. Therefore, city antiques became the treasures of the new nobility, and the paintings and calligraphic works of local artists hung on the living room walls of government officials. The Communist leaders and the cultural elite wished to find subjects of conversation beyond politics and to meet on artistic grounds. Famous opera actresses were invited to perform at the new nobility's homes or to escort them to dances. Distinguished writers and composers had the honor of being elected "people's representatives." In addition, even under censorship, professors were allowed to offer certain courses on Western philosophy, and temples and mosques around West Lake continued to be open to pilgrims and visitors. These cultural activities and contacts inevitably had a major impact on the aesthetic and ethical views of the southbound cadres.

Finally, the southbound cadres found that the city's scenic

beauty and cultural facilities could be a political resource for them to establish contacts with Beijing leaders and other important outsiders. In order to entertain their guests they had to know about the city's artistic works, historic treasures, and popular legends. They even studied classical Chinese literature so that they would be able to recite poems to their guests, as many previous mayors had done in the Tang or Song dynasties.[26] In a way, they gradually but inevitably absorbed the local elite culture. They were happy to accept their new identity as the "comrades of Hangzhou." While the peasant cadres tried to use their traditional weapons to obliterate the "degenerate" city, their urban experiences unwittingly undermined their own political definition of identity and reshaped the new rulers.

The southbound cadres were both peasant revolutionaries and the comrades of Hangzhou. The two identities were not parallel, with the latter depending upon the former as its source. People could not be "comrades" unless they were first considered revolutionaries. The identity of peasant revolutionaries was shaped by the political "biography" of the southbound cadres before 1949, in which lies their potential enthusiasm for Mao Zedong's "permanent revolution." In the 1950s, Mao first launched the campaign against Hu Shi's idealism and then mobilized criticism against Yu Pinbo's scholarship in *The Dream of the Red Chamber*. The CCP's cultural crusade later escalated into a wave of arrests of the independent-thinking writer Hu Feng and his friends. Although Hangzhou was not the center of the political whirlpool, the southbound cadres responded positively to Mao's every political campaign, reading each of his measures as one-step-forward progress that addressed their own concerns. Their sense of mission to purify Chinese society did not differ from the attitudes of the Red Guards toward the Chinese traditional culture or Western culture, which may well explain the fact that the majority of the Party's cadres warmly supported the Red Guards in destroying "the Four Olds" at the early stage of the Cultural Revolution of 1966.

The prejudice against urban culture within the CCP persisted and produced a complex contrapuntal policy with "orthodox" Marxist concepts. The issue of intellectuals and urban culture touched off political and factional struggles within the Party. As early as 1949, the differing visions of urban culture within the Hangzhou leadership had already emerged, but Communist cadres with an intellectual background were still able to survive the years of the takeover. They more quickly absorbed the urban culture and adopted the second identity of the "comrades of Hangzhou." However, although these intellectual cadres were veteran revolutionaries and held high positions in the Party and government, the peasant cadres still identified them as "the other people." The cultural gap between the two groups of cadres began to fragment the solidarity that had been formed in the common guerrilla experience before 1949. In the early days of the Communist takeover, most peasant cadres were at middle and lower-level posts. The growth of their influence in the following seventeen years made the Party's cultural program more radical, paving the way toward the Cultural Revolution.

This study of the Communist takeover of Hangzhou, in the end, has explored the unique pattern of China's post-revolutionary society. Why has the Chinese revolution never died? Why can terms such as "Thermidor" and "Bonapartism" not be used to describe stages in the life cycle of the Chinese revolution? How could the CCP sustain the revolution as a viable source for its social actions? Answers to these questions call attention to three inseparable properties of Chinese politics: opportunism, political ritual, and identity formation. Followed by Mao's political campaigns, State coercion was the foundation of the Communist takeover, cultural criticism its expression, and political control its aim. At each step, the CCP depended upon opportunist tactics and political rituals to both motivate and constrain people's political behavior, reminding them of the Party's glorious history and keeping its revolutionary ideals vibrant. The rituals constructed public identity with the Party leadership, and this public identity guided people to organize their lives around Mao's revolution without ever questioning the correctness of Mao's instructions or the Party's programs.

"How the people remember their past," notes Consuelo Cruz on post-colonial societies in Latin America, "shapes what they can make for their future."[27] Similarly, Mao's post-1949 revolutionary drama resulted from the collective memory of the country's heroic revolutionary past. This memory was ultimately of particular significance for the peasant revolutionaries, who strove to hold onto their original revolutionary identity. After many failures in reforms and revolutions in the previous hundred years, the Chinese Communists saw their mission as one of national salvation: changing the whole nature of traditional Chinese civilization and making vital changes in the social and cultural values that had been basic to the structure of this "semi-colonial" society. Both the radical young intellectuals in the New Culture Movement and the Communists in Yan'an had displayed this spirit of cultural iconoclasm. Although the Party's top leadership was comprised of elite intellectuals and a considerable number of students joined the CCP-led nationalist war in later years, the Chinese revolution had a purely peasant basis, and the peasant revolutionaries were the bannerbearers of Mao's revolutionary spirit. This spirit, in terms of both an ethos of asceticism and self-sacrifice and the values of egalitarianism and self-reliance, was required for the transformation of Chinese society, and the peasant cadres believed that they could maintain this spirit by upholding revolutionary practices rather than through economic development per se.

Maintaining their original identity was also vital for the peasant cadres in order to reposition themselves in the post-revolutionary society. It was, however, much harder for the former guerrilla fighters to learn professional management skills than to uphold their wartime traditions. The "permanent revolution," therefore, was not an intangible and abstract ideal of Mao Zedong but a requirement for establishing the moral and cultural authority of the peasant revolutionaries. With this authority the peasant revolutionaries could conquer the old urban elite and triumph over their rivals within the Party—the cadres of intellectual background.

Another major finding of this study is that the revolutionary and non-revolutionary cultures both confronted and compromised with each other. Mao's cadres believed that they could change the whole world but that nothing would change them. In fact, the transformers were also transformed. The peasant revolutionaries all over the country experienced cultural assimilation and changes in their identity. Their new identities were essential in their shift to new roles: sponsors of cultural undertakings and managers of a modern economy. The dual identity of the southbound cadres led to sadly ironic consequences: initially the southbound cadres led the masses to attack the urban bourgeoisie and its culture, while in the Cultural Revolution they were victimized for purportedly having themselves become bourgeois agents.

This irony had an ill omen. In 1962, Mao Zedong became openly skeptical about the success of the Communist takeover of the cities. He worried that urban life had made the southbound cadres smarter but softer, more intelligent but less revolutionary. The CCP's entry into the city, Mao concluded, "is also a bad thing because it caused our party to deteriorate."[28] Whether the deterioration is read as corruption or bureaucratization or civilization, it explicitly implied that the second identity of the southbound cadres had altered them for the worse—in other words, the term "the comrades of Hangzhou" (or of any other city) had lost its revolutionary meaning. According to Mao, when the Communists left their rural bases, they were uprooted from their revolutionary tradition. Mao needed a permanent revolution not only to consolidate Communist power, but also to retain or recover the revolutionary spirit of the Party. Consequently, if almost all political campaigns before the Cultural Revolution were directed against landlords, the bourgeoisie, liberal intellectuals, and the old culture, the most radical political attacks in the Cultural Revolution were doomed to extend to the Communist cadres themselves. This study of Hangzhou has simply touched on some aspects of this ironic evolution of Chinese politics. These links between the "golden age" of the People's Republic and the disastrous ten-year chaos of the Cultural Revolution merit further theoretical and empirical study.

Notes

Introduction

1. According to Maurice Meisner, the pattern of the post-revolutionary society was first put forward by Robert Michels, who predicted at the turn of the century, "The socialists might conquer, but not socialism, which would perish in the moment of its adherents' triumph." Cited in Meisner, *Mao's China and After: A History of the People's Republic* (New York: Free Press, 1986), 56.
2. Ibid.
3. See Xue Jianhua et al., eds., *Chengshi jieguan qinli ji* (The witnesses to the takeover of the cities) (Beijing: Culture and History Press, 1999); Lin Yunhui et al., eds., *Kaige xingjin de shiqi* (The period of triumphant march) (Zhengzhou: Henan People's Press, 1996); Shan Shaojie, *Mao Zedong zhizheng chunqiu 1949–1976* (Mao Zedong in power, 1949–1976) (Hong Kong: Mirror Books, 2000).
4. "Report to Second Session of Seventh Central Committee of the Communist Party of China" (March 5, 1949); in Mao Tse-tung, *Selected Works of Mao Tse-tung* (Beijing: Foreign Languages Press, 1969), 4: 374.
5. For India, see Louis Dumont, *Homo Hierarchicus: The Caste System and Its Implications* (Chicago: University of Chicago Press, 1977); for Africa, Max Gluckman, *Politics, Law and Ritual in Tribal Society* (Chicago: Aldine, 1965); for Latin America, Pedro Carrasco, "The Civil-Religious Hierarchy in Mesoamerican Communities: Pre-Spanish Background and Colonial Development," *American Anthropologist* 63 (1961): 483–497; for Iran, Mary Hegland, "Ritual and Revolution in Iran," in Aronoff, ed., *Culture and Political Change,* 75–94.
6. W. Lance Bennett, "Culture, Communication, and Political Control," in Aronoff, ed., *Culture and Political Change,* 39–52.
7. Lucian Pye, *The Spirit of Chinese Politics: A Psychocultural Study of the Authority Crisis in Political Development* (Cambridge, Mass.: MIT Press, 1968); Edward Friedman, *National Identity and Democratic Prospects in Socialist China* (Armonk, N.Y.: M. E. Sharpe, 1995); Tony Saich, *New Perspectives on the Chinese Communist Revolution* (Armonk, N.Y.: M. E. Sharpe, 1995); Ralph Thaxton, *China Turned Rightside Up: Revolutionary Legitimacy in the Peasant World* (New Haven, Conn.: Yale University Press, 1983); Richard Solomon, *Mao's Revolution and the Chinese Political Culture* (Ann Arbor: University of Michigan Press, 1998).

8. Steven Levine, *Anvil of Victory: The Communist Revolution in Manchuria, 1945–1948* (New York: Columbia University Press, 1987), 248.
9. CCP Work Team, "The Investigation of the First Hangzhou Textile Factory" (1949); Hangzhou Municipal Archives (HMA), 1/1/21. (Cited hereafter as HMA.)

Chapter 1: *On the Eve of the Takeover*

1. CCP Central Committee, Document Research Division, *Mao Zedong nianpu* (A chronological record of Mao Zedong), 4 vols. (Beijing: Central Documents Press, 1993), 3: 297.
2. Yan Changling, *Jingwei Mao Zedong jishi* (Records of guarding Mao Zedong) (Changchun: Jilin People's Press, 1998), 238–239.
3. Pang Song and Lin Yunhui, *Liguo xingbang: 1945–1956 nian de Mao Zedong* (Founding the state: Mao Zedong in 1945–1956) (Beijing: Chinese Youth Press, 1993), 113.
4. As early as December 1947, Mao Zedong said, "In contrast to the Kuomintang, the Communist Party of China not only has the confidence of the broadest masses of the people in the liberated areas but also has won the support of the broad masses in the areas and big cities under Kuomintang control." Mao Tse-tung, *Selected Works,* 4: 170. According to Suzanne Pepper, the situation in 1947 was not clear yet. She comments on Mao's statement: "Was this a reasonably accurate evaluation or was Mao perhaps indulging in a bit of rhetoric? Conflicting reports indicate that the question was a difficult one for foreign observers to answer even then." Suzanne Pepper, *Civil War in China: The Political Struggle, 1945–1949* (Berkeley: University of California Press, 1978), 89–90.
5. "Report to the Second Plenary Session of the Seventh Central Committee of the Communist Party of China"; in Mao Tse-tung, *Selected Works,* 4: 365.
6. See CCP Central Committee, Document Research Division, *Liu Shaoqi nianpu* (A chronological record of Liu Shaoqi), 2 vols. (Beijing: Central Documents Press, 1996), 141. This document did not release the exact number of people killed. As one informant told me in an interview in the summer of 1998, there were about three thousand innocents killed in one district in Hebei. Violence and the "left deviations" were hardly controlled until the Fourth Field Army crossed the Great Wall and the battle of Beijing-Tianjin started. Radical land reforms were postponed.
7. Cited in ibid., 141. Unless otherwise noted, translations from the Chinese are mine.
8. Pang Song and Lin Yunhui, *Liguo xingbang,* 119.
9. "The Work of Land Reform and of Party Consolidation in 1948"; in Mao Tse-tung, *Selected Works,* 4: 255.

10. Ibid., 252.
11. Ibid., 251–252.
12. See CCP Committee of Lunan District, "Decision on Stopping the Land Reform and Concentrating All Efforts on Production and Relief"; Linyi Municipal Archives (LMA), G1/2/11. (Cited hereafter as LMA.)
13. "On the Policy Concerning Industry and Commerce" (February 27, 1948); in Mao Tse-tung, *Selected Works*, 4: 203.
14. One of the five party secretaries, Ren Bishi, even gave firm orders to prohibit arbitrary arrests and killing and to protect industry and commerce in the newly liberated areas. See "Some Issues in Land Reform," *People's Daily*, March 28, 1948.
15. Located in Henan Province, central China, Luoyang was an important stronghold of the Guomindang troops. The PLA first stormed Luoyang on March 14, 1948, and then evacuated the city in order to destroy the GMD's effective strength in mobile warfare. On April 5, 1948, the PLA recaptured the city, and, as Mao Zedong reckoned, would securely hold it thereafter.
16. Mao Zedong, "Telegram to the Headquarters of the Luoyang Front after the Recapture of the City"; in Mao Tse-tung, *Selected Works*, 4: 247–249.
17. Ibid.
18. Bo Yibo, *Ruogan zhongda juece yu shijian de huigu* (A retrospect of some crucial decisions and events) (Beijing: Party School Press, 1991), 6.
19. Ibid., 6–7.
20. CCP Central Committee, *Mao Zedong nianpu*, 305.
21. Cited in Bo Yibo, *Ruogan*, 7.
22. "The Work of Land Reform"; in Mao Tse-tung, *Selected Works*, 4: 258.
23. "On the September Meeting: Circular of the Central Committee of the Communist Party of China" (October 10, 1948); in Mao Tse-tung, *Selected Works*, 4: 274.
24. Pang Song and Lin Yunhui, *Liguo xingbang*, 130.
25. Mao Tse-tung, *Selected Works*, 7: 110–111.
26. After a short-lived alliance against warlords, the GMD and CCP split up in spring 1927. Most Communist members in Shanghai were arrested and executed; the survivors were forced to give up urban revolution and went to rural areas to wage a guerrilla war.
27. "On the September Meeting"; in Mao Tse-tung, *Selected Works*, 4: 274. Also see CCP Central Committee, *Mao Zedong nianpu*, 343.
28. "Turn the Army into a Working Force" (February 8, 1949); in Mao Tse-tung, *Selected Works*, 4: 337.
29. CCP Executive Committee, "Summary of the Working Experience in Shijiazhuang" (August 1948); HMA, 1/1/54.
30. Ibid.
31. Chen Yun, *Selected Works of Chen Yun, 1926–1949*, 273–274.

32. CCP Central Committee, *Liu Shaoqi nianpu*, 146.
33. Telegram from the CCP Central Committee to the East China Bureau, December 18, 1948. In ibid., 170.
34. Secretariat of the CCP North China Bureau, "The Current Situation in North China and Our Tasks in 1949"; Shanghai Municipal Archives (SMA), 1/717. (Cited hereafter as SMA.)
35. James R. Townsend, "Intra-Party Conflict in China: Disintegration in an Established One-Party System," in *Elites in the People's Republic of China*, ed. Robert A. Scalapino (Seattle: University of Washington Press, 1972), 7.
36. "On the September Meeting"; in Mao Tse-tung, *Selected Works*, 4: 274.
37. These were the first instructions on preparing cadres for the takeover of the newly liberated areas (mainly South and Southeast China). Actually, it was impossible to recruit 53,000 cadres in a short time. On June 11, 1949, the CCP Central Committee issued another directive, "The Disbursement of 38,000 Cadres," for the takeover of nine provinces in Southwest and Northwest China. These cadres were mainly recruited from Manchuria and North China. See Wei Zhongyun et al., eds., *Zhongguo renmin jiefangjun xinan Fuwutuan Zuzhi Shi* (The organizational history of the PLA Southwest Service Regiment) (Chongqing: Society for History of the PLA Southwest Service Regiment, 1989), 3–4.
38. Ibid.
39. During the Sino-Japanese War, the Communists divided Shandong into five regions: Luzhongnan, Binhai, Luzhong, Jiaodong, and Bohai. Since the Communists did not come to power then, this informal division was basically for Communist guerrilla warfare and secret activities and was not recognized by the GMD government.
40. *The Art of War*, by Sun Zi (Sun Tzu), has been much admired in the West. The first translation was by a French missionary two hundred years ago, and many Western military leaders, including Napoleon and Nazi generals, have studied it and used what they learned in their battles. See Sun Tzu, *The Art of War*, trans. Ralph D. Sawyer (Boulder, Colo.: Westview Press, 1994), 79.
41. See Joseph W. Esherick, *The Origins of the Boxer Uprising* (Berkeley: University of California Press, 1987), especially chapter 4.
42. "History of the Linyi Normal School"; LMA, G4/1/1.
43. See Arif Dirlik, *The Origins of Chinese Communism* (New York: Oxford University Press, 1989).
44. According to local archives, the most popular schools for Luzhongnan students in the 1920s were the Qingdao Business School, the Jinan Normal School, the German-sponsored Tongji University, and the Transportation University in Shanghai.
45. The CCP leaders Li met included Wang Jinmei and Deng Enming, who

organized the first CCP branch in Shandong. See CCP Shandong Committee, *Zhonggong Shandong lishi dashi ji* (Chronology of the CCP in Shandong) (Jinan: Shandong People's Press, 1992), 18.

46. During the period of the GMD-CCP united front, Li Qingqi participated in the CCP-organized Shanghai workers' uprising. After the united front dissolved, Li Qingqi was arrested and executed at the age of twenty-six. Li Qingwei survived the first Civil War (1927–1937), and in 1938 he went to Yan'an to join the Communist army.
47. Committee for the Collection of Party History Materials, Ju County, "The Fule Mount Party Branch, Ju County"; Cangshan County Archives (CCA), G1/2/7. (Cited hereafter as CCA.)
48. Ibid.
49. "Report on an Investigation of the Peasant Movement in Hunan" (March 1926); in Mao Tse-tung, *Selected Works*, 1: 23.
50. "Instructions of the CCP Linyi Committee" (June, 1932), 3. LMA, G2/1/5.
51. Zhou Mengming and Zhuang Chuanzhang, eds., *Yimeng xinghuo* (Revolutionary spark in Yimeng) (Jinan: Shandong University Press, 1990), 49.
52. CCP Cangshang County Committee, "Collected Materials Relating to the Cangshang Uprising," 23; CCA, G1/1/11.
53. Ibid.
54. North China Bureau of the Communist Party, "Instructions to Shandong Party Organization," September 1937; CCA, G2/1/3.
55. On August 6, 1938, Mao Zedong sent a telegram to Liu Shaoqi, then secretary of the NCB: "The military forces in Shandong should be named as the guerrilla branch of the Eighth Route Army.... The Anti-Japanese Allied Army is not a good name." On August 8, Mao sent a second telegram reaffirming the existing decree: "For all guerrilla branches getting support from the broad mass of the people and stationed along with the allied Party and army, it is better to be renamed the Eighth Route Army. Otherwise they would be controlled by the Guomindang." See Xin Wei et al., eds., *Shandong jiefang qu dashi ji* (Chronology of events in Shandong liberated area) (Jinan: Shandong People's Press, 1982), 27–28.
56. See "Visit a Village, Liberate a Village, and Consolidate a Village," *Mass Daily*, editorial, January 21, 1942. *Mass Daily* was the newspaper of the CCP Provincial Bureau of Shandong; it started publication on January 1, 1939.
57. *Mass Daily*, June 25, 1944.
58. Xin Wei et al., eds., *Shandong jiefangqu dashi ji*, 71.
59. CCP Linyi Committee, *Zhonggong Yimeng dangshi dashi ji* (Chronological Record of Party History in the Yimeng Area) (Jinan: Shandong People's Press, 1992), 244.

60. CCP Linyi Committee, *Zhonggong Lunanqu dangshi dashi ji 1919 wuyue zi 1949 jiuyue* (Chronology of the CCP in Lunan, May 1919–September 1949) (Jinan: Shandong People's Press, 1991), 139–140.
61. Ibid., 165.
62. But Most victims were not acquitted until 1978. Ibid., 140.
63. CCP Shandong Bureau, "Decision on Reconstruction of Party Branches"; in Xin Wei et al., eds., *Shandong jiefangqu dashi ji,* 144.
64. CCP Linyi Committee, *Zhonggong Lunanqu,* 170.
65. Ibid., 165.
66. Ibid., 313.
67. "New Instructions on the Reexamination of Shandong Land Reform" (November 26, 1947); LMA, G4/1/82.
68. Interview with Zhu Mengming, Linyi, June 12, 1998. Zhu is the director of the research division for local Party history in the city of Linyi. He told me that he could not yet use these materials in the writing of local Party history.
69. See Jing Su and Luo Lun, *Landlord and Labor in Late Imperial China: Case Studies from Shandong,* trans. with an introduction by Endymion Wilkinson (Cambridge, Mass.: Harvard University Press, 1978).
70. See the introduction in ibid., 8.
71. The CCP Committee of the Linyi District pointed out that "Most sons and daughters of the landlords, local gentry, patriotic intellectuals, and even Guomindang members in the Yimeng revolutionary base had joined our Party and armies and made constructive contributions to the victory of the War of Resistance against the Japanese." CCP Linyi Committee, *Zhonggong Lunanqu,* 223.
72. In Luzhongnan people contributed in accordance with their annual income: peasants with annual incomes below 100 kilograms of wheat were exempt from payment; those with incomes of 100–200 kilograms of wheat paid 1–4 percent; those with incomes of more than 200 kilograms paid a 1 percent surcharge for every extra 50 kilograms. See "Measures for Fair Distribution of War Burden in Shandong," issued by the CCP Shandong Executive Committee in War Time (SECWT), October 20, 1941. The SECWT was renamed the Shandong Administrative Committee on August 30, 1943; Zaozhuang Municipal Archives (ZMA), 1/1/11. (Cited hereafter as ZMA.)
73. In May 1946, there were two anti-land reform revolts in the counties of Mengshan and Mengyin; they were quickly suppressed on May 29; ZMA, 4/5/3.
74. Mao Tse-tung, *Selected Works,* 4: 219.
75. In 1948, this view was propagated and circulated by Communist news agencies, newspapers, and radio stations. Mao Zedong pointed out that "this is a serious error of principle." See "Correct the 'Left' Errors

in Land Reform Propaganda"; in Mao Tse-tung, *Selected Works,* 4: 197.
76. The abbreviations for both Zhejiang and Guangdong Provinces are pronounced *"yue",* but they are two different words: Zhejiang is 越, while Guangdong is 粤. Zhejiang's local opera, *yueju* (also known as Shaoxing Xi), is 越剧, while Guangdong's *yueju* is 粤剧.
77. James Gao, *Meeting Technology's Advance: Social Change in the Railway Age* (Westport, Conn.: Greenwood Press, 1997), 160.
78. In 1936, archaeologists unearthed black pottery, stone tools, jade, and burlap. Known as artifacts of the Liangzhu Culture, these were dated back 4,700 years.
79. See Zhuge Ji and Ying Yuzhen, eds., *Wu-Yue shishi bian nian* (complete chronology of the Kingdom of Wu-Yue), vol. 2 (Hangzhou: Ancient Books, 1990). Also see Ouyang Xiu, *Ouyang wenzhonggong ji* (Selected works of Ouyang Wenzhong), ed. by Zhou Bida; n.p., 1195–1224.
80. Zhou Feng et al., eds., *Wu-Yue shoufu Hangzhou* (Hangzhou: The Capital of the Wu-Yue Kingdom) (Hangzhou: Zhejiang People's Press, 1988), 33–36.
81. Zhong Sulong, "Hangzhou binghuo" (War disaster in Hangzhou); manuscript copied by Xingxian; 2; Zhejiang Provincial Archives (ZPA), J1/1/24. (Cited hereafter as ZPA.)
82. See Li Hangyu, *Lao Hangzhou* (Old Hangzhou) (Nanjing: Jiangsu Art Press, 2000), 87–92.
83. Tan Qixiang, "Evolution of the Urban Development of Hangzhou," in Zhou Feng et al., eds., *Wu-Yue shoufu Hangzhou,* 13.
84. Based on three local annals *(Qiandong Annals of Lin'an, Cunyou Annals of Lin'an, and Xianchun Annals of Lin'an),* Lin Zhengqiu estimates that the population in Hangzhou (including adjacent counties) in 1102–1106 was 296,615. It increased to 552,507 in 1165–1173, grew to 767,739 in 1241–1252, and reached 1,240,760 in 1265–1274. See Ling Zhengqiu, "Jingshi jiu simin, renkou guan quanguo" (People from all parts poured into the capital, making it the city with the largest population in the country), in Zhou Fen et al., eds., *Nansong jingcheng Hangzhou* (Hangzhou: The Capital of the Southern Song dynasty) (Hangzhou: Zhejiang People's Press, 1988), 76–84.
85. Tao Gu wrote, "[Hangzhou] is a paradise on earth." Tao Gu in *Qingyi lu;* cited in Zhou Feng et al., eds., *Wu-Yue shoufu Hangzhou,* 235.
86. See Zhou Feng et al., eds., *Yuan Ming Qing mingchen Hangzhou* (Hangzhou: A famous city in the Yuan, Ming, and Qing dynasties) (Hangzhou: Zhejiang People's Press, 1997), 38.
87. David E. Mungello, *The Forgotten Christians of Hangzhou* (Honolulu: University of Hawai'i Press, 1994).
88. Gao, *Meeting Technology's Advance,* chapter 4.

89. Leng Xiao, "Overview of the Socialist Transformation of Capitalist Industry and Commerce in Hangzhou"; in *Zhejiang zibenzhuyi gongshangye de shehuizhuyi gaizhao* (A selection of materials on the socialist transformation of capitalist industry and commerce in Zhejiang) (Hangzhou: CCP Zhejiang Committee, Department of Propaganda, 1959), 503.
90. Leng Xiao, "The Socialist Transformation of the Hangzhou Silk Industry"; in *Zhejiang zibenzhuyi*, 513.
91. "The Transportation Business in Hangzhou" *Zhejiang Daily*, November 18, 1950, 3.
92. See manuscript dated October 11, 1953, 1–5, in *Hangzhoushi chaye, chaguanye tong ye gonghui dangan shilian xuanbian, 1939–53* (A selection of archival materials on professional associations of tea commerce and teahouses in Hangzhou, 1939–53) (HMA, 1996).
93. See files from 1954 and 1959, 18–33, in *Hangzhoushi sichouye tongye gonghui dangan shiliao xuanbian, 1937–60* (A selection of archival materials on professional associations in the silk industry in Hangzhou, 1937–60) (HMA, 1996). Cited hereafter as *Sichouye gonghui*.
94. Guandi (the emperor of Guan) is a legendary hero named Guan Yu who lived in the period of the Three Kingdoms (220–263). His bravery and loyalty made him a Chinese god worshipped among businessmen and police officers.
95. Cao Juren, *In Front of the Yuanminglou*. Cited in Li Hangyu, *Lao Hangzhou*, 137.
96. Wen-Hsin Yeh, *Provincial Passages: Culture, Space, and the Origins of Chinese Communism* (Berkeley: University of California Press, 1996), 7.
97. Guo Moruo, "On Gu Mount" (January 30, 1925). Cited in Wu Zhanlei, ed., *Yi Jiangnan: Mingren bixia de lao Hangzhou* (In memory of Yi Jiangnan: Hangzhou penned by famous writers) (Beijing: Beijing Press, 2000), 154. Guo Moruo (1892–1978) was a poet, historian, and social activist. He was the president of the Chinese Academy of Science and a deputy prime minister of the PRC.
98. Zhong Sulong, "Hangzhou binghuo"; ZPA, J1/1/24.
99. Mao Tse-tung, *Selected Works*, 4: 364.
100. CCP Central Committee, *Liu Shaoqi nianpu*, 142, 144, 158–159.
101. The book, *Jia Shen San Bai Nian Ji*, was a must-read in the Yan'an Rectification Movement in the 1940s. Mao Zedong to Guo Moruo, November 21, 1944. In CCP Central Committee, *Mao Zedong nianpu*, 2: 559.
102. Ibid.
103. In the ZMA, there is an advertisement by the cultural troupe of the Luzhongnan Military District for its opera performance of *The King Li Zicheng*, December 1948.
104. Cited in Pang Song and Lin Yunhui, *Liguo xingbang*, 171.

105. "Report to Second Session of Seventh Central Committee of the Communist Party of China" (March 5, 1949); in Mao Tse-tung, *Selected Works*, 4: 362.
106. Ibid.

Chapter 2: *Training the Cadres*

1. ECB, "Instructions on Sending 15,000 Cadres from Shandong Province to Newly Liberated Areas"; SMA, D1/711.
2. CCP Zaozhuang Committee, "Lunan geming shi" (A revolutionary history of Lunan), unpublished manuscript, 600.
3. "Notice of the Front-Supporting Committee of the ECB" (November 17, 1948); ZMA, G1/1/7.
4. Cited in CCP Zaozhuang Committee, "Summary of Logistic Work at the Huaihai Battle" (February 1949); ZMA, G1/2/7.
5. CCP Luzhongnan Committee, "Notice on Enlarged Party Committee Meeting" (December 1948); Shandong Provincial Archives (SPA), 30/1/14. (Cited hereafter as SPA.)
6. CCP Linyi Committee, *Zhonggong Lunanqu*, 383.
7. ECB, "Plan for Implementing Instructions of the Central Committee on the Land Reform and Party Rectification in 1948" (July 10, 1948); SMA, D1/718. In this document, the ECB reported the progress of the Production and Relief Campaign in Shandong and emphasized that "the Production and Relief Campaign is the desperate demand of all social classes in Shandong."
8. CCP Luzhongnan Committee, "A Circular on the Famine Situation" (December 1948); CCA, 1/1/14.
9. ECB, "Instructions on Implementing the Directive of the CCP Central Committee for the Preparation of 53,000 Cadres" (December 25, 1948); SMA, D1/711.
10. Ibid. Also see the CCP Luzhongnan Committee, Organizational Department, "A Summary Report on Assembly and Preparation" (March 7, 1949); Jinan Municipal Archives (JMA), 30/1/59/2. (Cited hereafter as JMA.) The "leaders at the district level" are deputies to the governors and other leading officers in a provincial government.
11. ECB, "Instructions on Implementing the Directive of the CCP Central Committee for the Preparation of 53,000 Cadres" (December 25, 1948); SMA, D1/711.
12. See Tan Zhenlin, "Some Elaboration on the Current Situation and Policy" (February 1949); ZPA, 46/1/181/5.
13. CCP Luzhongnan Committee, "Instructions of the District Committee: Implementation of ECB Instructions" (February 1, 1949); ZMA, 1/12/1.

14. CCP Zaozhuang Committee, "Lunan geming shi," 601.
15. CCP Luzhongnan Committee, "Instructions of the District Committee: Implementation of ECB Instructions" (February 1, 1949); ZMA, 1/12/1. See also CCP Zaozhuang Committee, "Lunan geming shi," 185–187.
16. CCP Luzhongnan Committee, "Education Outline on Transferring Cadres to the South" (February 7, 1949); CCA, 1/1/14.
17. Minutes of the CCP Zhaobo County Committee (February 11, 1949); CCA, 1/1/8.
18. CCP Luzhongnan Committee, "Summary Report on the Assembly and Preparation of Cadres" (March 7, 1949); SPA, 30/1/59/2.
19. Other leaders of the two brigades were as follows: for the Fifth Brigade, political commissar—Wang Xing; secretary of organizational department—Cui Xiaodong; secretary of propaganda—Zhou Lin; general secretary—Shang Xiangqian; for the Seventh Brigade, political commissar—Lu Zhixian; secretary of organizational department—Zhang Tao; secretary of propaganda—Yang Yuanshi; general secretary—Sun Wencheng. CCP Luzhongnan Committee, "The Allocation of Transferred Cadres (District Committee, District Government, and Military District)"; SPA, 46/2/242/2. Later, some cadres from these two brigades did not go to Hangzhou, but some cadres from other brigades were transferred to Hangzhou. For example, Lin Hujia, the director of the propaganda department of Luzhongnan District, was the head of the Third Brigade. After the arrival of his brigade in Zhejiang, he was also transferred to Hangzhou.
20. Cited in CCP Zaozhuang Committee, "Lunan geming shi," 601.
21. CCP Luzhongnan Committee, "Education Outline on Transferring Cadres to the South" (February 7, 1949); CCA, 1/1/14.
22. Ibid.
23. Ibid.
24. CCP Linyi Committee, *Zhonggong Lunanqu*, 381.
25. Minutes of the CCP Zhaobo County Committee (February 11, 1949); CCA, 1/1/8.
26. "Instructions of the Executive Committee of the Fifth Prefecture" (June 15, 1949); ZMA, 1/30/6.
27. Telegram from ECB to CCP Luzhongnan Committee, February 9, 1949; CCA, 1/1/8.
28. Interview with Li Xingsheng, Hangzhou, March 15, 1998. Li was among the rural cadres who moved to Hangzhou in 1949.
29. Telegram from ECB to CCP Luzhongnan Committee, February 10, 1949; CCA, 1/1/14.
30. Propaganda Department of the Sixth Prefecture, "The Prefectural Organ Established a Formal School" (March 5, 1949); LMA, 3/1/114.

31. "Final Report on Literacy Study of *Xian, Qu,* and *Xiang* Party Cadres in Binhai District" (December 1949); LMA, 3/1/114.
32. CCP Fifth Prefecture Committee of Luzhongnan, "A Decision on Mobilization and Assembly of the Transferred Cadres" (February 12, 1949); CCA, 1/1/14.
33. See Meisner, *Mao's China,* 85.
34. In the scholarly debate on Chinese peasant culture, I share Thaxton's argument that Chinese peasants did have an anti-Confucian tendency and a tradition of "subsistence practices carried out separately from the supervision of the dominant classes in the towns and cities and peasant ideas about reality, justice and authority conceived independently of any belonging to the dominant Confucian state." Thaxton, *China Turned Rightside Up,* xv. Thaxton writes that he would not go so far as to argue that the "little tradition values" with which the CCP originally interacted were institutionalized to become the dominant values shaping the PRC state, but it seems to me that this argument has some truth.
35. CCP Sixth Prefecture Committee, "Work Report for February" (February 4, 1949).
36. Interview with Gao Ke, Shanghai, January 10, 1998.
37. ECB, "Instructions on Sending 15,000 Cadres from Shandong Province to Newly Liberated Areas"; SMA, D1/711.
38. The anti-American movements included demonstrations protesting the rape of a Chinese girl by American soldiers on December 25, 1946, in Beijing and the demand that American Marines withdraw from the city of Qingdao.
39. "The Chiang Kai-shek Government Is Besieged by All the People"; in Mao Tse-tung, *Selected Works,* 4: 135.
40. Interview with Liu Bo, Hangzhou, May 20, 1997.
41. Ibid.
42. "Chinese Revolution and the Chinese Communist Party"; in Mao Tse-tung, *Selected Works,* 2: 301–334.
43. Interview with Xiao Yi (former secretary of Tan Qilong), Hangzhou, May 20, 1997.
44. See "Orientation of the Youth Movement"; in Mao Tse-tung, *Selected Works,* 2: 247–248.
45. "Talks at the Yan'an Forum on Literature and Art" (May 1942); in Mao Tse-tung, *Selected Works,* 3: 73.
46. *Dagong Daily,* June 24, 1949.
47. Tan Qilong, "Leading the Southbound Team to Take over Hangzhou"; in *Chengshi de jieguan yu shehui gaizao, Hangzhou juan* (The takeover of the cities and transformation of society, Hangzhou vol.) (Beijing: Modern China Press, 1996), 329.

48. Ibid., 329–330.
49. Yang Siyi, minister of the Provincial Organizational Department, mentions the conflict between the southbound cadres and the local cadres in his diary (entry for May 23, 1949), pointing out that the southbound cadres wanted to dominate everything (August 10, 1949). He also mentions a tendency toward localism and that some local leaders did not welcome the arrival of the southbound cadres (June 24, 1949). Yang Siyi, Diary (Hangzhou: Society for History of the New Fourth Army, 1997).
50. Mao's report is in Mao Tse-tung, *Selected Works*, 4: 361–375.
51. Interview with Xiao Yi, Hangzhou, May 20, 1997.
52. The first trade union organization was a cooperative of the workers in the Zhejiang Publishing House, which published a newspaper to advocate the "liberation of workers." The first peasant association, the Xiaoshang Yaqian Peasant Association, was established on September 27, 1921. It declared that it was "confronting the landlords and all landowners." See CCP Zhejiang Committee, *Zhongguo gongcandang Zhejiang lishi dashi ji, 1919–1949* (Chronology of the CCP in Zhejiang, 1919–1949) (Hangzhou: Zhejiang People's Press, 1990), 12–14.
53. The eastern Zhejiang base involved sixteen counties and was one of nineteen Communist-controlled areas during the war against Japan. The commander of the guerrillas at this base was He Kexi, and the political commissar was Tan Qilong. In the western Zhejiang base the Communists controlled ten counties. Their chief commander was Su Yu. See ibid., 3.
54. Yang Siyi, *Diary*, entry for May 12, 1949.
55. Central China Bureau (CCB), "Instructions to CCP East Zhejiang Committee"; ZPA, 23/7/1/6.
56. CCP South Zhejiang Committee, "Manifesto on Meeting the PLA Marching to Jiangnan" (April 22, 1949); SMA, 1/1254.
57. CCP East Zhejiang Committee, "Resolution on Urban Work" (February 1949); ZPA, 23/7/16.
58. See CCP Zhejiang Committee, "Second Instruction on the Unity of Cadres" (July 15, 1949); ZPA, 23/8/1/29.
59. Yang Siyi, *Diary*, entry for May 12, 1949.
60. Ibid.
61. See chapter 1.
62. Interview with Cui Bo, Hangzhou, March 19, 2001.
63. ECB, "Instructions on the Takeover of Jiangnan Cities" (April 21, 1949); ZPA, 23/8/1/1.
64. "Order of the Third Field Army" (April 1, 1949); cited in Zhong Qiguang, *Zhong Qiguang huiyilu* (Memoir of Zhong Qiguang) (Beijing: PLA Press, 1995), 384.

65. Ibid., 385.
66. "Recruit Large Number of Intellectuals"; in Mao Tse-tung, *Selected Works*, 2: 303.
67. Pepper, *Civil War in China*, 416.
68. CCP Central Committee, "Instructions on the Proposal to Take over Jiangnan Cities" (April 25, 1949); ZPA, 23/8/1/1.
69. Interview with Liu Xin, Hangzhou, May 19, 1997.
70. "Report to the Second Plenary Session of the Seventh Central Committee of the Communist Party of China," March 5, 1949; in Mao Tse-tung, *Selected Works*, 4: 364.

Chapter 3: *The First Efforts*

1. On October 1, 1949, the PRC was established and a new national flag was introduced—red with five gold stars. According to the government, the largest star stands for the CCP leadership and the four others represent the four social classes: workers, peasants, the petty bourgeoisie, and the national bourgeoisie. The national flag symbolizes Mao Zedong's idea of a "people's democracy."
2. Zhang Tianli, "Mr. Zhang Heng before and after His Term as President of the Hangzhou Municipal Congress," *Hangzhou wenshi ziliao* 18 (Reference materials on the local culture and history of Hangzhou, vol. 18), 3.
3. For an analysis of the "ambiguous feelings among the urban populace," see Meisner, *Mao's China*, 88.
4. Tan Zhenlin et al., "Report on Entering the City of Hangzhou" (May 4, 1949); ZPA, 23/8/1/2.
5. Municipal Bureau of Public Security, "Report on Work in the Second Half of 1949"; ZPA, 23/1/4/6.
6. Interview with Sun Tingfang by Chinese TV-radio; cited in documentary film *Liberating Nanjing, Shanghai, and Hangzhou* (PLA Studio, 1999).
7. *Dangdai Daily*, May 5, 1949. Also see Ke Li, "The Activities of the CCP Underground Organization before and after the Takeover of Hangzhou," in *Chengshi de jieguan*, 344.
8. Tan Zhenlin et al., "Report on Entering the City of Hangzhou" (May 4, 1949); ZPA, 23/8/1/2.
9. Cited in ECB, "Instructions on the Takeover of Jiangnan Cities" (April 1, 1949); SMA, D1-086.
10. Tan Zhenlin, "Speech at the Inaugural Meeting of the Hangzhou Municipal Military Control Committee" (May 7, 1949); ZPA, 23/1/1/1.
11. ECB, "Instructions on the Study of City Policies" (May 5, 1949); ZPA, 23/8/1/1.

12. ECB, "Instructions on the Takeover of Jiangnan Cities" (April 1, 1949); SMA, D1-086.
13. "Announcement of the Military Control Committee of the East China Military District of the Chinese People's Liberation Army, No. 1" (May 7, 1949); ZPA, 23/1/4/6.
14. Shiping Zheng offers a good analysis of dual rule in China, although we have different views on its origin. See Shiping Zheng, *Party vs. State in Post-1949 China: The Institutional Dilemma* (Cambridge: Cambridge University Press, 1997).
15. "Summary of City Security in the Previous Two Months" (August 24, 1949); ZPA, 23/3/8/8.
16. It was the storytellers in Hangzhou who first compiled and told stories about rural rebels in Shandong and provided the original oral version for what became *On the Margin of Water*.
17. Wu Song is a hero in *On the Margin of Water*, which was adapted for various local operas. A local actor in Hangzhou, Gai Jiaotian, gained a national reputation by performing in this drama and got the nickname of "the living Wu Song."
18. Interview with Liu Bo, Hangzhou, May 25, 1997. Liu Bo graduated from Huadong University and followed the PLA to Hangzhou. In 1949 he was a secretary in the Military Control Committee of Hangzhou.
19. Interview with Bian Pengfei, Hangzhou, June 1998.
20. Wang Liangxing, "Report to the GMD City Committee" (October 20, 1948); HMA, J1/1/108.
21. See Zhang Shichang, "The Society of Local Educators on the Eve of the Liberation," *Hangzhou wenshi ziliao* 17 (Reference materials on the local culture and history of Hangzhou, vol. 17), 103. See also Wu Yixun, "Local Finances of the City of Hangzhou, 1927–1947," in ibid., 240. Both silver dollars and paper currency were in circulation, but people preferred the former because they believed silver dollars were far less likely to devaluate.
22. "West Lake in Transformation," *Zhejiang Daily*, May 17, 1950, 3. The *Zhejiang Daily* started publication as the first official newspaper of the CCP Zhejiang Committee on May 9, 1949, six days after the PLA took over Hangzhou.
23. The volunteer police force was formed on April 23, 1949. Its commanders were the secretary of the Chamber of Commerce, Xu Wenda, and the chamber trustee, Sun Jitai. The force was dismissed by the PLA on May 3, 1949, as soon as it entered the city. See Tan Chong, "The Activities of the Hangzhou Volunteer Police Force before the Liberation," *Hangzhou wenshi ziliao* 3 (Reference materials on the local culture and history of Hangzhou, vol. 3), 100–105.

24. Mao Zedong warned the Communists that they must maintain a sharp vigilance against the "sugar-coated bullets" of the urban bourgeoisie. See "Report to Second Session of Seventh Central Committee of the Communist Party of China" (March 5, 1949); in Mao Tse-tung, *Selected Works*, 4: 374.
25. CCP City Works Department, "General Summary of Work in July" (July 1949); HMA, 1/1/10.
26. CCP Zhejiang Committee, "Report of the Urban Situation a Week after Entering the City of Hangzhou"; ZPA, 23/1/4/1.
27. Ibid.
28. Liu Shaoqi's speeches in Tianjin (April–May 1949); in CCP Central Committee, *Liu Shaoqi nianpu*, 164.
29. For Liu's visit to Tianjin and his policy recommendations, see Kenneth G. Lieberthal, *Revolution and Tradition in Tientsin, 1949–1952* (Stanford, Calif.: Stanford University Press, 1980), 40–52. Liu's major points are included in several government documents. See Liu Shaoqi et al., *New Democratic Urban Policies* (Hong Kong: Wencai Publishing, 1949). There were different voices within the Party leadership. In the 1950s the Communist leader in Manchuria, Gao Gang, criticized Liu's policy as "right opportunism." Gao once got support from Mao Zedong, but Mao finally stood with Liu and purged Gao from the Party. In the Cultural Revolution of 1966, Liu Shaoqi became the first target of the anti-revisionist crusade, and his talks in Tianjin became criminal evidence against him.
30. Cited in Lieberthal, *Revolution and Tradition*, 40–52.
31. "Jiang Hua and Lin Feng to Tan Zhenlin and Tan Qilong" (May 19, 1949); HMA, 1/1/15.
32. Labor Bureau, "Report of Work in June" (June 1949); HMA, 1/1/20.
33. "Report by Wang Pingyi to the City Government" (December 19, 1949); HMA, 1/1/15.
34. Ibid.
35. CCP Hangzhou Committee, "Report on Nine Months of Work of the United Front" (January 1950); HMA, 1/23/8/2/6.
36. Ibid.
37. CCP Zhejiang Department of the United Front, "Discussion Meetings on the Non-Party Personages of Various Circles" (1950); HMA, 4/1/2.
38. Hang Jinggang et al., "The Rebirth of the Private Minsheng Pharmaceutical Factory" (1956); HMA, 197/1/7.
39. "Draft of the Organization of the Hangzhou Military Control Committee" (May 1949); ZPA, 23/1/69.
40. Li Fengping and Wang Fang, "Brief Report on Public Security Work in May" (May 29, 1949); ZPA, 23/3/6/4.

41. Department of Public Security, Military Control Committee of Hangzhou, "A Circular of the Department of Public Security" (July 16, 1950); ZPA, 23/3/6/2.
42. Ibid. See also the CCP Zhongcheng District Committee, "Ten-Day Work Plan of the Zhongcheng District" (May 26, 1949); HMA, 1/1/36.
43. Tan Zhenlin, "Speech at the Inaugural Meeting of the Hangzhou Municipal Military Control Committee" (May 7, 1949); ZPA, 23/1/1/1.
44. CCP Zhejiang Committee, "The Decision on Ending the Work of the Previous Municipal Committee and Establishing a New Municipal Committee of Hangzhou" (May 11, 1949); ZPA, 23/1/14/1.
45. This Chinese practice is commonly described as "two signboards but one group of people." One of the purposes of this confusing structure (Party vs. government) is that one signboard is for the public while the other is for internal use.
46. CCP Zhejiang Committee, "Notice on Member List of CCP Zhejiang Provincial Committee" (June 2, 1949); ZPA, 23/1/2/1. The CCP Central Committee approved the composition of the Zhejiang Committee on May 26, a week after the notice was issued.
47. Military Control Committee, "Report on Government Institutions"; ZPA, 23/1/42.
48. CCP Hangzhou Committee, "Summary Report of Seven Months of Work" (March 8, 1950); HMA, 1/1/30. Like the eight urban districts, two county governments (Xiaoshan and Hangzhou) were under the jurisdiction of the Hangzhou municipal government.
49. "Primary Summary Report on the Takeover of the City of Hangzhou" (May 30, 1949); ZPA, 23/8/2/1.
50. Files from 1960 in *Sichouye gonghui*, 34.
51. CCP Zhejiang Committee, "Instructions on Handling the Employees of the Old Institutions in the Process of Takeover" (May 29, 1949); ZPA, 23/1/14/3.
52. Ibid.
53. Ibid.
54. CCP Hangzhou Committee, "Summary Report of Seven Months of Work" (March 8, 1950); HMA, 1/1/30.
55. City Study Committee, "Education Plan for Retained Employees," *Zhejiang Daily*, July 25, 1949.
56. Ibid.
57. "Report to Second Session of Seventh Central Committee of the Communist Party of China" (March 5, 1949); in Mao Tse-tung, *Selected Works*, 4: 361.
58. Ibid., 365.
59. Department of Social Welfare, General Trade Union of Hangzhou,

"Report on Estimated Rice Relief for Unemployed Workers" (September 28, 1949); HMA, 1/3/35.
60. City General Trade Union, "Report of Work in the Last Fifteen Months"; HMA, 1/3/17.
61. "Collection of Papers of the Conference on Urban Works in Manchuria" (February 1949); SMA, 1/728.
62. "Collection of Papers of the Conference on Urban Works in Manchuria" (February 1949); SMA, 1/728.
63. Labor Bureau, "Report of Work in June" (June 1949); HMA, 1/1/20.
64. CCP Zhejiang Committee to the ECB, "Summary Report on the City Situation One Week after Our Entry into Hangzhou" (May 11, 1949); ZPA, 23/1/4/1.
65. Ibid.
66. Ibid.
67. Li Daigen, Jin Ling, and Hu Zhiming, "Investigation on Unemployed Workers in the Silk Industry" (May 5, 1955); HMA, 1/3/19.
68. Department of Propaganda, "Summary on Propaganda Work" (May 1949); HMA, 3/1/1.
69. "Uphold the Correct Line for the Labor Movement against Left Deviation," editorial by the Xinhua News Agency, *Zhejiang Daily,* May 16, 1949.
70. CCP Zhejiang Committee, "Instructions on Factory Work" (May 1949); HMA, 1/1/20. According to the provincial committee's telegram to the First Prefectural Committee, the workers in Nanjing and Wuxi got 6 *jin* of rice (6.6 pounds) per day, so the workers in Hangzhou should have a similar daily wage. The First Prefectural Committee replied that it had finally decided to give workers and college professors the same monthly pay of ¥3,000. See CCP First Prefectural Committee, "Some Additional Suggestions on the Takeover" (undated); ZPA, 23/8/1/32.
71. Cited in Lei Lei, "A Survey of the Silk Industry and Business in Hangzhou," in *Sichouye gonghui,* 40.
72. ECB, "Instructions on the Takeover of Jiangnan Cities" (April 1, 1949); SMA, D1-086.
73. The GMD sentenced Wang Wuquan to twelve years in prison in September 1945. After the Communists took over Hangzhou, his case was reviewed, and Wang was shot in December 1950.
74. Cai Jinxian, "Takeover of the Wufeng Silk Factory," in *Chengshi de jieguan,* 391.
75. Cited in Lei Lei, "A Survey of the Silk Industry and Business in Hangzhou," in *Sichouye gonghui,* 41.
76. Party History Research Group of Zhejiang Province and Party History Research Group of Hangzhou, in *Chengshi de jieguan,* 25.

77. Cai Jinxian, "Takeover of the Wufeng Silk Factory," in ibid., 388.
78. Ibid., 389–393. One old RMB = ¥10,000. On February 28, 1955, the national bank issued new RMB and retrieved the old ones; one new RMB = ¥1. Unless otherwise noted, in this book all monetary denominations are based on the old RMB system.
79. Tan Zhenlin, "Summary of Nine Months of Work after the Liberation of Zhejiang and the Party's Task in 1950" (March 3, 1950); ZPA, 23/8/1/34.
80. Ibid.
81. Ma Xiangping, "Rebirth of the Yuli Ironwork Workshop," in *Chengshi de jieguan*, 396–399.
82. Ibid.
83. See CCP Central Committee, *Liu Shaoqi nianpu*, 199.
84. "The Fulfillment of the Takeover of the City of Hangzhou," in *Chengshi de jieguan*, 10.
85. "Summary of the Struggle against the Silver Dollar Hawkers" (May 17, 1949); ZPA, 23/5/5/1.
86. Song Depu, "The Takeover of the Financial and Economic Institutions of Hangzhou: Recollections of A Participant," in *Chengshi de jieguan*, 378–383.
87. "Announcement of the Military Control Committee of the City of Hangzhou" (No. 3) (May 16, 1949); ZPA, 23/1/4/10.
88. On May 9, 1949, the Military Control Committee published a second announcement banning the JYJ. No circulation of JYJ was allowed in the market, but holders could exchange JYJ for RMB, issued by the Communist People's Bank, at the rate of 135,000:1. The Military Control Committee declared that this rate could change because the GMD continued to issue JYJ in areas it controlled. It also stipulated that all businesses must use RMB for settling accounts and that market prices would no longer skyrocket in accordance with the JYJ's devaluation. On the other hand, the rate between the silver dollar and the RMB could not be fixed. "Announcement of the Military Control Committee of the City of Hangzhou" (No. 2) (May 9, 1949); ZPA, 23/1/4/10.
89. Li Fengping, "Reminiscences of Public Security in the Early Years of Liberated Hangzhou," in *Chengshi de jieguan*, 336–341.
90. CCP Hangzhou Committee, "Summary of the Struggle against the Silver Dollar Hawkers" (May 17, 1949); ZPA, 23/5/5/1.
91. Ibid.
92. "Speculators Who Manipulate the Silver Dollar and Cause Disorder in the Money Market, Wake Up!" Editorial in *Jiefang Daily*. Cited in *Dangdai Daily*, June 8, 1949. *Dangdai Daily* started publication on June 1, 1949. Professing itself to be a private newspaper and "to hold a nongovernmental position," it was actually under the leadership of the CCP Department of Propaganda.

93. *Dagong bao*, June 11, 1949.
94. Propaganda Department, "Summary of Three-Day Propaganda on the Banning Silver Dollar Deals" (June 1949); HMA, 23/5/5/3.
95. *Zhejiang Daily*, January 4, 1950.
96. Ibid., April 9, 1950.
97. Ibid., June 27, 1949.
98. CCP Hangzhou Committee, "Summary of the Struggle against the Silver Dollar Hawkers" (May 17, 1949); ZPA, 23/5/5/1.
99. "Be Concerned with the Well-Being of the Masses, Pay Attention to Methods of Work"; in Mao Tse-tung, *Selected Works*, 1: 149.
100. Tan Zhenlin, "Speech at the Inaugural Meeting of the Hangzhou Municipal Military Control Committee" (May 7, 1949); ZPA, 23/1/1/1.

Chapter 4: One Step Back, Two Steps Forward

1. According to the mailing list of the CCP Hangzhou Committee (June 1949), the first deputy secretary, Lin Feng; the second deputy secretary, Zhang Jinfu; the director of the Office of the Chief Secretary, Chen Boliang; the leaders of the Organizational Department; the head of the Department of Propaganda, Gu Dehuan; and other city leaders all lived at 27 or 15 Shentang Street; HMA, 1/1/6.
2. Tan Zhenlin, "Speech at the Discussion Meeting with Trade Union Cadres and Worker Activists of the City of Hangzhou" (April 28, 1950); ZPA, 23/8/2.
3. Trade Union of the City of Hangzhou, "Investigation of Workers in Various Enterprises of Hangzhou" (April 4, 1950); HMA, 1/13/19.
4. CCP Zhejiang Committee, *Zhongguo gongcandang Zhejiang lishi dashi ji, 1949–1993* (Chronology of the CCP in Zhejiang, 1949–1993) (Beijing: CCP History Press, 1996), 10.
5. Lin Biao, "Report on the Future Work of the Central China Bureau," *Changjiang Daily*, July 4, 1949. Lin Biao made the speech on June 6, 1949. CCB deputy secretary Deng Zihui reiterated the argument on other public occasions. About a month later, Lin's speech was published in the Communist organ newspaper, *Changjiang Daily*, indicating approval from the CCP Central Committee.
6. Mao Tse-tung, *Selected Works*, 4: 363.
7. Tan Zhenlin, "Speech at the First Enlarged Meeting of CCP Provincial Committee"; cited in CCP Zhejiang Committee, *Zhongguo gongcandang Zhejiang, 1949–1993*, 10–11.
8. Ibid., 11.
9. After the campaign to eliminate bandits was completed, the PLA withdrew from the work teams in spring 1950.

10. Cited in *Chengshi de jieguan*, 28.
11. Tan Zhenlin, "Speech at the Inaugural Meeting of the Hangzhou Municipal Military Control Committee" (May 7, 1949); ZPA, 23/1/1/1.
12. CCP Hangzhou Committee, "Report on Government Institutions in the City of Hangzhou"; in *Chengshi de jieguan*, 100.
13. CCP Zhejiang Committee, "Summary Report on the Urban Situation a Week after Entering the City of Hangzhou" (May 11, 1949); HMA, 1/6/2.
14. CCP Zhejiang Committee, Policy Research Division, "On Leadership Problems in the Hangjiang Textile Factory" (June 9, 1949); HMA, 1/1/21.
15. Zhang Wensong, "Scraps of Memory of the Early Days after Beiping's Liberation," in Xue Jianhua, *Chengshi jieguan Qinli ji*, 266. Zhang Wensong was the director of the Propaganda Department at South Hebei Prefecture before 1949. After the Communist takeover of Beijing, he held several important positions, including director of the Policy Research Division of the CCP Beijing Committee and standing member of the committee, director of the city's Education Department, and deputy minister of the Education Department of the PRC.
16. "Instructions on Subsidies to Retained Employees" (May 26, 1949); HMA, 23/5/11/19.
17. Liu Jiqin, "Summary of the Party's Work and Work among the Masses of the Hangzhou People's Court in July" (July 1949); HMA, 1/1/8.
18. CCP Propaganda Department, "Report on Monthly Work in December" (December 1949); HMA, 3/1/1.
19. During the revolutionary war and in the early days of the PRC, the supply system (*gongji zhi*) was used to provide the state cadres and their dependents with the basic necessities of life—that is, cadres received payments in kind rather than salaries. The system was abandoned by the government and the army in 1953–1954 (see chapter 7).
20. CCP Zhejiang Committee, "Summary Report of Seven Months of Work in 1949" (March 8, 1949); HMA, 1/1/30.
21. Mao Tse-tung, *Selected Works*, 4: 374.
22. For the Manchu case, see Philip Kuhn, *Soulstealers: The Chinese Sorcery Scare of 1768* (Cambridge, Mass.: Harvard University Press, 1990), chapter 3.
23. In Mao Zedong's terms, as noted above, the "sugar-coated bullets."
24. CCP Propaganda Department, "Report on Monthly Work in December" (December 1949); HMA, 3/1/1.
25. Ibid.
26. Ibid.
27. Meisner, *Mao's China*, 85.
28. Zhang Youyu, "I Was Appointed to Be the Deputy Mayor of Beijing," in Xue Jianhua et al., eds., *Chengshi jieguan Qinli ji*, 259. On January 15, 1949, Zhang was appointed to be the deputy mayor of Tianjin. But

before he went to this post, he was transferred to Beijing to be the acting deputy mayor in February 1949.
29. Editorial in *Tianjin Daily*, 1948; cited in Liu Shaoqi et al., *New Democratic Urban Policies*, 32–33.
30. Tan Zhenlin, "Speech at the Inaugural Meeting of the Hangzhou Municipal Military Control Committee" (May 7, 1949); ZPA, 23/1/1.
31. It was reported that by the end of 1949, forty-seven thousand bandits had been eliminated and in early 1951, another thirty-six thousand; also, the GMD troops had been wiped out. See CCP Zhejiang Committee, *Zhongguo gongcandang Zhejiang, 1949–1993*, 15, 17.
32. The major religious and semi-religious secret organizations in rural Zhejiang included Christian churches, Buddhist temples, the Green Gang, Yi Guan Dao, and Tongshan Tang. In the Campaign for the Suppression of Counterrevolutionaries all these organizations were banned.
33. Interview with Zhong Ru, Hangzhou, May 29, 1997. Also see Jin Yanfeng et al., *Zhejiang jiaofei jishi* (The True Record of the Elimination of Bandits in Zhejiang) (Hangzhou: Zhejiang People's Press, 1990), 331–336.
34. Mao Zedong sharply criticized this argument. See Mao Zedong, "Closing Address at the Second Session of the First National Political Consultative Conference" (June 23, 1950), in *Jianguo yilai Mao Zedong wengao* (Mao Zedong's manuscripts since the founding of the People's Republic of China) (Beijing: Central Documents Press, 1987–1999), 1: 416.
35. According to the Chinese Law of the Land (1948), a landlord is one who has land but hires others to till it for him and thereby lives from the exploitation of hired labor.
36. Tan Zhenlin, "General Summary of Nine Months of Work after the Zhejiang Liberation and the Party's Tasks in 1950" (May 3, 1950); ZPA, 23/1/1/5.
37. The Fifth Brigade of the southbound cadres arrived in the district on May 4, 1949, and took over the local government five days later. The brigade leader, Qi Yaohua, was appointed the head of the district, and its political instructor was the Party secretary of the district committee. See Qi Yaohua, "How We Took Over the Sixth District of Hangzhou"; in *Chengshi de jieguan*, 353–359.
38. Ibid.
39. Interview with Sun Wencheng, Hangzhou, May 18, 1997.
40. CCP Zhejiang Committee, *Zhongguo gongcandang Zhejiang, 1949–1993*, 23.
41. See CCP Zhejiang Committee: "Decision on Dispatching Government Officials to the Land Reform" (July 1950), and "Decision on Recruiting Intellectual Youth for the Land Reform" (July 1950), cited in ibid.

42. "Primary Summary Report of the Overtake of Hangzhou" (May 30, 1950), ZPA, 23/8/2/2.
43. Interview with Liu Yifu, Hangzhou, January 10, 1997. Liu Yifu (1919–1997) held many important positions in Zhejiang: president of Zhejiang Medical University, chairman of the Zhejiang Provincial Committee on Science and Education, and deputy governor of Zhejiang Province.
44. "Zhejiang" and "Zhijiang" are rather confusing. Zhejiang University was a public school established in 1901 by the Qing government. In 1948, there were 1,872 students (22 graduates, 1,850 undergraduates) and 652 professors and staff. Zhijiang University was founded by an American doctor at Ningbo in 1845, registered in Washington, D.C., in 1920, and then registered with the Chinese government in 1930. The college was associated with the Chinese Christian Association, and most members of the university board were Chinese, but American donations remained its main source of funding. In 1952, the college was closed and its departments merged with other universities.
45. Zhijiang University, "Report on University Affairs (second semester, 1949)" (May 12, 1950); HMA, 52/2/16.
46. The few changes that were made included the dismissal of the previous director of education, Zhong Boyong, and two of his chief assistants, Jin Cheng and Yan Yiwen. The former was the principal of Yushenguan School, and the latter, principal of GaoYenxiang School. Department of Education "Monthly Summary Report of the Department of Education" (July 1949); HMA, 1/1/8.
47. Zhijiang University, "Report on University Affairs (second semester, 1949)" (May 16, 1950); HMA, 52/2/16.
48. Ma Zihua, "The Old Anding, Full of Vigor," in *The Ninetieth Anniversary of the Hangzhou No. 7 School,* ed. Hangzhou No. 7 School (Hangzhou, 1992), 40.
49. Ibid., 37.
50. Ibid., 33.
51. Zhijiang University, "Report on University Affairs (second semester, 1949)" (May 16, 1950); HMA, 52/2/16.
52. Interview with Bian Pengfei, Hangzhou, August 5, 1998.
53. Interview with Liu Bo, Hangzhou, May 20, 1997.
54. Later this slogan was changed to "Education serves proletarian politics and combines with production."
55. Hangzhou Normal School, "Outline of the University Affairs Reform in the First Semester, 1949" (1949); ZPA, 23/1/63.
56. Ibid.
57. General Trade Union, "Summary Report on Workshops for Shop Assistants" (1950); HMA, 1/3/10.

58. Leng Xiao, "An Overview of the Reorganization and Transformation of the Department Stores in the City of Hangzhou" in *Zhejiang zibenzhuyi,* 587.
59. Han Shaoyi, "Preparation for the People's Night School in the Shangcheng District" (June 23, 1949); HMA, 1/1/27.
60. CCP Tianzhang Branch, "How Does the Party Branch in the Tianzhang Silk Factory Lead Production?" HMA, 1/3/9.
61. Ibid.
62. CCP Zhejiang Committee, "Minutes of the Meeting on the Industry and Labor Movement in May" (May 17, 1949); ZPA, 23/8/2.
63. CCP Zhejiang Committee, "Instructions on Dealing with Current Labor-Capital Relations" (February 8, 1950); ZPA, 23/8/2.
64. CCP Zhejiang Committee, "Instructions on Factory Work" (May 24, 1949); ZPA, 23/8/2.
65. See Hangzhou Military Control Committee, "Provisional Regulations on Labor-Capital Relations" (October 31, 1949); ZPA, 23/8/1.
66. Ibid.
67. Tan Zhenlin, "Speech at the First Convention of Worker Representatives of the Province of Zhejiang" (October 4, 1949); ZPA, 23/8/3.
68. For the early Communist labor movement in China, see Jean Chesneaux, *The Chinese Labor Movement, 1919–1927* (Stanford, Calif.: Stanford University Press, 1968), part 3.
69. Pang Song and Lin Yunhui, *Liguo xingbang,* 3: 264–265.
70. *Zhejiang Daily,* October 11, 1949, 6.
71. Ibid.
72. See the following articles in the *Zhejiang Daily:* "The Hangzhou School of Art Is Remodeling," November 1, 1949, 6; "New Zhejiang University, New Atmosphere," November 14, 1949, 5; "The Monks at Ling Ying Temple Begin to Change," November 21, 1949; "The Social Value of Hangzhou Is Changing," January 4, 1950, 6; "The Hangzhou Market Is Changing," May 3, 1950; "West Lake Is Changing," May 17, 1950; "The Acrobats Remold Themselves," May 14, 1950, 3.
73. Tan Zhenlin, "Speech at the First Convention of Worker Representatives of the Province of Zhejiang" (October 4, 1949); ZPA, 23/8/3.
74. General Trade Union, "Work Report for June" (July 1949); HMA, 1/7/84; district unions reports, HMA, 1/1/36.
75. CCP Zhejiang Committee, "On the Socialist Transformation of Capitalist Industry" (November 1954); ZPA, 23/8/2.
76. Tang Tsou, "Interpreting the Revolution in China: Macrohistory and Micromechanism," *Modern China* 26, no. 2 (April 2000): 205–238.
77. See also Pepper, *Civil War in China.*

Chapter 5: *The Korean War and the City*

1. The Zhongshan Road, the major north-south thoroughfare in Hangzhou, was named after Sun Yat-sen (Sun Zhongshan in the new spelling system). Hangzhou is a city of water and bridges, so a lot of places were identified via the bridges.
2. Eugenia Barnett Schultheis, *Hangchow, My Home: Growing up in Heaven Below* (Fort Bragg, Calif.: Lost Coast Press, 2000), 127.
3. All six articles were written for the Xinhua News Agency: "A Confession of Helplessness" (August 12); "Cast Away Illusions, Prepare for Struggle" (August 14); "Farewell, Leighton Stuart!" (August 18); "Why It Is Necessary to Discuss the White Paper" (August 28); "'Friendship' or Aggression?" (August 30); and "The Bankruptcy of the Idealist Conception of History" (September 16). "Farewell, Leighton Stuart" appears in Mao Tse-tung, *Selected Works*, 4: 438.
4. A. Doak Barnett, *Communist China: The Early Years, 1949–1955* (New York: Praeger, 1964), 11. See also Pepper, *Civil War in China*, chapter 5.
5. "Cast Away Illusions, Prepare for Struggle"; in Mao Tse-tung, *Selected Works*, 4: 427.
6. See "The Bankruptcy of the Idealist Conception of History"; in Mao Tse-tung, *Selected Works*, 4: 451.
7. Stuart's father, John Linton Stuart, had done forty-six years of missionary work in this city, and his mother, Mary Stuart, had worked even longer—fifty years. Both of Leighton's parents were buried in the Hangzhou Foreign Cemetery near West Lake. John Leighton Stuart, *Fifty Years in China: The Memoirs of John Leighton Stuart* (New York: Random House, 1954), 9–20.
8. Ibid., 36.
9. John Leighton Stuart, cited in Yu-ming Shaw, *An American Missionary in China: John Leighton Stuart and Chinese-American Relations* (Cambridge, Mass.: Harvard University Press, 1992), 24.
10. "Stuart—An Honorable Citizen of Hangzhou," *Hangzhou wenshi ziliao* 7 (Reference materials on the local culture and history of Hangzhou, vol. 7), 13.
11. Ding Rongguan, "Huilan Private High School," in Zhou Feng et al., eds., *Minguo shiqi Hangzhou*, 577–578.
12. There were four major colleges in Hangzhou in the early 1950s: Zhejiang National University, Zhijiang University, the Zhejiang Medical School, and the National School of Art. The summer institute was to discuss four topics: the international situation (the Korean War), the country's financial situation, the land reform, and educational reform.
13. Zhijiang University, "Summary of the Summer Institute of the Faculty and Staff" (August 21, 1950); ZPA, 52/2/9.

14. Zhijiang University, "Minutes of the Board of Trustees of Zhijiang University" (August 19, 1950); ZPA, 52/2/9.
15. "How Did Zhejiang University Launch the Campaign to Resist America, Aid Korea, Defend Home, and Defend the Motherland?" *Hangzhou Work* 6 (December 2, 1950); HMA, 1/3/9.
16. CCP Hangzhou Committee on Middle School Affairs, "Summary Report on Models in the Ideological Reform of Middle School Teachers" (July 22, 1952); HMA, 1/7/21.
17. Department of Transportation, "Report on Mass Mobilization in the Resist America, Aid Korea Campaign" (1952); HMA, 48/2/7.
18. For a political analysis of China's goals and strategies in the Korean War, see Chen Jian, *Mao's China and the Cold War* (Chapel Hill: University of North Carolina Press, 2001), chapter 4.
19. For a detailed discussion about how propaganda and the popular culture served the mobilization during the Korean War, see James Z. Gao, "War Culture, Nationalism, and Political Campaigns, 1950–1953," in *Chinese Nationalism in Perspective: Historical and Recent Cases,* ed. C. X. George Wei and Xiaoyuan Liu (Westport, Conn.: Greenwood Press, 2001), 179–204.
20. Shen Shanhong et al., eds., *Hangzhou Daxue xiaoshi, 1897–1988* (A history of Hangzhou University, 1897–1988) (Hangzhou: Hangzhou University Press, 1989), 21, 36.
21. Luo Yi, "The Resist America, Aid Korea, Protect Home and Defend Motherland Campaign of the People in Zhejiang Is Deepening and Broadening Step by Step," in *Carry the Resist America, Aid Korea Campaign to a New Stage,* ed. Chinese People's Committee for Defending World Peace against American Aggression (Beijing: People's Press, 1951), 106.
22. Ibid. Also see "New Developments of the Patriotic Movement in the Province of Zhejiang," *Jiefang Daily* (Shanghai), April 10, 1951.
23. State Council, "Resolution on Policy toward Cultural, Educational, and Charitable Institutions and Religious Groups Accepting American Sponsorship (December 29, 1950)"; cited in Chinese Association for the Resist America, Aid Korea Campaign, ed., *The Great Resist America, Aid Korea Campaign* (Beijing: People's Press, 1954), 797.
24. Ibid.
25. Ibid., 798–799.
26. State Council, "Registration Regulations for Cultural, Educational, and Charitable Institutions and Religious Groups that Receive Foreign Financial Aid or Are Owned by Foreigners" (December 29, 1950), approved by the sixty-fifth session of the State Council; HMA, 86/1/33.
27. "Joint Declaration of the Representatives of the Chinese Christian

Churches and Christian Groups" (April 21, 1951); cited in Chinese Association for the Resist America, Aid Korea Campaign, ed., *The Great . . . Campaign,* 804–805.
28. Ibid., 805.
29. Ibid.
30. "Wipe Out the Influence of American Cultural Imperialism"; in Chinese Association for the Resist America, Aid Korea Campaign, ed., *The Great . . . Campaign,* 801.
31. Ibid., 800.
32. Ibid., 802.
33. Ibid.
34. Ibid., 802–803.
35. Ministry of Education, "A Circular Letter on Cutting off Ties with UNESCO" (1951), No. 1447; ZPA, 52/2/169.
36. State Council, "Tentative Regulations on the Invitation of Foreign Advisers and Experts" (August 18, 1951), Order 601; ZPA, 52/2/169.
37. "Notice of the State Council" (September 11, 1951), No. 677; see also Zhejiang Department of Culture and Education, "Notice: Strictly Check Books and Periodicals" (October 8, 1951); both in ZPA, 52/2/169.
38. CCP Hangzhou Committee, "Arrangements for the Further Implementation of the Directive on the Suppression of Counterrevolutionaries" (March 10, 1951); HMA, 1/3/10. In this document, the city committee reported that in 1950 some aliens and their churches and schools had spread counterrevolutionary messages and engaged in counterrevolutionary activities but had not been punished accordingly. It argued that the policy of leniency had to be corrected.
39. Hangzhou Bureau of Civil Administration, "Semi-Annual Report on the Registration of Foreign-Sponsored and Foreign-Run Cultural, Educational, and Charitable Institutions and Religious Groups" (July 14, 1951); ZPA, 86/1/23.
40. Yu Zhongwu, "On the Issue of the Takeover of Schools that Receive Foreign Financial Aid" (March 6, 1951); HMA, 86/1/33.
41. Ibid.
42. Hangzhou Bureau of Civil Administration, "Semi-Annual Report on the Registration of Foreign-Sponsored and Foreign-Run Cultural, Educational, and Charitable Institutions and Religious Groups" (July 14, 1951); ZPA, 86/1/23.
43. *Office Work* (April 1950), 1; ZPA, 52/2/164.
44. Zhijiang University, "Draft Plan for the Improvement of University Affairs"; ZPA, 52/2/32.
45. CCP Hangzhou Committee, "Instructions on the Abolition of the *Bao-Jia* System and Establishment of Residents' Committees" (December 1, 1949); ZPA, 23/1/25.

46. "Annual Report of the City's Security and Administration" (December 1950); in *Chengshi de jieguan*, 205.
47. CCP Hangzhou Committee, "Instructions on the Abolition of the *Bao-Jia* System and Establishment of Residents' Committees" (December 1, 1949); ZPA, 23/1/25.
48. "The Work Plan of the Shangcheng District in June" described how to find and train activists at night schools for workers and residents; HMA, 1/1/36.
49. Since the Residents' Committees were actively involved in Communist purges and social control, people did not like them, and "Bound-foot scouts" was a derogatory term. Very few of them were actually women with bound feet.
50. "Annual Report of the City's Security and Administration" (December 1950); in *Chengshi de jieguan*, 200–201.
51. Ibid. YGD, a religious organization, is discussed further below.
52. Ibid., 202.
53. CCP Hangzhou Committee, "Report on the Suppression of Counterrevolutionaries" (May 5, 1951); HMA, 1/3/10.
54. Xin Guanqiao Police Station, "How to Organize an Accusation Meeting in a Residential Area" (June 8, 1951), and CCP Committee of the Hangzhou Waterworks, "How the Waterworks Proceeded with the Suppression of Counterrevolutionaries Campaign" (May 8, 1951); both in HMA, 1/3/10.
55. CCP Hangzhou Committee, "Report on the Suppression of Counterrevolutionaries" (May 11, 1951); HMA, 1/3/10.
56. Cited in Bai Xi, *Da zhenya* (The great suppression) (Beijing: Jincheng Press, 2000), 864.
57. Zhang Shixiang et al., "The War of Annihilation Destroying the Remains of the Counterrevolutionaries"; in *Chengshi de jieguan*, 366–377.
58. CCP Central Department of Propaganda, "Instructions on How to Use Propaganda to Implement the Central Directives on the Suppression of Counterrevolutionaries," *Struggle* 57 (October 1950): 2–3.
59. Feng Jiping, "Report on Cases of Suppressing Counterrevolutionaries in Beijing" (March 15, 1951); cited in Bai Xi, *Da zhenya*, 356–357.
60. *Hangzhou Work*, December 1950, 12.
61. For detailed information about the YGD and its suppression in North China, see Lieberthal, *Revolution and Tradition*, 366–377.
62. "Endorse the Order of the Hangzhou Military Control Committee to Ban the Reactionary YGD," *Zhejiang Review*, December 16, 1950, 3.
63. Ibid.
64. One of the department's findings indicates that in the Genshan district, a suburb of Hangzhou, more than 60 percent of the villagers were believers of the YGD.

65. "Resolutely Support the Decree of the City Military Control Committee on Disbanding Reactionary Cliques," *Zhejiang Daily*, December 16, 1950, 3.
66. Department of Public Security, "Report on Disbanding Reactionary Cliques" (December 31, 1950); in *Chengshi de jieguan*, 197.
67. Hangzhou City Government, "Annual Report of the People's Government in 1950"; in *Chengshi de jieguan*, 152.
68. "Resolution on the Strict Suppression of Counterrevolutionaries" (April 18, 1951), approved by the second session of the First Zhejiang Provincial Congress of People's Representatives; ZPA, 23/3/5/20.
69. *Zhejiang Daily*, April 30, 1951. See also Bai Xi, *Da zhenya*, 630–633.
70. "Resolution of the Third Conference on Public Security" (May 15, 1951); HMA, 1/3/10.
71. "First Report on the Public Trial in Hangzhou" (May 13, 1951); HMA, 1/3/10.
72. Zhang Tianli, "Mr. Zhang Heng before and after His Term as President of the Hangzhou Municipal Congress," in *Hangzhou wenshi ziliao*, 18: 1–11.
73. CCP Hangzhou Committee, "Summary Report on the Suppression of Counterrevolutionaries Campaign in the Last Ten Days" (May 14, 1951); HMA, 1/3/10.
74. CCP Hangzhou Committee, "Assignments for Carrying Out the Suppression of Counterrevolutionaries Campaign" (May 14, 1951); HMA, 1/3/10.
75. The CCP Hangzhou Committee, Committee on School Affairs, "Summary of Experiments of the Ideological Reform Campaign of the Faculty and Staff" (July 22, 1952); HMA, 1/7/21.
76. CCP Hangzhou Committee, "Assignments for Carrying Out the Suppression of Counterrevolutionaries" (May 14, 1951); HMA, 1/3/10.
77. See *Hangzhou Work*, no. 14 (1951).
78. *China Youth Daily*, May 8, 1951, 3.
79. Lei Feng was a PLA soldier who died in a car accident while on duty. In his diary he expressed his love for Mao Zedong and recorded every good thing he had done for the people according to Mao's teaching. Mao called on everyone to "learn from comrade Lei Feng" after his death. Cited in *People's Daily*, March 5, 1963. Lei's diary was published, and passages from it were recited by thousands of Chinese youngsters. Lei wrote: "Be warm to comrades like the spring; be cruel to the enemy like a severe winter." Lei Feng, *Diary* (Beijing: People's Press, 1963), 17.
80. *People's Daily*, October 24, 1951.
81. Lin Yunhui et al., eds., *Kaige xingjin de shiqi*, 215.
82. CCP Committee of Zhejiang University, Political Division, "Summary Report" (February 1953); Zhejiang University Archives (ZUA), 52/11/1/2. (Cited hereafter as ZUA.)

83. CCP Central Committee, *Zhou Enlai nianpu* (A chronological record of Zhou Enlai), 2 vols. (Beijing: Central Documents Press, 1996), 1: 178–179.
84. *Jianguo yilai Mao Zedong wengao*, 2: 448.
85. CCP Central Committee, *Zhou Enlai nianpu*, 1: 182–183.
86. Meng Xianchen (minister of education), "Notice of the East China Military and Administrative Committee, JG (2): 200402" (January 24, 1952); ZPA, 52/2/89.
87. CCP Committee of Zhejiang University, "Reflections on Enhancing Teaching Excellence by Organizing the Faculty and Staff for Political Study" (1952); ZUA, 52/11/1/2.
88. Returning students (also called transferred cadre students [*diao gan sheng*]) were Party workers or government employees who were sent and paid by the government to study at various universities.
89. CCP Committee of Zhejiang University, "Summary Report of Party Recruitment" (1952); ZUA, 0044.
90. "How Does Zhejiang University Implement the Resist America, Aid Korea, Protect Home and Defend the Motherland Campaign?" *Hangzhou Work*, December 2, 1950; HMA, 1/3/9.
91. Ibid.
92. Ibid.
93. CCP Committee of Zhejiang University, "Report on the Three Antis and the Thought Reform Campaign"; ZUA, 52/11/1/2.
94. CCP Committee of Zhejiang University, "Annual Report of Party Work" (1951–1952 Academic Year); ZUA, 00081.
95. CCP Hangzhou Committee, Committee on School Affairs, "Summary of Experiments of the Ideological Reform Campaign of the Faculty and Staff" (July 22, 1952); HMA, 1/7/21.
96. Ibid.
97. For the changing understanding of and attitude toward the Thought Reform Campaign by Chinese intellectuals in the 1950s and following years, see Perry Link, *Evening Chats in Beijing: Probing China's Predicament* (New York: W. W. Norton, 1992), 139–144.
98. CCP Committee of Zhejiang University, "Annual Report of Party Work" (1952–1953 Academic Year); ZUA, 00082.
99. CCP Committee of Zhejiang University, "Annual Report of Party Work" (1951–1952 Academic Year); ZUA, 00081.
100. George Taylor, *The Struggle for North China* (New York: Institute of Pacific Relations, 1940), 101. Also see the discussion in Mark Selden, *China in Revolution: The Yen'an Way Revisited* (Armonk, N.Y.: M. E. Sharpe, 1995), 225, 230–235.
101. See Lieberthal, *Revolution and Tradition*, 97–124.
102. Lo Yi, "Zhejiang Resist America, Aid Korea Campaign," *Jiefang Daily*, April 10, 1951.

Chapter 6: The Trial of Strength

1. In Li Hangyu, *Lao Hangzhou*, 107.
2. See Chen Yun, "The High-Ranking Leaders Must Increase Their Vigilance," in *Selected Works of Chen Yun* (Beijing: People's Press, 1987), 230.
3. Private industrial output had increased by 31.58 percent and the volume of private commerce by 29.38 percent. CCP Zhejiang Committee, "Socialist Transformation of Capitalist Industry and Commerce in Hangzhou"; in *Zhejiang zibenzhuyi*, 9. See also Wu Xian, "Investigation of Basic Changes in Urban Industry and Commerce" (September 25, 1951); HMA, 1/5/55.
4. In 1961, as China was about to overcome the three years of "natural disaster," Mao Zedong put forward the slogan "Never forget the class struggle." Years later, in 1975, Mao again claimed, "Class struggle is the guiding principle."
5. Chen Wenjin, *Xihu Wenwu* (Cultural relics of West Lake) (Hangzhou: Zhejiang Photography Press, 1997), 40–41.
6. Interview with Sun Wencheng, Hangzhou, May 18, 1997.
7. Interview with Sun Wencheng, Hangzhou, August 13, 1998.
8. "Zhou Enlai to Deng yingchao" (March 31, 1951); cited in Chen Wenjin, *Xihu Wenwu*, 35.
9. *People's Daily*, November 10, 1951. Hao Jianxiu later became a famous model worker. She was elected to be a member of the CCP Central Committee and even promoted to be the minister of the textiles industry.
10. In *Jianguo yilai Mao Zedong wengao*, 2: 514.
11. Zhang Jianwei, *Keguo diyi dao* (The first surgery after the founding of the PRC) (Beijing: China Radio-TV Press, 1990), 41–43.
12. *Jianguo yilai Mao Zedong wengao*, 2: 535.
13. Ibid., 2: 528–529. The two officials were Liu Qingshan (deputy Party secretary of the city of Shijiazhuang) and Zhang Zishan (Party secretary of Tianjin Prefecture). Both were in their late thirties but had served in the Party for more than twenty years. Because they had practiced graft in connection with the relief funds for flooded areas, they were executed on February 10, 1952. A lot of literature describes the details of the case. See, for example, Zhang Jianwei, *Keguo diyi dao*.
14. Bo Yibo, *Ruogan*, 152.
15. "Conversation with Zhai Zuojun" (spring 1952); in Mao Zedong, *The Writings of Mao Zedong, 1949–1976* (Armonk, N.Y.: M. E. Sharpe, 1986), 1: 254.
16. *Jianguo yilai Mao Zedong wengao*, 2: 513.
17. "New Year's Greetings" (January 1, 1952); in ibid., 3: 1.
18. Lieberthal, *Revolution and Tradition*, 125.

19. Barnett, *Communist China*, 138–139.
20. Interview with Zhong Ru, Hangzhou, May 29, 1997.
21. In Zhang Jianwei, *Keguo diyi dao*, 56.
22. In Hangzhou, *yueju* roles are all performed by actresses. The main themes of the opera are traditional love stories. For more on *yueju*, see chapter 8.
23. Interview with Yang Xueyan (former head of division of social work, Bureau of Civil Administration of Hangzhou), Hangzhou, May 22, 1997. Also see Zhang Jianwei, *Keguo diyi dao*, 108–110.
24. *Jianguo yilai Mao Zedong wengao*, 3: 87.
25. Ibid., 3: 115.
26. Ibid., 3: 145.
27. Ibid., 3: 154–155.
28. Ibid.
29. Ge Hongsheng et al., eds., *Fengyu chang xiangyi: Jinian Liu Jian tongzhi wenji* (The lasting memory in the storm: Selected papers in memory of Comrade Liu Jian) (Beijing: CCP History Press, 1994), 144.
30. Lin Yunhui et al., eds., *Kaige xingjin de shiqi*, 250.
31. Interview with Sun Wencheng, Hangzhou, May 18, 1997.
32. Interview with Liu Bo, Hangzhou, May 20, 1997.
33. Lin Yunhui et al., eds., *Kaige xingjin de shiqi*, 251.
34. CCP Zhejiang Committee, "First Summary Report on the Current Progress and Further Plans for the Five Antis Campaign" (March 8, 1952); in *Zhejiang zibenzhuyi*, 115. Here I have followed the original document and refer to the old RMB.
35. CCP Zhejiang Committee, *Zhongguo gongcandang Zhejiang, 1949–1993*, 33–34.
36. Ibid.
37. CCP Zhejiang Committee, "First Summary Report on the Current Progress and Further Plans for the Five Antis Campaign" (March 8, 1952); in *Zhejiang zibenzhuyi*, 115.
38. Ibid.
39. *Zhang Jianwei, Keguo diyi dao*, 167.
40. CCP Zhejiang Committee, Department of the United Front, "A Report on Conveying and Implementing the Spirit of the Sixth Meeting of the Provincial Political Consultative Conference" (July 5, 1952); in *Zhejiang zibenzhuyi*, 142–147.
41. *Liberation Daily*, February 9, 1952. *Liberation Daily* is the official newspaper of the CCP Shanghai Committee.
42. Typical comments were made by Huang Yanpei, who was not a Party member but was appointed deputy prime minister of the state council on February 13, 1952; see Lin Yunhui et al., eds., *Kaige xingjin de shiqi*, ch. 2. According to the Common Program of the Chinese Political

Consultative Conference, the four friends of the working class were peasants, the petty bourgeoisie, the national bourgeoisie, and other patriotic democratic elements.
43. Interview with Zhong Ru, Hangzhou, May 29, 1997.
44. Zhang Jianwei, *Keguo diyi dao*, 205.
45. CCP Zhejiang Committee, "First Summary Report on the Current Progress and Further Plans for the Five Antis Campaign" (March 8, 1952); in *Zhejiang zibenzhuyi*, 115.
46. CCP Central Committee, "Instructions on the Classification and Treatment of Industrialists and Merchants in the Five Antis Campaign" (March 5, 1952); in *Jianguo yilai Mao Zedong wengao*, 3: 308–312. See also Barnett, *Communist China*, 141.
47. CCP Zhejiang Committee, "First Summary Report on the Current Progress and Further Plans for the Five Antis Campaign" (March 8, 1952); in *Zhejiang zibenzhuyi*, 115.
48. ECB, "Reply to the First Report by the Zhejiang Committee on the Five Antis Campaign" (March 11, 1952); in *Zhejiang zibenzhuyi*, 120.
49. CCP Zhejiang Committee, "Instructions on Implementing the Instructions of the ECB on the Five Antis Campaign" (March 13, 1952); in *Zhejiang zibenzhuyi*, 121.
50. *Jianguo yilai Mao Zedong wengao*, 3: 97.
51. Chen Yun, *Selected Works*, 172.
52. CCP Zhejiang Committee, *Zhongguo gongcandang Zhejiang, 1949–1993*, 34; CCP Central Committee, *Liu Shaoqi nianpu*, 1: 305.
53. ECB, "Comments on the Summary Report by the CCP Hangzhou Municipal Committee on the Five Antis Campaign" (April 22, 1952); in Zhejiang zibenzhuyi, 120.
54. According to Cheng Chu-yuan, the Three Antis and Five Antis Campaigns were responsible for financing 23 percent of Beijing's government budget. Cheng Chu-yuan, *New Trends in Chinese Communist Fiscal Economic Policies* (Hong Kong: Zuyu Press, 1953), 35–40.
55. CCP Zhejiang Committee, "Instructions on Implementing the Instructions of the Central Committee on the Adjustment of Commerce" (November 21, 1952); in *Zhejiang zibenzhuyi*, 148. For the economic impact of the campaign on other cities, see, for example, Lieberthal, *Revolution and Tradition*, 170–172.
56. Interview with Cui Bo, Hangzhou, March 19, 2001.
57. CCP Hangzhou Committee, "Summary Report on the Five Antis Campaign" (April 18, 1952); in *Zhejiang zibenzhuyi*, 123.
58. Ibid.
59. "Report on the Five Antis Campaign in Shanghai and Hangzhou"; internal report by the Xinhua News Agency, 1952.

60. CCP Central Committee, *Zhou Enlai nianpu*, 1: 235.
61. Rong Yiren had a very successful political career with the Communist Party. He was elected vice chairman of the Shanghai Political Consultative Committee and later became vice president of the PRC.
62. Cited in Bo Yibo, *Ruogan*, 173–174.
63. Cited in ibid., 167.
64. CCP Hangzhou Committee, "Summary Report on the Five Antis Campaign" (April 18, 1952); in *Zhejiang zibenzhuyi*, 123.
65. Cao Xiangju, "A Warm Concern and Earnest Teachings," in *Wuxian jinian wenji* (Selected papers in memory of Wu Xian), ed. Chen Fawen et al. (Hangzhou: Hangzhou Press, 1998), 170.
66. Jin Runxiang, "Speech at the Third Session of the First People's Congress of the Province of Zhejiang" (January 1956); in *Zhejiang zibenzhuyi*, 539–543.
67. Ibid.
68. Ibid.
69. Cited in Bo Yibo, *Ruogan*, 165–166.
70. Interview with Liu Bo, Hangzhou, May 20, 1997.
71. Ibid.
72. "Instructions of the Central Committee on the Struggle against Bureaucratism, Commandism, and the Violation of Laws and Discipline" (January 5, 1953); in *Jianguo yilai Mao Zedong wengao*, 4: 8–9.
73. Tan Qilong, "Speech at the Seventy-fourth Work Meeting of the Zhejiang Provincial Government" (January 30, 1963); cited in CCP Zhejiang Committee, *Zhongguo gongcandang Zhejiang, 1949–1993*, 40.
74. CCP Central Committee, "Comments on Report by CCP North China Bureau on Continuing the New Three Antis Campaign" (March 6, 1953); in *Jianguo yilai Mao Zedong wengao*, 4: 94–95.
75. Yang Siyi, *Diary*, February 3, 1955.
76. "Liberalism" was usually defined as a lack of discipline and disobedience to the Party's leadership.
77. Yang Siyi, *Diary*, July 30, 1953; August 4 and 9, 1953; May 2 and 9, 1954. In 1953, Yang Siyi was a member of the CCP Provincial Standing Committee, director of the provincial Organizational Department, director of the Personnel Division of the provincial government, and secretary of the Discipline Committee of the CCP Zhejiang Committee. For more information about Yang, see chapter 2.
78. Ibid., August 4 and 9, 1953.
79. Ibid., July 19, 1954.
80. In the following years Yang was repeatedly accused of bourgeois liberalism, localism, and anti-Party factionalism. Because of his intellectual background, he was also suspected of having historical

"black spots." In 1957 Yang Siyi again became a victim, this time of the Anti-Rightist Campaign. A week after he was purged from the Party, he died of a cerebral hemorrhage.

81. Frederick C. Teiwes, *Politics and Purges in China: Rectification and Decline of Party Norms 1950–1965* (Armonk, N.Y.: M. E. Sharpe, 1993), 124.

Chapter 7: Women Cadres

1. This worker-peasant-soldier emblem was designed to represent Mao Zedong's dictum that literature and the arts must serve the broad mass of workers, peasants, and soldiers.
2. For these images of women, see Huang Yuanling, ed., *Cartoons of the Century*. (Beijing: Modern Press, 2000), 101, 103. Also see Hua Mei, "Fashions of the Century," *People's Daily,* May 17, 2001, 7.
3. The Marriage Law was promulgated on April 13, 1950. On April 30, the PRC central government announced that the law would come into force on May 1, 1950. In May the Zhejiang provincial government issued "Instructions on the Correct Implementation of the Marriage Law" and established the marriage registration system in seven cities and seventy-seven counties of the province. Zhejiang Provincial Women's Federation Archives (ZPWFA), 10/5/1. (Cited hereafter as ZPWFA.) For an English translation of the law, see Neil J. Diamant, *Revolutionizing the Family: Politics, Love, and Divorce in Urban and Rural China, 1949–1968.* (Berkeley: University of California Press, 2000), 342–343.
4. The All-China Women's Federation claimed that 84 percent of Chinese women voted in the 1954 elections. *New Women of China* 3 (1953): 5.
5. For a general discussion of the Marriage Law and the 1953 Marriage Law Campaign in China, see Kay Ann Johnson, *Women, the Family and Peasant Revolution in China* (Chicago: University of Chicago Press, 1983), 115–154.
6. For a discussion, see Judith Stacey, *Patriarchy and Socialist Revolution in China* (Berkeley: University of California Press, 1983).
7. See K. Johnson, *Women*.
8. Victoria Cass makes a similar argument that urbanization in the Ming dynasty brought new employment opportunities and consequent independence to women. See *Dangerous Women: Warriors, Grannies and Geishas of the Ming* (Lanham, Md.: Rowman and Littlefield, 1999).
9. CCP Zaozhuang Committee, *Lunan geming shi,* 30.
10. CCP Linyi Committee, *Zhonggong Binhai dangshi dashi ji* (Chronology of the CCP in Binhai) (Jinan: Shandong People's Press, 1988), 24.
11. CCP Zaozhuang Committee, *Lunan geming shi,* 56.
12. See Christina K. Gilmartin, "Gender, Political Culture, and Women's

Mobilization in the Chinese Nationalist Revolution, 1924–1927," in Gilmartin et al., eds., *Engendering China*, 195–225.
13. Interview with Ren Xiurong, Hangzhou, August 25, 2001.
14. Interview with Wang Huaizhen, Hangzhou, May 24, 1997.
15. "School Admissions Brochure of the Shandong Anti-Japanese Military and Political College," *Mass Daily*, January 10, 1939.
16. Liu Qi, "Father Sent Me to the Cadre School," in Xin Wei, ed., *Fenhuo yu yingcai*, 166–167.
17. Zhang Xia, "Recollections of the Third Class of the Women's Brigade at the Cadre School," in Xin Wei, ed., *Fenhuo yu yingcai*, 170.
18. Both Mulan and Mu Guiying are legendary heroines in Chinese oral history. Mulan, well known in the West, was a brave soldier, while Mu Guiying was a female general in command of an army who had more dramatic experiences in Chinese literature.
19. *Lunan Times*, January 8, 1947.
20. Interview with Ren Xiurong, Hangzhou, August 25, 2001.
21. Interview with Cui Bo, Hangzhou, August 25, 2001.
22. CCP Cangshan Committee, *Zhonggong Cangshan dangshi dashi ji* (Chronology of the CCP in Cangshan, 1927–1949) (Linyi: District Publishing House, 1993), 42.
23. *Lunan Times*, January 8, 1947.
24. "The Model of Women in the Anti-Japanese War," *Mass Daily*, February 2, 1947.
25. Interview with Cui Bo, March 19, 2001.
26. The CCP Central Committee issued instructions on "Promoting the Campaign for Rent Reduction and Cherishing the People" on October 1, 1943. The following January the campaign unfolded in seven districts of Luzhongnan.
27. *Lunan Times*, January 15 and 17, 1947.
28. See chapter 1.
29. CCP Linyi Committee, *Zhonggong Lunanqu dangshi dashi ji*, 381.
30. Minutes of the CCP Zhaobo Committee (February 11, 1949); CCA, 1/1/8.
31. Interviews for this section were conducted with (among others) the historians of local Party history in Shandong (1999) and with southbound women's cadres in Hangzhou (2000).
32. For details, see Gao Hongxing, *Chanzhu shi* (A history of foot binding) (Shanghai: Wenyi Press, 1995).
33. See "Declaration of the Feminist Movement Association," *Women's Journal* 8, no. 8 (1922): 127.
34. CCP Cangshan Committee, *Zhonggong Cangshan dangshi dashi ji*, 50.
35. Interviews with women who came from the same county as Liu Lan: Fang Jingshu, Fang Min, and Xu Jingxin, Hangzhou, March 19, 2001.

36. Zhang Xia, "Recollections," 170.
37. Interview with Cui Bo, Hangzhou, March 19, 2001.
38. Ibid.
39. Wen-hsin Yeh writes about the CCP's early experience and Chen Duxiu, who rented a house in the French Concession in Shanghai. His residence was very different from other middle-class homes because of its absence of children, the elderly, and women, and all the visitors were male bachelors. Yeh writes: "The frequent coming and going of numerous young males, each speaking with a distinct provincial accent, readily attracted the attention of the police, whose surveillance further restricted [the Communists'] field of action in the city." *Provincial Passages*, 210–212. From this lesson, in later years CCP secret institutions in the cities, local headquarters, and liaison officers were usually disguised in the form of a mundane normal family.
40. See Ross Terrill, *Madame Mao: The White-Boned Demon*, rev. ed. (Stanford, Calif.: Stanford University Press, 1999), 17.
41. The famous Chinese woman writer Ding Ling described the harrowing experience of her mother, who started to unbind her feet at the age of thirty: "Removing the layers of cloth wrappings, taking the first anguished steps, bathing the feet in cold water every night to lull the pain, exercising regularly, she found that her feet slowly began to straighten out, and finally she was able to wear regular footwear." Cited in Jonathan Spence, *The Gate of Heavenly Peace: The Chinese and Their Revolution, 1895–1980*. (New York: Penguin, 1982), 164.
42. Interview with Ren Xiurong, Hangzhou, August 25, 2001.
43. Because of her bound feet, Liu Lan was persuaded to "return to production" in 1949. Later, she was given honorary membership in the county's Political Consultative Council, with a monthly stipend of ¥30. More often than not, she did not get the pay. By the end of the twentieth century, when the glory of the revolution had faded, she was ninety-two years old and living with her daughter in the city of Kuming. The monthly payments of ¥30 remained her only income; this sum could buy only meals for one day in the city. Interviews with women who came from the same county as Liu Lan: Fang Jingshu, Fang Min, and Xu Jingxin, Hangzhou, March 19, 2001.
44. CCP Bohai Committee, Organization Department, "Report on Dependents of the Southbound Cadres Who Fled from Famine" (December 31, 1949); SPA, 26/121/9.
45. CCP Yi Committee, Division of Internal Affairs, "Report on How We Take Care of the Families of the Southbound Cadres" (June 7, 1949); ZMA, 1/1/102.
46. CCP Cangshan Committee, "Report on Production of the Families of the Southbound Cadres" (June 24, 1949); CCA, 1/1/71.

47. "Notice of the Personnel Department, CCP Luzhongnan District Committee" (May 2, 1949); CCA, R1/1/15.
48. Ibid.
49. Interview with Xu Jingxin, Hangzhou, March 19, 2001.
50. Interview with Ren Xiurong, Hangzhou, August 25, 2001.
51. See chapter 1.
52. Marriage Law, Article 8.
53. Interviews with Fang Jingshu and Cui Bo, Hangzhou, March 19, 2001.
54. Supreme Court, "Circular Order Regarding the Divorce Cases of the Southbound Cadres"; Fa Du 138 (March 1951).
55. Interview with Zhang Lifa, Cangshan, June 15, 1998. Zhang is the chairman of the Party History Committee, Cangshan County.
56. For example, the southbound team from Luzhongnan that arrived at Xiaoshan (a suburb of Hangzhou) to establish a new local government in May 1949 had thirty-one cadres, only three of whom were women—Zhang Xiuyuan, Zheng Xiulan, and Yang Suixian. See "The List of the Southbound Cadres to Xiaoshan, May 1950," unpublished manuscript.
57. Interview with Shen Yi, Hangzhou, August 25, 2001.
58. The Lenin suit is a Russian-style coat—double-breasted with a turned-down collar. It was first a uniform of the Communist civilian cadres and then became a women's fashion in Chinese cities in the 1950s.
59. *Modern Evening Paper*, December 10, 1949.
60. "Brief Report on the Takeover of Educational Institutions and Promotion of Social Education in Hangzhou" (December 1949); ZPA, 23/8/2/4.
61. Yang Siyi, *Diary*, May 4, 1952.
62. Many of the names of the newborn children are clues to their family background and their parents' expectations. For example, names such as Hangshen (which literally means "born in Hangzhou," implying that the parents were southbound cadres who came from the north), Xinhua (New China), Yuancao (Support Korea), and Weike (Bolshevik) were most popular among the second generation of southbound cadres.
63. "Order of the Minister of Defense, Peng Dehuai" (1953).
64. See Qin Dong and Ya Ping, *Sa Wenhan yu Chen Xiuliang* (Sa Wenhan and Chen Xiuliang) (Ningbo: Ningbo Press, 1999).
65. Wu Zhongliang is one of the few women soldiers who joined Mao Zedong's guerrilla army in Jinguangshan. When the CCP took over Hangzhou, her husband, Jiang Hua, became the deputy major and she became an associate director of the Organizational Department of the CCP Zhejiang Committee and later became president of the provincial court.
66. The First Congress of the All-China Women's Federation was held in Beijing March 24–April 3, 1949. On March 7, 1950, the All-China Women's Federation issued the "General Organizational Principles of

the Women's Federation," which served as guidelines for the Women's Federations at various levels throughout the country. Interview with Cui Bo, Hangzhou, March 19, 2001.
67. See Phyllis Andors, *The Unfinished Liberation of Chinese Women, 1949–1980* (Bloomington: Indiana University Press, 1983), 30.
68. Zhejiang Women's Federation, "Reorganize and Give Play to the Rural Women's Organization"; ZPWFA, 10/1/13.
69. Zhejiang Women's Federation, "Women in Social Transformation"; ZPWFA, 10/1/3.
70. Tan Zhenlin, "Speech at the Standing Committee of the Provincial Women's Federation" (August 1951); ZPWFA, 10/6/1.
71. Zhejiang Women's Federation, "Active Roles in the Patriotic Campaign for Increasing Production and Practicing Economy"; ZPWFA, 10/3/3.
72. Cited in Zhejiang Women's Federation, "Women in the Democratic Reform and the Three Antis and Five Antis Campaigns"; ZPWFA, 10/4/1.
73. Ibid.
74. Ibid.
75. Ibid.
76. Tan Zhenlin, "Speech at the Standing Committee of the Provincial Women's Federation" (August 1951); ZPWFA, 10/6/1.
77. The nightstool is a wooden container used as a chamber pot at night in rural China. When it is new or clean, it is also used for other purposes.
78. According to a report by Cixi County, 1,242 women became members of village committees by the end of the land reform. ZPWFA, 10/1/1.
79. In 1953 girls made up 26, 29.1, and 33.8 percent of the student population in colleges, high schools, and primary schools respectively.
80. Zhejiang Women's Federation, "Active Participation in Developing the Country's Democracy" (1953); ZPWFA, 11/1/2.
81. Tan Qilong, "Closing Speech at the Second Provincial Women's Congress," *Zhejiang Daily,* July 1, 1953.
82. Zhejiang Women's Federation, "Women in the Socialist Transformation of the Crafts Industry" (1953); ZPWFA, 11/3/1.
83. Zhejiang Women's Federation, "Active Participation in Developing the Country's Democracy" (1953); ZPWFA, 11/1/2.
84. Li Liang, "Equality between Men and Women in Socialist Countries," *New Women of China* 6 (1953): 8.
85. For example, Chen Xiuliang was the secretary of the CCP Nanjing Committee before the city was liberated by the PLA. As a radical urban intellectual, Chen was not foot-bound and had joined the CCP as early as 1927. Living in the enemy city and doing secret work, she had to dress as a "modern, urban, middle-class woman." When the PLA troops stormed the city, both the soldiers and the cadres were surprised at

Chen's hairstyle and dress. They did not believe that it was this dainty, petty bourgeois lady who had headed all the CCP underground activities under the most dangerous circumstances in the GMD's capital. And Chen was not assigned to a major government office after 1949.

Chapter 8: *The "Geneva of the East"*

1. The State Planning Commission had worked out the outline of this plan in 1952; it was revised many times and finally released in July 1955.
2. CCP Zhejiang Committee, "Outline of City Work in 1954"; in CCP Zhejiang Committee, *Zhongguo gongcandang Zhejiang, 1941–1993*, 45.
3. Li Fuchun, "Report on the First Five-Year Plan for the Development of the National Economy of the People's Republic of China"; Second Session of the First Chinese People's Congress; cited in *People's Daily*, July 6, 1955, 1. Li Fuchun was the chair of the State Planning Commission in 1955.
4. See Gu Dehuan, "Speech at the Conference of the Directors of the Departments of City Industry in Zhejiang Province" (May 1956). Cited in Le Zixing et al., eds., *Lixiang fengxian fengfan: Huainian Gu Dehuan tongzhi* (Ideal, devotion, and style: In memory of Comrade Gu Dehuan) (Ningbo: Ningbo Press, 1995), 260. Gu was the director of the Zhejiang Bureau of Industry and Mines at that time. In this speech, he argued that the central government's policy on coastal-inland divisions "had negative side effects."
5. According to Doak Barnett, industrial and commercial taxes were the largest source of state revenue. From 1950 to 1954, they increased 3.5 times, from U.S. $1.3 billion to U.S. $4.4 billion. The increase mainly resulted from the Communists' efforts to regularize and rationalize the tax system in the coastal cities. Barnett, *Communist China*, 218–221.
6. Minutes of the City Planning Meeting (September 1, 1953); HMA, 1/9/47.
7. Ibid.
8. Ibid.
9. Schultheis, *Hangchow*, 157.
10. Lin Fengmian, *Artistic Hangzhou* (1932); cited in Wu Zhanlei ed., *Yi Jiangnan*, 292–293. Lin Fengmian (1900–1991) was an artist and educator who studied art in France. When he returned to China, he served as president of the National Art School in Beijing and founded the Chinese Art School in Hangzhou. In the 1970s he moved to Hong Kong and lived out his life there.
11. On the "morbid prosperity," see *Zhejiang Daily*, May 17, 1950, 3.
12. Yu Senwen, "Urban Construction in the Past Year" (1950); HMA,

23/3/53. Yu was director of the Bureau of Urban Construction in 1950.
13. "Announcement of the People's Government of the City of Hangzhou" (November 16, 1949); HMA, 23/1/60.
14. Yu Senwen, "A Report to Mayor Jiang Hua and Deputy Mayor Wu Xian on the Plan for Fish Production in West Lake (Draft)" (November 1949); HMA, 23/1/60.
15. *Zhejiang Daily*, October 1, 1950, 6.
16. All these assistants served Mao Zedong as his secretaries. Tian Jiaying always worked closely with Mao, but Hu and Chen had other positions in the Party and government. For example, in the 1950s, Hu was the acting minister of the Party propaganda department, and Chen was the president of the Academy for Marxist-Leninist Studies. The three secretaries had quite different fates in the Cultural Revolution. Chen became a Politburo member, Hu was dismissed from office, and Tian committed suicide.
17. In his last visit in 1975, when he was eighty-one years old, Mao stayed at Wang Zhuang.
18. Zhong Xiangping, *Xihu mingren guju* (Former residences of eminent persons around West Lake) (Hangzhou: Hangzhou Press, 2000), 19–21.
19. The *qing* is a seven-stringed plucked musical instrument in some ways similar to the zither.
20. Zhong Xiangping, *Xihu mingren guju*, 95–96.
21. For details, see Teiwes, *Politics and Purges in China*, 130–165. Available Chinese accounts on this event include Bo Yibo, *Ruogan*, 308–325, and Lin Yunhui et al., eds., *Kaige xingjin de shiqi*, 318–336. Also see Shi Dongbing, *Gao Gang mengduo Zhongnanhai* (Gao Gang's Nightmare in Zhongnanhai) (Hong Kong: Tiandi Books, 1995).
22. Liu Shaoqi's ideas for the consolidation of the "New Democratic Order," and the encouragement of capitalist development in China were highly admired by the Party and by public opinion during and after the Cultural Revolution (1966–1976). However, Mao Zedong had quite different views on these issues in the early 1950s (see note 6 in chapter 9). These differences support the earliest interpretation of the Gao-Rao affair by Harold C. Hinton, *The "Unprincipled Dispute" within the Chinese Communist Top Leadership* (Washington, D.C.: U. S. Information Agency, IRI Intelligence Summary, No. LS-98-55, July 1955). They also reveal the fact that although the CCP leadership was stable in that period, the "broad policy consensus" suggested by Teiwes in *Politics and Purges in China* actually did not exist.
23. In a meeting with Pavel Yudin, Mao said, "Somebody is against me." Mao meant Gao Gang. See Shi Zhe, *Zai lishi juren shenbian* (At the side of the historic giant) (Beijing: Central Documents Press, 1991). It is my

opinion that other charges against Gao, such as his wanting an independent kingdom in Manchuria, his Soviet connections, and his arguments on Party-army relations, were secondary reasons for Mao Zedong's decision to purge him from the Party. A detailed discussion of the Gao-Rao affair, however, is beyond the scope of this book.

24. An unconfirmed source in the Cultural Revolution stated that Mao regretted Gao's early suicide and said, "Gao Gang knew many things about Liu Shaoqi." This might be a rumor; Liu Shaoqi's advocacy of the "capitalist road" was the primary attack against him by Gao Gang and Rao Shushi in 1953.
25. On January 7, 1954, Mao told Liu Shaoqi that he had talked with Lin Biao in Hangzhou and that Lin fully agreed with the resolution of the CCP Central Committee on the Gao-Rao affair. See *Jianguo yilai Mao Zedong wengao*, 4: 432.
26. Qiu Shi, ed., *Gongheguo zhongda shijian he juece neimu* (Inside stories on crucial events and decisions of the Republic) (Beijing: Economic Daily Press, 1997), 188.
27. On March 19, 1980, Deng Xiaoping had a talk with the writing team for the "Resolution on Several Historical Issues after the Founding of the PRC." He said, "After Comrade Mao Zedong suggested that the Central Committee be divided into the first and second tiers at the end of 1953, Gao Gang became very active. He first got support from Lin Biao, which made him dare to do so." Deng Xiaoping, *Deng Xiaoping wenxuan (1975–1982)* (Selected works of Deng Xiaoping, [1975–1982]) (Beijing: People's Press, 1984), 257.
28. Mao's instructions included (among others) letters to Liu Shaoqi and Zhou Enlai on the CCP Fourth Plenum (January 7, 8, 15, 18, 22, 27; February 28; and March 12, 1954); telegrams about the drafting of the PRC constitution (February 24, 26, 27, 1954); and telegrams to Zhu De and Peng Dehuai on a meeting of high-ranking PLA officers (January 23 and 25, 1954). See *Jianguo yilai Mao Zedong wengao*, 430–467.
29. For example, the Party's first secretaries of Shandong, Shanxi, and Tianjin Provinces; the president of the PRC's Supreme Court; and the minister of justice (among others) were recruited from Hangzhou.
30. General Office of Hangzhou, "Report on the Requisition of Land by the Navy to Build a Sanatorium" (September 26, 1951); ZPA, 1/5/49.
31. Zhang Qijun, "A History of Scenic West Lake," in Wu Zhanlei, ed., *Yi Jiangnan*, 210.
32. In 1949, the Hangzhou Dujinshen Silk Factory started to print the portraits of Communist leaders—Marx, Lenin, Stalin, Mao, Zhu, and Zhou—on silk scarves. Demand for such silk portraits began to rise in 1953, and the sales volume increased by 37 percent in 1954. See Wu Penyan and Lin Ziqing, "Before and after the Nationalization of

the Hangzhou Dujinshen Silk Factory"; in *Zhejiang zibenzhuyi*, 525–530.
33. According to the statistics of the Buddhist Association of Hangzhou, there were 282 temples and 257 nunneries. See *Zhejiang Daily*, May 14, 1950, 3.
34. Li Shutong, "The Course of My Conversion to Buddhism in West Lake"; cited in Li Hangyu, *Lao Hangzhou*, 3.
35. Zhou Feng et al., eds., *Nansong jingcheng Hangzhou*, 165.
36. Lin Fengmian, cited in Wu Zhanlei ed., *Yi Jiangnan*, 287.
37. For example, Master of Law Wenhui was a famous artist and poet in the Sung dynasty. His poems (most were collected in a book, *Shiyuan ji*) were admired by Emperor Gaozhong, who used the same rhyme scheme to write poems in reply. See Zhou Feng et al., eds., *Nansong jingcheng Hangzhou*, 160–171.
38. Several books on Master Hongyi have been published in China. One is Lin Tiao, *Yonghen de chenxi* (Permanency in silence) (Beijing: Beiyue Press, 2000).
39. Li Hangyu, *Lao Hangzhou*, 17.
40. *Zhejiang Daily*, November 21, 1949, 3.
41. *Zhejiang Daily*, May 3, 1950, 6.
42. Ibid.
43. Ibid.
44. *Zhejiang Daily*, November 21, 1949, 3.
45. CCP Zhejiang Department of the United Front, "Primary Measures for Implementing the Instructions of the Provincial Committee on the Temples in the City of Hangzhou" (July 22, 1953); ZPA, 4/1/59.
46. Ibid.
47. According to my interviews in Shaoxing County (about forty miles from Hangzhou) in 1998, rural women sixty years or older were all involved in pilgrimage activities, and they told me of their experiences with great excitement. The activities were stopped during the Cultural Revolution. After 1978, the activities were restored but they never regained their former momentum, and few of the young girls in the villages of the county were interested in them.
48. Li Hangyu, *Lao Hangzhou*, 21.
49. Ibid., 16.
50. Zhang Qijun, "A History of Scenic West Lake," 228.
51. CCP Zhejiang Department of the United Front, "Primary Measures for Implementing the Instructions of the Provincial Committee on the Temples in the City of Hangzhou" (July 22, 1953); ZPA, 4/1/59.
52. *Zhejiang Daily*, November 23, 1949, 3.
53. See Zhou Feng et al., eds., *Minguo shiqi Hangzhou*, 422–423; Mao Shan,

"From Singing Story to Yueju Opera," *Global Journal*, November 12, 1995, 18.
54. "Propaganda Department of Zhejiang Requires Opera Reform," *Zhejiang Daily*, October 23, 1953, 2; "Veteran Performers Talk about Opera Reform," *Zhejiang Daily*, March 29, 1954, 2.
55. *Zhejiang Daily*, May 14, 1950, 3.
56. Here I refer to the oral version of *On the Margin of Water*, which is an embryonic form of the classic novel by Shi Nai'an. See Ma Chengsheng, "Hangzhou and *On the Margin of Water*," in Zhou Feng et al., eds., *Yuan Ming Qing mingchen Hangzhou*, 343–358.
57. See Ju Yizhong, "Storytellers in Hangzhou, the Mainland," *Global News*, October 19, 1995, 23.
58. Not all the comments, however, met the government's requirements. Sometimes, trouble came from a loose tongue and a joke ruined an actor's career. The storyteller Zhang Yiming was good at detective stories, especially legends about an ancient and prestigious Chinese judge named Bao Gong, who used all means to crack criminal cases. In his performances, Zhang would say that Bao Gong never investigated a case but always cheated or threatened in order to trap criminals into a confession. Then he added that this was exactly what the Communist cadres had done in the Five Antis Campaign: they did not have any evidence, but they bluffed the capitalists and merchants, who did not have political experience and were easily fooled, into confessions. On another occasion, Zhang made a joke about public bonds *(gong zhai)*, remarking that the Chinese character *gong* (public) looked like a crying face. The government called on everyone to buy public bonds, but those who bought the bonds would taste a bitter pill and want to cry. These words obviously offended the government. At political study meetings, Zhang Yiming was condemned for attacking the Five Antis Campaign and being against Party policy. The Bureau of Culture and Education declared that "his counterrevolutionary ideas could not be tolerated" and sent him to the countryside for "ideological remolding through labor." Most storytellers were used to using the past to disparage the present and could not always follow government instructions; they were doomed to be persecuted in later political campaigns. See Department of Culture and Education, "Summary Report on Cultural Work in 1952"; HMA, 86/1/40.
59. Wu Xian (chairman of the city's Financial and Economic Committee), "A Notice on the Takeover of Big World" (May 23, 1952); HMA, 86/1/49. The owner of Big World, Chen Shenfu, was scared by the public criticism in the Five Antis Campaign and feared serious punishment for tax evasion. Ironically, a month after his suicide, Chen's Big World was

classified as a "basically law-abiding establishment." See the Municipal Committee for Increasing Production and Practicing Economy, "Notice No. 9268" (May 29, 1953); HMA, 86/1/49.
60. In the end, eighteen of the fifty-two Big World employees were retained.
61. City Government of Hangzhou, "Temporary Regulations for Managing Cultural and Recreation Places and Organizations in the City of Hangzhou" (1951); HMA, 23/5/74.
62. For example, the Dazhong Theater criticized the Movie *Only for Love*, which was shown at that theater on February 25, 1952. It suggested that the Department of Culture and Education provide movies "full of educational implications." Dazhong Theater, "Work Report, January–July 1952"; HMA, 86/1/40.
63. See "Remarkable Progress on Drama Reform, New Focus on *Yueju* Reform," *Zhejiang Daily*, November 23, 1949, 3.
64. Ibid.
65. Bureau of Culture and Education, "Summary Report on Cultural Work in 1952"; HMA, 86/1/40. *Hangju* first emerged on the stage in 1923 but never became very popular in Hangzhou. *Qu yi* includes various forms of performance: ballad singing, storytelling, comic dialogues, and clapper talks.
66. Ibid.
67. Ibid.
68. Interview with Wang Tugen, Hangzhou, March 19, 1998; interview with Mao Liren, Hangzhou, August 17, 1998. The government report applauded the efforts in reforming *yueju* but was dissatisfied with the changes in *The White Snake*. See "Conference on Drama Performance," *Zhejiang Daily*, May 4 and 7, 1954, 3.
69. "*Yueju* 'Liang Shanbo and Zhu Yingtai' in Hong Kong," *Zhejiang Daily*, December 14, 1954, 3.
70. Yang Siyi, *Diary*.
71. Related by Bian Pengfei in interview, Hangzhou, August 5, 1998.
72. Guang Weiran, "The Heritage of Realism in Traditional Chinese Opera"; cited in Zhao Qingge, *Liang Shanbo yu Zhu Yingtai* (Liang Shanbo and Zhu Yingtai) (Beijing: New World Press, 1999), 1.
73. The graves and monuments include those of Xu Xilin (1873–1907), who was a Republican martyr; Tao Chengzhao (1878–1912), a revolutionary leader who was assassinated after the victory of the 1911 revolution; and Li Shutong (1880–1942) and Su Manshu (1884–1918), famous scholars and Buddhist masters. The story of Su Xiaoxiao was well known in the city. The first part of her story was similar to that of any talented and beautiful geisha: she fell in love with a young man, but the man abandoned her. Su was praised by generations of Confucian scholars for her generosity after her heartbreak. Despite her own suffering, Su Xiaoxiao

gave a poor student, Bao Ren, a hundred teals of silver, making it possible for him to go to the capital for the civil service exam. After Su's death in Hangzhou, Bao Ren buried her by the lakeside. From a Communist perspective, Su Xiaoxiao could not be ranked with the revolutionary heroine Qiu Jin.
74. Len Xiao, "Overview of the Socialist Transformation of Capitalist Industry and Commerce in Hangzhou"; in *Zhejiang zibenzhuyi,* 503.
75. ECB, "Comments on Zhejiang's Report on Commerce and Markets" (June 23, 1953); ZPA, 14/8/1/7.
76. Ibid.
77. Tan Zhenlin, "Speech at the Fourth Provincial Convention of the CCP in Zhejiang" (October 23, 1953); ZPA, 14/8/1/6.
78. ECB, "Comments on Zhejiang's Report on Commerce and Markets" (June 23, 1953); ZPA, 14/8/1/7.
79. CCP Zhejiang Committee, "Instructions for the Implementation of a State Monopoly for the Purchase and Marketing of Grain" (November 12, 1953); ZPA, 14/8/1/8.
80. CCP Zhejiang Committee, "Instructions on the Socialist Transformation of Private Industry and the Handicrafts Industry through State Capitalism" (March 1954); ZPA, 14/8/1/7.
81. ECB, "Urgent Instructions on Strengthening the Control over Markets in Zhejiang" (January 11, 1954); ZPA, 14/8/1/8.
82. CCP Zhejiang Committee, "Additional Instructions on the Socialist Transformation of Private Industry through State Capitalism in 1954" (April 2, 1954); ZPA, 14/8/1/7.
83. Finance Committee of Zhejiang Province, "Report on Some Issues in Joint State-Private Enterprises (Industry) and Proposed Measures" (March 6, 1954); ZPA, 14/8/2/3.
84. Finance Committee of Zhejiang Province, "Report on the First Provincial Meeting on Joint State-Private Industrial Ventures" (July 6, 1954); ZPA, 14/8/2/3.
85. CCP Zhejiang Committee, "Instructions on the Socialist Transformation of Private Industry through State Capitalism" (December 10, 1953); ZPA, 14/8/2/3.
86. CCP Zhejiang Committee, "Report on Joint State-Private Ownership of the Mingfen and Huafen Paper Mills" (September 12, 1953); ZPA, 14/8/1/7.
87. CCP Hangzhou Committee, "Report on Application for Institution of Joint State-Private Ownership in Minshen Pharmacy and Four Other Factories" (November 26, 1953); CCP Zhejiang Committee, "Approval of the Report by CCP Hangzhou Committee on Institution of Joint State-Private Ownership in Minshen Pharmacy and Four Other Factories" (December 3, 1953); ZPA, 14/8/1/7.

88. Tan Zhenlin, "Speech at the Fourth Provincial Convention of the CCP in Zhejiang" (October 23, 1953); ZPA, 14/6/1.
89. Ibid.
90. Interview with Xiao Yi, Hangzhou, May 20, 1997.
91. On January 16, 1956, the CCP Hangzhou Committee called a discussion meeting with the representatives of factory owners and merchants, calling on them to follow Beijing's example to institute joint state-private ownership within three days. In the meantime the CCP Zhejiang Committee passed a resolution on joint ownership. Students and workers poured into the streets to urge the capitalists to take action. The provincial Women's Federation organized the wives of capitalists and merchants to persuade or support their husbands to take action. The Association of Industry and Commerce called an urgent meeting to respond to the Party's call. Next, 5,998 enterprises applied for joint state-private ownership; 2,533 were approved, and the rest became collective enterprises. See Leng Xiao, "Overview of the Socialist Transformation of Capitalist Industry and Commerce in the City of Hangzhou"; in *Zhejiang zibenzhuyi*, 511.
92. Mao Zedong, *On the Correct Handling of Contradictions among the People* (February 27, 1957) (Beijing: People's Press: 1957), 12.

Chapter 9: *Conclusion*

1. See Meisner, *Mao's China*. Stuart Schram also argues that the substance of Mao Zedong's contribution to the theory of building socialism, known as "mainstream Maoism," is not found in the early 1950s but in 1955–1965. See Stuart Schram, *The Political Thought of Mao Tse-Tung* (New York: Praeger, 1969).
2. The concept of "permanent revolution" is often linked with Trotskyism, but the CCP argues that the term was employed by Mao earlier. Mao's "permanent revolution" includes the concept of a "revolution in stages," but that is totally different from the Trotskyist heresy of "leaping over stages." See Liu Shaoqi, *Address at the Meeting in Celebration of the Fortieth Anniversary of the Founding of the Communist Party of China* (Beijing: Foreign Languages Press, 1961).
3. "On the People's Dictatorship"; in Mao Tse-tung, *Selected Works*, 4: 422.
4. This idea was also expressed in Mao's early works. See "The Chinese Revolution and the Chinese Communist Party"; in Mao Tse-tung, *Selected Works*, 3: 326–331.
5. It was called a "gradualism with a clear blueprint" in *The Cambridge History of China*, ed. Roderick MacFarquhar and John Fairbank (Cambridge: Cambridge University Press, 1987), 78.

6. In "Outline of Speech at Politburo Meeting" (June 15, 1953), Mao Zedong wrote: "Several confusing points: (1) consolidation of New Democratic social order; (2) New Democracy leads to socialism; (3) guarantee of private ownership." In *Jianguo yilai Mao Zedong wengao,* 4: 251. Bo Yibo and Zhou Enlai took detailed notes of this speech; see Bo Yibo, *Ruogan,* 65–66. Mao's comments were an implicit criticism against Liu Shaoqi, who encouraged capitalist development and emphasized the protection of private industry and commerce. According to Liu, this was basic Party policy, known as the "New Democratic Order." Mao Zedong, however, believed that the New Democracy was but a temporary Party tactic in the transition period; the New Democratic Order should not be consolidated, and private ownership must be eliminated.
7. Although Gao Gang in Manchuria served as a trailblazer for CCP policy implementation, he was also condemned for developing policies at variance with the programs of the CCP Central Committee in 1949 and 1954. See Bo Yibo, *Ruogan,* 57, 308–321. Also see Teiwes, *Politics and Purges in China,* 145–150, 152–155.
8. For example, it was reported that "all counterrevolutionaries in the 126 cities and towns of the province of Zhejiang had been arrested or killed" by February 1951. See CCP Zhejiang Committee, *Zhongguo gongcandang Zhejiang, 1949–1993,* 28.
9. See Schram, *Political Thought of Mao Tse-Tung,* 54.
10. David Kertzer, *Ritual, Politics, and Power* (New Haven, Conn.: Yale University Press, 1988), 54.
11. Sally F. Moore and Barbara Myerhoff, eds., *Secular Ritual* (Assne: Van Gorcum, 1977), 226.
12. In discussing the forced confessions of Chinese intellectuals in various political campaigns, Perry Link writes, "In exchange for a sense of security, people become willing to proffer their 'guilt,' and the state reinforces this psychology by demanding confessions and promising leniency to those who confess well." Perry Link, *Evening Chats in Beijing,* 215.
13. Bennett, "Culture, Communication, and Political Control." Transaction Books.
14. The song about Mao is "Dongfang hong" (The East is red).
15. Ted C. Lewellen, *Political Anthropology: An Introduction* (Westport, Conn.: Bergin and Garvey, 1992), 73.
16. Most people were labeled anti-Party or anti-socialism rightists in 1957 just because they criticized some Party cadres.
17. Pye, *The Spirit of Chinese Politics,* 67. Pye is right to argue that "the Chinese Communists have carried [this philosophy] to new extremes." Nevertheless, his generalization that "No other political culture puts

as much stress upon the emotion of hate as does the Chinese" is problematic.
18. The so-called "four categories of evil" were defined as the people's enemies and comprised landlords, rich peasants, counterrevolutionaries, and bad elements (criminals or persons with bad records). In 1957, the term was replaced by the "five categories of evil" to include the rightists.
19. Lucian Pye, *Asian Power and Politics: The Cultural Dimension of Authority* (Cambridge, Mass.: Harvard University Press, 1985), x.
20. Ibid., 118–124.
21. Schram, *Political Thought of Mao Tse-Tung*, 8.
22. Mao repeatedly emphasized the necessity for revolutionary intellectuals and revolutionary youth to learn from peasants. See "The Chinese Revolution and the Chinese Communist Party" (December 1939); in Mao Tse-tung, *Selected Works*, 2: 322, and "Talks at the Yen'an Forum on Literature and Art" (May 1942), in ibid., 3: 87.
23. Pye, *The Spirit of Chinese Politics*, 23. Pye also mentions Susan Shirk's argument on "virtuocracies" in Maoist China. See Susan L. Shirk, *Competitive Comrades* (Berkeley: University of California Press, 1982).
24. Edwin Hubbell Chapin, *Humanity in the City*; cited in Gunther Barth, *City People: The Rise of Modern City Culture in Nineteenth-Century America* (Oxford: Oxford University Press, 1980), 11.
25. It was common practice in China, especially in periods of regime change, for cultural celebrities to use their cultural capital to deal with the problems of everyday life. See Qianshen Bai, "Calligraphy for Negotiating Everyday Life: The Case of Fushan (1607–1684)," *Asia Major* 12, no. 1 (1999): 67–118.
26. In January 1958, Mao Zedong said, "The various departments of the center, and the three levels of the province, the prefecture, and the village group *(xiang)* must train and make their cadres *xiu cai*. These *xiu cai* must understand relatively more about Marxism-Leninism, and they must also be well educated in terms of scientific knowledge and literary training." "Sixty Points on Methods of Work"; in *Jianguo yilai Mao Zedong wengao*, 7: 62. *Xiu cai* were Confucian students who passed the lowest level government exam in traditional China. The Chinese usually refer to well-educated scholars as *xiu cai*.
27. Consuelo Cruz, "Identity and Persuasion: How Nations Remember Their Pasts and Make Their Futures," *World Politics*, 2000.
28. Mao Zedong, *Mao Zhuxi he youren de tanhua* (Chairman Mao's talks with friends) (Beijing: Chinese Youth Press, 1968), 288.

Glossary

Anhui	安徽	Deng Xiaoping	邓小平
Bai Juyi	白居易	Deng Zihui	邓子恢
Bai She Zhuan	白蛇传	*diwei*	地委
bai zu nan qian	百族南迁	*dongyuan hui*	动员会
bao jia system	保甲制	*dou*	斗
bao jia wei guo	保家为国	*douzheng hui*	斗争会
Baodugu	抱犊崮	Du Yuesheng	杜月笙
Bengbu	蚌埠	Dunyitang	敦义堂
Bianlian Xian	边联县	*fang zu*	放足
bie san	瘪三	Fanzhi	繁峙
Binhai Zhuanqu	滨海专区	*Fei xiao*	非孝
Bo Yibo	薄一波	*fenliang renren youfen, canjun renren youze*	分粮人人有份，参军人人有责
Bohai	渤海		
Boqiang	伯强		
bu ru min zhai	不入民宅	Feng Yindong	冯荫东
bu shi bing ge	不事兵戈	*fu gui qi rong*	夫贵妻荣
Cai Jingxian	蔡敬贤	*fu mu guan*	父母官
Cangshan	苍山	Fu Qiutao	傅秋涛
Chen Boda	陈伯达	Fujian	福建
Chen Duxiu	陈独秀	*funü shiziban*	妇女识字班
Chen Xiuliang	陈修良	Gai Jiaotian	盖叫天
Chen Yi	陈毅	*gai zu*	改足
Chen Yongzao	陈永造	*gai zu pai*	改足派
Chen Yun	陈云	*gan shu*	干属
Chenzhong	晨钟	*gan, guan, guan*	赶，关，管
chong mei	崇美	Gao Gang	高岗
Chouye Huiguan	绸业会馆	Genshan district	艮山区
Chu	楚	*gongji zhi*	供给制
Cui Bo	崔波	*gong zhai*	公债
cuncun dianhuo	村村点火	*gongzi zhi*	工资制
Dadaohui	大刀会	*gongnong ganbu*	工农干部
Dadian	大店	Gongshu Qu	拱墅区
dan	石	*gou lou*	佝偻
dang ke	党课	Gu Dehuan	顾德欢
Dangdai Ribao	当代日报	*guan taitai*	官太太
dangdi ganbu	当地干部	*guan zhi*	管制
daqu	大区	Guanchengtang	观成堂

Guandi	关帝	*lao balu*	老八路
Guo Chunlin	郭春霖	*lao geming*	老革命
Guo Moruo	郭沫若	Li Daigen	李代耕
Guomindang	国民党	Li Dazhao	李大钊
Han	汉	Li Desheng	李得胜
Handan	邯郸	Li Fengping	李丰平
hangju	杭剧	Li Fuchun	李富春
Hangzhou	杭州	Li Qingqi	李清绮
Hao Jianxiu	郝建秀	Li Qingwei	李清潍
Hebei	河北	Li Qingyu	李青余
Hongyi	弘一	Li Shutong	李叔同
Hu Haiqiu	胡海秋	Li Xiannian	李先念
Hu Qiaomu	胡乔木	Li Yu	黎玉
Hu Zongnan	胡宗南	Li Zhaohuan	黎照寰
Huadong University	华东大学	Li Zicheng	李自成
Huaihai Battle	淮海战役	Liang Shanbo and Zhu Yingtai	梁山伯与祝英台
Huaiyin	淮阴		
huhu maoyan	户户冒烟	Liangzhu Wenhua	良诸文化
Hunan	湖南	Liangzhu	良诸
Hupao	虎跑	*lihun bu lijia*	离婚不离家
Ji Pengfei	姬鹏飞	Lin Biao	林彪
Jia Shen San Bai Nian Ji	甲申三百年祭	Lin Feng	林枫
		Lin Hujia	林乎加
Jianggan district	江干区	Lincheng	临城
Jiangnan	江南	Lingyin temple	灵隐寺
Jiangxi	江西	Linyi	临沂
Jianqiao district	笕桥区	Liu Bang	刘邦
jiantao hui	检讨会	Liu Bo	刘博
Jiaodong	胶东	Liu Jian	刘建
Jiaozuo	焦作	Liu Lan (Ren Daniang)	刘蓝 (任大娘)
Jiaxing	嘉兴		
Jin Runxiang	金润庠	Liu Qingshan	刘青山
jin	斤	Liu Shaoqi	刘少奇
Jinan	济南	Liu Yifu	刘亦夫
Jining	济宁	*liuyong renyuan*	留用人员
Ju Xian	莒县	Long Yue	龙跃
jun shu	军属	Longjing	龙井
kai cang ji pin	开仓济贫	Lu Zhixian	吕志先
Kaifeng	开封	Lunan	鲁南
Ke Li	柯里	Luoyang	洛阳
kong mei	恐美	Luzhong	鲁中
kongsu hui	控诉会	Luzhongnan	鲁中南
kuaiban	快板	Ma Yinchu	马寅初

Glossary

Mao Zedong	毛泽东	Suzhou	苏州
Meijiawu	梅家坞	Taierzhuang	台儿庄
Moganshan	莫干山	Taizao Diqu	台枣地区
Mu Guiying	穆桂英	Tan Jiazhen	谈家桢
muji sichen	牡鸡司晨	Tan Qilong	谭启龙
Mu He	沐河	Tan Zhenlin	谭震林
mu	亩	*te kong*	特控
nanxia ganbu	南下干部	Tian Jiaying	田家英
nianpu	年谱	Tianjin	天津
Nie Rongzhen	聂荣臻	*tianshi dili renhe*	天时地利人和
Ningbo	宁波		
Peng Dehuai	彭德怀	*wa kugen*	挖苦根
pipan hui	批判会	*waihang lingdao neihang*	外行领导内行
Qiantang	钱塘		
qin mei	亲美	Wang Daohan	汪道涵
Qing Bang	青帮	Wang Jian'an	王建安
Qiu Jin	秋瑾	Wei Siwen	魏思文
qu	区	Weixian	潍县
quyi	曲艺	*wu du*	五毒
Qufu	曲阜	Wu Jinan	吴锦安
qunzhong guanzhi	群众管制	Wuqihui	五旗会
Rao Shushi	饶漱石	Wu Xian	吴宪
Rong Yiren	荣毅仁	Wuhe Xian	五合县
ruseng	儒僧	Wu Xun	武训
Sanfanzi	三番子	Wu-Yue Guo	吴越国
sao di chu men	扫地出门	Xiacheng district	下城区
Shajiadian	沙家店	Xi'an	西安
Shanbei	陕北	*xian*	县
Shandong	山东	*xiang*	乡
Shangcheng district	上城区	Xiang Yu	项羽
Shanxi	山西	*Xiangdao*	向导
Shaoxing	绍兴	*xiangsheng*	相声
Shenyang	沈阳	Xiao Fangzhou	肖方洲
Shi Nai'an	施耐庵	Xiaoshan	肖山
Shijiazhuang	石家庄	Xibaipo	西柏坡
shui	税	Xihu district	西湖区
Song	宋	*Xiongdihui*	兄弟会
song lang can jun	送郎参军	*xuan qiang liu ruo*	选强留弱
Su Dongpo	苏东坡	Xun Zi	荀子
suku hui	诉苦会	Xuzhou	徐州
Suiyuan	绥远	Yan'an	延安
Sun Wencheng	孙文成	Yang Shangkun	杨尚昆
Sun Zi	孙子	Yang Siyi	杨思一

Yang Yuanshi	杨源时	Zaozhuang	枣庄
Yantai	烟台	Zhang Deng	张登
Yanzhou	兖州	Zhang Heng	张衡
Ye Jianying	叶剑英	Zhang Jinfu	张劲夫
yi cha dai jiu	以茶代酒	Zhang Youyu	张友渔
Yi Guan Dao	一贯道	Zhang Zishan	张子善
Yi He	沂河	Zhao Liangkun	赵亮昆
Yi Xian	峄县	Zhao Yiman	赵一曼
Yimeng	沂蒙	Zhaobo Xian	赵博县
Yishui Xian	沂水县	Zhejiang	浙江
yong bu wang ben	永不忘本	Zhejiang University	浙江大学
youji zuofeng	游击作风	*zhen*	镇
Yu Jimin	俞济民	Zheng Jinfang	郑锦芳
Yu Zisan	于子三	*zhengzhi xuexi hui*	政治学习会
yuan feng bu dong	原封不动	Zhijiang University	之江大学
yuan feng yuan yang	原封原样	*zhishifenzi ganbu*	知识分子干部
Yuan Ming (Fu Daniang)	袁明 (付大娘)	Zhong Qiguang	钟期光
Yuncheng	运城	*Zhongshan Zhuang*	中山装
yue fa san zhang	约法三章	Zhongcheng district	中城区
Yue Guo	越国	Zhou Enlai	周恩来
yueju	越剧	*zongjie hui*	总结会
zai zhou zhi shui yi fu zhou	载舟之水亦覆舟	*zuzhi*	组织

Selected Bibliography

Archival Sources

CCA Cangshan Xian Dangan Guan (Cangshan County Archives)
HMA Hangzhou Shi Dangan Guan (Hangzhou Municipal Archives)
HUDA Hangzhou Shi Chengjian Dangan Guan (Hangzhou Urban Development Archives)
JMA Jinan Shi Dangan Guan (Jinan Municipal Archives)
LMA Linyi Shi Dangan Guan (Linyi Municipal Archives)
SMA Shanghai Shi Dangan Guan (Shanghai Municipal Archives)
SPA Shandong Sheng Dangan Guan (Shandong Provincial Archives)
ZMA Zaozhuang Shi Dangan Guan (Zaozhuang Municipal Archives)
ZPA Zhejiang Sheng Dangan Guan (Zhejiang Provincial Archives)
ZPWFA Zhejiang Sheng Fulian Dangan Shi (Zhejiang Provincial Women's Federation Archives)
ZUA Zhejiang Daxue Dangan Shi (Zhejiang University Archives)

Documentary Collections (Printed for internal circulation)

Chengshi de jieguan yu shehui gaizao, Hangzhou juan (The takeover of the cities and transformation of society, Hangzhou vol.). Beijing: Modern China Press, 1996.
Hangzhou diqu nongye ziranzaihai shiliao huibian (A selection of historical materials on agriculture and natural disasters in Hangzhou). Hangzhou Municipal Archives, 1994.
Hangzhou Lijie Dangdaihui (Materials on all previous CCP Hangzhou Municipal Congresses). Hangzhou Municipal Archives, 1995.
Hangzhou shi jiguan jigou yange (The evolution of Hangzhou municipal institutions). Hangzhou Municipal Archives, 1995.
Hangzhoushi chaye, chaguanye tong ye gonghui dangan shiliao xuanbian, 1939–53 (A selection of archival materials on professional associations of tea commerce and teahouses in Hangzhou, 1939–53). Hangzhou Municipal Archives, 1996.
Hangzhoushi sichouye gaikuang (An overview of the silk industry in Hangzhou). Hangzhou Municipal Archives, 1996.
Hangzhoushi sichouye shiliao (Historical materials on the silk industry in Hangzhou). Hangzhou Municipal Archives, 1996.

Hangzhoushi sichouye tongye gonghui dangan shiliao xuanbian, 1937–60 (A selection of archival materials on professional associations in the silk industry in Hangzhou, 1937–60). Hangzhou Municipal Archives, 1996.

Jianguo yilai Liu Shaoqi wengao (Liu Shaoqi's manuscripts since the founding of the People's Republic of China). Beijing: Central Documents Press, 1999.

Jianguo yilai Mao Zedong wengao (Mao Zedong's manuscripts since the founding of the People's Republic of China). Beijing: Central Documents Press, 1987–1999.

Jianguo yilai zhongyao wenxian xuanbian (A selection of important documents since the founding of the People's Republic of China). Beijing: Central Documents Press, 1992–1998.

Jieguan Shanghai (The takeover of Shanghai). Shanghai Municipal Archives, 1993.

Minguo shiqi Hangzhou shiqu gequ quhua yanbian gaikuang (An overview of the district changes in Hangzhou in the republican period). Hangzhou Municipal Archives, 1994.

Minguo shiqi Hangzhou shizhenfu dangan shiliao xuanbian (A selection of archival materials of the Hangzhou municipal government in the republican period). Hangzhou Municipal Archives, 1995.

Shandong shizhi ziliao, 1–6 juan (Reference materials on Shandong local history, vols. 1–6). Jinan: Shandong People's Press.

Shanghai geming lishi wenjian huiji (A collection of historical materials on the revolution in Shanghai). Shanghai Municipal Archives, 1986–1991.

Zhejiang zibenzhuyi gongshangye de shehuizhuyi gaizhao (A selection of materials on the socialist transformation of capitalist industry and commerce in Zhejiang). Hangzhou: CCP Zhejiang Committee, Department of Propaganda, 1959.

Zhonggong dangshi jiaoxue cankao ziliao, 16–22 juan (Reference materials on teaching CCP history, vols. 16–22). Beijing: Defense University, n.d.

Zhonggong zhongyang jiefang zhangzheng shiqi tongyi zhanxian wenjian xuanbian (Selected documents on the CCP united front in the liberation war). Beijing: Archives Press, 1988.

Zhonggong zhongyang wenjian xuanji (Selected documents of the CCP Central Committee). Beijing: CCP Party School Press, 1989–1992.

Zhongguo difangzhi minsu ziliao huibian: Huadongjuan (Selected references on folk customs from the annals of local history: East China volume). Beijing: Bibliography Press, 1995.

Zhongguo gongcandang lishi ziliao congshu: Hangzhou juan (Series of historical materials of the CCP: Hangzhou volume). Beijing: Modern China Press, 1996.

Zhongguo gongcandang zuzhishi ziliao huibian (A selection of reference materials on the organizational history of the CCP). Beijing: Red Flag Press, 1981.

Books and Articles

Andors, Phyllis. *The Unfinished Liberation of Chinese Women, 1949–1980.* Bloomington: Indiana University Press, 1983.

Aronoff, Myron J., ed. *Culture and Political Change.* New Brunswick, N.J.: Transaction Books, 1983.

Bachman, David M. *Bureaucracy, Economy, and Leadership in China.* Cambridge: Cambridge University Press, 1991.

Bai Xi. *Da Zhenya* (The great suppression). Beijing: Jincheng Press, 2000.

Barnett, A. Doak. *Communist China: The Early Years, 1949–55.* New York: Praeger, 1964.

Barth, Gunther. *City People: The Rise of Modern City Culture in Nineteenth-Century America.* Oxford: Oxford University Press, 1980.

Bennett, W. Lance. "Culture, Communication, and Political Control." In Aronoff, ed., *Culture and Political Change*, 39–52.

Bianco, Lucien. *Origins of the Chinese Revolution, 1915–1949.* Stanford, Calif.: Stanford University Press, 1971.

Bo Yibo. *Ruogan zhongda juece yu shijian de huigu* (A restrospect of some crucial decisions and events). Beijing: Party School Press, 1991.

Cao Xiangju. "A Warm Concern and Earnest Teachings." In Chen Fawen et al., eds., *Wuxian jinian wenji*.

Carrasco, Pedro. "The Civil-Religious Hierarchy in Mesoamerican Communities: Pre-Spanish Background and Colonial Development." *American Anthropologist* 63 (1961): 483–497.

Cass. Victoria. *Dangerous Women: Warriors, Grannies and Geishas of the Ming.* Lanham, Md.: Rowman and Littlefield, 1999.

CCP Cangshan Committee. *Zhonggong Cangshan dangshi dashi ji* (Chronology of the CCP in Cangshan, 1927–1949). Linyi: District Publishing House, 1993.

CCP Central Committee. Document Research Division. *Liu Shaoqi nianpu* (A chronological record of Liu Shaoqi). 2 vols. Beijing: Central Documents Press, 1996.

———. *Mao Zedong nianpu* (A chronological record of Mao Zedong). 4 vols. Beijing: Central Documents Press, 1993.

———. *Zhou Enlai nianpu* (A chronological record of Zhou Enlai). 2 vols. Beijing: Central Documents Press, 1996.

CCP Linyi Committee. *Zhonggong Lunanqu dangshi dashi ji 1919 wuyue zi 1949 jiuyue* (Chronology of the CCP in Lunan, May 1919–September 1949). Jinan: Shandong People's Press, 1991.

———. *Zhonggong Binhai dangshi dashi ji* (Chronology of the CCP in Bingai). Jinan: Shandong People's Press, 1988.

———. *Zhonggong Yimeng dangshi dashi ji* (Chronological record of Party history in the Yimeng area). Jinan: Shandong People's Press, 1992.

CCP Shandong Committee. *Zhonggong Shandong lishi dashi ji* (Chronology of the CCP in Shandong). Jinan: Shandong People's Press, 1992.
CCP Zaozhuang Committee. "Lunan geming shi" (A revolutionary history of Lunan). Unpublished manuscript.
CCP Zhejiang Committee. *Zhongguo gongcandang Zhejiang lishi dashi ji, 1949–1993* (Chronology of the CCP in Zhejiang, 1949–1993). Beijing: CCP History Press, 1996.
——. *Zhongguo gongcandang Zhejiang lishi dashi ji, 1919–1949* (Chronology of the CCP in Zhejiang, 1919–1949). Hangzhou: Zhejiang People's Press, 1990.
Cell, Charles. *Revolution and Work: Mobilization Campaigns in China*. New York: Academic Press, 1977.
Chen Fawen et al., eds. *Wuxian jinian wenji* (Selected papers in memory of Wu Xian). Hangzhou: Hangzhou Press, 1998.
Chen, Jian. *Mao's China and the Cold War*. Chapel Hill: University of North Carolina Press, 2001.
Chen Wenjin. *Xihu Wenwu (Cultural relics of West Lake)*. Hangzhou: Zhejiang Photography Press, 1997.
Chen Yun. "The High-Ranking Leaders Must Increase Their Vigilance." In *Selected Works of Chen Yun*. Beijing: People's Press, 1987.
Chen, Yung-fa, *Making Revolution: The Communist Movement in Eastern and Central China, 1937–1945*. Berkeley: University of California Press, 1986.
Cheng, Chu-yuan. *New Trends in Chinese Communist Fiscal Economic Policies*. Hong Kong: Zuyu Press, 1953.
Chesneaux, Jean. *The Chinese Labor Movement, 1919–1927*. Stanford, Calif.: Stanford University Press, 1968.
Chinese Association for the Resist America, Aid Korea Campaign, Propaganda Department, ed. *The Great Resist America, Aid Korea Campaign*. Beijing: People's Press, 1954.
Cruz, Consuelo. "Identity and Persuasion: How Nations Remember Their Pasts and Make Their Futures." *World Politics*, 2000.
"Declaration of the Feminist Movement Association." Women's Journal 8, no. 8 (1922).
Deng Xiaoping. *Deng Xiaoping wenxuan (1975–1982)* (Selected works of Deng Xiaoping [1975–1982]). Beijing: People's Press, 1984.
Diamant, Neil J. *Revolutionizing the Family: Politics, Love, and Divorce in Urban and Rural China, 1949–1968*. Berkeley: University of California Press, 2000.
Ding Rongguan. "Huilan Private High School." In Zhou Feng et al., eds., *Minguo shiqi Hangzhou*.
Dirlik, Arif. *The Origins of Chinese Communism*. New York: Oxford University Press, 1989.
Dittmer, Lowell. *China's Continuous Revolution: The Post-Liberation Epoch 1949–1981*. Berkeley: University of California Press, 1987.

Dumont, Louis. *Homo Hierarchicus: The Caste System and Its Implications.* Chicago: University of Chicago Press, 1977.
Esherick, Joseph W. *The Origins of the Boxer Uprising.* Berkeley: University of California Press, 1987.
———, ed. *Remaking the Chinese City: Modernity and National Identity, 1900–1950.* Honolulu: University of Hawai'i Press, 2000.
Friedman, Edward. *National Identity and Democratic Prospects in Socialist China.* Armonk, N.Y.: M. E. Sharpe, 1995.
Gao Hongxing. *Chanzhui shi* (A history of foot binding). Shanghai: Wenyi Press, 1995.
Gao, James Z. *Meeting Technology's Advance: Social Changes in China and Zimbabwe in the Railway Age.* Westport, Conn.: Greenwood Press, 1997.
———. "War Culture, Nationalism, and Political Campaigns, 1950–1953." In *Chinese Nationalism in Perspective: Historical and Recent Cases*, ed. C. X. George Wei and Xiaoyuan Liu. Westport, Conn.: Greenwood Press, 2001.
Ge Hongsheng et al., eds. *Fengyu chang xiangyi: Jinian Liu Jian tongzhi wenji* (The lasting memory in the storm: Selected papers in memory of Comrade Liu Jian). Beijing: CCP History Press, 1994.
Gilmartin, Christina K. "Gender, Political Culture, and Women's Mobilization in the Chinese Nationalist Revolution, 1924–1927." In Gilmartin et al., eds., *Engendering China.*
Gilmartin, Christina K. et al., eds. *Engendering China: Women, Culture, and the State.* Cambridge, Mass.: Harvard University Press, 1994.
Gluckman, Max. *Politics, Law and Ritual in Tribal Society.* Chicago: Aldine, 1965.
Harding, Harry. *Organizing China: The Problem of Bureaucracy, 1949–1976.* Stanford, Calif.: Stanford University Press, 1981.
Hegland, Mary. "Ritual and Revolution in Iran." In Aronoff, ed., *Culture and Political Change.*
Hinton, Harold C. *The "Unprincipled Dispute" within the Chinese Communist Top Leadership.* Washington, D.C.: U.S. Information Agency. IRI Intelligence Summary no. LS-98-55, July 1955.
Hua Mei. "Fashions of the Century." *People's Daily,* May 17, 2001.
Huang Yuanling, ed. *Cartoons of the Century.* Beijing: Modern Press, 2000.
Jin Yanfeng et al. *Zhejiang jiaofei jishi* (The true record of the elimination of bandits in Zhejiang). Hangzhou: Zhejiang People's Press, 1990.
Jing Su and Luo Lun. *Landlord and Labor in Late Imperial China: Case Studies from Shandong.* Trans. with an introduction by Endymion Wilkinson. Cambridge, Mass.: Harvard University Press, 1978.
Johnson, Kay Ann. *Women, the Family, and Peasant Revolution in China.* Chicago: University of Chicago Press, 1983.
Ju Yizhong. "Storytellers in Hangzhou, the Mainland." *Global News,* October 19, 1995.

Kertzer, David. *Ritual, Politics, and Power*. New Haven, Conn.: Yale University Press, 1988.
Kuhn, Philip A. *Soulstealers: The Chinese Sorcery Scare of 1768*. Cambridge, Mass.: Harvard University Press, 1990.
Lei Feng. *Diary*. Beijing: People's Press, 1963.
Levine, Steven. *Anvil of Victory: The Communist Revolution in Manchuria, 1945–1948*. New York: Columbia University Press, 1987.
Lewellen, Ted. C. *Political Anthropology: An Introduction*. Westport, Conn.: Bergin and Garvey, 1992.
Li Fuchun. "Report on the First Five-Year Plan for the Development of the National Economy of the People's Republic of China." *People's Daily*, July 6, 1955.
Li Hangyu. *Lao Hangzhou* (Old Hangzhou). Nanjing: Jiangsu Art Press, 2000.
Li Liang. "Equality between Men and Women in Socialist Countries." *New Women of China* 6 (1953).
Lieberthal, Kenneth G. *Revolution and Tradition in Tientsin, 1949–1952*. Stanford, Calif.: Stanford University Press, 1980.
Lin Biao. "Report on the Future Work of the Central China Bureau." *Changjiang Daily*, July 4, 1949.
Lin Tiao. *Yonghen de chenxi* (Permanency in silence). Beijing: Beiyue Press, 2000.
Lin Yunhui et al., eds. *Kaige xingjin de shiqi* (The period of triumphant march). Zhengzhou: Henan People's Press, 1996.
Lin Zhengqiu. "Jingshi jiu simin, renkou guan quanguo" (People from all parts poured into the capital, making it the city with the largest population in the country). In Zhou Fen et al., eds., *Nansong jingcheng Hangzhou*.
Link, Perry. *Evening Chats in Beijing: Probing China's Predicament*. New York: W. W. Norton, 1992.
Link, Perry, Richard Madsen, and Paul G. Pickowicz, eds. *Unofficial China: Popular Culture and Thought in the People's Republic*. Boulder, Colo.: Westview Press, 1989.
Liu Qi. "Father Sent Me to the Cadre School." In Shandong Kangdai, ed., *Fenhuo yu yingcai*.
Liu Shaoqi. *Address at the Meeting in Celebration of the Fortieth Anniversary of the Founding of the Communist Party of China*. Beijing: Foreign Languages Press, 1961.
Liu Shaoqi et al. *New Democratic Urban Policies*. Hong Kong: Wencai Publishing, 1949.
Lo Yi. "Zhejiang Resist America, Aid Korea Campaign." *Jiefang Daily*, April 10, 1951.
Luo Yi. "The Resist America, Aid Korea, Protect Home and Defend Motherland Campaign of the People in Zhejiang Is Deepening and

Broadening Step by Step." In *Carry the Resist America, Aid Korea Campaign to a New Stage.* Ed. Chinese People's Committee for Defending World Peace against American Aggression. Beijing: People's Press, 1951.

Ma Chengsheng. "Hangzhou and *On the Margin of Water.*" In Zhou Feng et al., eds., *Yuan Ming Qing mingchen Hangzhou.*

Ma Zihua. "The Old Anding, Full of Vigor." In *The Ninetieth Anniversary of the Hangzhou No. 7 School.* Ed. Hangzhou No. 7 School. Hangzhou, 1992.

MacFarquhar, Roderick, and John Fairbank, eds. *The Cambridge History of China.* Cambridge: Cambridge University Press, 1987.

Mao Shan. "From Singing Story to Yueju Opera." *Global Journal,* November 12, 1995.

Mao Tse-tung. *Selected Works of Mao Tse-tung.* Beijing: Foreign Languages Press, 1969.

Mao Zedong. *Mao Zhuxi he youren de tanhua* (Chairman Mao's talks with friends). Beijing: Chinese Youth Press, 1968.

———. *On the Correct Handling of Contradictions among the People (February 27, 1957).* Beijing: People's Press, 1957.

———. *The Writings of Mao Zedong, 1949–1976.* Armonk, N.Y.: M. E. Sharpe, 1986.

Meisner, Maurice. *Mao's China and After: A History of the People's Republic.* New York: Free Press, 1986.

Moore, Sally F., and Barbara Myerhoff, eds. *Secular Ritual.* Assne: Van Gorcum, 1977.

Mungello, David E. *The Forgotten Christians of Hangzhou.* Honolulu: University of Hawai'i Press, 1994.

Pang Song, and Lin Yunhui. *Liguo xingbang: 1945–1956 nian de Mao Zedong* (Founding the state: Mao Zedong in 1945–1956). Beijing: Chinese Youth Press, 1993.

Pepper, Suzanne. *Civil War in China: The Political Struggle, 1945–1949.* Berkeley: University of California Press, 1978.

"Propaganda Department of Zhejiang Requires Opera Reform." *Zhejiang Daily,* October 23, 1953.

Pye, Lucian W. *Asian Power and Politics: The Cultural Dimension of Authority.* Cambridge, Mass.: Harvard University Press, 1985.

———. *The Spirit of Chinese Politics: A Psychocultural Study of the Authority Crisis in Political Development.* Cambridge, Mass.: MIT Press, 1968.

Qin Dong and Ya Ping. *Sa Wenhan yu Chen Xiuliang* (Sa Wenhan and Chen Xiuliang). Ningbo: Ningbo Press, 1999.

"Remarkable Progress in Drama Reform, New Focus on *Yueju* Reform." *Zhejiang Daily,* November 23, 1949.

Saich, Tony. *New Perspectives on the Chinese Communist Revolution.* Armonk, N.Y.: M. E. Sharpe, 1995.

Scalapino, Robert A., ed. *Elites in the People's Republic of China.* Seattle: University of Washington Press, 1992.
Schram, Stuart. *The Political Thought of Mao Tse-Tung.* New York: Praeger, 1969.
Schultheis, Eugenia Barnett. *Hangchow, My Home: Growing Up in Heaven Below.* Fort Bragg, Calif.: Lost Coast Press, 2000.
Selden, Mark. *China in Revolution: The Yen'an Way Revisited.* Armonk, N.Y.: M. E. Sharpe, 1995.
Shan Shaojie. *Mao Zedong zhizheng chunqiu 1949–1976* (Mao Zedong in power, 1949–1976). Hong Kong: Mirror Books, 2000.
Shaw, Yu-ming. *An American Missionary in China: John Leighton Stuart and Chinese-American Relations.* Cambridge, Mass.: Harvard University Press, 1992.
Shen Shanhong et al., eds. *Hangzhou Daxue xiaoshi, 1897–1988* (A History of Hangzhou University, 1897–1988). Hangzhou: Hangzhou University Press, 1989.
Shi Dongbing. *Gao Gang mengduan Zhongnanhai* (Gao Gang's Nightmare in Zhongnanhai). Hong Kong: Tiandi Books, 1995.
Shi Zhe. *Zai lishi juren shenbian* (At the side of the historic giant). Beijing: Central Documents Press, 1991.
Shirk, Susan L. *Competitive Comrades.* Berkeley: University of California Press, 1982.
Skocpol, Theda. *States and Social Revolutions: A Comparative Analysis of France, Russia, and China.* Cambridge: Cambridge University Press, 1979.
Solomon, Richard. *Mao's Revolution and the Chinese Political Culture.* Ann Arbor: University of Michigan Press, 1998.
Spence, Jonathan. *The Gate of Heavenly Peace: The Chinese and Their Revolution 1895–1980.* New York: Penguin, 1982.
Stacey, Judith. *Patriarchy and Socialist Revolution in China.* Berkeley: University of California Press, 1983.
Stuart, John Leighton. *Fifty Years in China: The Memoirs of John Leighton Stuart.* New York: Random House, 1954.
Sun Tzu. *The Art of War.* Trans. Ralph D. Sawyer. Boulder, Colo.: Westview Press, 1994.
Tan Chong. "The Activities of the Hangzhou Volunteer Police Force before the Liberation." *Hangzhou wenshi ziliao* 3 (Reference materials on the local culture and history of Hangzhou, vol. 3).
Tan Qilong. "Leading the Southbound Team to Take over Hangzhou." In Jin Yanfeng et al., eds., *Takeover of the Cities and Transformation of Society (Hangzhou).* Beijing: Modern China Press, 1996.
Tan Qixiang. "Evolution of the Urban Development of Hangzhou." In Zhou Feng et al., eds., *Wu-Yue shoufu Hangzhou.* Hangzhou: Zhejiang People's Press, 1988.

Taylor, George. *The Struggle for North China.* New York: Institute of Pacific Relations, 1940.
Teiwes, Frederick C. *Politics and Purges in China: Rectification and Decline of Party Norms 1950–1965.* Armonk, N.Y.: M. E. Sharpe, 1993.
Terrill, Ross. *Madame Mao: The White-Boned Demon.* Rev. ed. Stanford, Calif.: Stanford University Press, 1999.
Thaxton, Ralph. *China Turned Rightside Up: Revolutionary Legitimacy in the Peasant World.* New Haven, Conn.: Yale University Press, 1983.
Townsend, James R. "Intra-Party Conflict in China: Disintegration in an Established One-Party System. In Scalapino, ed., *Elites in the People's Republic of China.*
Tsou, Tang. "Interpreting the Revolution in China: Macrohistory and Micromechanism." *Modern China* 26, no. 2 (April 2000): 205–238.
"Veteran Performers Talk about Opera Reform." *Zhejiang Daily,* March 29, 1954.
Vogel, Ezra F. *Canton under Communism: Programs and Politics in a Provincial Capital, 1949–1968.* Cambridge, Mass.: Harvard University Press, 1969.
Wei Zhongyun et al., eds. *Zhongguo renmin jiefangjun xinan Fuwutuan Zuzhi Shi* (The organizational history of the PLA Southwest Service Regiment). Chongqing: Society for History of the PLA Southwest Service Regiment, 1989.
Wu Zhanlei, ed. *Yi Jiangnan: Mingren bixia de lao Hangzhou* (In memory of Jiangnan: Hangzhou penned by famous writers). Beijing: Beijing Press, 2000.
Xin Wei, ed. *Fenhuo yu yingcai* (The Flames of battle make heroic soldiers). Linyi: Shandong Provincial Press, 1988.
Xin Wei et al., eds. *Shandong jiefangqu dashi ji* (Chronology of events in Shandong liberated area). Jinan: Shandong People's Press, 1982.
Xue Jianhua et al., eds. *Chengshi jieguan qinli ji* (The witnesses to the takeover of the cities). Beijing: China Culture and History Press, 1999.
Yan Changling. *Jingwei Mao Zedong jishi* (Records of guarding Mao Zedong). Changchun: Jilin People's Press, 1998.
Yang Siyi. *Diary.* (Printed for internal circulation.) Hangzhou: Society for History of the New Fourth Army, 1997.
Yeh, Wen-Hsin. *Provincial Passages: Culture, Space, and the Origins of Chinese Communism.* Berkeley: University of California Press, 1996.
"*Yueju* 'Liang Shanbo and Zhu Yingtai' in Hong Kong." *Zhejiang Daily,* December 14, 1954.
Zhang Jianwei. *Keguo diyi dao* (The first surgery after the founding of the PRC). Beijing: China Radio-TV Press, 1990.
Zhang Qijun. "A History of Scenic West Lake." In Wu Zhanlei, ed., *Yi Jiangnan.*
Zhang Shichang. "The Society of Local Educators on the Eve of the

Liberation." *Hangzhou wenshi ziliao* 17 (Reference materials on the local culture and history of Hangzhou, vol. 17).
Zhang Tianli. "Mr. Zhang Heng before and after His Term as President of the Hangzhou Municipal Congress." *Hangzhou wenshi ziliao* 18 (Reference materials on the local culture and history of Hangzhou, vol. 18).
Zhang Wensong. "Scraps of Memory of the Early Days after Beiping's Liberation." In Xue Jianhua et al., eds., *Chengshi jieguan qinli ji*.
Zhang Xia. "Recollections of the Third Class of the Women's Brigade at the Cadre School." In Xin Wei, ed., *Fenhuo yu yingcai*.
Zhang Youyu. "I Was Appointed to Be the Deputy Mayor of Peking." In Xue Jianhua et al., eds., *Chengshi jieguan qinli ji*.
Zhao Qingge. *Liang Shanbo yu Zhu Yingtai* (Liang Shanbo and Zhu Yingtai). Beijing: New World Press, 1999.
Zheng, Shiping. *Party vs. State in Post-1949 China: The Institutional Dilemma*. Cambridge: Cambridge University Press, 1997.
Zhong Qiguang. *Zhong Qiguang huiyilu* (Memoir of Zhong Qiguang). Beijing: PLA Press, 1995.
Zhong Xiangping. *Xihu mingren guju* (Former residences of eminent persons around West Lake). Hangzhou: Hangzhou Press, 2000.
Zhou Feng et al., eds. *Minguo shiqi Hangzhou* (Hangzhou in the republican period). Hangzhou: Zhejiang People's Press, 1997.
———. *Nansong jingcheng Hangzhou* (Hangzhou: The capital of the Southern Sung dynasty). Hangzhou: Zhejiang People's Press, 1988.
——— et al., eds. *Wu-Yue shoufu Hangzhou* (Hangzhou: The capital of the Wu-Yue Kingdom). Hangzhou: Zhejiang People's Press, 1988.
——— et al., eds. *Yuan Ming Qing mingchen Hangzhou* (Hangzhou: A Famous City in the Yuan, Ming, and Qing dynasties). Hangzhou: Zhejiang People's Press, 1997.
Zhu Mengming and Zhuang Chuanzhang, eds. *Yimeng xinghuo* (Revolutionary spark in Yimeng). Jinan: Shandong University Press, 1990.
Zhuge Ji and Ying Yuzhen, eds. *Wu-Yue shishi bian nian* (Complete chronology of the Kingdom of Wu-Yue). 2 vols. Hangzhou: Ancient Books, 1990.
Zweig, David. *Agrarian Radicalism in China, 1968–1981*. Cambridge, Mass.: Harvard University Press.

Interviews

Bian Pengfei	Hangzhou, August 5, 1998.
Cui Bo	Hangzhou, March 19 and August 25, 2001.
Fang Jingshu	Hangzhou, March 19 and August 25, 2001.
Fang Ming	Hangzhou, March 19 and August 25, 2001.

Gao Ke	Shanghai, May 9, 1997, and January 10, 1998.
Le Zixing	Hangzhou, May 28, 1997, and August 4, 1998.
Li Xingsheng	Hangzhou, March 15, 1998.
Liu Bo	Hangzhou, May 20, 1997.
Liu Tao	Hangzhou, May 23, 1997.
Liu Xin	Hangzhou, May 19, 1997.
Liu Xingwu	Linyi, June 12, 1998.
Liu Yifu	Hangzhou, January 10, 1997.
Mao Liren	Hangzhou, August 17, 1998.
Qi Guangben	Zaozhuang, June 13, 1998.
Qi Juling	Zaozhuang, June 13, 1998.
Qiu Bingzhong	Zaozhuang, June 13, 1998.
Ren Xiurong	Hangzhou, August 25, 2001.
Shen Yun	Hangzhou, August 25, 2001.
Sun Wencheng	Hangzhou, May 18, 1997, and August 13, 1998.
Wang Huairui	Cangshan, June 11, 1998.
Wang Huaizhen	Hangzhou, May 24, 1997.
Wang Mingchi	Xuzhou, June 18, 1998.
Wang Tugen	Hangzhou, March 19, 1998.
Xiao Yi	Hangzhou, May 20, 1997.
Xu Daming	Zaozhuang, June 13, 1998.
Xu Jingxin	Hangzhou, March 19 and August 25, 2001.
Yang Xueyan	Hangzhou, May 22, 1997.
Zhang Hongxiang	Hangzhou, June 22, 1998.
Zhang Lifa	Cangshan, June 15, 1998.
Zhang Ling	Xuzhou, June 18, 1998.
Zhong Ru	Hangzhou, May 29, 1997.
Zhu Fangmin	Hangzhou, May 25, 1997.
Zhu Mengming	Linyi, June 12, 1998.

Index

accusation meetings (*kongsu hui*), 83, 111, 140, 148. *See also huiyi*
agrarian socialism, 87, 105, 120. *See also* rural socialism
American culture, 126, 237
American imperialism: cultural, 9, 132–135; and demonstration, 52, 273n. 38; and the Korean War, 125, 128, 207, 254; and suppression of counter-revolutionaries, 140–143; and thought reform, 148–149, 151–152; and Three Antis, 162
Anding Middle School, 114–115
Anhui, 25, 27, 55, 71
Anti-Japanese Military and Political College, 187–188
Anti-Japanese War: in Luzhongnan, 24–25, 27–28, 160; and merchants, 176, 177–178; and nationalism, 130, 140; and peasants, 61, 75, 106; women in, 186–187, 190–196, 212; in Zhejiang, 37, 89, 225, 231–232
Anti-Rightists Campaign, 63, 248
archives, 7–8
Association of Industry and Commerce, 90–91, 166–168, 173, 176

Bai Juyi, 32
bai zu nang qian, 31
bandits, 80, 100, 108, 124
Bao Jia, 137, 142
Baodugu, 24
Battle of Yichuan, 11–12
Beijing, 91, 107, 221–224; central government in, 116, 128, 217–218, 259; conferences in, 131–136, 141; move to, 38–40; schools in, 79, 128–129, 147–148; in Three Antis and Five Antis, 169, 172, 294n. 54
Bengbu, 55
Bianlian Xian, 26
Big Sword Society, 13–14, 21, 23–24
Big World, 233, 305n. 59
Binhai, 45, 50, 197, 266n. 39
Bo Yibo, 15, 167, 174, 309n. 6

body search, 208, 215
Bohai, 19, 266n. 39
Bolsheviks, 25
Boqiang, 14
bourgeois culture, 41, 107, 116, 121–122, 149, 182, 184, 258
bourgeois-democratic revolution, 246
bu ru min zhai, 70
bu shi bing ge, 31
Bureau of Culture and Education, 233–234
Bureau of Industry and Mines, 91
Bureau of Internal Affairs, 110
Bureau of Public Security, 77, 80, 81, 104, 137, 139, 142–143, 198, 229
bureaucratism, 157–159, 163, 179–182, 213, 249
bureaucrats, 84, 86, 89, 105, 113–114, 149, 156, 183

cadre recruiting, 17, 102, 108, 180, 266n. 37; in cities, 18, 55, 95, 121–122, 130, 140, 165, 174, 182, 214; in rural areas, 19, 23–26, 124; among students and intellectuals, 19, 22, 52–53, 57, 62–63, 102, 103, 161, 182, 187; among women, 121, 186–187, 193, 201, 214–215; by women, 189, 194
Cai Jingxian, 89–91
Cangshan, 44, 193
Canton, 5, 6, 23, 134
Canton Holy Baby Nursery, 134
Cao Daishan, 198
capitalism, 76, 122, 178, 222, 239, 243, 257
CCP Central China Bureau (CCB), 14, 99
CCP Central Committee: and policy, 28, 88, 254; and political campaigns, 58, 141, 144, 162, 171, 174, 180; on retreat, 58, 99–100; and rural revolution, 23–24, 58, 112, 192; and socialist transformation, 241, 339; on the takeover, 18–19, 43–44, 56, 62, 71–72, 266n. 37; on the White Paper, 126. *See also* Mao Zedong

CCP East China Bureau (ECB): in the Civil War, 42–43; and Five Antis, 169–170, 172; and land reform, 27; and private commerce, 239–240; and the Production and Relief Campaign, 271n. 7; and the Silver Dollar War, 93, 96; and the takeover, 59, 62, 72, 76, 89, 99; and the Thought Reform Campaign, 148; and transfer cadres, 19–20, 44–46, 50, 57–58, 102, 182; on urban policy, 72
CCP Executive Committee, 18. *See also* Liu Shaoqi
CCP Hangzhou Committee: and anti-American policy, 135–136, 140, 288n. 38; on education, 113, 128–129, 135–136; establishment of, 81, 281n. 1; and labor campus, 145; on socialist transformation, 308n. 91; on Three Antis and Five Antis, 170–171, 173, 175; on women, 199
CCP Politburo, 1, 16, 17, 19, 221–223, 227
CCP Shandong Bureau, 26, 268n. 62
CCP Zhejiang Committee: and cadres, 57, 102; and CCP Hangzhou Committee, 81–82; and entertainment, 237; on labor issue, 88, 119–120; and Military Control Committee, 82, 278n. 45; on New Three Antis, 180–181; and religion, 229–230; on rural programs, 99–100, 108, 112; on socialist transformation, 239–240, 308n. 91; on Three Antis and Five Antis, 162–165, 169–171; on women, 198, 206, 209–210
Chamber of Commerce, 29, 37, 75, 241, 242, 276n. 23
Chen Boda, 149, 221, 302n. 16
Chen Xiuliang, 205, 300n. 85
Chen Yi, 44, 60
Chen Yun, 18, 171, 221–222, 224
Chenzhong, 22
Chiang Kai-shek: in the Civil War, 12, 17, 52; and suppression of counterrevolutionaries, 141, 143, 146; and urban people, 71, 114, 239
Chinese Communist Party (CCP): and anti-American campaigns, 126–127, 132, 259; behaviors and strategies of, 245, 246, 247–250, 251–255, 256, 260–261; and bourgeoisie, 28, 153, 158, 171, 174, 175, 178–179, 240; cadres of, 4, 9, 19, 41, 43, 45, 51–52, 80, 96, 101–104, 106, 152, 160, 163, 180, 183–184, 192, 257; in the Civil War, 3, 4, 43; and Mao Zedong, 14, 17, 38, 243; policies of, 8, 9, 10, 40, 73, 97, 109–110; and post-revolutionary society, 1, 2, 3, 4, 8, 9, 64, 159, 183, 246, 257, 258, 260; rural experiences of, 39, 75, 101, 107–108, 111, 246; in Shandong, 20, 22, 24–25, 26–28, 35, 44, 49, 71; and students and intellectuals, 52–55, 61, 63, 115–116, 126, 146–148, 150, 151, 167; and suppression of counterrevolutionaries, 140, 142–143, 145–146; on the takeover, 71, 72, 81, 112; urban programs of, 41, 44, 58, 75, 78, 89, 92, 96, 99, 112, 124, 137, 155, 241, 259, 262; and women, 186–187, 191, 193–195, 197–198, 206, 208, 211–212, 213–215; and workers, 117–119, 120–121, 123, 173; in Zhejiang, 57, 71, 73, 74, 81–82, 113, 274nn. 52, 53
Chinese People's Volunteers (CPV), 129–131, 146, 224
chong mei, 146
Chouye Huiguan, 35
Christian organizations, 131–137, 288n. 38
civil service examination, 14
Civil War: and archives, 7; in history, 31, 37, 251; intellectuals in, 127, 248; and Mao Zedong, 86, 126; in Shandong, 19–20, 28, 44–45, 52, 61, 160; Women in, 186, 188, 190–192, 194; in Zhejiang, 55, 57, 75, 176, 208, 219
collectivization, 216, 239, 246
commandism, 180–181
communications, 4, 20, 29–30, 101, 194–195, 202
Communism, 257; in Hangzhou, 29, 247, 266; international, 128, 248; in Shandong, 24, 63
Communist Youth League, 206; in early years, 22; and mass mobilization, 74, 112, 126, 174, 241; in political campaigns, 131, 163, 233
"comrades of Hangzhou," 225, 231, 236, 243–244, 259–260, 262. *See also* identity
confession meetings (*jiantao hui*), 150–151, 162, 254. *See also huiyi*

Index 329

confessions, 84, 150–151, 152, 162, 166–171, 178, 309n. 12
criticism meetings (*pipan hui*), 254. *See also huiyi*
Cui Bo, 59, 189–190, 201–203, 205–206, 210
cultural aggression, 132, 137
cultural capital, 258
cultural crusade, 9, 152, 259
cultural elite, 258
cultural identity, 5
cultural programs, 41
Cultural Revolution, 63, 146, 222, 224, 230–231, 238, 252, 259–262
cultural shock, 5
"*cuncun dianhuo, huhu maoyan,*" 28

Dadaohui, 21
Dadian, 27
dang ke, 123
Dangdai Daily, 94, 280n. 88
dangdi ganbu, 16, 28
daqu, 46
Democratic Army, 70
democratic reform, 14, 173
Deng Xiaoping, 13, 222, 303n. 27
Deng Zihui, 281n. 5. *See also* Lin Biao
discipline, 1, 9, 15, 47, 59–62, 71–72, 105, 180
divorce, 50, 185, 199, 200, 214–215
Du Yuesheng, 177
dual rule, 72–73
Dujinshen Silk Factory, 225, 303n. 32
Dunyitang, 35

East China Bureau (ECB): and cadres, 19–20, 27, 42–46, 49–50, 56–59, 199; on economy, 93, 96; on education 102; on political campaigns, 148, 169–172, 182; on socialist transformation, 239–240
Education Bureau, 114, 116, 120, 136
education: Confucian, 20, 116; institutions of 132–133, 135, 161, 233–234; policy of, 115, 150, 284n. 54; political, 85, 96, 103, 105, 114, 116, 124–125, 130, 134, 136–137, 148–149, 163, 166; reform, 116–117; rural, 25; and southbound cadres, 43, 47, 48, 50, 72, 76, 151, 160, 179, 257; and students and intellectuals, 25, 32, 54, 151, 161; takeover of, 17, 20, 80, 82, 102, 112–113, 151; urban, 36, 43, 115, 139, 218; Western, 54, 126, 127, 128; of women, 185, 188, 199, 203, 206, 211–212, 214, 300n. 79. *See also* ECB; Education Bureau; CCP Hangzhou Committee
Eighth Route Army, 24, 187–188, 191, 267n. 55
enemies without guns, 2, 75
entrepreneur, 174–175
Executive Committee, 13–14, 18, 28, 192

fa bu ze zhong, 168
family-arranged marriages, 186, 199
fang zu, 196, 298n. 41
Fanzhi county, 14
Fei Xiao, 36
Feng Yindong, 136
fenliang renren youfen, canjun renren youze, 43
First Five-Year Plan, 216–217
First Hangzhou Textile Factory, 8
Five Antis Campaign: and confession, 252; and economic struggle, 164–167, 169, 294n. 54; and the Korean War, 248; and new fashion, 256; and political message, 172–176, 178, 305n. 58; and women, 213
Five Flags Society, 21
"five poisons" (*we du*), 64, 166–168, 171, 173, 176
foot-bound, 193–196, 214, 298n. 41
four categories of evil, 255, 310n. 18
Four Limitations, 122
Four Olds, 259. *See also* Cultural Revolution
Fu Daniang, 193
fu gui qi rong, 205
fu mu guan, 256
Fu Qiutao, 48
Fujian, 30, 35, 46
funu shiziban, 188

gai zu pai, 196
gai zu, 196
gan shu, 201
Gao Gang: and the Cultural Revolution, 303n. 24; and innerparty struggle, 222–223, 277n. 29, 302nn. 22, 23, 303nn. 25, 27; in Manchuria, 247, 309n. 7; and Three Antis, 157–158, 161. *See also* Mao Zedong; Liu Shaoqi; New Democracy

General Trade Union, 77–78, 112, 202, 206, 224
Geneva of the East, 216, 218, 238, 243
Genshamen Power Station, 218
Genshan district, 110, 289n. 64
gentry: in the Anti-Japanese War, 24, 28, 187, 188, 191–192, 195, 268n. 72; children of, 23, 26, 115–116, 268n. 71; and early CCP, 23, 26; and elimination of bandits, 109; in the land reform, 28, 34; and merchants, 34, 89; and the Taipings, 123
gentry culture, 51
GMD Youth League. *See* Three People's Principles Youth League
Golden Age, 2, 262
Gongshu district, 218
grandma Fu. *See* Yuan Ming
grandma Pilgrims, 229–230, 304n. 47
grandma Ren. *See* Liu Lan
Green Gang, 35, 118, 177, 283n. 32
Green Jade Hairpin, 234–235
Gu Dehuan, 81, 91, 220, 301n. 4
guan taitai, 205
Guandi, 36, 270n. 94
guan zhi, 139, 141
Guanchengtang, 35
Guandi, 36, 270n. 94
Guo Chunlin, 136
Guo Moruo, 36–37, 39, 131–132, 270n. 97, 270n. 101
Guomindang (GMD): and America, 127, 177; in the Anti-Japanese War, 35; and capitalists, 78, 79, 177–178; in the Civil War, 3, 7, 11–12, 16–19, 25, 27–29, 42–44, 46, 49–54, 62, 87–88, 106, 186, 194, 201, 265n. 26; and Hangzhou, 43, 51–52, 54, 57, 75, 78, 217, 238; and intellectuals, 126, 149–150, 248; and JYJ, 94–95; and labor, 35, 118; remnants of, 100–101, 108–109; and students, 37, 53–54; and suppression of counterrevolutionaries, 137–146, 249; after the takeover, 9, 57, 69, 70, 71, 80–85, 89, 92, 102–103, 113; taxes of, 251–252; and Three Antis, 101, 179

Hangchow Christian College, 129. *See also* Zhijiang University
Hangju, 234
Hao Jianxiu, 156, 292n. 9

Hebei, 12
Hollywood movies, 132, 137, 237
Hongyi. *See* Li Shutong
Hu Haiqiu, 175–176, 179
Hu Qiaomu, 221, 302n. 16
Hu Zongnan, 11
Huadong University, 52–53, 89
Huaihai Battle, 42–44, 48, 192–193
Huang Yangpei, 293n. 42
huhu maoyan, 28
Huilan High School, 127–128
huiyi (or *hui*), 83, 251–255
Hunan, 23, 223
Hupao Temple, 226, 228–229, 231

idea revolutionary, 257. *See also* peasant cadres and rural revolutionaries
identity, 5, 9, 29, 255–262
images, 9, 55, 185, 235
imperial examination, 38–40
inner-Party struggle, 181
intellectuals, 9, 12, 36, 255; mobilization of, 18–19, 42–43, 45, 52–55, 135; in political campaigns, 63, 110, 115, 117, 135, 147, 153, 161, 167, 182, 309n. 12, 310n. 18; political education of, 102–104, 126–127; revolutionary, 4, 28, 39, 61, 82, 185, 268n. 71; urban, 21–22, 25–26; women, 185. *See also* Thought Reform Campaign
internal control (*nei kong*), 40, 139

Ji Pengfei, 82
Jia Shen San Bai Nian Ji, 39, 270n. 101
Jiang Hua, 220, 299n. 65
Jianggan district, 211, 218, 234
Jiangnan, 48–51, 59, 62, 72, 109–110, 197, 230, 258
Jiangxi, 35, 96
Jiaodong, 19, 20, 266n. 39
Jiaozuo, 15
Jiaxing, 57, 178
Jin Runxiang, 176–179
Jinan, 16, 18, 42, 53, 59, 71, 82, 172
Jining, 46
jinyuanjuan (JYJ), 92–94, 280n. 88
joint state-private ventures, 240–243
Ju Xian, 22, 24, 27
jun shu, 201

"*kai cang ji pin*," 86
Kaifeng, 32

Ke Li, 81
kong mei, 146
kongsu hui, 83
kuaiban, 232
Kuomintang, 13–14, 39, 127, 264n. 4. See also Guomindang (GMD)

Labor Bureau, 77–78, 87, 90–91, 98–99, 102, 119–120
labor movement, 19, 22, 36, 41, 120–122, 212
land of Buddha, 225
land of rice and fish, 7, 29, 48
land reform, 123–124, 135, 254; and left deviations, 12–13, 268nn. 73, 75; in Luzhongnan, 27–28, 47, 61, 106; policy, 15–16; women in, 191–192, 210–211; in Zhejiang, 99, 108, 110, 112, 142, 228. See also landlords
landlords: in the Anti-Japanese War, 191–192; condemnation of, 210, 254, 262; and Land reform, 27–28, 61; and left deviations, 13–14, 192; policy to, 16; and students, 149; and the Taipings, 124; in Zhejiang, 100, 109–111. See also gentry; land reform
lao balu, 203
lao geming, 49, 203
lecture on the Party (*dang ke*), 123
left deviations, 12–13, 16, 27–28, 40, 264n. 6, 268nn. 73, 75. See also land reform; landlords
Lei Feng, 146, 290n. 79
Lenin suits, 74
Li Daigen, 81
Li Desheng, 11
Li Fengping, 81
Li Qingqi, 22, 267n. 46
Li Qingwei, 25, 267n. 46
Li Qingyu, 106
Li Shutong, 38, 226, 306n. 73
Li Xiannian, 221
Li Yu, 27
Li Zhaohuan, 113
Li Zicheng, 39–40, 157, 270n. 103
Liang Shanbo and Zhu Yingtai, 236–237
Liangzhu Wenhua, 29, 269n. 78
"liberal gentry," 187
lihun bu lijia, 200
Lin Biao, 99–100, 281n. 5
Lin Feng, 81–82
Lin Fengmian, 219, 301n. 10

Lin Hujia, 112, 272n. 19
Lincheng, 47–48, 59
Lingyin Temple, 99, 225–228, 229–231
Linyi Normal School, 23, 268n. 71
Liu Bo, 53–54, 276n. 18
little tradition. See peasant culture
Liu Jian, 47
Liu Lan, 194–195, 298n. 43
Liu Qingshan, 292n. 13
Liu Shaoqi: in the Anti-Japanese War, 267n. 55; in Beijing, 221, 224; on bourgeoisie, 76–77; in the Civil War, 12, 18, 28, 52; and Gao Guang, 222–223, 277n. 29, 303n. 24, 303n. 25; on new democratic order, 247, 302n. 22; on the takeover, 92. See also CCP Executive Committee
Liu Yifu, 113, 284n. 43
Liu Zhuang, 221–225
liuyong renyuan, 82–84
local culture, 234
localism, 16, 47, 56, 58
Longjing, 145
Lu Zhixian, 272n. 19
Lunan, 20, 186, 190
Luoyang, 14–15, 30–31, 61, 265n. 15
Luzhong, 20, 266n. 39
Luzhongnan, 19–20, 75, 109, 266n. 39; in the Anti-Japanese War, 24–26; cadres from, 19, 38, 42–51, 54, 56, 75, 82–83, 85, 95, 97, 112, 160–166, 299n. 56; in the Civil War, 27, 42–43, 268n. 72; early CCP activities in, 20–24; and peasant roots, 106; women in, 186–189, 191–198, 200, 202. See also the Civil War; peasant revolutionaries; peasant cadres

Ma Yinchu, 132, 147–148, 166. See also Thought Reform
Manchuria, 18, 40, 59, 62, 87, 91, 95–96, 99, 128, 157, 194–195, 212, 222, 247, 266n. 37
Mandate of Heaven, 3, 251
Mao, tse-tung. See Mao, Zedong
Mao, Zedong: in the Anti-Japanese War, 24, 267n. 55; on cadres, 17, 19, 154, 310n. 26; in the Civil War, 11–13, 38–41, 52–54, 264n. 4; on class struggle, 292n. 4; and Gao Gang, 157–161, 221–223, 277n. 29, 302nn. 22, 23, 303nn. 24, 25, 27;

Mao, Zedong (cont.)
and Hangzhou, 155–156, 222–225, 230; and intellectuals, 259, 309n. 6, 310n. 26; on "left deviations," 28, 87, 192; and new democracy, 247, 309n. 6; and the New Three Antis Campaign, 180–181; and optimism, 246–250; and peasant movement, 23; and permanent revolution, 1–2, 182–184, 259–262, 308n. 2; and political ritual, 251–255; Schram on Mao, 257; and Suppression of Counterrevolutionaries, 141, 148–149; and Three Antis and Five Antis Campaigns, 162–164, 170, 175, 177, 179, 242–243; on urban policy, 14–16, 56, 61, 63, 71, 75–77, 81–83, 85–86; on the White Paper, 125–127, 133–134; and women liberation, 186–188, 193. See also CCP Central Committee
Marriage Law, 185–186, 199, 206, 211, 214, 296n. 3
Marxism, 21, 110, 115
Marxist: organizations, 36, 39, 113; theories, 3, 6, 22, 103, 114, 117, 134, 142, 149, 238, 239, 255, 257, 259; and women, 186. See also Marxism
Mass Daily, 25, 191, 267n. 56
mass line, 90, 97
Maxim, A. C., 218
Meijiawu, 155
membership system, 207
Mencius, 20
midwives, 209–210
Military Control Committee, 79, 202; and cadres, 105, 160; and counterrevolutionaries, 139, 141–142; and culture, 231; and labor, 120; organization of, 72, 80–82; and student recruits, 53, 59; and urban economy, 87–89, 92–93, 176, 280n. 88. See also CCP Hangzhou Committee; military representatives
military representatives: in factories, 74, 87, 89, 91–92, 120, 122; in government, 83, 86; in schools, 112; and the Silver Dollar War, 92
military service, 43–44
Mingfen and Huafen Pager Mills, 241
Minsheng Pharmaceutical Factory, 79
missionaries, 125, 128, 133, 147, 219

mobilization meetings (*dongyuan hui*), 45, 47, 254
model worker, 207, 212
Moganshan Conference, 181–182, 237. See also Yang Siyi
Mu Guiying, 189, 297n. 18
muji bu sichen, 215
mystification of the CCP, 253

national flag, 69, 275n. 1
new China, 3, 50, 53, 54, 63, 73, 83, 115, 117, 159, 185, 201, 256
New Culture Movement, 261
New Democracy, 114–115, 147, 175, 302n. 22, 309n. 6. See also Mao Zedong; Liu Shaoqi; and Gao Gang
New Fourth Army, 57, 274n. 53
New Three Antis Campaign, 179–182, 248
Nie Rongzhen, 13
Ningbo, 114
Ninth Corps, 55, 128
"no war" policy, 31
North China Bureau (NCB), 12, 15, 18–19, 24, 162

old liberated areas, 18, 19, 91, 96, 122, 192–193
On the Margin of Water, 21, 73, 233, 250, 254, 276nn. 16, 17
opportunism, 247–251, 260

party school, 18, 165
patriarchal rule, 181–182, 255
peasant cadres, 4–9; change of, 5, 157, 180, 205; cultural shock of, 5, 6, 107; identities of, 9, 259–261; and intellectuals, 43, 55, 61, 63, 151, 161–162, 183; and leadership, 5, 9, 123; and Mao Zedong, 250, 251; mobilization of, 47, 51, 59; perspectives of, 6, 7, 51, 63, 104, 106; Revolutionary tradition of, 9, 52, 104–105, 121; and transformation of city, 5, 6, 8, 38, 41; and urban programs, 9, 41, 61, 73, 83, 85, 95–97, 104, 123, 152. See also rural revolutionaries
peasant culture, 51, 273n. 34
peasant virtue, 78, 105, 106, 257
Peng Dehuai, 204, 222
People's Congresses, 186, 212–213

People's Daily, 146, 156–157
People's Liberation Army (PLA): in the Civil War, 3, 37, 42–45, 48, 54, 232; disciplined, 70–74, 97, 105; and economic order, 92, 95; in factories, 88–89; and intellectuals, 84; and Mao, 223; new soldiers of, 26, 52–53; and rural works, 45, 108; and the takeover, 7, 18, 55, 57–60, 62, 69, 76, 80–81, 99–100, 145, 216, 228; and urban policy, 14–15; and women, 185, 191–192, 197, 200–201, 213
People's Republic of China (PRC), 1, 7–8, 51, 124, 126, 152, 185–186, 221–222, 229, 246, 247, 275n. 1
permanent revolution, 182, 222, 246, 251, 259, 261–262, 308n. 2
pilgrims, 75, 87, 219, 225–230, 258, 304n. 47
policy of rich peasants, 27
Politburo, 1, 16–17, 19, 222–223, 237
political culture, 5, 10, 243
political study meetings (*zhengzhi xuexi hui*): and anti-American crusade, 126, 178; institutionalized, 83–86, 122–123, 126, 147, 241, 252; and psychological offence, 160; ritualized, 160, 242. *See also huiyi*
population in Hangzhou, 29, 31, 33, 218–219, 269n. 84
post-revolutionary society, 2, 257–258, 260–261
private commerce, 239–240, 292n. 3
pro-American sentiments *(qin mei, chong mei,* and *kong mei),* 146, 148–149
pro-American groups, 152; and speeches, 133
Production and Relief Campaign, 44–45, 271n. 7
professionals, 63, 84, 159, 183, 209. *See also* intellectuals
Propaganda Department, 47, 104–106, 143, 205, 233
public bond *(gong zhai),* 232
public control (guan zhi), 139, 141
purges, 63, 183, 254; of cadres, 25–16, 104, 158, 161; of Gao Gang, 222–223, 237, 277n. 29, 302–303n. 23; of intellectuals, 55, 113, 182; in political campaigns, 134, 161; of retained employees, 86

Qiantang, 29–30, 218–219
qin mei, 146
Qing Bang. *See* Green Gang
Qiu Jin, 186, 238
qu yi, 234, 306n. 65
Qufu, 20
Quick Literacy, 211
qunzhong guanzhi, 140

Radical programs, 14
Rao Shushi, 222
Regulations on the Punishment of Counterrevolutionaries, 144
remin, 256
Ren Bishi, 265n. 14
Renminbi (RMB), 90, 92–94, 96, 160, 165, 280nn. 78, 88
rent and interest rate reduction, 13, 24, 26, 28, 138–139, 143, 167
representative system, 207
Residents' Committee, 137–138, 289n. 49
Resist America, Aid Korea Campaign, 129, 131, 135–136, 138, 152
restoration of production, 76, 78, 89, 91, 97, 176, 197, 248
rich peasants, 13, 16, 27, 100, 110–111, 115, 191–192
ritual, 3–4, 9, 196, 228, 246, 251–252, 256–257, 260. *See also huiyi*
Rong Yiren, 174–175, 295n. 61
rural campaigns, 100, 112, 124
rural revolutionaries, 4, 6, 9, 19, 47–48, 73, 117, 121, 182, 184, 246. *See also* peasant cadres
rural socialism, 15. *See also* agrarian socialism
ruseng, 138, 304n. 37. *See also* Li Shutong (Hongyi)

salary: of cadres, 104, 206, 282n. 19; of retained employees, 84, 104; of workers, 87, 89, 279n. 70
Sanfanzi, 21
sao di chu men, 13
Seventh Corps, 80–81, 89, 100, 108
Shanbei, 11–13
Shandong: in the Anti-Japanese War, 26, 58; cadres of, 39, 41, 45–53, 61, 71, 73, 81, 85; in the Civil War, 16–17, 82; and Hangzhou, 257–258; Huadong University in, 116;

Shandong (cont.)
mass mobilization, 111, 173; people of, 7, 21, 22; rural bases in, 6, 19–20, 43–44, 186; rural reforms, 12, 26, 27; support from, 96, 101; and Three Antis, 162; women of, 186–188, 192–196, 201, 214. *See also* Luzhongnan
Shangcheng district, 218
Shanghai: cadres from, 82; capitalism in, 94–95, 97, 231–232; CCP in, 22, 36, 39, 57–58, 298n. 39; Five Antis in, 164, 167, 170, 174–175; GMD in, 130; and Hangzhou, 33–36, 38, 79, 88, 167, 177, 217, 219, 230; reception center in, 198; the takeover of, 18, 19, 46, 48, 71–73, 91, 94, 164, 167, 170, 174–175. *See also* Jiangnan
Shanxi, 12–14, 167
Shanxi-Shuiyuan area, 13
Shenyang, 18
Shijiazhuang, 15, 18, 58–59, 62, 87
silk business, 59, 62, 87, 88
Silk Guild Hall, 35
Silver Dollar War, 92, 94–97, 276n. 21, 280n. 88
Sino-Japanese War. *See* Anti-Japanese War
socialism: and Mao Zedong, 175, 242–243; and practice, 238–239, 242–243, 245; and women liberation, 186. *See also* agrarian socialism; rural socialism
socialist revolution, 3, 240, 246. *See also* Socialism and Socialist transformation
socialist transformation, 9, 123, 216, 239, 242, 244, 246, 308n. 91
song lang can jun, 189
southbound cadres: and bourgeoisie, 120; identity of, 255, 257–259, 262; and intellectuals, 53, 55, 103, 149, 150; leadership of, 102, 119–120, 152, 171, 181; and local cadres, 57, 58, 182; and mass line, 99, 101, 111, 143, 173; and opportunism, 247, 249–251; and organization of, 46–47, 217n. 10, 272n. 19; in political campaigns, 126, 182–183; recruiting of, 47–49, 55–58; and revolution, 220, 242, 243, 246; and rituals, 254; in the takeover, 53, 56, 62, 73, 75, 78, 81–82; and temple, 225–231; training of, 52, 56, 61, 116–117; and urban culture, 231–232, 235–237, 243; and urban environment, 103–105, 107–108, 122, 124, 224–225; and wives, 138, 197–201, 202, 215; and women, 220–203, 299n. 56; and workers, 121, 123, 206–207. *See also* peasant cadres; rural revolutionaries
Soviet Union, 91, 123, 129, 148–149, 217, 223
speak with bitterness, 192
special control (*te kong*), 139
State Council, 131, 133, 135
Story of Wu Xun, 124
storytellers, 21, 233, 305n. 58, 306n. 65
struggle meetings (*douzheng hui*), 83, 111, 210, 254. *See also* huiyi
Stuart, John Leighton, 125–127, 286n. 7
students, 3; and the Anti-Japanese War, 25, 187, 261; and CCP, 36, 187, 195, 214; in the Civil War, 25, 26, 37, 74; in education reform, 112–117, 211; and the Korean War, 129–131; in political campaigns, 108–109, 112, 124, 144, 165, 232; recruiting, 18–19, 21–24, 102, 187, 217; and the takeover, 43, 49, 71, 73, 74, 95; and thought reform, 148–149, 151; traditional, 5, 40–41, 236; training of, 51–55, 203; at Western schools, 136, 176, 227. *See also* intellectuals
Su Dongpo, 32
Su Xiaoxiao, 238, 306n. 73
sugar-coated bullets, 121, 158, 277n. 24, 282n. 23
Suiyuan, 13
suku hui, 83
sum-up meetings (*zongjie hui*), 254
Sun Wencheng, 122
Sun Zi, 20, 222n. 40
supply system (*gongji zhi*), 104, 205, 282n. 19
suppression of counterrevolutionaries, 81, 135, 140, 144–145, 283n. 32, 288n. 38, 309n. 8
Suzhou, 33

Taierzhuang, 47, 51, 59
Taipings, 123–124
Taiwan, 7, 79, 95, 128, 217
Tan Jiazhen, 150
Tan Qilong, 55–56, 71–72, 82, 180, 211

Tan Zhenlin: and bourgeoisie, 78, 122, 175–176; and cadres, 102, 108; and criticism of America, 208; on economy, 89; an inner Party struggle, 5, 239; on retreat, 100; in the takeover, 55, 58, 71–72, 81–82; and women, 207; and workers, 98–99, 120. *See also* CCP Zhejiang Committee; Military Control Committee
Tax Bureau, 80–81, 93, 104
tax of CCP, 62, 79, 92, 104–105, 114, 122, 233, 301n. 5; evasion of, 105, 110, 164, 174, 177, 241; of GMD, 137, 251; imperial, 27, 29, 39
te kong, 139
Tea Business Association, 35
temples: in the Civil War, 74–75, 87; in history, 31, 32, 304n. 33; after the takeover, 110, 219, 220, 225–231
tea culture, 155, 156, 226–227
tea parties, 78–79, 156, 176
ten points for attention, 60–62
textile industry, 33–35, 207
The Romance of the Three Kingdoms, 233, 250
Third Field Armies, 17
third group of people, 248. *See also* intellectuals
Third Women's Normal School, 186
Thought Reform Campaign, 63, 117, 132, 146–149, 151–153, 167
Three Antis Campaign, 158–164, 166, 213, 248
Three People's Principles Youth League, 14, 53
three pledges, 60–62
Three Rotations Society, 21
Three Self-Principles, 133
three word policy (*guan, guan, guan*), 135
Tian Jiaying, 221
Tianjin, 5–6, 19, 77, 91, 94, 108, 148, 156, 222, 247
tianshi dili renhe, 250
Tianzhang Silk Factory, 118–119
tiger-hunting, 159–163, 166, 168. *See also* Three Antis Campaign
Trotskyist elements, 25, 238n. 2
Twenty-third Army, 70, 81

unionism, 117–118, 274n. 52
urban culture, 3, 5, 9, 21, 50, 97, 106, 124, 156, 227, 257–260

urban dwellers: and CCP, 154; cynical, 1, 37, 75, 83; identity of, 255–256; life of, 31, 33–34, 155, 219; and PLA, 69, 70–71, 73–34; reorganization of, 137–140; and rural cadres, 6, 8, 9, 107, 173, 203
urban policy, 12–15, 40–41, 47, 51, 109, 246
Utopian, 2, 257

Voice of America (VOA), 138

waihang lingdao neihang, 63, 183
Wang Daohan, 72
Wang Jian'an, 82
Wang Jinmei, 266n. 45
Wang Wuquan, 89, 279n. 73
Wang Zhuang, 221–222, 302n. 17
War against Japanese Aggression. *See* Anti-Japanese War
Wei Siwen, 26
Weixian, 18
West Lake: and buildings, 34, 38, 105; and business, 33, 220; and city development, 218–220; and Mao Zedong, 222, 225; and roads, 75, 80; reform of, 146, 220; and scenery of, 30, 37, 88, 98, 100, 218; and temples, 226, 229, 258; and tradition, 217; and *White Snake*, 235
Western style schools, 22, 36, 54, 266n. 44. *See also* Huiland High School
White Paper, 126–128
White Snake (*Bai she zhuan*), 235. *See also* West Lake
Women's Federation, 190, 193, 205–214, 299–300n. 66
workers, 30, 41, 238, 255; and capitalists, 8, 34, 77, 87, 88, 107 176; and CCP, 18, 19, 25, 57, 89; in commerce, 34, 119; economic demands of, 86–87, 88, 98, 119, 120; education of, 77–78, 85, 103, 117, 119; in industry, 34, 45, 200; and intellectuals, 54–55, 61, 117, 149; mobilization of, 121–123, 131, 159, 173, 174; organization of, 6, 36, 118; in rural programs, 27, 108, 124, 165; salary of, 87–89, 279n. 70; and secret society, 35; in the takeover, 71, 76; in Three Antis and Five Antis, 166–169, 173; and urban culture, 18; and women, 118, 185, 207–208, 217

Wu Song, 73, 276n. 17
Wu Xun, 124
Wu Xian, 176
Wu Zhongliang, 206, 299n. 65
Wufeng Silk Factory, 89–90
Wuqihui, 21
Wu-Yue Guo, 30–32

Xiacheng district, 88, 122, 143, 218
Xiangdao, 22
Xiao Fangzhou, 47
Xiaoshan, 209, 228, 278n. 48
Xibaipo, 28, 38, 316
Xiongdihui, 118
xuan qiang liu ruo, 49
Xun Zi, 20
Xuzhou, 18, 42

Yan'an, 11, 25, 28, 192, 223, 261
Yang Shangkun, 223
Yang Siyi, 274n. 49, 295n. 77; criticism against, 58, 295–296n. 80; and in Mogansan, 237; and the New Three Antis, 181–182; in the takeover, 57–58, 81–82; and his wife, 204
Yang Yuanshi, 44
Yangtze River, 18–19, 31, 37, 43, 48, 55, 62, 74, 89, 100, 201, 229, 232
Yanzhou, 46
Ye Jianying, 221
Yellow River, 11–12, 14, 29, 38
"yellow union," 119
yi cha dai jiu, 77–78
Yi Guan Dao (YGD), 141–143, 148, 283n. 32, 289n. 64
Yifen Silk Factory, 77–78
yong bu wang ben, 105–106
youji zuofeng, 103
Yu Jimin, 74
Yu Zisan, 37, 144

yuan feng bu dong, yuan feng yuan yang, 15, 71, 83, 85
Yuan Ming, 193–195
yue fa san zhang, 60–62
Yue Guo, 30
Yueju, 160–161, 231–237, 293n. 22, 269n. 76

zai zhou zhi shui yi fu zhou, 12
Zhang Deng, 82
Zhang Heng, 69, 145
Zhang Jinfu, 81
Zhang Wensong, 282n. 15
Zhang Youyu, 107, 282n. 28
Zhang Zishan, 292n. 13
Zhao Liangkun, 22
Zhao Yiman, 212
Zhaobo Xian, 49
Zhaoqing Temple, 216
Zhejiang clique, 29
Zhejiang Daily, 121–122, 135, 227–228, 276n. 22
Zhejiang New Tide Weekly, 36
Zhejiang University, 7, 71, 129–130, 144, 147–151, 284n. 44, 286n. 12
Zheng Jinfang, 233
Zhijiang University, 113–115, 129–133, 136, 284n. 44, 286n. 12. *See also* Hangchow Christian College
zhishifenzi ganbu, 61–62, 82, 182, 214, 260. *See also* intellectuals
Zhong Qiguang, 61
zhongshan zhuang, 79
Zhou Enlai: and America, 128; and dancing party, 237; and Gao Gang, 222; and intellectuals, 148; and *Liang Shanbo and Zhu Yingtai*, 236; and Linying Temple, 231; and Mao Zedong, 40; and national bourgeoisie, 174; and New Democracy, 309n. 6; and tea, 156

About the Author

James Z. Gao holds a Master's degree in international relations from Peking University and a doctorate in history from Yale University. He is the author of a number of articles on Chinese politics and foreign policy and one book, *Meeting Technology's Advance: Social Changes in China and Zimbabwe in the Railway Age.* He previously taught at Peking University and Christopher Newport University and was a research associate at the Institute of East Asian Studies at the University of California, Berkeley. Professor Gao is currently on the history faculty at the University of Maryland, College Park.

Studies of the Weatherhead East Asian Institute

Selected Titles

Taxation without Representation in Rural China: State Capacity, Peasant Resistance, and Democratization, Thomas P. Bernstein and Xiaobo Lü. Modern China Series, Cambridge University Press, 2003

The Reluctant Dragon: Crisis Cycles in Chinese Foreign Economic Policy, by Lawrence Christopher Reardon. Seattle: University of Washington Press, 2002

Spanning Japan's Modern Century: The Memoirs of Hugh Borton, Hugh Borton. Lexington Books, Inc., 2002

Korea Between Empires, 1895–1919, Andre Schmid. New York: Columbia University Press 2002

The North Korean Revolution: 1945–50, Charles Armstrong. Cornell University Press, 2002

Consumer Politics in Postwar Japan: Institutional Boundaries of Citizen Activism, Patricia Maclachlan. Columbia University Press, 2001

Abortion before Birth Control: The Politics of Reproduction in Postwar Japan, by Tiana Norgren. Princeton University Press, August 2001

Cadres and Corruption: The Organizational Involution of the Chinese Communist Party, by Xiaobo Lü. Stanford University Press, 2000

Japan's Imperial Diplomacy: Consuls, Treaty Ports, and War with China, 1895–1938, by Barbara Brooks. Honolulu: University of Hawai'i Press, 2000

China's Retreat from Equality: Income Distribution and Economic Transition, Carl Riskin, Zhao Renwei, Li Shi, eds. M. E. Sharpe, 2000

Nation, Governance, and Modernity: Canton, 1900–1927, by Michael T. W. Tsin. Stanford: Stanford University Press, 1999

Assembled in Japan: Electrical Goods and the Making of the Japanese Consumer, by Simon Partner, University of California Press 1999

Civilization and Monsters: Spirits of Modernity in Meiji Japan, by Gerald Figal, Duke University Press, 1999

The Logic of Japanese Politics: Leaders, Institutions, and the Limits of Change, by Gerald L. Curtis. New York: Columbia University Press, 1999

Contesting Citizenship in Urban China: Peasant Migrants, the State and Logic of the Market, by Dorothy Solinger. Berkeley: University of California Press, 1999

Bicycle Citizens: The Political World of the Japanese Housewife, by Robin LeBlanc. Berkeley: University of California Press, 1999

Chaos and Order in the Works of Natsume Sōseki, by Angela Yiu. Honolulu: University of Hawai'i Press, 1998

Production Notes for
Gao/THE COMMUNIST TAKEOVER OF HANGZHOU

Design by the University of Hawai'i Press Design &
Production Department

Composition by Asco Typesetters

Text set in Palatino, display set in Gill Sans and Bolt Bold

Printing and binding by The Maple-Vail Book
Maufacturing Group

Printed on 60# Text White Opaque